SACRED JOURNEY OF THE MEDICINE WHEEL

-How To Prepare for the Coming Earth Changes-

By

Myron Old Bear

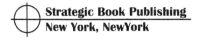

Strategic Book Publishing
New York, NewYork

Strategic Book Publishing
An imprint of AEG Publishing Group
845 Third Avenue, 6th Floor - 6016
New York, NY 10022
www.StrategicBookPublishing.com

ISBN: 978-1-60693-232-2   1-60693-232-2

Printed in the United States of America

Photography by: Dale Perkins

Book Design: SP

ACKNOWLEDGEMENTS

This book is the cumulative efforts of many people, and I am very grateful to them for their valuable input.

First, I thank grandfather Old Bear because he is the actual source of most of the information in this book.

I thank my wonderful wife and best friend, Angelitta, for her encouragement and patience during the long days and frequent sleepless nights while I was preparing this material.

I also thank Judy Perkins for editing the manuscript, and my good friend, Rhonda Cordonnier for her tireless work in sending and receiving e-mails on my behalf while I was at home on Medicine Wheel Mesa.

Thank you David Litell and Archie Wilson for your valued input and evaluation of the material as it was being assembled.

I also thank my sister, Judy, for her prodding, valuable suggestions, and for always believing in this project.

And finally, and most importantly, I thank our Creator for helping my wife and I walk this Sacred Path referred to in this book as The *Way of the Medicine Wheel*.

DEDICATION

This book is dedicated to my wife, Angelitta, who is my best friend and wonderful partner on this Sacred Journey called Life.

During the time we lived in Indonesia, Angelitta was able to arrange for me to meet with numerous "medicine people" living in remote mountain villages, and she served as my advisor and interpreter during those meetings. With her assistance, I was able to discover the similarities between certain aspects of Native American spirituality and the spiritual principles applied by those indigenous peoples in remote Indonesian jungle village, including their understanding of the basic concepts of the medicine wheel.

Without Angelitta's valuable help, encouragement, and support, this book would not have been written.

A Personal Letter from Myron and Angelitta Old Bear

Dear Friend and Relative,

We consider it a great honor—as well as an inescapable obligation—to be able to pass on to you what our Creator and some of His Helpers have taught us over the years concerning the ancient sacred path referred to as *The Way of the Medicine Wheel.* During the most ancient of times, indigenous tribes and clans on every continent have followed this sacred path that combined the physical and Spiritual realms into a single reality, and enabled their people to live balanced lives in harmony with all creation.

Unfortunately, about all we have left today of *The Way of the Medicine Wheel* are the prehistoric stone circles found at various sacred sites in many countries, on remote islands, and even on the ocean floor. For many years anthropologists, archeologists and scientists from many other disciplines have been studying these ancient sites in an effort to learn what they represented, how they were used, and if they offer any clues about how the cultures and societies lived that constructed them.

Many years ago, while living in Indonesia, I learned to *Spirit Travel* to a place I now refer to as "My Private World". There, I met a very old Indian, who, over the years, has taught me about this ancient sacred path that he calls *The Way of the Medicine Wheel.* He has also shared with me many prophecies concerning The Coming Earth Changes, and how we can prepare for them by following this Sacred Path.

This book presents the ancient wisdom, spiritual songs, powerful sacred ceremonies, and step-by-step instructions that collectively reveal the long forgotten mystical pathway to our Creator. It brings the physical realm and Spiritual Realm together into a single reality for those who follow this Sacred Path. However, it is only fair to warn you that as you read the following pages, learn the spiritual songs, and begin conducting the sacred ceremonies, your current personal value system and world view may be shaken to it's core.

As you begin your Sacred Journey on this ancient Spiritual Path toward our Creator, you will discover that each small step taken helps free you from the strangling grip that modern society's deceptive and extremely destructive materialistic values have had on you. And, as you continue along this Sacred Path, you will feel yourself being re-born. The negative values and belief systems that permeate almost every facet of our technologically advanced, modern world can be systematically replaced in your life with powerful spiritual tools and ancient sacred ceremonies. These tools and ceremonies will strengthen your connection to our Creator, and help mend the Sacred Circle of Life here on Mother Earth.

The Way of the Medicine Wheel is not what is commonly referred to today as a Native American spiritual path; even though in very ancient times, Native Americans followed this Sacred Path. In the beginning, it was given to all two-leggeds in every tribe and clan around the world. It was a universal Spiritual Path that all of our ancient ancestors—both yours and mine—followed in the far distant past when the physical realm and the Spiritual Realm were inseparable.

This Sacred Journey was given to the Ancient Ones at the dawn of the First Age in order to help them live in peace, harmony and balance here on Mother Earth. Once again, as the curtain of time begins closing on this current age, Mother Earth prepares to cleanse herself from all of the various kinds of pollution that is rapidly destroying her. Our Creator's helpers from the spiritual realm are attempting to restore this ancient Sacred Path called *The Way of the Medicine Wheel*. In doing so, those two-leggeds entering the next age will have the Sacred Tools necessary in order to once again live in peace, harmony, and balance with our Creator's Sacred Circle of Life.

So, dear relative, we welcome you to this exciting Sacred Journey, and may this Path provide the same peace, harmony, and balance in your life as it has in ours.

Myron and Angelitta Old Bear
Medicine Wheel Mesa
Bed Rock, Colorado

TABLE OF CONTENTS

INTRODUCTION

Many years ago, while living in Indonesia, I was taught how to journey to a place I now refer to as "My Private World"; and later in this book, you will be given instructions concerning how to make the journey to your own Private World. It is a wonderful world, much like this one, with beautiful, snow-capped mountains, meandering rivers, rolling hills, thick forests, and all kinds of animals—even those that have been extinct for a long time in our current age. Fluffy white clouds float lazily across a deep blue sky, and the air is always clean and fresh with the smell of mountain flowers. Oh, how I love going there, because I always seem to learn something new and wonderful from our Creator and his Helpers during those sacred journeys.

A few years later I returned to Colorado with my wife, Angelitta, a beautiful and wise Indonesian lady, my best friend and wonderful life partner, who has patiently taught me a great deal concerning the ancient spiritual wisdom of her indigenous culture. I have learned many things from her world, and she has learned much from mine. And together, we continue to learn wonderful things from our Creator concerning how to walk this sacred path called *The Way of the Medicine Wheel.*

Shortly after we moved from Indonesia back to my home state of Colorado, I had an experience in My Private World that changed the course of our lives forever. People develop their own personal method for getting to their Private World. I will briefly share mine with you now and go into much more detail later in the book.

I begin my preparation to journey to My Private World by taking several deep breaths to help me relax and focus on what I'm about to do. Then I visualize myself standing on the edge of a high, very narrow canyon filled with fog. I step out onto the fog and float gently down through it, landing far below on a small trail that winds its way through a thick forest of very tall evergreen trees. The trail crosses a small stream, and on the other side of the stream there is a high, rock-faced cliff on the south side of a mountain.

There is a big, angling crack in the side of the cliff. I walk through it and come out into a large round cave inside the mountain. Three huge stone doors are on the west wall of the cave. And intuitively, I have always known that as I face that wall, the door on the left goes into the future, the door in the center takes me into the present, and the door on the right leads back into the past.

While living in Indonesia, out of curiosity, one day I decided to go through the door on the right. However, as I entered the cave, I saw what appeared to be a security guard sitting behind a desk in front of that door.

As I approached the door, he stood and said, "Myron, where are you going?"

I was shocked that he knew my name and stammered, "I—I'm going to go through the door on the right."

He shook his head and sternly replied, "No. I'm sorry, I can't let you do that. It isn't time for you to go through that door. And besides, someone must help you make that journey." He smiled warmly and continued, "Don't be discouraged. You'll be told when it's time to go through this door."

The time for me to go through the door on the right came one spring evening in the mountains of Colorado.

Earlier that day, my secretary had received a strange telephone call while I was out to lunch, and when I returned to the office, she handed me a telephone message note, and said with a frown, "I hope you can make more sense out of this message than I could." She paused and shook her head in disbelief, then continued. "The man who called wouldn't give me his name, nor would he explain what he meant by the message."

The short, mysterious message my secretary had hurriedly written on her telephone message pad was as follows: "It's time for you to go through the door on the right." The message startled me, so I slowly read it again. "It's—time—for—you—to—go—through—the—door—on—the—right."

I glanced at my secretary who was inquisitively staring at me. I smiled, trying to hide the feelings of shock, confusion and concern starting to boil up inside of me and said in as calm a voice as I could muster, "I know what the message means, but I have no idea who told you to give it to me." Not knowing who had made that call created my greatest concern, because my wife was the only one who knew about my journeys to My Private World and my encounter with the security guard that day in Indonesia when I tried to go through the door on the right.

That night, Robert Talltree, an Objibwa Indian spiritual leader and close personal friend, assisted me as I journeyed to My Private World behind the door on the right. The life-changing journey I experienced that night is described below.

As I walked through the door on the right, I was shocked to find myself entering a cold, dark night because it had always been a bright, warm day each time I entered the world behind the center door. I was also startled, and became quite fearful, when I realized I was standing on the side of a very steep mountain. In fact, the slope was so steep I felt myself starting to fall forward into the terrifying, black abyss.

As I grabbed at a nearby bush to stop my fall, I suddenly realized I was a young boy about twelve years of age. Then, just as suddenly, I became keenly aware that people were chasing me.

Terrified, I began running blindly through the darkness, stumbling over countless unseen obstacles as I tried in vain to escape my pursuers. I could hear them getting closer and closer behind me. And suddenly, I felt a searing, hot pain shoot through my back as a spear struck me just below my right shoulder blade, knocking me to the ground. Then the whole world seemed to break up into tiny, white mist particles, which slowly evaporated as I lapsed into unconsciousness.

When I awoke I was lying on a ragged, dusty old buffalo robe in a small smoke filled tipi that had several small holes in the hide covering.

As I took a deep breath and sniffed the smoky air, a terrible pain shot through my back and into my chest, causing me to cry out in pain.

The smell of burning sage and sweet grass was strong in the air, and I slowly turned my head from side to side, trying to locate the source of the smoke. Bright orange rays of early morning sunlight had found their way through the small holes in the tipi cover and were dancing lazily above me as they mixed with the billows of sage and sweet grass smoke. I tried to concentrate on their eerie movements in an effort to forget about the throbbing pain in my back, but it didn't work, and the pain was getting more severe with each breath I took.

The sound of approaching footsteps drew my attention to the door flap. A very old woman with long, gray hair stuck her head in the door, and seeing that I was awake, she made a low "huuummph" sound. My eyes were starting to burn and get watery from so much smoke in the air, so I had to blink them several times to clear my vision.

Frightened by her ugly appearance, I let out a gasp and turned away. I had never seen such an old, frail-looking woman in my life. Her stooped shoulders made her long, unkempt gray hair seem even longer, and her face was covered with deep, almost canyon-like wrinkles. Her tattered deer skin dress was soiled with numerous dark stains of animal fat, and her wrinkled, leathery skin matched the brown, dirty color of her dress.

She hobbled over and peered down at me through squinting, beady, black eyes. "So you finally decided to wake up," she said, with a great deal of impatience. "Well, get up. Your grandfather is waiting for you."

Before I could tell her I couldn't get up because I was wounded, and that my grandfather couldn't be waiting for me because he was dead, she reached down and grabbed me by my arm and yanked me to my feet.

When I let out a scream and pleaded with her to stop because I was wounded, she yanked on my arm even harder and snorted, "Huuummph! You look fine to me." She wouldn't stop pulling on my arm as she led me stumbling out the tipi door. "It isn't polite for children to keep their elders waiting. You must learn to be more respectful when you come to visit your grandfather," she growled.

Once outside the tipi, she continued leading me through the small village. I noticed that most of the skin covered tipis were even more worn and tattered than the one I had been lying in.

My eyes quickly scanned the surrounding area in an effort to see if any of the landmarks looked familiar. They didn't. The small, poorly kept village was scattered along an equally small grove of large cottonwood trees strung out along the bend in a river that meandered down a long, narrow valley. A high rocky bluff blocked the view to the south.

However, I had time to see a rugged range of snow capped mountains off in the distance to the east before the old woman yanked on my arm again, and I went stumbling after her toward the western edge of the little village.

I noticed that the villagers were busy with their early morning routines. A few women were building small fires in preparation to cook the first meal of the day, and several children were already playing down by the river. Some of the men were congregated in front of one of the small lodges closer to the river, apparently in light hearted conversation, because their laughter could be heard, even from that distance.

As I was being led through the village by the old woman, my immediate reaction to the scene unfolding around me was that these people were extremely poor. In fact, they seemed almost destitute.

When we came to the western edge of the village, I saw a big bear standing on its hind legs with a very tall and skinny elderly man standing beside it. I let out a scream and tried to yank my arm free from my captor's grip, but she was much stronger than she looked. The harder I tried to free myself the tighter she gripped my arm. So, exhausted and in terrible pain, I finally gave in to the fate I was sure awaited me—she was going to feed me to that big bear!

However, as we approached the bear, I saw that it wasn't a bear at all. It was a very old man—even older than the old woman who held me captive—almost completely hidden inside the bear robe. The huge bear's head was sitting atop the old man's head, and his arms were covered with the front legs and paws of the bear hide.

15

As I screamed in fear and pulled and kicked to free myself from the old woman, she suddenly yanked me up to her side and said to the old man almost hidden in the bear robe, "Well, you wanted him, so here he is." She yanked on my arm again to bring me to full attention as she continued. "Why you wanted this scrawny little weasel, I'll never know. We have a lot of fine young boys right here in our own village eager for this opportunity, and just look how disrespectful this one is!" She gave my arm another hard yank and I gritted my teeth and clenched my fists, determined not to scream out in pain after her humiliating insult.

The old man cocked his head to one side and peered down at me in silence for a long time. I became even more frightened as I realized that the power radiating from his deep set, black eyes seemed to be casting a spell on me. His magnetic stare actually had control of me now. How could he do that, I wondered? How could he control me by simply looking into my eyes?

My fear was quickly being replaced with a calm, pleasant feeling of peace and security. I no longer felt the need to fight to free myself from the old woman's vice-like grip and run away. In fact, I felt content to simply stand there and look back into his warm, loving eyes. And then, to my surprise, I realized the pain in my back was gone. How had that happened? Had that old man been able to heal me simply by looking into my eyes? Those eyes—they were so reassuring, warm and loving. I began to feel like I had known this old man forever, even though I didn't even know his name.

He smiled and patted the top of my head. But, instead of feeling his hand, I felt the bear's paw—and it was alive! At least, it felt alive! Instead of feeling like a cold, limp paw attached to a bear hide, it felt warm and soft. In fact, I was sure I felt the claws slowly flexing and combing through my hair as the heavy paw gently patted my head.

As I looked into the old man's eyes, they began to twinkle mischievously as if to ask, "Did you really feel that bear or was it only your imagination?"

I was about to say that I really did feel a live bear's paw on my head, when, to my surprise, he suddenly flung the bear robe off his own shoulders and wrapped it around me. I let out a gasp as I instantly became swallowed up inside the enormous bearskin.

While the old man balanced the huge, heavy bear head on top of my small head, I heard him say, "I've been waiting a long time to do this, and now you've finally come." Then, as I peered out from inside the bear robe, I saw him turn to the other elderly man beside him and say, "It's time for me to go now." He paused, then looked at me and continued. "But I'll be back to visit you from time to time because we have much to talk about."

Then, turning to the old woman, he said, " Bring the boy and follow Two Feathers and me back to the lodge."

As we started back toward the village, suddenly I realized that with the bear robe around me, somehow, mysteriously, I was actually feeling the needs of the people in the village. When I looked at a person, I seemed to know if they were happy or sad, hurting or contented, sick or well. Shocked, and not believing what I was experiencing, I stopped and began staring at the people, one person at a time. It was true! As I looked at each person, I was keenly aware of what he or she was feeling and thinking.

I became frightened and tried to yank off the bear robe, but it wouldn't move. It was as if it had become a part of me and I a part of it. I tried to yell for help, but no sound came out of my mouth. I started to panic. Then, the old man turned and smiled at me and I realized we had arrived at the door of the tipi I had been laying in when I woke up.

"Come on inside my lodge, little cub," he said, "and I'll take that big bear off of you before it decides to swallow you whole." He laughed as he ducked his head and entered the tipi, and I knew that he had been reading my mind. He somehow knew what I was thinking, even without the bear robe wrapped around him. As I followed the old woman into the lodge, I shuddered, not liking the idea of someone knowing my thoughts and feelings without my permission.

The old man took the bear robe from my shoulders and wrapped it *around himself, then he lay down on the ground. He pulled the robe up around his thin body and face until he was completely hidden from view. The one he called Two Feathers handed the old woman a large shell and asked her to go and fill it with burning coals. When she returned, he sprinkled cedar leaves on the coals, then began smudging the old man and chanting in a high pitched voice.*

With a somber look of concern on her face, the old woman motioned for me to go and stand next to Two Feathers. He had moved up close to the bear skin and was holding the shell filled with smoking cedar leaves out over the robe while he continued to sing.

I was afraid to get to close to the bear robe with the old man inside, but I reluctantly moved up beside Two Feathers because, at that moment, I feared the wrath of the old woman more.

I loved the smell of the cedar smoke. It was sweet and pleasant, and seemed to have a calming effect on my fear, as well as the ability to open my mind to the meaning of the song Two Feathers was singing. I felt that the tall, skinny, old singer was singing some kind of a farewell or good-bye song, but I didn't understand why. Suddenly I looked down at the robe at my feet, and it appeared empty. I couldn't believe my eyes—the old man was gone! But, that was impossible, wasn't it?

I blinked several times, thinking the smoke must be blurring my vision. But no, the bear robe was really empty! Now it was laying flat on the floor, and the old man who had been hidden inside it had escaped, or vanished, or something had happened to him, but I wasn't sure what, or where he had gone.

I quickly looked around the tipi but he wasn't there. I decided that he must have quietly slipped outside undetected while I was caught up in my thoughts and enjoying the smell of the cedar smoke. Searching for answers, I looked first up at Two Feathers and then over at the old woman, but they had their eyes closed and contented smiles on their faces as if they knew where he had gone, and that all was as it should be.

After a while Two Feathers stopped singing and opened his eyes. He looked down at me and said, "Little Cub, its now your turn."

I frowned, not knowing what he meant—my turn for what? Were they going to make me disappear too? Where had the old man gone, anyway? Suddenly an overwhelming fear of these people gripped me again. I glanced over toward the door, and was ready to make a run for it, but my moment of indecision cost me the opportunity. Two Feathers put his big, bony hand on my shoulder and at the same time, the old woman stepped up beside me as if to prevent my escape.

Caught in the tight grip of panic, I could no longer move. My mind screamed at my legs to run, but they seemed frozen to the ground. I looked again at Two Feathers, then over at the old woman. Why did they want to hurt me? I had never done anything to them. I had never even seen them until today.

I could hear my heart pounding wildly as the blood rushed to my head. My cheeks suddenly felt as hot as fire. Why was my face so hot when my feet felt so cold? What were these two old savages doing to me?

All of these questions exploded in my mind at once as confusion joined the fear that had already turned me into a mummy-like state. I heard Two Feathers voice as if it was echoing from somewhere deep inside a cave. He kept talking, but I couldn't understand him. I was getting dizzy, like I was about to pass out. Then I felt my knees buckle, but I never felt myself hit the ground.

When I came to I was wrapped inside the bear robe and Two Feathers and the old woman were gone. I threw off the robe, propped myself up on an elbow and looked around. I had no idea how long I had been lying inside the bear robe. I pushed the robe away and sat up. I felt fine, so I stood up and glanced around the tipi once more, afraid my captors were still lurking somewhere nearby, but I was alone.

Suddenly, I remembered the door I had gone through back at the cave. Terror consumed me—panic like I had never known before. It felt like a vise squeezing the very life out of me. My whole body was shaking with fear, and I could hardly breathe.

Where was the door—and where was I? How did I get here, and who were these strange people? As these unanswered questions flooded my mind, at the same time, I became overwhelmed with despair. I felt trapped in some foreign, unknown world with no way to escape.

I dropped to my knees and started to bury my face in my hands, when, suddenly, I saw movement out of the corner of my eye. I whirled around and gasped in dismay as I saw a huge bear standing just inside the door looking at me.

I screamed, convinced I was about to die. How did that bear get in the tipi? I glanced over in the direction of the bear robe—it was gone! Somehow that bear robe must have suddenly become a real live bear! How could that be? It was impossible, wasn't it? I didn't know. After all, hadn't I thought the paw on the bear robe felt alive—like it was running its claws through my hair? I wasn't sure of anything any more. But, I did know I needed to get away from this giant bear.

However, before I had time to jump to my feet in an effort to run, I heard the bear speak! "Come, my friend, and I'll take you to the door."

Suddenly I felt myself inside the bear! My mind could no longer comprehend what was happening to me. Was I really inside the bear now? Yes. In fact, I was not only inside the bear, it was as if somehow I had become part of the bear. The bear and I were now one and the same.

I could feel its powerful muscles as well as the ground under its (or my) paws. Now I was aware of all kinds of new smells. And in my own ear I could hear the buzzing of a fly as it flew close to the bear's ear.

Then, suddenly we were running. I had never run so fast in my life—and it was so effortless. It seemed like it only took a few seconds for us to run through the small village and across the river. Then we were moving fast up a mountain and through a dense evergreen forest. We ran faster and faster until our surroundings became a blur.

I could feel the wind against my fur and hear it roaring in my ears as we seemed to be running through the air. I had never experienced such an exhilarating feeling. It was as if I could fly anywhere in the twinkling of an eye by just thinking about it.

We came to a stop, and I was instantly outside the bear. I looked around and saw the door in the side of the mountain I had come through, and when I looked back to where the bear had been he was gone.

Off in a distant valley far below me I saw a river winding its way through a thick, green forest. Was that the same river that flowed by the village I had just left? I didn't know, nor did I really care. All I wanted to do was go back through the door and leave this place far behind.

When I stepped through the door into the cave in the mountain, I was immediately back to being me as I am now. I, as a young boy, was locked behind the door on the right in some distant place, far back in time...

For the most part, the book you are about to read is the result of many additional meetings I have had over the years with the old man in the bear robe. Many years have passed since I traveled through the door on the right and out into My Private World. As of the writing of this book, I have never gone through that door again because I haven't felt the need to.

Shortly after my first encounter with the old man (as I described it above), he started appearing to me when I traveled to My Private World and went through the center door—the door to the present. That was when he started teaching me about the sacred path he refers to as *The Way of the Medicine Wheel.*

A few years ago, he suddenly appeared beside me while I danced at Sun Dance. He spent part of one Round dancing with me and talking about one of the most difficult aspects of walking this Sacred Path, *The Way of the Medicine Wheel*, as he called it. And since that day at Sun Dance, he now appears to me on a regular basis, both here in this physical reality and on the other side of the center door in My Private World.

During our first few meeting several years ago I was very reluctant to listen to what he had to say because many of his comments, statements and teachings appeared to be in direct conflict with the values and belief systems I had grown up with in modern-day America. However, as time went by, I began to see the wisdom and powerful truth in what he had to tell me.

21

I never knew either of my biological grandfathers. However, over the years, I have come to consider this warm, loving and caring old man my grandfather. And rightly so, because he told me his name is Old Bear.

BOOK ONE

*Laying the Foundation
for This Sacred Path*

Teaching Session – 1
BEGINNING THE SACRED JOURNEY

It was only a few weeks after my first encounter with grandfather Old Bear that he began meeting with me almost every time I went through the doorway to the present (the center door) in My Private World. At first, I resented his presence in what I considered to be my own private space. But as time went by, I not only became more comfortable around him, I actually looked forward to our meetings.

The first time Grandfather Old Bear talked to me about this Sacred Path he lovingly refers to as *The Way of the Medicine Wheel*, we were sitting in his tipi. We were near a trail that follows along the bank of a beautiful river that winds its way through My Private World. I often walk along that trail because the crystal clear water seems to sing to me as it flows over the multi-colored rocks in the riverbed. The grassy, rolling hills beside the river are home to many kinds of birds and animals. I often see Bald Eagles swoop down and snatch fish from the river with their razor sharp talons, then fly off to feast on a good meal, or maybe share part of it with their young.

That particular day, Grandfather seemed to be in an unusually somber mood, and I sensed that we were about to have a very serious discussion. I had no idea that what he was about to tell me would be the first of many teaching sessions that would change my life forever. And his instructions have continued to this day. Part of that first discussion between grandfather Old Bear and myself is presented below.

Grandfather poured us a cup of juniper berry tea and, after studying me for a while as if to determine if I was ready to receive what he was about to say, he began. "You know, grandson, things have gotten very bad in your world."

Using a forked stick, he picked a round hot rock out of the small fire in front of us and smiled at me. He dropped the stone in the water bag made from the stomach of a large animal. "Gotta keep the water hot because we're going to drink lots of tea today."

He chuckled mischievously as he continued. "You think the microwave oven crowd in your world will be able to learn to heat water again the right way?" Then, he became very serious. "I know what you're thinking. You don't think this is the right way to heat water. Well, some day you'll understand that this is not only the right way—it's the sacred way. It's the way that helps maintain our spiritual connection with our Creator and all of his sacred creation."

He blew on the hot tea in his wooden cup. "When the sacred stones make the water hot, it stays hot for a long time, not like water heated in your microwave ovens. Water heated that way gets hot fast, but it also cools off fast." He laughed when he saw the questioning look on my face. "No," he said. "I haven't drank water heated in a microwave oven, but that doesn't mean that I don't know how it works, and what it does to food and water."

Grandfather took another sip of hot tea. "Let me explain why my way of heating water is the right way," he said. "For me to be able to heat water, I first must kill an animal. Then I must prepare its stomach to be used as a container to put water in. This takes time, and while I'm preparing the stomach, I'm being reminded of my dependence on the animal for my existence."

He paused and looked over at me to make sure I was paying attention, and then continued. "Every time I use the stomach as a water container, my love and respect for the animal grows, and I am reminded to say a prayer of thanks to the animal that gave its life so mine could continue and be better. You see, every time I put water in this old buffalo stomach, it serves as a lesson in how we are all dependent on each other for our continued existence. It helps keep me humble and respectful of the Sacred Circle of Life. The same is true of the stone, the wood and the fire. They become my teachers. They teach me powerful lessons in how I need them daily. So you see, grandson, when I made this tea for us, it was a sacred activity. It helped keep me focused on the Sacredness of all Life. It was a lesson in humility. It reminded me that our Creator has made everything for the benefit of all his children."

He was silent for a while, letting the powerful truth of his words sink deep into my mind, then he asked, "And what about you, grandson, what spiritual lessons do you learn when you heat water in your microwave oven?"

I sat there speechless and humiliated, staring at the flames in the small fire, and too ashamed to look up into grandfather Old Bear's questioning eyes. I had no answer to his question, and he knew it. So I sat there silently, not sure of what to say because no response of mine could begin to match the powerful wisdom that had just been shared with me.

After a while, he reached over and patted me on the leg and smiled that warm, loving smile that radiates from deep within his spirit, and always makes me smile back in return. "Now we didn't call this meeting to discuss whose method of heating water is better, did we? But, in a way it serves to illustrate the need for what I'm going to share with you."

At that point, grandfather Old Bear introduced me to a Sacred Path he referred to as, *The Way of the Medicine Wheel*. And in this first chapter, to the best of my ability, I will pass on to you the main points he shared with me in My Private World that day long ago as we sat in his tipi having several cups of juniper berry tea.

DEFINING *"THE WAY OF THE MEDICINE WHEEL"*

Since this first chapter is titled, *Beginning The Sacred Journey*, I will start by giving you a working definition of this Sacred Path, as grandfather Old Bear shared it with me.

But first, I want to caution you to do what grandfather always tells me to do—*"Don't just listen to my words—listen to your heart. Our Creator will confirm to your spirit whether my words are true or not. After all, no*

27

two-legged can teach you any spiritual truth. Spiritual truth can only come from our Creator, and he's the one who confirms it to your spirit."

Grandfather Old Bear has spoken those words to me many times, and I pass his advice and wisdom on to you because it is the best advise one can receive when walking a Spiritual Path. In addition, I want to make it very clear that I am just a simple two-legged, and do not claim to be a "medicine man" or special spiritual leader, nor do I attach any titles to my name. I am simply trying to serve our Creator and my relatives in the Sacred Circle of Life any way I can. So, with that point of clarification out of the way, let's continue.

When our Creator first made the two-leggeds, he gave them *The Way of The Medicine Wheel* as a "lifestyle" that helped them maintain a strong spiritual connection with him and the rest of his Sacred Creation. Notice that I said, "a lifestyle". *The Way of the Medicine Wheel* is NOT a religion. **It is a lifestyle that helps bring the physical realm and the spiritual realm together into a single reality.**

In the beginning, clans and tribes all over the earth followed this Sacred Path. I want to emphasize to you, as Grandfather Old Bear emphasized to me, that this is not a Sacred Path that was followed only by Native American Indians. In the far distant past, all ancient two-leggeds everywhere lived by these same Spiritual Principles and values. However, the ceremonies used to express these principles and values varied from clan to clan and tribe to tribe.

As time went by, the two-leggeds became more and more self-centered and greedy. This led to a weakening of their connection to our Creator, and as a result, they were no longer able to maintain harmony between the spiritual and physical realms. Selfishness caused the two-leggeds to start living mostly in the physical realm, and thus they lost more and more of their knowledge and understanding of the spiritual realm.

As Grandfather Old Bear emphasizes, *"The more time we spend focusing on the physical realm, the more our connection to the spiritual realm is weakened".*

Because of that Universal Spiritual Truth, about all we have left today of the ancient Sacred Path are a few prehistoric circles of stone at various sacred sites found on all the continents, on remote islands, and even on the ocean floor.

However, Grandfather Old Bear has told me that this Sacred Path must be revived during the few remaining years left before the earth cleanses itself. He says that The Cleansing is necessary because of the contamination that has been created by the two-leggeds due to their selfishness and greed. He has told me that The Time of Cleansing will eliminate all modern societies. Those few people who survive The Cleansing period will suddenly find themselves living as their ancient ancestors lived at the beginning of this age—in harmony and balance with the Sacred Circle of Life, just the way our Creator intended.

THE FOUR "LIFESTYLE" CEREMONIES

The Way of The Medicine Wheel isn't simply making and using a medicine wheel—that is only one of the many "tools" we use when walking the Sacred Path. And in a later Teaching Session I will explain, step-by-step, the ceremony for constructing and using a medicine wheel.

This sacred path consists of four "lifestyle ceremonies". A *lifestyle* ceremony is not like other ceremonies that may last a few hours or even up to a few days. These four lifestyle ceremonies make up the way we live our lives throughout the year, and they correspond with the four Sacred Seasons.

The first lifestyle ceremony is called The Ceremony of New Beginnings, and lasts from the Spring Equinox to the Summer Solstice. The second lifestyle ceremony is called The Ceremony of Growth and starts on the Summer Solstice and continues to the Fall Equinox. The Ceremony of Reaping and Harvesting is the next lifestyle ceremony, and it begins on the Fall Equinox and continues to the Winter Solstice. The fourth lifestyle ceremony is called The Ceremony of Renewal and starts at the beginning of the Winter Solstice and continues until the Spring Equinox.

These four powerful lifestyle ceremonies enable us to once again learn to live in peace, harmony and balance with all creation, and merge the physical realm and spiritual realm together into a single reality. The more we recognize the spiritual significance and meaning of every activity we are involved with day by day, week by week and season by season, the faster we become aware that the physical and spiritual realms are becoming a single reality in our daily lives.

In addition to these four lifestyle ceremonies, there are many "event" ceremonies that we perform in the course of walking this sacred path season after season. Event ceremonies are conducted in honor of, or to give recognition to, a special time or activity that occurs within the lifestyle ceremonies, and they become part of the overall lifestyle ceremonies that are lived during the annual Sacred Cycle of Seasons. The smaller event ceremonies are extremely important because they help magnify the connection between the physical and spiritual realms.

At this point I should point out that much of the information in the remainder of this chapter might seem quite basic and rudimentary to some of you. However, for others, this could be the first time you have been exposed to this type of material. Therefore, even though it will be review for some of you, it is necessary to cover the following information because for beginners we must start at the beginning.

TAKING THE FIRST STEPS ON THIS SPIRITUAL PATH

The first step we take when walking this Sacred Path is to recognize that the Creator of All Things is our spiritual father and Mother Earth is our physical mother. I use the term, "Creator of All Things" instead of the more commonly used word, "God", so that there won't be any misunderstanding as to whom I am referring. When I use the word, "Creator", I mean the Creator of the universe. On the other hand, some religions have many gods. But this spiritual path recognizes only the

Creator of All Things as being God. However, our Creator has many "helpers or "angels", as they are called in some religions, assisting him in his work.

All of us are aware that we have a biological father and mother. However, many people are unaware that the Creator is our spiritual father and Mother Earth is our physical mother.

Our Creator made the tree, and the Creator made us. We both have the same spiritual father, so we are relatives of the trees. Our Creator made the four-leggeds, and he made us, so we are also relatives of the four-leggeds. The same is also true of the winged people, the water people and the rock people—we are their relatives because we all have the same spiritual father.

We not only have the same spiritual father, we also have the same physical mother—the earth. We all came from the earth. Our bodies contain the same minerals as found in the earth. **So since all life on earth has the same spiritual father and physical mother, we are all related to each other.** Go back and read the previous sentence again, because that Spiritual Truth is at the very core of everything we do on this sacred path.

We must not only understand this powerful Spiritual Truth with our heads, we must deeply understand it with our hearts. It isn't just a neat, modern day environmental principle that is the "in" thing to believe; it is a fundamental Spiritual Truth that permeates all our attitudes, decisions, actions and sacred ceremonies as we walk this Sacred Path.

I can't emphasize enough how important it is for us to make this powerful Spiritual Truth *the* focal point of all our actions. For example, when you walk through a forest, you aren't just walking among trees— you are walking among you relatives. Therefore, when you cut down a live tree, you are taking the life of one of your relatives.

When you see a herd of buffalo, elk or deer grazing on the side of a hill, you aren't looking at "dumb animals", as most people think, you are looking at some of your relatives. When you kill one of these animals for food, you are killing one of your relatives.

When we truly grasp this powerful Spiritual Truth, it will not only change the way we view our world; it will also change the way we relate within it.

WE LIVE IN A SACRED WORLD

Webster's Collegiate Dictionary defines the word "sacred" as something "dedicated or set apart for the service or worship of a deity."

We are not only related to all creation; everything our Creator has made is sacred. That is, all creation is directly related to, and connected with, its Creator, and he has put some of his Sacred Essence into everything he has made. Unfortunately, most modern day two-leggeds do not understand the meaning and importance of sacred things. In fact, they tend to believe that nothing is sacred.

To help us understand what the word "sacred" means, we first must have an understanding of our Creator's character. It is amazing how overly intellectual modern man often tends to have great difficulty trying to accept the concept of a Creator of All Things. This is due, in part, to many intellectual people today having a hard time accepting the idea that there might be a power greater than their own intelligence. To do so would mean that they would have to face the issue of whether or not they were subject to that Greater Power, and many modern day intellectuals tend to resist the idea of being subject to any power above their own intelligence.

Many people today are so involved in, and controlled by, the physical realm that they have little, if any, connection to the spiritual realm. In fact, such people know so little about the spiritual realm they tend to seriously doubt its existence.

On the other hand, our ancient ancestors who followed *The Way of The Medicine Wheel* simultaneously lived in both the physical realm and the spiritual realm. As a result, they never questioned the reality of a Creator, because they experienced, first hand, his influence and presence in their lives every day.

These Ancient Ones learned about the character and nature of our

Creator by living among and studying his natural creation. They not only lived close to nature; they became part of it. This Sacred Path taught them to live in peace, harmony and balance with all their relatives within the Sacred Circle of Life. As a result, they knew our Creator and his helpers on an intimate, personal basis.

As the Ancient Ones studied the intricate details and interconnectedness of nature around them, and then stared out into the vastness of the night sky, they became keenly aware of the incomprehensible power and intellect of our Creator. As the Old Ones experienced how our Creator provided everything they and all their relatives needed to sustain their lives, they learned of his unconditional compassion and love for all his children within the Sacred Circle of Life.

Our ancient ancestors had an intimate, personal relationship with their Spiritual Father. Their ideas of our Creator weren't based on theory or philosophy. They were based on daily practical experience. Even the book of Genesis in the Old Testament describes God's relationship to Adam and Eve as a face-to-face experience. Genesis chapter three describes personal conversations between our Creator and Adam and Eve. Whether you believe the Bible or not, this passage illustrates how the Ancient Ones recognized the close, interpersonal relationship between the two-leggeds and their Creator.

If you want to know our Creator, study his creation. Just as artists put some of their creativity and personality into their paintings, so the Creator of All Things puts some of his essence in all he creates. And since some of our Creator's essence is in all he creates, all his creations are sacred, including the two-leggeds, four-leggeds, winged people, green people, water people, and the earth itself.

We were created as Sacred Beings, containing a small part of our Spiritual Father's own holy and pure Sacred Essence. And, our physical mother, the earth, is sacred. She was given part of our Creator's Sacred Power to produce Sacred Life. As I said earlier, as these Spiritual Truths not only fill our minds, but find their way deep within our hearts, souls and spirits, they not only change the way we see our world, but also the way we relate to it.

For example, all the food we eat comes from either animals or plants. As we have previously said, these are not only sacred life forms, they are also our relatives. Therefore, everything we eat is not only sacred, but we are actually eating our relatives.

The Ancient Ones had a deep understanding of this fact. When the men hunted for food, or the women gathered plants to eat, they recognized that they were taking the lives of their sacred relatives. So to them, hunting and food gathering were also sacred, spiritual activities. Prayers were offered to the spirits of their relatives before the hunt, and the taking of life was done with great respect because they knew they were killing their relatives. Even the preparation, serving and eating of the food became a sacred activity.

But today, most people are totally unaware of the sacredness of the food they eat—let alone comprehend that their food was once one of their living relatives. As people buy "processed foods" from supermarkets that have been filled with all kinds of harmful chemicals and preservatives and placed in attractive packages, it never crosses most of their minds that the foods they are buying were once their living relatives. That is why they tend to have so little regard for what they eat, and often waste almost as much food as they consume.

In addition, man has contaminated most of the plants and animals we eat by adding chemicals to the soil, injecting the animals with growth hormones, or adding harmful chemicals to make the meat tender or preserve the food. As a result, the two-leggeds have destroyed the natural sacredness of most of their relatives used for food. Because of his greed, man has even destroyed the ability of plants to produce seeds with the sacred reproductive life force in them

It is true that everything our Creator makes is sacred. However, nothing we two-leggeds make is sacred—and therein lies a great problem. We have covered our sacred Mother's body with sprawling, man-made

34

cities, and these seemingly endless concrete jungles are cesspools of pollution that contaminate our Sacred Mother Earth.

If you take a drive out into nature, far from the man-made cities, you actually begin to feel the spiritual power of sacred creation radiating around you, calming your spirit, and creating peace within your being. Then, when you leave the natural world and return to the man-made city, you begin losing that feeling of peace and serenity, which is replaced with negative feelings such as physical tenseness, frustration and impatience.

In the world made by our Creator, we are surrounded by positive, spiritual power that strengthens our bodies, minds and spirits. On the other hand, in the world made by man, we are surrounded by negative spiritual power that weakens our bodies, minds and spirits. That is why Grandfather Old Bear told me that it is impossible to maintain the strong spiritual connection with our Creator, as he intended, as long as we remain in the man-made cities.

THE IMPORTANCE OF SYMBOLISM

This sacred path is saturated with symbolism, and it permeated virtually every activity in the daily routines of the Ancient Ones.

Symbolism is a form of communication. It reveals, as well as hides, spiritual truths. To the informed, or initiated, one simple symbol may reveal volumes of information. On the other hand, to the uninformed, or to those not initiated into the ways of the sacred, symbolism serves as a camouflage—hiding instead of revealing deep spiritual truths and principles.

From antiquity, mystics have used symbolism to keep Sacred Knowledge hidden from those not yet initiated. However, as The Time of Great Cleansing draws nearer, many Mystics and Sages feel it is imperative for the masses to be informed of Sacred Knowledge, ceremonies, and the spiritual tools that previously were not available to the public.

Symbolism is the bridge over which we walk to get to the reality that is hidden behind the symbol. The more of the symbolism we understand, the more of the reality hidden behind the symbol we may experience. On the other hand, the opposite is true—if we understand very little of the symbolism, then we won't experience much of the reality expressed by the symbol.

The further you travel on the Sacred Path, the deeper you will become immersed in symbolism. In reality, it will become your tutor and master teacher. It will reveal to you more and more of the limitless Spiritual Truths available as you take this Sacred Journey. A two-legged may point you in the direction of this Spiritual Path, showing you where it begins, but symbolism will become one of your most important instructors, helping you maintain the daily connection between the physical and spiritual realms.

Our ancient ancestors used to say that every step they took on Mother Earth was a sacred step. They could say that because they had learned the spiritual lessons taught them by the symbolism that constantly surrounded them. They used symbolism to unlock the Mystical Secrets that enabled them to merge the physical realm and the spiritual realm into a single reality—and, as you progress on this sacred path, you will learn to do the same.

For example, Sunrise and Sunset are the two most important times of the day because of their powerful symbolism that reveals the very nature and character of our Creator. Closely observing the Sunrise and Sunset are two of the most important times in my daily routine. As you learn more and more of the symbolism that permeates these two events, I'm sure they will become the most significant times of day for you also.

The rising sun is the most powerful symbol of our Creator's Unconditional Love for us that we have. First of all, the sun never fails to come up each new day in the east, does it? The faithfulness of the sun to rise in the east each morning is one of the best symbols we have to remind us of our Creator's faithfulness to be with us each and every day. So, the sunrise becomes a powerful sacred event, not just another routine activity

36

in nature. It teaches us that just as the sun never forsakes us, neither does our Creator. Even on cloudy, dreary days when we can't actually see the sun, we know it is there in the sky because we see its light all around us. That is a great symbolic reminder that, even when we are the most discouraged, and we can't actually see our Creator at work in our lives, we know that he is because the evidence of his power is all around us in creation.

In addition, the sun shines on the good and bad—the saint and the sinner—alike. The sun shines the same amount of light on the prisons as it does on the temples and churches. The sun does not discriminate. It doesn't say, "You were a bad person today, therefore, I won't shine on you very much." Nor does it say, "You didn't show me enough respect, so I won't give you as much light as those who do."

The sun is a powerful symbol of the character, nature and power of our Creator. Just as the sun shines its light on the good and bad, alike—so our Creator gives his Unconditional Love equally to the deserving and undeserving. The sun illustrates that our Creator doesn't discriminate—he loves us all the same.

Every time I glance up at the sun, I don't just see a bright, orange disk in the sky. I see our Creator's Unconditional Love for me and I smile and say, "Thank you, Creator. Help me to also pass your Unconditional Love on to others the same way you give it to me—without discrimination."

The sun also symbolizes our total dependence on our Creator for our lives. Just as nothing on earth can continue to live without the sun, so nothing would exist without our Creator. Just as we owe our continued existence to the sun, so we owe our creation and daily existence to our Creator.

On this Sacred Path, the lifestyle ceremony we call The Ceremony of New Beginnings is the ceremony of the East on the medicine wheel. And, as the sun rises in the East, it not only brings a new day, it also brings us new life. Yesterday is gone forever. It was covered over by the night, and cannot be retrieved. The sunrise brings us a new beginning—a new life. A wonderful and powerful lesson in living can be learned by watching the rising sun. Our present lives and our future is before us, not behind us. The sunrise tells us to look to the future—not the past.

These are some of the many reasons why I try to watch the sunrise every morning.

It has great spiritual significance for me in my life, containing powerful symbolism that teaches me and reminds me daily about our Creator's nature, and what he does for me each day. Often with tears in my eyes, I sing the Morning Prayer Song (the words to this song are in the Appendix of this book) as I face the east and watch the gift of new life being given to me. And as this awesome, powerful sacred event unfolds on the eastern horizon, I am overwhelmed with humility, gratitude and awe as I once again am reminded of the wonderful spiritual truths revealed in the symbolism present in the Sunrise.

And the same can be said about the Sunset, which contains equally powerful and important symbolism that teaches us the true meaning of our Creator's Unconditional Forgiveness.

The Sunrise brings with it new beginnings, new life and new lessons and opportunities. However, during the course of the day, we frequently make mistakes. We say things we shouldn't have said, and we do things we shouldn't have done—that is why the Sunset is so important.

The sun sets in the West and opens the doorway for the night to enter. Then the night covers the day with its blanket of darkness. It blots out and erases the activities of the day. The things we did and said through the day are gone forever—they can never be brought back to be repeated or undone. Therefore, there is no need to brag about the great things we accomplished during the day because they are gone, covered by the night. And likewise, it does no good to worry and fret about the mistakes we made during the day, because they can't be undone.

Unfortunately, many people carry the guilt, frustration and other negative feelings and attitudes resulting from the mistakes they made during the day forward into tomorrow, and on into the weeks, months and years to come in the future. However, there is no need to do that if we understand the powerful symbolism of the Sunset and approaching night.

38

The night symbolizes the awesome forgiveness of our Creator. Just as the night blots out and erases the activities of the day, the night also symbolizes our Creator's power to forgive and erase our negative words and actions from his memory, as if they had never happened.

That is why I also am just as eager to watch the Sunset as I am to watch the Sunrise. Both become equally important and powerful sacred events when I understand the symbolism they contain. The Sunset opens the door to the night, which symbolizes our Creator's forgiveness. And the following Sunrise not only brings a new day, it brings a whole new life. So, now I am free from the negative feelings and guilt I might have had because of the wrong things I said and did yesterday (and every day all of us say and do things that we shouldn't have).

Therefore, in the evening as the sun is going down, I make every effort to quietly observe that sacred event. I stand facing the setting sun and with uplifted arms to the sky, I ask our Creator to forgive me for my negative words and actions during the day, and take them away like the night removes the day. Then, using my drum, I sing the Evening Prayer Song and sometimes The Thank You Song (all songs mentioned in this book are printed out in the appendix, and can be ordered on CD from our web page at "medicine wheelmesas.com").

I can tell you from personal experience that the Sunrise and Sunset are the highlights of my day. The sunrise teaches me that our Creator is not only giving me a new day, but new life, and that truth helps keep me focused on this Sacred Path throughout the day. During the day, as I see the sun shining, I am reminded of our Creator's Unconditional Love for all of his children, and that he loves us unconditionally whether we deserve it or not. Each day, the Sunset gives me an opportunity to experience first hand our Creator's forgiveness when I blow it and say or do something that hurts others.

As I said earlier, symbolism is the bridge over which we walk to get to the reality behind the symbol. The more of the symbolism we understand, the more of the power and reality represented by the symbol we will experience. This Sacred Path is filled with symbolism. It is constantly all around us.

Symbolism is the focal point of all our ceremonies. It is the foundation on which this Sacred Path is laid. There is no end to what symbolism can teach us about our Creator and his Sacred Circle of Life. It speaks volumes of Sacred Information to our spirits, if we are alert and listening. It is blowing in the wind, standing in the shade, hiding in the rocks, singing in the streams, floating in the clouds, riding on the lightning, calling from the thunder—constantly showing us how to bring the physical and spiritual realms together into a single reality.

Never tire of sitting at the feet of symbolism and learning all you can, for if you do, it will never tire of teaching you more and more about our Creator, and how to walk this Sacred Path toward him.

Teaching Session-2
THE SELF-OFFERING CEREMONY

In this teaching session, we will take you through the step-by-step process of performing the Self-Offering ceremony. However, first it is important to understand the purpose of conducting a ceremony.

THE PURPOSE OF CEREMONY

Ceremony is the passageway that connects the physical realm with the spiritual realm. Ceremony helps merge the physical and spiritual realms together into a single reality—that is its purpose.

On this Sacred Path, ceremony is an important part of all daily activity. In fact, life itself becomes a continuous sacred ceremony as we take the Sacred Journey we refer to as *The Way of The Medicine Wheel*.

As was pointed out in the first teaching session, this Sacred Path consists of four lifestyle ceremonies that correspond with the Four Sacred Seasons. These are called "lifestyle" ceremonies because every activity we are involved in day by day and week by week takes on spiritual meaning and significance.

On the other hand, within the lifestyle ceremonies there are special "event" ceremonies. These event ceremonies are of short duration—from a few hours to a few days in length—and place special spiritual emphasis on specific activities.

THE FOUR PHASES OF A CEREMONY

All sacred ceremonies consist of four phases, each equally important to its overall success. These four phases are:

41

4. Personal preparation of the individual or people conducting and participating in the ceremony.

5. Preparation of the sacred items to be used in conducting the rituals involved in the ceremony.

6. Conducting the sequence of rituals.

7. Showing gratitude for the results of the ceremony.

Failure to give proper attention to any one of the above phases of a ceremony may not only result in its failure, but may actually produce a negative result. Therefore, it is extremely important to give proper attention to all four aspects of conducting a sacred ceremony.

Phase One: A novice on this sacred path may assume that preparations for a ceremony are not a part of the actual ceremony. That is not true. The ceremony begins with the preparation of the people, or person, conducting it. And, in reality, personal preparation plays a major role in the ceremony's outcome.

Personal preparation almost always includes some form of individual purification such as conducting the Self-Offering ceremony, participation in a Purification ceremony, or smudging and special prayers. Prior to some major ceremonies the participants may even go on what is commonly called a Vision Quest to properly prepare themselves for the event.

No matter what method of personal preparation is used, the purpose of that preparation is to purify body, mind and spirit so that the individual doesn't inhibit the flow of our Creator's power during the ceremony. In virtually all instances involving ceremony, the better the personal preparation, the more effective the results will be.

Phase Two: Once the personal preparation is completed, the next step is to properly prepare all sacred items to be used in conducting the ceremony. Each item symbolizes or represents a power invoked, or a reality produced, as a result of conducting the ceremony. Therefore, ceremonial items are a necessary and extremely important part of any ceremony.

In the previous teaching session I said that symbolism is the bridge

42

over which we walk to get to the reality behind the symbol. The ceremonial items, themselves, have no power. However, they often represent tremendous power, and the more of the item's symbolism we understand, the more power will be present during the ceremony. Never forget that the symbolism represented by the ceremonial item is the bridge to the power invoked, and the ceremony opens the doorway for that power to flow through.

A ceremony consists of bringing together sacred items with deep symbolic meaning, and then using those items in a specific way. Always remember that every action taken in conducting a ceremony has important symbolic meaning. Therefore, it is extremely important that every ceremonial item is properly prepared, and every action taken in conducting the ceremony is properly performed—I can't emphasize the importance of this enough.

So, later in this teaching session, when we go through the step-by-step process of preparing one's self and the items needed to perform the Self-Offering Ceremony, make sure you follow the instructions exactly as given. Also, make sure you properly understand the symbolic meaning of every item used, and every action taken when conducting the ceremony, because that is the key to the desired results.

Phase Three: Our Creator gives us spiritual ceremonies for our benefit. Spiritual ceremonies open the passageway between the physical and spiritual realms, merging them together into a single reality. However, to accomplish this, the ceremony must be performed exactly as our Creator instructs us. **Never take shortcuts when performing ceremonial rituals.**

Keep in mind that a ceremony is for our benefit, not our Creator's. By that I mean that our Creator gives us a ceremony to meet a specific need and produce a specific result. However, our Creator and his helpers pay very close attention to the way we perform a ceremony and its rituals, because this is how they determine our worthiness to receive the intended benefit.

For example, the way we perform a ceremony shows our Creator our willingness to obediently follow his instructions. If we won't follow instructions in performing a ceremony, we probably can't be trusted to follow other plans or instructions our Creator wants to give us. In addition, the ceremony is a test of our faith in our Creator to produce the desired result. By properly performing the ceremony, we are demonstrating faith in our Creator to produce the needed result.

On the other hand, if we ignore his instructions and inject our own ideas into the ceremony we are saying that we know more than our Creator does. By our actions we are insinuating that we have the power, knowledge and ability to solve our own problems and produce our own results. Failing to follow our Creator's instructions concerning how to perform a ceremony is the ultimate insult to him and his Helpers, and we usually pay a high price for our disobedience and defiance—so never forget that.

I am not saying that there is only one way to perform a ceremony. Our Creator has an infinite number of ways to solve a problem. And as time goes by, he may instruct us to change a ceremony by adding to it or deleting some part of it. He may even ask us to stop performing it altogether. The important thing to remember is that we must always be listening to our Creator's instructions to us. And one thing we can be sure of, if he asks us to change a ceremony, it is never to simply make it easier to perform: it is always to make it more relevant and effective in meeting our immediate needs.

Over the years, a lot of my "traditional" Native American relatives have asked me if I follow the "old traditional ways". I always reply that I'm not sure that I know what they mean by "traditional". And if you consider yourself a "traditionalist", I ask you the same question I always ask my "traditional" Indian relatives. What does "traditional" mean? How far back are you tracing your "traditions"? Are you going back to pre-reservation days, pre-dominant society days, or all the way back to the arrival of your people here on Mother Earth? How far back in history are you tracing your so-called "traditional ways"?

I am the first to admit that tradition is important. However, obedience to our Creator is far more important. So, as you perform ceremonies, always listen to our Creator and follow his instructions concerning how you are to conduct the ceremony.

Tradition is very important when it comes to performing Sacred Ceremony. A Sacred Ceremony is one given to us by our Creator. However, not all ceremonies are sacred. Two-leggeds can—and often do—develop ceremonies that may be very impressive to watch. However, only ceremonies given to us by our Creator and his Helpers are sacred, and open the passageway that allows the physical and spiritual realms to merge into a single reality.

A ceremony given to us by our Creator should never by changed or altered in any way unless he tells us to make those changes. From time to time, he may ask us to make certain changes. But, we have no right to take it upon ourselves to alter any Sacred Ceremony unless Grandfather (our Creator) or his Helpers communicate to our spirit the specific changes to be made.

Phase Four: Showing gratitude for the results is the fourth and final phase of any ceremony. I can't emphasize enough the importance of this part of the ceremony. And, I am surprised at how many people seem to be unaware of the importance of this final step. Ceremony invokes our Creator's power on our behalf. Therefore, it is extremely important to let him know how much we appreciate all he does for us. That is why each ceremony concludes with a display of our gratitude for our Creator's help.

The showing of gratitude can take many forms, but one of the most common methods is the "give away". Often the ceremony concludes with people giving away various items to the elderly, the needy, or the children. Things given away are usually practical items such as blankets, food, money, etc. In addition, a give away may include a pledge of service to someone, such as providing a winter's supply of firewood for the elderly in the community who are unable to get the wood for themselves.

The more gratitude we show Grandfather (our Creator) for how he works on our behalf, the more he is willing to continue helping us. On the other hand, if all we say to our Creator is, "Give me, give me," and we

45

rarely say, "Thank you", we are demonstrating to him our lack of gratitude.

Keep in mind that our gratitude must be genuine—not just words. As the second verse of the "Thank You" song says, "Oh, Grandfather, how I thank you for providing for us each day. So I will help those who are needy that I meet along life's way." This song teaches us important principles of gratitude. If we are truly thankful for what our Creator does for us, then we will eagerly do for others, because this is the proof of our gratitude for the way Grandfather provides for us.

THE ROLE OF SMUDGING

Smudging is an important practice in all indigenous people's spiritual pathway. And among different tribes and clans, different natural materials are used when smudging. For example, in Southeast Asia dried coconut husk is a common smudging material. On the other hand, most Native Americans consider sage, sweet grass and cedar leaves to be the best plants to use for smudging.

Smudging is the process of burning a sacred natural substance in order to create sacred smoke for the purpose of helping purify people, ceremonial items or a specific space or area.

The Ancient Ones understood that the spirits of the plant people, or "green people" as they are often called, have been given special powers by our Creator to help their two-legged relatives. Some of the green people have the power to heal certain sicknesses, some have the power to open the doorway to the spiritual realm and others have the ability to drive away negative energy and forces.

46

Our Creator gave sage the power to drive away negative forces. Sweet grass was given the power to attract positive and good energy, while cedar was given the ability to help cleanse and purify things it came in contact with.

Therefore, Grandfather taught the Ancient Ones to smudge themselves, their ceremonial items and the space around the area where the ceremony was to be performed with sage, sweet grass and cedar. This was done to help drive away negative energies, attract positive powers and help purify and cleanse people and items involved in the ceremony.

So, as we walk this Sacred Path, we use sage, sweet grass and cedar daily for smudging. In the morning, we smudge our homes with sage to drive away any negative powers that may have come around during the night. We burn sweet grass to help attract positive powers to the area and we put cedar leaves in the fire before cooking our meals to help keep the food we eat pure as we prepare it and eat it.

Therefore, since these sacred herbs are used daily, you will need to either go out into the surrounding countryside and collect your own sage, sweet grass and cedar for smudging, or go to a local store or supplier to purchase it. Stores that carry herbs often carry these items.

CONDUCTING THE SELF–OFFERING CEREMONY

The Self-Offering ceremony is the first, and one of the most important ceremonies, we learn as we walk *The Way of the Medicine Wheel.*

PURPOSE OF THE SELF-OFFERING CEREMONY

The purpose of the Self-Offering ceremony is to help develop and maintain a strong connection between our spirit and our Grandfather, the Creator of All Things.

I will say it again—the purpose of this Sacred Path is to bring the physical and spiritual realms together into a single reality. For this to happen, we must constantly maintain a strong spiritual connection with Grandfather.

The physical world is the great distracter. By that I mean it is constantly distracting our attention away from the Spiritual Realm. The physical or material world feeds and promotes the ego. Everything we do in the physical realm is designed to make us "feel good". That is why I call the physical realm "the feel good world".

The more we focus on the material world, the more time we spend doing things to make ourselves feel good and create a life of leisure. Unfortunately, the life of leisure makes us more and more self-centered. And, the more self-centered we become, the more our appetite grows for things that make us feel good, and provides us with what we consider to be an even better life of leisure.

The feel good world is also the great deceiver. It deceives many people into thinking the most important thing in life is to acquire more and more material possessions, because they believe that peace, happiness and security are acquired through them. Unfortunately, just the opposite is true. The more people focus on the material world, the farther they remove themselves from the Spiritual World.

Peace, happiness, security and the meaning of life are found only by developing and maintaining a strong connection with our Creator and his Spiritual Realm—and that is the ultimate goal of the Self-Offering ceremony. It removes any negative thoughts, intentions and motives we may have, and fills us with our Creator's Unconditional Love so we can pass it on to other relatives within the Sacred Circle Of Live.

When we perform the Self-Offering ceremony we are committing ourselves to be of service to the Sacred Circle of Life. We submit our will and our total being to be used by our Creator to help restore the Sacred Circle of Life to its original, undefiled state. We are affirming our commitment to serve our fellow relatives in Creation instead of always seeking to be served. In order to accomplish this, we first must let our

Creator remove the things our self-centered egos have created in our lives that hinder us from being of service to Creation's Sacred Circle.

ITEMS NEEDED TO CONDUCT THE SELF-OFFERING CEREMONY

You will need the following items in order to conduct the Self-Offering ceremony:

- Sage, sweet grass and cedar for smudging.
- A large seashell (abalone shells work quite well).
- A large feather from a wild bird (turkey, duck or goose feathers will work if you are not Native American and allowed to use eagle feathers).
- Natural tobacco (no chemicals added).
- Corn meal.
- Small pieces of black, red, yellow, white, green and blue cotton cloth (these pieces need to be about one inch square).
- A piece of red felt large enough to make a circle 12" – 14" in diameter.
- Hand drum.
- Small blanket (approximately 24" x 36").

PERSONAL PREPARATION IS THE FIRST STEP IN CONDUCTING THE SELF-OFFERING CEREMONY

Personal preparation is a very important part of any ceremony. You don't prepare yourself to conduct a ceremony—the ceremony begins with your preparation. Begin your personal preparation by taking several deep breaths and exhaling slowly. This will help you relax. As you do this focus your mind and thoughts on the ceremony and its purpose.

Next, put a mixture of sage, sweet grass and cedar in the abalone shell and light it. Let it continue to flame up for a few seconds so that it is burning well, and then blow it out. This will create plenty of smoke. After running the feather through the smoke, use it to push the smoke around you. Smudge yourself from head to toe, front and back. As you do this, thank the sage, sweet grass and cedar for participating in the ceremony, and for driving away any negative energy that may be near. Take your time, using plenty of smoke to smudge yourself. Keep in mind that your personal preparation is a very important part of the ceremony, and greatly influences its results.

PREPARING THE ITEMS TO BE USED IN THE SELF-OFFERING CEREMONY

Preparing the items to be used during the ceremony is the second step in conducting the Self-Offering ceremony.

- First, smudge all the items to be used.
- Cut out a circle of red felt 12" – 14" in diameter. This circle of felt will be saved and used each time you conduct the ceremony.
- Place the small rug facing East.
- Next, place the circle of red felt at the eastern end of the rug. This red circle of felt has many powerful symbolic meanings. First, it symbolizes you and the commitment of your whole being to our Creator for his service. Make sure you are willing to make such a commitment before doing the ceremony, because failure to do so will constitute a lie on your part as you conduct the ceremony.
- Hold the blue square of cotton cloth up toward the sky and ask Grandfather to help you perform the ceremony, and then place it at the center of the circle of red felt. The blue square of cloth symbolizes our Creator, and placing it at the center of the circle of red cloth symbolizes your commitment to letting our Creator control all you do and say. The act of placing the blue cloth in the center of the red felt

circle also symbolizes your commitment to having Grandfather at the very center of your life so that he can help you walk this Sacred Path in peace, harmony and balance with the Sacred Circle Of Life.

- Next, hold the green square of cloth down toward the ground and thank Mother Earth for providing all that you have, including your food, shelter and clothing. Promise to always respect the earth as your mother and then place it next to the blue square of cloth. The green cloth symbolizes Mother Earth and placing it at the center of the red felt circle symbolizes our recognition that the earth is our physical mother.

- The black cloth symbolizes our Creator's sacred power of the West. Hold it up toward the west and ask Grandfather's power of the West to come and join you and help you as you perform the Self-Offering Ceremony. As you place the black cloth on the Western side of the circle, thank our Creator's power from the West for coming to help you.

- The square of red cloth symbolizes our Creator's sacred power of the North. Hold it up toward the North and ask Grandfather's power of the North to come and help you as you perform the ceremony and then place the it on the northern side of the circle of felt.

- You will repeat this process for the yellow and then the white squares of cloth. First, hold the yellow cloth up to the East and ask Grandfather's power from the East to come and help you during the ceremony and place it on the eastern side of the circle. Repeat this for the South with the white cloth and place it on the southern side of the felt circle.

- Placing these little squares of colored cloth in the Four Sacred Directions symbolizes your commitment to obey all that our Creator asks of you as you walk the circle of your life.

- Next, hold the cornmeal down to the earth and thank Mother Earth for the way she takes care of you, meeting all your physical needs. Hold the cornmeal up to our Creator and commit to serve the needs of others. Now, place a small pinch of cornmeal on each of the colored pieces of cloth, beginning with blue and continuing with green, black, red, yellow and white, in that order. The cornmeal symbolizes the bringing together of the physical and Spiritual Realms into a single reality.

THE SELF-OFFERING RITUAL

Once all of the ceremonial items have been properly prepared, you are ready to conduct the Self-Offering ritual.

Begin by kneeling on the rug. The circle of red felt will be in front of you. Take several deep breaths as you focus your attention on the meaning of the circle and the squares of colored cloth with cornmeal on them.

Next, ask Grandfather to reveal the things in your life that displease him, and hinders you from being of service to your relatives in the Sacred Circle of Life.

As our Creator brings these things to mind, ask him to remove them from your life, and visualize yourself removing them and throwing them away. For example, if you have a bad habit of cursing, visualize yourself reaching into your mouth and throwing the curse words far away from you as you actually go through the physical motions of doing that.

Continue this process until all the negative things Grandfather reveals to you have been removed. Once all these things have been removed, ask our Creator to fill you with his Unconditional Love. Sit quietly and visualize a beam of white light entering the top of your head and completely filling your whole being. As I do this, I began to feel warm all over.

It is important to remember that our Creator fills us with his Unconditional Love so we can pass it on to others. Once we are full of Grandfather's Love, the only way we can receive more of his Love is to give that Love away to others within the Sacred Circle of Life. It is like filling a glass with water. Once the glass is full, we can't add more water until some of that water has been poured out of the glass. So, it is with our Creator's Love, once he fills us with his Love, that we must pass that Love on to others before we can receive more.

The final step is to ask our Creator to reveal to you those relatives within the Sacred Circle of Life that you should pass his Love on to. Grandfather will begin bringing to mind those who need your help. The only way we can share our Creator's Love with others is to serve them and meet a need they have. Therefore, ask our Creator to show you how you are to serve the relatives he brings to mind, and visualize taking the actions needed to meet the needs that have been shown to you. Commit to start taking those actions immediately.

End the Self-Offering ceremony by singing the Thank You Song. At the end of the ceremony, the small pieces of colored cloth and the cornmeal on them should be burned or buried, and the rest of the items wrapped up in the small blanket for use the next time you conduct the ceremony.

I perform the Self-Offering ceremony on a regular basis in order to maintain a strong connection between my spirit and our Creator. I often use it as a form of prayer and I find that it helps keep me focused on serving others instead of wanting to be served.

Teaching Session - 3
THE PURIFICATION CEREMONY

I walked through the center doorway and followed the little stream down the gently sloping hillside toward the river in the broad valley below. I loved coming to this place that I call My Private World. Until grandfather Old Bear pitched his lodge down around the bend in the river, this had been my own private place.

I chuckled to myself as I recalled how irritated I had been when I first discovered he had moved his old buffalo skin lodge from that far off world behind the door on the right, and pitched it beside "my river" behind the center door. However, not only had I quickly adjusted to his being in my secluded world, I soon found myself eagerly anticipating each visit.

And now I was headed to his little tipi to inquire about how the sweat lodge was used on the Sacred Path he kept referring to as The Way of The Medicine Wheel. I felt a little apprehensive because I had never initiated a topic for discussion with him. He had always been the one to introduce a new topic, and I wondered how he would react to my questions concerning the sweat lodge.

I felt compelled to discuss the sweat lodge with him, because certain people back in my hometown were complaining that the way I ran a sweat lodge ceremony wasn't "traditional" enough. They believed every sweat lodge ceremony should be conducted the way they had been taught, and since I wasn't from their tribe, and didn't speak their Native language, they thought I couldn't possibly know the proper way to run a sweat lodge ceremony.

When I reached the river, I was surprised to see grandfather Old Bear walking up the path from his lodge toward me. "You're late," he said, with his patented warm smile..

55

"I'm late?" I asked, questioning his comment. "I didn't know you were expecting me."

He turned and started back down the trail. "Come on. The Sacred Stones are also tired of waiting for you."

I frowned and asked, "What sacred stones?" as I hurried down the trail after him.

He stopped and waited for me to catch up with him. "The Sacred Stones I've been heating so we could do a Purification Ceremony," he replied. "You did come here to talk about the Purification Ceremony, didn't you?"

His answer stopped me in my tracks, and my mouth fell open. Before I could gather my thoughts to answer him, he continued. "Well, the best way to learn about the Purification Ceremony is to DO the ceremony, not just TALK about it." He laughed at the shocked look on my face. "What's the matter—you afraid to do the Purification Ceremony?"

"No," I said, as I started following him again. "I've been in lots of sweat lodges, so why should I be afraid?"

"Huh! So you call it a 'sweat lodge' too." He started walking faster. "It's NOT a sweat lodge!" he exclaimed. "The white man gave that degrading name to a very sacred ceremony." He shook his head in disgust, and continued. "And now, even most of our Indian brothers and sisters refer to the Purification Ceremony as a sweat lodge. It's a disgrace, I tell you—a disgrace!"

We rounded the bend in the river and walked up the little knoll to his tipi. Since my last visit, he had built a small Purification Lodge about twenty yards to the south of his tipi, and the red hot Sacred Stones were getting even hotter in the fire blazing in the fire pit several feet to the west of the little lodge.

The Purification Lodge was constructed of willow poles placed in the ground about every two feet to form a circle about eight feet in diameter. Poles from opposite sides of the circle were then bent over and tied together using long, rope-like strips of willow bark. Once all of the poles were bent over and tied together, they formed a rigid framework shaped

56

like an upside down bowl. Grandfather had then covered the willow framework with animal skins so that the inside of the lodge would be completely dark when the small door, which was also made of animal skins, was closed.

Grandfather Old Bear told me to take off my clothes, and then he smudged me with sage smoke. With a nod of his head, he motioned me to go into the Purification Lodge. Using a long forked stick, he placed seven red-hot stones in the round hole in the ground at the center of the little lodge.

Crawling on his hands and knees through the small doorway, grandfather entered the lodge and sat on the ground just to the right of the doorway. He reached outside and got his drum and a buffalo stomach, which was partially filled with water. He pulled the animal skin door closed, and instantly it was pitch dark in the tiny lodge, except for the faint red glow of the hot Sacred Stones.

"If you're going to follow this Sacred Path then you must stop referring to this as a sweat lodge," grandfather said very sternly. "Such a term is degrading to this very sacred ceremony."

He sat across from me and silently stared into the glowing sacred stones for a long time, and I was getting more and more uncomfortable with the silence.

"In the time of my people, all the two-leggeds around the world had some form of a Purification ceremony," he finally continued. "Some were performed in small caves, some in man-made holes in the ground, some in little lodges like this one and some were even made of logs. My people preferred using small caves when we could find them, but that won't be very practical for you today."

"The form of the ceremony differed from place to place, but the meaning and purpose was all the same—to purify mind and body so the Sacred Circle of Life would remain strong," he said. He poured water on the hot stones and it instantly burst into steam.

He opened the door and went out and brought in the rest of the hot stones, and soon I was sweating from every pore in my body.

57

After he sang a song in a language I didn't understand, and poured more water on the hot stones, he continued. "You came here to today to learn how to conduct the Purification Ceremony the way it is done on The Way of the Medicine Wheel. Once you begin walking this Sacred Path toward the Creator of All Things, you will perform the Purification Ceremony the way I will show you."

During the remainder of this teaching session, I will pass on to you the things grandfather Old Bear taught me concerning the Purification Ceremony as it is performed on *The Way of The Medicine Wheel*. I want to make it clear, however, that there are many ways of conducting the Purification Ceremony. The following information only applies to the ceremony as it is performed on this Sacred Path.

You may have learned to conduct the Purification Ceremony differently from the way it is described in this teaching session. That is fine, and I am not suggesting that you change. However, grandfather has instructed me to pass on to people the way the Purification Ceremony is conducted on this Sacred Path in case some people are interested in performing it this way.

If you have never been exposed to the Purification Ceremony before, then I suggest you follow this method. However, as you are exposed to other ways of performing the ceremony, you may find one of them better meets your needs.

PURPOSE OF THE PURIFICATION CEREMONY

Several years ago, while living in Indonesia, a man who referred to himself as "a powerful medicine man" came to our house and said he had heard about our Purification Lodge, and asked if he could participate in the ceremony. We were having a Purification Ceremony that night, so rather reluctantly, I invited him to stay and join us.

After the ceremony was over, he stayed until everyone else had left, and then asked if I would teach him how to have the power he felt during the ceremony. He said that he wanted to learn how to conduct the ceremony, and control its power, so he could improve his standing with the people back in his village.

When I refused to teach him how to conduct the Purification Ceremony, and asked him not to come back as long as he continued to have that kind of attitude, he became very angry, and threatened to use Black Magic to kill me and destroy the Purification Lodge. Needless to say, his efforts were in vain.

I share that experience with you because, unfortunately, there are many people who are attracted to various sacred ceremonies thinking it is a way to enhance their own personal power, and gain prestige among their peers. Such people often acquire lots of "head knowledge" about these Sacred Ways, but they tend to never let our Creator's power change their hearts and lives.

Throughout these teaching sessions, I will remind you over and over again that the purpose of *The Way of The Medicine Wheel* is to help us learn how to live in peace, harmony and balance with our Creator and all of his Sacred Creation. Our Creator uses his unlimited power to help us achieve this—and that power is Unconditional Love.

Love is the power behind all of the ceremonies on this Sacred Path. Love serves others, not self. Therefore, we perform each ceremony for the benefit of all our relatives in the Sacred Circle of Life, not to acquire more personal power, or enhance our standing among our peers.

Grandfather Old Bear explained to me that the Purification Ceremony was given to the two-leggeds in ancient times to help our pre-historic ancestors develop and maintain pure intentions and actions as they performed their daily tasks, or conducted other ceremonies on this Sacred Path. It removed the impurities from their minds and bodies so our Creator's Unconditional Love could empower them to live in peace, harmony and balance with all creation.

What does it mean to live in peace, harmony and balance with all creation? First, it means our motives and actions will change. Our Creator's Unconditional Love will transform us into servants of the people

59

instead of servants of our own egos. We will become givers instead of takers, peace makers instead of trouble makers, self controlled instead of self indulgent, encouragers instead of fault finders, seekers of wisdom instead of seekers of pleasure, and guardians of truth and justice instead of manipulators and deceivers. We will be known for our humility, not our arrogance. And, our actions will draw people's attention to our Creator instead of bringing attention to ourselves. In addition, we will see ourselves as part of nature, not controllers of it.

The purpose of the Purification Ceremony is to help us become servants of our Creator instead of servants of our own will and ego. During the Purification Ceremony, the knowledge we have of this Sacred Path's spiritual principles is transferred from our heads into our hearts, and Grandfather's power transforms how we think, act and live. Our Creator is the embodiment of purity and love. So, in order for us to have a strong connection to him, we also must take on those same qualities in our nature. Our spirituality must become more than an intellectual pursuit. It must change our self- centered nature to that of being of service to the Sacred Circle of Life. Our Creator's power of Unconditional Love must transform our minds and hearts into the embodiment of his purity and love —and that is why he gave us the Purification Ceremony.

Unfortunately, much of the Purification Ceremony's true purpose and meaning has been lost, and today it is commonly referred to as a "sweat lodge" ceremony. As a result, the powerful Purification Ceremony frequently is reduced to little more than a ceremony to produce sweat as we pray. That is evident in the way many people refer to the Purification Ceremony. I frequently hear people say, "I need to do a sweat." Or they will ask, "Are you going to make it to the 'sweat' tonight?"

Sweating may have a temporary physical benefit, but it doesn't purify us. That is why many people attend "sweat lodge" ceremonies on a regular basis, but their basic self-centered natures fail to change. They continue to be controlled by the same bad habits and personal problems, and live their lives controlled by their egos instead of by our Creator's purity and Unconditional Love.

If you have a deep understanding of all of the powerful symbolism associated with the Purification Ceremony, and properly perform its rituals, you will be filled with our Creator's power of Unconditional Love, which will purify your mind and heart as well as your body.

Our Creator's purity and Unconditional Love enables us to live in peace, harmony and balance with him and all of his Creation. That is the purpose of the Purification Ceremony. That is why our Creator gave it to us. And, that is why it is one of the most important ceremonies on this Sacred Path.

LIVING IN PEACE, HARMONY AND BALANCE WITH OUR CREATOR

Grandfather Old Bear spent a lot of time that day in the Purification Lodge talking to me about what it means to live in peace, harmony and balance with the Creator of All Things. The main points of that conversation are presented below.

"Today, in your world, very few people are at peace with themselves, their neighbors and their Creator," grandfather said as he poured more water on the hot stones. *"That is because they no longer know how to have peace. To be at peace with yourself and the rest of your relatives, you first must be at peace with our Creator."*

More hot steam exploded into the air around me as he continued to pour water on the Sacred Stones. "And, to be at peace with our Creator, you must first submit to living under his laws that govern all Creation. This is our Creator's world, not yours, grandson. You are not in charge-- he is. You do not determine what is right and wrong—he does. He is not only the Creator of all things, he is the supreme authority over all things, and you must humbly and willingly submit to his authority. Do you understand that, grandson?"

I shook my head indicating that I did, then realized he couldn't see me in the dark, so I softly said, "Yes."

"Well, it's not enough to just understand it. You must submit your will

to our Creator's authority over you, and commit to living under his Universal Laws, then you will be at peace with yourself, your relatives within the Sacred Circle of Life, and with your Grandfather, the Creator of All Things."

Grandfather Old Bear chuckled mischievously. "I can tell you from personal experience that it's far better to submit to our Creator's Laws For Right Living and his authority, and be at peace with him, than to fight against those laws and his authority and be at war with him—because you lose every time. So, grandson, be sure to make peace with our Creator. Submit to his Universal Laws that govern you and all the rest of your relatives, and don't fight against them. They are there for our good—for our protection—and to insure the good and protection of future generations within the great Sacred Circle of Life."

Grandfather sat across from me in silence for a long time, letting the truth of his words sink deep into the fertile soil of my mind. Finally he spoke again. "Well grandson, who's going to be in charge of your life— you or our Creator?" Then he fell silent again, but his words continued to ring in my ears like the heavy beating of a drum. I knew he expected an answer. However, I also knew that he expected the truth. This certainly was no time for mind games with this Mystic Elder of the Old Ones. Besides, he could read me like a book, and I could feel him probing deep into the hidden closets of my mind.

"The Creator of All Things will be in charge of my life," I finally said with as much commitment ringing in my voice as I could muster. "I submit to his authority over my will and ego, because I want to always be at peace with him and the rest of my relatives within the Sacred Circle of Life."

I heard grandfather Old Bear grunt his approval. He then continued, "Once you've made peace with our Creator by submitting to his Universal Laws For Right Living, and you give him authority over your will, you will find it much easier to live in harmony with all your relatives. In fact, as we follow our Creator's Universal Laws, they produce harmony between us and the rest of Creation. You will soon discover that disharmony is the result of violating one or more of our Creator's Universal Laws."

"What do you mean by "our Creator's Universal Laws?" I asked.

"Our Creator places his Universal Laws of right and wrong and good and bad within the consciousness of all of his children," grandfather explained. "He has specific Universal Laws for the two-leggeds; different laws for the four-leggeds; and still other laws for the winged people, green people, water people and rock people. Those laws dictate what is right and wrong or good or bad for each family group within the Sacred Circle of Life. You see, the green people have different Universal Laws governing how they are to live and relate to one another than the rest of their relatives within Creation, and the two-leggeds have their own Universal Laws For Right Living that are different from those of the green people. To live in peace, harmony and balance with our relatives in Creation we must follow the Universal Laws our Grandfather, the Creator, gave us.

"But he knows that no matter how hard we two-leggeds try to always follow his Universal Laws, we regularly break them. That is why he gave us the Purification Ceremony. It is a way of purifying our spirits, minds and bodies again when we break the Universal Laws we're to live by. Unfortunately, we break them all too often."

Grandfather Old Bear picked up the drum and started a slow methodical beat as he softly sang a song. When he finished, he said, "That was the Purification Song, and you will sing it in the Purification Lodge. It's a prayer asking our Creator to purify our spirits, minds and bodies. It's a powerful prayer when we sing it from our hearts, and mean what we're saying". (The song is on the CD that is available at our web page, "medicinewheelmesas.com".)

He laid the drum on the ground beside him, then poured more water on the hot stones. I was already sweating profusely, and the new blast of hot steam made the sweat start running from every pore in my already sweat-soaked body.

"Following our Creator's Universal Laws creates peace and

harmony in our lives," grandfather said. "And performing the ceremonies he gave us keeps us in balance as we move along this Sacred Path's ever-changing life cycle.

"Our ceremonies keep us walking in step with the changing seasons. They also help maintain a strong connection between the physical and Spiritual Realms, forming them into a single reality."

Grandfather was quiet for a while as if reflecting on what he had told me, and I got the impression he wanted to make sure he hadn't left out anything of importance. Finally he said, "So, Little Cub, that's how you develop peace, harmony and balance as you walk this Sacred Path."

SYMBOLISM OF THE PURIFICATION CEREMONY

As was previously mentioned, symbolism is the bridge over which we walk to get to the power behind the symbol, and ceremony is the doorway that connects the physical and spiritual realms into a single reality. Therefore, thoroughly understanding the symbolism associated with the Purification Ceremony is the key to tapping into its power. And as we conduct the ceremony, we open the passageway between the physical and Spiritual Realms, enabling our Creator's purity and Unconditional Love to flow freely into us.

We never learn all there is to know about a ceremony, and that's certainly true of the Purification Ceremony. The more we perform this ceremony, the more we learn about its symbolism, and the power hidden behind it.

The fire pit where the sacred stones are heated: The fire pit where the sacred stones are heated is rich in symbolic meaning. It symbolizes the place where the Creator lives. It represents the place from which the Creator of All Things sent out his power to create the universe and all that is within it. Therefore, great care must be taken when picking the location for the fire pit and preparing it for use.

The fire pit is not just a place to safely heat rocks. It symbolizes the holiest of all holy places, the place from which our Creator's power was sent out to bring all things into existence. It represents the most holy and powerful spot in the universe. That is why it is so important to keep the fire pit and surrounding area very clean and in order at all times. Never throw trash in the fire pit, not even cigarette butts or gum wrappers. Since this area is such a sacred place, it must be treated with the utmost respect.

The wood used to heat the sacred stones: The wood that is used to heat the sacred stones symbolizes us. Placing the wood in the fire pit symbolizes the giving of our selves to the Creator for his use and service. The act of lighting the wood on fire symbolizes that moment in time when you actually made the commitment to give our Creator control over your life, and to be of service in helping keep the Sacred Circle of Life strong.

The person lighting the wood on fire is reaffirming that commitment, and demonstrating for all to see that he or she has actually given our Creator control over his or her life. Only those who have made such a commitment should be permitted to place the wood in the fire pit and light the fire. Never forget that. It would be a great mockery of this sacred ceremony to allow people to do that if they haven't made a commitment to give our Creator control over their lives.

Gathering the firewood is a very sacred act. Those collecting the wood should smudge themselves and any saws or other tools that may be used to collect the wood. Before leaving to gather the wood, prayers should be made to our Creator, asking him to guide the wood gatherers to the right pieces of dead wood to be used for the fire. In addition, before taking the wood, tobacco offerings should be made to the trees in the area, thanking them for their help and participation in conducting the Purification Ceremony. As the firewood is taken, tobacco should be placed on the spot where the wood was laying on the ground as a "thank you offering" to the spirit of the dead tree for the use of its body in making the sacred fire.

The Sacred Stones: The stones are part of Mother Earth's body. They are pieces of her sacred bones. When possible, lava rock should be used because it comes from deep with our Mother's body, and contains large amounts of her energy. However, other types of stones will work if lava rock is not available in your area. But never use "river rock" (stones that you find in the riverbed, or along riverbanks), because they frequently have moisture trapped inside, and can explode when heated in a fire.

These sacred stones symbolize Mother Earth's love and care for us. They represent our total dependence on her for our existence. They remind us that all we have came from her.

Once the stones are heated, they are called "Grandfathers", because our Creator's power has entered them. That power will be released inside the Purification Lodge so it can purify our minds and bodies.

When you go to gather the stones, ask Mother Earth to lead you to the ones she wants you to use in the ceremony. These stones will be about the size of a human head. Smudge yourself and those helping you. Before taking each stone, offer tobacco to Mother Earth as a thank you offering. Rub the tobacco on the stone you took, thanking it for helping you perform the Purification Ceremony, and then place the tobacco on the spot on the ground where the stone was resting. Also, remember that you are taking the stone away from its family and friends who may be nearby watching. Therefore, thank them for allowing the stone to go with you, and promise to always respect your stone people relatives.

The willows used to build the Purification Lodge: The willows used to build the Purification Lodge are small in diameter, yet strong and limber. They bend without breaking. They are powerful symbols of the attitude we are to have towards the traditions in our ceremonies. Like the willow, we must be flexible, yet not break away from the ancient ceremonies that connect us to the spiritual realm. That is why the willow is often used in the construction of the Purification Lodge framework. As we sit in the lodge, we are totally encircled by willows. They hold the lodge together. They have the power to bend, but not break. They teach us the importance of not giving in under pressure.

While we sit in the Purification Lodge we are surrounded by the willows' power of endurance while under pressure. The little willow teaches us a very important lesson—we must be flexible, and remain tolerant of others and their ways, while keeping true to the sacred path our Creator gave us.

The cover for the Purification Lodge: Symbolism determines the power of the ceremony. And one of the reasons the Purification Ceremony is so powerful is because its symbolism is so strong.

As has been stated many times during these teaching sessions, symbolism is the bridge over which we walk to get to the power, or reality, behind the symbol. The more of the symbolism we understand, the more of the ceremony's power we experience, and that certainly applies to the Purification Ceremony with its layer upon layer of symbolism.

The Purification Lodge's cover is just one example of the powerful symbolism contained within the Purification Ceremony. Long ago, animal skins were used to cover the Purification Lodge's dome-shaped willow framework. Today, however, the cover usually consists of blankets and/or canvas.

Regardless of the material used, the cover symbolizes how our Creator's Unconditional Love covers, surrounds and protects us from the negative forces at work in the physical realm. When we are inside the Purification Lodge, its dome-shaped cover protects us from the physical elements outside. That is a powerful symbol of how our Creator's Unconditional Love surrounds us and protects us from the negative forces that constantly try to draw us away from our Creator.

Since symbolism is the bridge to get to the reality, or power, behind the symbol, when we crawl into the Purification Lodge, we aren't really sitting inside its protective, physical cover of canvas or blankets. In reality, we are actually sitting within the protective covering of our Creator's Unconditional Love. His love is all around us, protecting us from anything that might harm our spirits, minds or bodies.

Understanding the symbolism of the Purification Lodge cover changes our whole perspective of the little dome-shaped, willow framed hut. It also has a tremendous positive effect on our experience while in the lodge. For example, I have had people peer inside the Purification Lodge, frown, and say, "Oh, I don't think I could go in there. I can't stand to be in small, enclosed spaces."

After I had explained the symbolism associated with the Purification Lodge, they were not only eager to go in, they had a very positive experience while inside our Creator's protective cocoon of Unconditional Love.

The hole in the ground inside the Purification Lodge: The hole in the ground inside the Purification Lodge symbolizes the place where our Creator took some of Mother Earth's body to make us and our other "earth-bound" relatives.

Placing the "Grandfathers" in the hole in the ground symbolizes placing our Creator's power (Unconditional Love) within us so we can be reborn with pure spirits, minds and bodies as we emerge from the Purification Lodge.

The area inside the Purification Lodge: The area inside the Purification Lodge symbolizes Mother Earth's womb. When we enter the Purification Lodge, we are reentering our Mother's womb to be reborn with pure spirits, minds and bodies.

The Purification Lodge's doorway: The Purification Lodge doorway symbolizes the passageway between the physical and Spiritual Realms. Unlike the entrances to churches and other religious temples that allow those entering to walk upright as they go inside, the doorway to the Purification Lodge is very low. This forces those entering to get down on their hands and knees and crawl inside. This symbolizes the need for us to humble ourselves in order to enter such a holy place.

The door faces the West because, on the medicine wheel, West is the direction from which we receive the power and ability to know and understand our own motives, motivations and internal truths. From the West comes the ability to be honest with our selves. Our conscience was given to us by our Creator's power from the West. Any time we are involved in spiritual ceremony it is very important for us to be honest with our selves, and have the proper motives for conducting the ceremony so we can do it with a clear conscience.

The path between the fire pit and the Purification Lodge: There is a pathway about four to six feet wide between the fire pit and the doorway of the Purification Lodge that is rich in powerful symbolism.

First of all, it represents the "pathway of creation". This is the path the Creator's power traveled when coming to earth to impregnate Mother Earth with all her children.

It also symbolizes the "road of life" we travel while living here on earth. And third, it signifies the "Spirit Path" we travel to our spirit homeland to be with our Creator after our physical death.

The path between the fire pit and the Purification Lodge is bordered on each side with tobacco, cornmeal or a small berm of gopher dirt. These borders are formed before people enter the lodge and are removed after they come out.

Once these borders along each side of the path have been put in place no one is allowed to step inside the sacred path until it is time to enter the lodge. In order to enter the lodge, people start on the sacred path at the fire pit and walk along it to the doorway to the Purification Lodge. The fire keeper also carries the heated stones (Grandfathers) along this sacred path as he or she takes them from the fire pit to the Purification Lodge's doorway.

The Altar: A round altar, made of the dirt taken to form the hole in the center of the Purification Lodge, is constructed in the middle of the sacred path, about half way between the fire pit and the doorway to the lodge. The borders marking the edges of the pathway extend outward about three feet on both the north and south sides of the altar. A buffalo skull is placed on the altar facing West toward the fire pit. The buffalo is a symbol of the way our Creator provides all our needs. Medicine Pipes, Cornhusk Pipes and other sacred objects are also placed on the altar prior to the tobacco, cornmeal or berms of gopher dirt being put in place to mark the boundaries of the Sacred Path.

The altar symbolizes the connection between the physical and Spiritual Realms. It also signifies our commitment to give our Creator control over all we do and say. It is placed on the Sacred Path in recognition of our need to continually reaffirm our commitment to our Creator, as well as the need for the physical and Spiritual Realms to be combined into a single reality.

The sacred fire: Lighting the fire to start heating the stones is a very sacred act, and people should be quiet and respectful while the fire keeper lights the fire. The fire symbolizes our Creator's power. His power of Unconditional Love is entering the stones through the fire and transforming them into what we call "Grandfathers". Once the stones are heated, they are referred to as Grandfathers because they have been filled with our Creator's power.

When the fire keeper carries the red-hot stones down the sacred path to the Purification Lodge, he or she is actually transporting our Creator's power into the lodge. That is why great care must be taken when carrying the Grandfathers. If a Grandfather is dropped while being transported to the lodge, it must be returned to the fire pit and another stone selected. This is done so that all of our Creator's power in the stone will be brought into the lodge instead of going into the ground where it fell.

The first seven Grandfathers: The first seven stones to be placed on top of the wood in the fire pit have a very important symbolic meaning. The first four also symbolize our Creator's power of the "Four Winds" or Four Sacred Directions.

The first stone represents our Creator's power in the West. The second stone represents his power in the North. The third symbolizes our Creator's power in the East, and the fourth stone is for his power in the South. The fifth stone represents our Creator. The sixth stone is for Mother Earth and the seventh stone represents our ancestors who were faithful to pass on these sacred ways so we could have them today.

The fire keeper: The fire keeper plays a very important and powerful role in the Purification Ceremony. This person is responsible for making sure that all aspects of the ceremony occurring outside the lodge are performed correctly. First, he or she makes sure the area is clean and neat, and then smudges the entire area, including the inside and outside covering of the Purification Lodge. Next, the person prepares the altar, places the wood and stones in the fire pit, and lights the fire. As people arrive, the fire keeper greets them and smudges them and any items they may have brought. He or she also prepares the water to be used inside the Purification Lodge and makes sure all items to be used inside the lodge are available. Prior to people entering the lodge, the fire keeper marks the boundaries of the Sacred Path with cornmeal, tobacco or gopher dirt. And finally, when all is ready, he or she carries the Grandfathers from the fire pit to the Purification Lodge.

The fire keeper is a symbol of our Creator's Unconditional Love in action. Our Creator takes care of us, provides for us, and watches over us. This is also the fire keeper's role during the ceremony. He or she is there to serve the needs of the people participating in the ceremony. Therefore, the fire keeper becomes a visual representation of the way our Creator takes care of us and meets our needs on a daily basis. So, with that in mind, the fire keeper must always perform the tasks and serve the people to the best of his or her ability.

The person who pours the water inside the Purification Lodge: The leader of the ceremony is the one who pours the water on the Grandfathers inside the lodge. He or she sets the date and time for the ceremony and selects the person to be the fire keeper. The leader is also responsible for insuring that all items needed to perform the ceremony are present, unless that responsibility has been specifically delegated to the fire keeper.

The ceremony leader will inform the fire keeper concerning any special issues to be dealt with during the ceremony (such as physical healing for a specific individual) or special purposes of the ceremony (such as preparing people for a Spirit Quest, etc). The leader will then tell the fire keeper how many stones are to be used during the Purification Ceremony.

The ceremonial leader symbolizes the life of humility that is required of all those who would walk the Sacred Path called *The Way Of The Medicine Wheel.* The leader's life should be the ultimate example of living to serve the needs of others.

The Sacred Water: Water is the sacred "Life Force" of Mother Earth.

Pouring the water on the sacred stones represents our Creator impregnating Mother Earth with his power so we can be "reborn" with pure spirits, minds and bodies.

The heat in the Purification Lodge: During the Purification Ceremony it gets very hot inside the lodge. When the sacred water is poured on the red-hot stones, our Creator's power is released into the lodge through the hot steam. The heat symbolizes our Creator's power that surrounds us and enters our spirits, minds and bodies to make them pure again. Therefore, we should not fight against the heat, but welcome it into us. In so doing, we are welcoming our Creator's power of Unconditional Love to enter us and purify us.

The sweat that pours from our bodies: We sweat profusely during the Purification Ceremony. Sweat literally runs from every pore in our bodies. The sweat symbolizes all of the impurities that have contaminated our spirits, minds and bodies, thus hindering us from effectively walking this Sacred Path.

Again I remind you that symbolism is the bridge over which we walk to get to the power behind the symbol. The more we understand the symbolism associated with the Purification Ceremony, the more of its power we will experience. That is why it is so important for us to meditate on the symbolism described above, and ask our Creator to reveal more and more of its meaning so that we can reap the full benefit of this powerful ceremony.

BUILDING THE PURIFICATION LODGE

Building the Purification Lodge is a very sacred activity, and in many ways, is similar to performing a ceremony. Therefore, great care must be taken to make sure that every action taken is properly performed.

Personal preparation: Personal preparation is an important part of any ceremony, and it is especially important when preparing to construct a Purification Lodge.

Begin by asking our Creator to guide you in each activity involved in

72

building the lodge. Make sure your motives for building the lodge are to serve the people, not to promote your own ego.

There is a great responsibility associated with being the caretaker of a Purification Lodge. The lodge does not belong to you, it belongs to the people, just like a church or temple belongs to the people. You must be willing to put the needs of the people ahead of your own needs. Unless you are willing to make such a commitment, you should not build the lodge.

So you can see that a great deal of "soul searching" needs to be done before you build a Purification Lodge. You must make sure this is something Grandfather is asking you to do, and not something you want to do in an attempt to improve your standing among your peers.

Selecting and preparing a site for the lodge: Once you have determined that our Creator wants you to build a Purification Lodge and become its caretaker, the next step is to choose a location. Smudge yourself with sage and ask Grandfather and Mother Earth to direct you in choosing the site. The site should be as level as possible and located where there will be no danger of the fire in the fire pit getting out of control and burning surrounding trees and other vegetation. It should also be easily accessible by the people who will attend the ceremony.

Once the site has been chosen, tobacco or cornmeal should be offered to the Four Winds, Our Creator and Mother Earth and sprinkled over the site. Next, the selected site should be smudged with sage and then cleared of all small stones, stickers and weeds. As you do this, apologize to your relatives for disturbing them.

Marking the site for the lodge, altar and fire pit: The Purification Lodge ranges in size from very small to very large, the average size being about eight to ten feet in diameter. The size of the lodge will depend on how many people you expect to use it at any one time. (It has been my experience that smaller groups seem to accomplish more than large groups).

Make a circle on the ground to mark the spot for the Purification Lodge. The door to the lodge will face the West. Mark a space about two feet wide on the western side of the circle to indicate where the door will go. Next, in the center of the circle, mark a small circle on the ground about two and one half feet in diameter to indicate where the pit for the Grandfathers will be dug.

Starting at the place in the lodge circle where the door will go, step off about twenty to twenty five feet to the west. This is approximately where the fire pit will be dug. Offer tobacco or cornmeal to the Four Winds, our Creator and Mother Earth, then sprinkle the offering on the ground at the spot where the fire pit will be located. As you do this, ask Mother Earth for permission to dig the fire pit, and then mark a circle on the ground approximately six to seven feet in diameter to indicate where the pit will be dug.

The fire pit should have gently sloping sides and be about twelve inches deep in the center. The pit should have a flat bottom at least four feet long. The dirt removed from the fire pit should be used to form a half-moon shaped berm on the western side of the fire pit.

Making the altar: The altar will be situated along a straight line about half way between the fire pit and the doorway to the lodge. The dirt removed from the pit in the center of the lodge where the Grandfathers will be placed during the ceremony will be used to form the altar into a round circle of Earth. The pit in the center of the lodge should have straight walls and a flat bottom, and be about twenty to twenty-four inches deep.

Gathering the willows for the framework: Ask our Creator to guide you to a village of willows that wish to offer assistance in the construction of the Purification Lodge. The willows consider it a great honor to be able to help you perform this sacred ceremony, and they will be eagerly waiting your arrival.

When you arrive at their village, talk to the willows, explaining your need for their help in construction the Purification Lodge. They have already identified members of their community who wish to help with the construction.

Offer tobacco or cornmeal to the Four Winds, our Creator, and Mother

Earth; then, sprinkle the offering on the ground among the willows. As you do this, ask the elders of the village to take you to the willows wanting to participate in the lodge's construction. Your attention will be drawn to the volunteers, and you will know which willows to cut. The willows will be approximately one inch to one and one half inches in diameter and eight to ten feet tall.

Before cutting each willow, thank it for its help. Rub tobacco or cornmeal on its skin, then sprinkle the offering on the ground at the base of the willow. As you cut the willows, thank them for their participation in making the lodge.

Building the lodge: First, cut all the branches off the willows and strip the bark off for the first two feet up from the base. This symbolizes the willow's purity of spirit, and how our impurities must also be stripped away during the Purification Ceremony.

Next, re-mark the circle on the ground, making it about ten feet in diameter (a lodge this size will comfortably have room for ten to twelve people). Offer tobacco or cornmeal to Mother Earth, and ask her permission to dig holes in her skin in which to place the willows.

The first two holes will be dug on the western side of the circle, one on each side of the doorway, marking its width. These two holes should be about thirty inches apart. Each hole along the circle should be ten to twelve inches deep, and an offering of tobacco or cornmeal and a small amount of water (about one cup) should be placed in each hole. The holes will be dug on a slight angle, with the bottom sloping in towards the pit in the center of the lodge. This will make it easier to bend the poles and keep the back of the lodge straight for the first couple of feet.

Once the first two holes have been dug, willows will be placed in them and dirt tamped tightly around them to make them sturdy. The next two willows will be placed in holes on the eastern side of the circle, directly opposite those in the west.

You will need two people to bend the willows. One person will very slowly bend the willows on the west toward those in the east, while another person will slowly bend those on the east toward the west. The willows will be bent until they are about four feet off the ground at the center of the circle, then tied together so they will stay in place.

Keep in mind that it is important to bend the willows very slowly to keep them from breaking.

Once the willows on the East and West sides of the circle have been bent and tied together, you will repeat the same process for the North and South sides of the circle. Once those have been bent and tied together, you will place two willow poles half way between those on the West and North, then two between those on the East and South, two between those on the North and East and two between those on the South and West. Once those have been bent and tied together, the next step is to place two rows of poles horizontally around the structure. The first row should be about six inches off the ground and the second just below the point where the poles bend sharply inward. The horizontal poles should be tied securely to the vertical poles with cotton cord. This will make the structure very strong.

Covering the lodge: Our ancestors used animal skins to cover their Purification Lodges. Today, however, blankets and tarps are the most common forms of lodge covers. Cover the lodge with blankets first. Then, place a tarp over the top of the blankets. The tarp should be large enough to cover the lodge and extend out onto the ground a few inches. Place dirt over the tarp on the ground to keep light from entering the lodge at ground level.

Make the door covering out of a combination of blanket and tarp. The door cover should be shaped in a square and the top of the door cover should have a willow pole sewn into it. The willow should extend about six inches beyond each end of the cover. A rope should be tied to each end of the willow and be long enough to go over the top of the lodge and down the East side, then staked in the ground. This will hold the door cover in place. You can use the rope to adjust how high the top of the door cover will be above the doorway (about ten to twelve inches). There should be enough door cover at the bottom so that it will easily lie flat on the ground.

When the door is closed it should be totally dark in the lodge—not even a pinhole of light should show through.

RESPONSIBILITIES OF A LODGE KEEPER

The Purification Lodge belongs to the people. It is constructed for the people, and becomes a focal point of spiritual activity involving the people. Therefore, the lodge keeper has a great responsibility to the people.

The Purification Lodge sits on holy ground, and the surrounding area is a very sacred site. The lodge keeper not only has a great responsibility to the people, he or she is also responsible for the protection and upkeep of the Purification Lodge and surrounding sacred site.

In many respects, the lodge keeper is like a security guard charged with the security and protection of the lodge. The lodge keeper insures that drugs and alcohol are kept away from the area, that the site is kept clean and neat, and foul language and negative conversations are avoided by people while on the sacred site. He or she tries to insure that people always treat the sacred site with the proper honor and respect it deserves.

In addition, the lodge keeper is responsible for the maintenance and up keep of the lodge and sacred site. He or she organizes a "workday" as needed, so people can help repair the lodge and do general clean up of the area. The lodge keeper is also responsible for insuring that there are always enough stones and firewood available for use in the ceremony.

A lodge keeper must have a servant's heart, and be an example of our Creator's unconditional love in action. A person interested in becoming a lodge keeper should first do lots of soul searching, and spend lots of time in prayer to determine if our Creator wants him or her to keep a Purification Lodge for the people.

CONDUCTING THE PURIFICATION CEREMONY

Remember that there are four parts to any ceremony:

- 1) Personal preparation
- 2) Preparation of the items to be used in the ceremony
- 3) Conducting the rituals of the ceremony
- 4) Showing our thanks to our Creator for what he did for us during the ceremony.

I can't emphasize enough how important it is to make sure all four parts are present in any ceremony we perform.

THE CEREMONY BEGINS WITH PERSONAL PREPARATION

Conducting a spiritual ceremony is a great responsibility. The ceremony belongs to the people, and is for their benefit. Spiritual ceremonies, when performed properly, contribute to the restoration of the Sacred Circle Of Life. Ceremonies given to us by our Creator not only benefit the two leggeds—they benefit all of creation. We must never forget that very important aspect of sacred ceremony.

The ceremony begins with personal preparation. One of the first things the ceremony leader should do in preparing for the ceremony is to decide on the time it will be conducted and then arrange for someone to be the fire keeper. Both the ceremony leader and fire keeper should spend time alone praying for a successful ceremony. The ceremony leader will ask our Creator how many stones should be used and if there are specific songs that should be sung.

Keep in mind that the ceremony actually begins with personal preparation. Those attending the ceremony should also spend the proper amount of time with personal preparation. The more time spent in prayer prior to entering the Ceremonial Lodge, the more effective the ceremony will be.

This is a Purification Ceremony, not a "sweat lodge" ceremony. The purpose is personal purification of spirit, mind and body. Our whole focus should be on preparing ourselves for purification.

The proper attire for attending the Purification Ceremony are long skirts or dresses for the women and cut-off pants or sweat pants for the men. This is extremely important, and people should not be allowed to participate in the ceremony unless they have the proper attire.

Scantily clad women and men should never be allowed to participate in—or even attend—any sacred ceremony on this Sacred Path. There should never be any room for compromise on this rule because people's full attention and focus should be on the purpose of the ceremony, and not on the sex appeal of those in attendance. We should never attend a Sacred Ceremony to draw attention to ourselves. We aren't there to make a fashion statement. We're there to support, participate in, and benefit from the ceremony. Always refrain from wearing suggestive clothing or excessive cosmetics and jewelry when attending a Sacred Ceremony. Such distractions can have a very negative and detrimental effect on any ceremony. So keep in mind that having the proper attire (that includes a towel for drying off) is a very important part of each individual's preparation for a Purification Ceremony.

PREPARING THE ITEMS TO BE USED DURING THE CEREMONY

You will need the following items in order to conduct a Purification Ceremony:

- Wood (enough to heat the stones for about two hours).
- At least twenty eight stones about the size of a human head (preferably lava rock).
- A five gallon water bucket filled with water.
- Water dipper.
- Sage, sweet grass, cedar and a shell for smudging.
- Pitchfork for carrying the Grandfathers.

- Set of deer antlers.
- Buffalo skull for the altar.
- Black, red, yellow, white, green, purple and blue cotton cloth for flags about three inches wide and two feet long.
- Tobacco or corn meal.
- Ceremonial tobacco (mixture of natural tobacco, inner white bark of the red willow, bear berry leaves and sage leaves or seeds).
- Corn husks.
- Matches.
- Drum.
- A bag of natural tobacco for people to use as a prayer offering.

- Food for the ceremonial feast.

Either the ceremony leader or fire keeper must be responsible for insuring all of the above items are available for the Purification Ceremony. All of the items must be smudged with sage before they can be used, or the food prepared or eaten.

When everything has been prepared, place the flags in the Purification Lodge directly above the pit in the ground. Start with the black flag, hanging it directly above the West edge of the pit. Next, place the red flag directly above the North edge of the pit. Place the yellow flag above the pit's eastern edge. Then, the white flag should be set above the Southern edge, and the green flag slightly in toward the center of the pit from the yellow flag. Finally, put the purple flag slightly in from the white flag, and the blue flag directly above the center of the pit.

The black, red, yellow and white flags symbolize the Four Sacred Directions, the green flag symbolizes Mother Earth, the purple flag represents our ancestors and the blue flag symbolizes our Creator.

Prepare a separate flag to honor the current season (black for fall, red for winter, yellow for spring or white for summer), and place it on the appropriate wall of the lodge. During the fall, the black flag will go on the west wall, during winter the red flag will go on the north wall, during spring the yellow flag will go on the east wall and during summer the white flag will hang from the south wall. This is done to show our commitment to live in harmony with the four seasons on the medicine wheel.

You will then place four willow poles, each with a "V" shaped fork in the top and approximately six feet tall, in the ground several feet beyond the actual Purification Lodge site. These poles will be placed in each of The Four Sacred Directions. Each time a ceremony is conducted, new "Directional Flags" will be tied in the "V" at the top of each pole. This will mark the boundary of the sacred site.

I continually emphasize that the ceremony begins with personal preparation because it has such a profound influence on the ceremony's outcome. Make sure all those planning to enter the Purification Lodge are there well before it is time to start the fire so they can spend the proper amount of time with their own personal preparation. As people arrive, smudge them with sage and ask them to go off alone for a few minutes to reflect on the purpose of the ceremony and their personal need for purification.

PLACING THE WOOD IN THE FIRE PIT

Make sure everyone planning to enter the Purification Lodge is present when you place the wood in the fire pit because it is a very important part of the ceremony.

Everything we do during a Sacred Ceremony has powerful symbolic meaning. This is especially true in placing the wood in the fire pit. Have the people gather around the fire pit for this part of the ceremony. First, smudge the fire pit area with sage. As you do this, discuss with those in attendance what the fire pit symbolizes. Pray to our Creator, thanking him for all he has made, and ask for help to live in peace, harmony and balance with the Sacred Circle of Life.

Next, select the first eight pieces of wood to be used and smudge them. As you do this, thank the green people for their participation in the ceremony. Place four pieces of wood (approximately three to four feet long and six to eight inches in diameter) in the fire pit facing east and west. Then, place four pieces the same size on top of them facing north and south. While you do this, remind the people that the wood symbolizes all of the people in attendance. It also represents their commitment to live in peace, harmony and balance with all their relatives within the Sacred Circle of Life. Placing the wood in the fire pit symbolizes our commitment to allow our Creator to purify us so that we can better serve others.

The fire keeper will then ask the people to get a small piece of wood from the wood pile and place it in the fire pit on the ground around these eight big logs as a way to affirm their commitment to serve others within the great Sacred Circle of Life.

This is a very important part of the Purification Ceremony because it draws our attention to the fact that in order to live in peace, harmony and balance with all creation, we must first be willing to serve others. Just as the wood gives itself to be used to heat the Sacred Stones, we must give ourselves to be of service to one another. This is the purpose of life on *The Way of The Medicine Wheel.*

PLACING THE SACRED STONES ON THE WOOD

When the people have completed their affirmation of service, the next ritual involves the selection of the stones to be placed on the wood in the fire pit.

First, offer a prayer, thanking Mother Earth for providing some of her sacred bones to be used in this ceremony. Also, thank her for providing all that we have, and affirm your commitment to always honor and respect her for the way she continually provides for us.

Next, select the number of stones to be used in this ceremony. The number of stones may vary from ceremony to ceremony, and our Creator will tell you how many stones should be used each time.

Always keep in mind that these Sacred Ceremonies have been given to us by our Creator; they are his ceremonies, not ours. Each Sacred Ceremony has been given to us for our benefit, to meet specific needs and solve certain problems. Our Creator designed them to help us effectively walk this Sacred Path in a way that will be pleasing and honoring to him, and empower us to live in peace, harmony and balance with all of our relatives within the Sacred Circle.

Never forget that our Creator is in control of the ceremony, not us. He produces the results, we don't. If we were capable of producing the results, or solving the problems, we wouldn't need the ceremony to begin with. I remind you of this because once our Creator gives us a Sacred Ceremony we sometimes think it is ours. We are often tempted to think that we are in control now. We may even become deceived into believing that we produce the results. However, the facts are, we can do nothing. We are totally incapable of living in peace, harmony and balance with our other relatives without our Creator's help.

Never let your ego get in the way of what our Creator wants to accomplish through the ceremony. He knows each person's needs far better than we do. He is the only one totally cognizant of what happened in the past, completely aware of all that makes up the present, and sees all that is coming in the future.

Willard Fools Bull, a Lakota spiritual leader and close friend of mine, once told me, "If people run a Sweat Lodge ceremony the exact same way every time, I know they are in control—not the Creator." He went on to say, "Such people are usually unaware they have become deceived. They tend to brag that they are the only ones properly conducting the ceremony, when in fact, just the opposite is true." A sad expression crossed his face as he continued. "If we always use the same number of stones and sing the same number of songs each round, we are saying the Creator is limited in how he can achieve a result."

I have never forgotten the wisdom in what Willard said that day. Yes, our Creator gives us Sacred Ceremonies. Yes, we are to conduct the ceremonies the way our Creator told us. However, that does not mean our Creator is limited in what he can tell us concerning how the ceremony is to be performed each time. Just because he asked us to use twenty-eight stones during the Purification Ceremony last week doesn't mean he necessarily wants us to use twenty-eight stones this week.

Our Creator has many reasons for giving us Sacred Ceremonies. First, they are a way to test our faith. Second, they show how well we follow his instructions. Third, they point out how well we listen to new instructions he gives us. Fourth, they demonstrate who's in charge—our ego or our Creator. And fifth, if we pass the test, they produce the result as promised by our Creator.

Our Creator will talk to you, telling you how many stones you are to use during the ceremony. And the Sacred Stones will talk to you, telling you which of them are to be used this time. So, you must listen to both our Creator and the Sacred Stones. Set aside the stones you have been told to use, and have the fire keeper smudge them thoroughly. Then, ask that group of stones which ones among them have been chosen to be the first seven stones to be placed on the base of large logs in the fire pit. The stones will speak to your spirit, and you will intuitively be drawn to those seven specific stones.

These seven stones play a very special role in the ceremony. They are the ones who will help you call the Old Ones who faithfully passed on theses Sacred Ways, our Creator's power in the Four Winds, the spirit of Mother Earth and, most importantly, our Creator, to come and assist us during the ceremony.

Gently set these seven stones apart from the others. Have the fire keeper smudge them with a mixture of sweet grass and cedar. As this is being done, thank these seven stones for volunteering to play such an important role in the Purification Ceremony.

Ask the people to go the altar, take a pinch of natural tobacco from the bag, and return to the fire pit and face the West. Pick up the first of the seven sacred stones and cradle it gently in your arms as you take it to the fire pit. As you face the West, hold the sacred stone high toward the heavens. Ask our Creator's sacred power from the West to come and help all of those participating in the ceremony to be truthful and honest with themselves, our Creator and one another.

Our Creator's power from the West, often referred to as, "The West Wind", is the one who speaks to us through what we call, "our conscience", and provides us with discernment, intuition and internal truth. When we say our conscience is bothering us, that is our Creator's power of the West, or West Wind, speaking to our spirits, telling us what is right or wrong, good or bad. The more we seek guidance from our Creator's power from the West, the more we will understand what is right and wrong for us. The West Wind speaks to us through what we call, "our inner voice", telling us what we should, or should not, do or say. Therefore, it is necessary for our Creator's power of the West to be present in all of us during the Purification Ceremony in order for us to discern

Right from wrong and good from bad as we walk this Sacred Path.

As you hold the stone high overhead toward the West, the people will hold their pinch of tobacco up to the West and also pray, asking our Creator's power from the West to come and speak to them during the ceremony.

When you are finished with your prayer, gently place the sacred stone on the western side of the base of large logs in the fire pit, and have the people sprinkle their tobacco over the stone. They will then go to the altar and get another pinch of tobacco and return to the fire pit.

This process will be repeated for the remaining six stones. The next stone will be held up to the North, and the people will turn to the north as you ask our Creator's power from the North to come and participate in the ceremony. The North Wind brings with it our Creator's purity and wisdom to the ceremony. The North Wind is the great healer. It not only removes the bad, it heals the hurt and takes away the pain created by the bad or negative things within us. Without our Creator's power from the North there can be no Purification Ceremony.

It is important to understand that, even though our Creator sends in power from the North to the ceremony, unless we are willing to let go of those negative things in our lives, we cannot be purified. Once we let them go, we must ask our Creator's purity from the North to remain within our spirits, minds and bodies. The North Wind gives us the wisdom and power needed to avoid making the same mistakes in the future. There is no value in releasing the negative things in our lives, only to turn around and invite them back in again.

Our Creator's power from the East brings us "new beginnings". It is the source of the power to change. Our Creator's power of the North Wind removes the old, negative things and bad habits in our lives, and his East Wind brings us a new and right way to live. We must have our Creator's power from the East dwelling within us in order to make the changes necessary that enable us to live in peace, harmony and balance with all Creation.

Our Creator's power from the South—the South Wind—is the source of Unconditional Love and unity. It enables us to create harmony within our relationships, both with our Creator and his Sacred Circle of Life. The South Wind gives us the desire and power to serve others rather than serve self. It is impossible to live in peace, harmony and balance with the rest of Creation without the aid and assistance of our Creator's power from the South.

The South Wind brings rapid growth and development of the new insights, ideas, and beginnings that were given to us by our Creator's power from the East. As long as we are filled with our Creator's power from the South, things go well for us in all we do. However, if we shun our Creator's South Wind, we will quickly find ourselves falling prey to the conflict, turmoil and negative energies that are lurking in the shadows, waiting for an opportunity to trip us up.

The fifth stone symbolizes Mother Earth. Thank her for all she does for us. Everything we have came from her. She not only gave birth to us. Like any wonderful mother, she lovingly takes care of us. However, like most immature children, we sometimes disrespect her, and are very ungrateful for all she does for us. She unselfishly gives of herself for our benefit. She provides our shelter, food and clothing. We should always respect her and thank her for what she does for us. The stone representing

Mother Earth should be placed in the north west corner of the logs in the fire pit.

Take the sixth stone back to the fire pit, and facing southeast, hold it up to the sky. After going to the altar for more tobacco, the people will form a circle around you (or the person leading the ceremony). In forming the circle, the oldest person will stand in the south, and going in a clockwise direction, people will line up in descending order of age so that the youngest person will end up standing to the right side of the oldest person in the circle.

This sacred stone represents our ancestors who faithfully passed these Sacred Ways on to the next generation so that we can still perform them today. After thanking the ancestors for their faithfulness, affirm you commitment to our Creator to also faithfully pass these Sacred Ways on to the next generation. This is a very important part of the Purification Ceremony, because it illustrates how strongly the past and future are connected to the present.

This part of the ceremony also teaches us in a very powerful way that our present actions will not only have a tremendous impact on our lives now, but also on the lives of countless generations into the future.

Hand the sacred stone to the eldest member in the circle and have it slowly passed around clockwise until it ends up in the hands of the youngest person, who in turn, will place it gently on the southeast corner of the logs in the fire pit. As the stone slowly makes its way around the circle, explain to the people that the only way the sacred stone can make it to the fire pit is if each person passes it on to the next individual to his or her left. Point out that unless we are faithful in passing these Sacred Ways on to the next generation, this Ancient Sacred Path will be lost, and all of our relatives in future generations will suffer from that loss.

As the stone representing our ancestors is placed in the fire pit, ask the people if they are willing to help pass these Sacred Ways on to the next generation. Starting with the eldest and finishing with the youngest person in the circle, have those willing to make such a commitment place their tobacco on the sacred stone symbolizing our ancestors.

The seventh stone represents our Grandfather, the Creator of All Things. Carry it to the fire pit and slowly turn in a circle as you hold it high over your head. As you bring it slowly down and hold it firmly against your heart, have the people get more tobacco from the altar.

Our Creator is not only pure and holy, he is the source of all purity, and every thing he created was brought forth in a pure and perfect state— even we two leggeds. However, we have polluted and corrupted ourselves, as well as our environment, by following after our own self-centered egos. That is why our Creator has given us this powerful Purification Ceremony. It removes the impurities from our lives, and makes us like a hollow tube through which our Creator's Unconditional Love flows into us, through us, and out to others in the form of service to our relatives within the Sacred Circle of Life.

Explain to the people that it isn't enough for us to mentally accept the fact that our personal egos have led to the corruption of ourselves, as well as our environment. We must make a conscious commitment to change, giving our Creator control over our will, and empowering us with his Love so we can effectively help restore the Sacred Circle.

Having explained that, send the people away, individually, to a quiet place to reflect on the impurities that need to be eliminated from their lives. Tell them to hold the tobacco as they pray. Our Creator will reveal the things that need to be removed, or changed, in the people's lives so they will be more effective in serving their relatives within the Sacred Family Of Life. They will demonstrate their willingness to let go of those things, or make the necessary changes, by returning to the fire pit and placing their tobacco on the sacred stone representing our Creator, which has been placed on the altar.

Once the seventh stone has been placed on the altar, put the remaining stones in a pile on the logs in the fire pit. Next, take the stone representing our Creator from the altar and place it on top of all the other stones, and then sprinkle tobacco or cornmeal over the entire pile as you thank them again for their participation in this sacred ceremony.

PLACING THE WOOD AROUND THE SACRED STONES

The next step in the ceremony is for the fire keeper to place wood around the sacred stones. He or she will stand the pieces of wood upright and gently lean them against the pile of stones. This process will continue until the sacred stones have been totally enclosed within the pieces of wood.

As the fire keeper places the wood around the sacred stones, the people will get more tobacco from the altar. When all the wood is in place, the people will sprinkle the tobacco over the wood in honor of their commitment to offer themselves to our Creator for service in helping restore the Sacred Circle of Life.

As mentioned earlier, the wood symbolizes us. Just as the wood gives itself to be used to create the sacred fire, we are to give ourselves to our Creator to be of service to all our relatives within the Sacred Circle.

Most modern day two leggeds have been deceived into thinking the earth and everything in it belongs to them. They tend to view the earth as nothing more than "natural resources" to be used (and abused) to feed their unquenchable appetites for more and more material possessions. And tragically, they seem to be totally oblivious to the fact that they are in the process of destroying their Mother, and the rest of their relatives, because of their greed.

The Purification Ceremony draws our attention to this fact, and confronts us with the need to live in peace, harmony and balance with the rest of Sacred Creation. The wood symbolizes the commitment we make to serve our relatives within the Sacred Circle instead of serving our own egos.

Placing the wood in the fire pit is a very important part of the ceremony. It is a time for us to reflect on our commitment to serve others instead of self. It confronts us with the most important decision of our lives—who will be in charge, our egos or our Creator?

LIGHTING THE SACRED FIRE

When the people have finished sprinkling their tobacco over the wood, the fire keeper then leads them in singing the Sacred Stone Song (the words to the song are in the appendix of this book and it is on the CD that can be purchased from our web page at "medicinewheelmesas.com").

When the song is finished, the fire keeper will light the sacred fire as the people move in closer to the fire pit. Powerful symbolic meaning surrounds the lighting of the fire. First, it confirms to our Creator our desire and commitment to live in peace, harmony and balance with all our relatives within the Sacred Circle of Life. Second, it represents our Creator's overwhelming and awesome power as he responds to our invitation to actually come among us! From the time the fire is lit until the time people enter the Purification Lodge, the people's actions must be extremely respectful. Those present must avoid loud talk or disrespectful conversation because our Creator has arrived at the ceremony, and now is in the midst of the people.

The people must move back away from the fire because our Creator's power is consuming the wood and penetrating Mother Earth's sacred bones. Only the fire keeper is allowed near the fire, and then only to place more wood in the fire pit as needed, or remove any sparks that may have blown from the burning wood.

While our Creator consumes the wood and penetrates the sacred stones, making them red hot with his power, the people will go quietly to the altar and get a cornhusk and pinch of sacred tobacco and roll it into the form of a small "pipe". As they make the cornhusk pipe, they will pray, thanking our Creator in advance for the purification they will receive from him. Their prayers of thanksgiving are being placed within the sacred tobacco, and will later be released to our Creator.

As the people finish making their cornhusk pipes, they will place them on the altar. When all the cornhusk pipes are on the altar, the ceremony leader will go to the altar and load the Sacred Medicine Pipe, if he or she is a "Pipe Carrier" and using one during the ceremony. If the

Medicine Pipe is not being used, the leader will wait until everyone has finished making the cornhusk pipe, then he or she will go to the altar to make one that will be smoked by everyone in the Purification Lodge.

The ceremony leader will prepare a mixture of sage, sweet grass and cedar and smudge the parts of the Medicine Pipe and sacred tobacco mixture (or corn husk if the Medicine Pipe is not being used). As the leader does this, he or she will sing the Prayer Song for The Sacred Pipe. The people present who know the song will sing along with the leader.

Only those who have been initiated as "Pipe Carriers" know the ritual for filling the sacred Medicine Pipe, so I will not explain the ritual to the general public. However, since most of you reading this material are probably not Pipe Carriers, I will give you a ritual for preparing the Cornhusk Pipe. I encourage you to smoke the Cornhusk Pipe regularly as you pray.

Ritual For Preparing the Cornhusk Pipe

First, put just enough water on the cornhusk to dampen it slightly so it will be pliable enough to roll up without cracking. Next, tear off a small strip of the cornhusk about an eighth of an inch wide to be used for tying the rolled up cornhusk together. Place enough sacred tobacco in the corn husk to form a "pipe" about a half inch in diameter, then roll it up and tie it firmly with the strip of cornhusk. When the corn husk pipe has been made, offer it to the Four Sacred Directions, asking our Creator's power from the Four Winds to come into the corn husk pipe that will later be smoked. When you are finished with your prayer, place the cornhusk pipe on the top of the buffalo skull on the altar.

PREPARING THE SACRED PATH

When the sacred stones in the fire pit have become red hot they are called

91

"Grandfathers". The fire keeper will determine when the stones have become Grandfathers, and will inform the ceremony leader.

At that point, the fire keeper will prepare the Sacred Path. First, he will remove his shoes and then smudge the ground again between the fire pit and the entrance to the Purification Lodge. As he does this, all of the people will also remove their shoes. Next, he will smudge the container of tobacco or cornmeal. The ceremony leader will then smudge the fire keeper's hands.

Using his bare hands, the fire keeper will start at the fire pit and form a small line of tobacco or cornmeal that will mark the North side of the Sacred Path running from the fire pit to the North side of the lodge's doorway. He will repeat the process for the South boundary. The Sacred Path will be approximately four feet wide and connect the fire pit with the entrance to the Purification Lodge.

Once the Sacred Path has been created, no one is allowed to cross it. In order to move from one side to the other, people must either go around the Eastern end of the Purification Lodge, or around the Western side of the fire pit.

This Sacred Path is Holy Ground. Therefore, no one may wear shoes while walking on this path.

ENTERING THE PURIFICATION LODGE

The ceremonial leader will enter the lodge first. He or she will go to the fire pit to be smudged by the fire keeper, and then enter the Sacred Path there. The leader will slowly walk along the path and around the North side of the altar, and then stop at the lodge's entrance. The leader will raise his hands to the sky and slowly turn in a clockwise circle. As he does this, he will offer a prayer to our Creator, thanking him for this Sacred Ceremony, and asking him to purify the spirits, minds and bodies of all those present.

He will then drop to his hands and knees at the entryway. Here he will ask Mother Earth's permission for himself and the people to enter her holy womb so they can once again become purified. When his prayer is finished, the leader will enter the Purification Lodge on his hands and knees and crawl in a clock wise circle around the pit in the lodge floor and sit near the South entrance of the doorway.

Once the leader is inside the lodge, the people will line up at the fire pit to be smudged by the fire keeper before entering the Sacred Path. The women will line up first. The woman that the leader has asked to help him in the lodge will enter the Sacred Path first, followed by the rest of the women. Both women and men will follow the path around the North side of the altar, and when they arrive at the doorway, they will raise their arms and slowly turn in a clockwise circle. As they do, they will ask our Creator to purify them in spirit, mind and body. And as they drop to their hands and knees to enter they lodge, they will ask Mother Earth's permission to enter her holy womb. Then, like the leader, they will crawl in a clockwise circle around the pit to their place.

Once everyone is inside the lodge, the leader will ask the fire keeper to hand in the sacred items to be used during the rituals to be performed there. The cedar, sweat grass, drum, deer antlers and Sacred Medicine Pipe (if one is being used) will enter the lodge and travel around the circle in a clockwise position to the ceremonial leader. The leader will hand the cedar and sweet grass to the woman on his right who, in turn, will select one woman to sprinkle cedar on the Grandfathers as they are placed in the pit, and another woman to rub it with the sweet grass. The woman just to the right of the leader will be given the Medicine Pipe and she will touch the pipe stem to each of the first seven Grandfathers as they are placed in the center pit.

BRINGING THE FIRST SEVEN GRANDFATHERS INTO THE PURIFICATION LODGE

The leader will tell the fire keeper when he is ready to have the first seven Grandfathers brought into the lodge.

The fire keeper will use a pitchfork to carry the Grandfathers. He will shake the ashes off each Grandfather before removing it from the fire pit. This is very important because any ashes left on the stones may cause lots of smoke in the Purification Lodge.

The fire keeper will follow the Sacred Path around the North side of the altar to the lodge door as he carries each Grandfather. He will slowly stick the pitchfork through the doorway, and the ceremony leader will help guide it over the pit in the center of the lodge, then gently lower the Grandfather into the pit.

Using the deer antlers, the leader, or the man he appoints, will position the first Grandfather on the Western side of the pit because it symbolizes our Creator's power of the West Wind. The next Grandfather will be placed in the North side of the pit, symbolizing our Creator's power of the North Wind. The third one will be positioned on the East side, and represent the power of the East Wind. The fourth Grandfather will be placed on the South side and symbolize the South Wind's power. The fifth one will be placed in the center of the pit, representing our Creator's awesome, holy power that fills the center of the universe and moves out from there in the Four Sacred Directions. The next Grandfather represents Mother Earth and is placed in the northwest part of the pit. The seventh Grandfather represents the faithful ancestors who handed down these Sacred Ways from generation to generation and is placed in the southeast.

As each of these seven Grandfathers are brought in, the leader has the woman on his right who has been designated as the female helper during the ceremony, touch each sacred stone with the end of the Medicine Pipe stem (if one is being used). This symbolizes the people's acknowledgement that the Medicine Pipe is a sacred gift from our Creator, and it serves as a way to welcome the Grandfather into the Purification Lodge. If a Medicine Pipe is not used, the cornhusk pipe is held out over the top of the Grandfather instead.

As each of the first seven Grandfathers are positioned in the pit, the female helper sprinkles a few cedar leaves on it so the cedar smoke will purify the entire area inside the lodge. Next, she will wipe the sweet grass across the Grandfather. The sweet grass smoke will help attract some of our Creator's Helpers to the ceremony.

No one will be permitted to speak while the first seven Grandfathers are being brought into the lodge. Once those Grandfathers are in their proper place in the pit, the entire space within the lodge becomes very sacred and holy. Therefore, the people must act with the utmost reverence and respect. That does not mean people can't laugh. This is also a very joyous time, and laughter is certainly permitted when appropriate. However, people may not say anything negative about anyone inside or outside the lodge.

BRINGING THE REMAINING GRANDFATHERS INTO THE LODGE

After the first seven Grandfathers have been brought into the lodge, the leader will hand the Medicine Pipe (or cornhusk pipe) out to the fire keeper, and the pipe will be placed on the altar. The pipe bowl will be gently placed on the ground near the buffalo skull and the stem will be leaned against the skull, facing West.

The leader will then welcome all the people to this part of the ceremony and offer any special comments or instructions concerning how the remaining rituals will be performed. He will then instruct the fire keeper concerning how many remaining Grandfathers will to be brought in for each round. This will be according to the instructions the leader received from our Creator earlier. Our Creator will vary the details of the ceremony according to the needs of those in attendance. All of the remaining Grandfathers may sometimes be brought in before the first round begins. On the other hand, our Creator may instruct the leader to bring in a certain number of remaining Grandfathers before the beginning of each round.

THE FIRST ROUND OF THE PURIFICATION CEREMONY

Before discussing the rituals that occur inside the Purification Lodge, I want to emphasize again that our Creator is in charge of the ceremony. He has given certain things that are to occur during each round. He will determine the details that occur based on the specific needs of those attending the ceremony. This is extremely important to keep in mind; otherwise, it is easy to fall into the trap of doing things the same way during each ceremony.

It is true that the rituals that occur outside the lodge may be more predictable than the things that occur inside the lodge. This is a very personal ceremony. People have come to be purified in spirit, mind and body. Each person has specific issues and needs that relate to his or her purification, and our Creator will meet those needs in very specific ways. Therefore, it is imperative for the ceremony leader to focus his attention on listening carefully to our Creator, and do and say only those things Grandfather instructs.

I want to emphasize that this Purification Ceremony is performed quite differently from sweat lodge ceremonies. On this Sacred Path, the Purification Lodge is referred to as a "medicine wheel lodge", and the focus of each round is quite different from the focus of the rounds in what is commonly referred to as a "sweat lodge" ceremony.

Once the Grandfathers have been placed in the pit, the leader will ask the fire keeper to close the lodge door. The fire keeper may come inside the lodge to participate in the rituals, or he may stay outside to look after the fire. This will have been determined ahead of time between the leader and fire keeper.

When the door has been closed, the leader will thank everyone for coming, and explain that his role is simply to pour the Sacred Water. He will remind the people that this is our Creator's ceremony, and he will actually be in charge of all that occurs inside the lodge.

In most instances, the leader will begin by leading the group in singing the Sacred Direction Song. This song is usually sung at the beginning of the first round because it is asking our Creator to send his sacred power of the Four Winds into the lodge to help all of those

96

participating in the ceremony. However, I caution you not to get caught in the trap of thinking you must always sing certain songs at specific times during the ceremony. Listen to our Creator. He will tell you which songs should be sung, if any. Keep in mind that this ceremony is not a "sing fest". It is a Purification ceremony in which our Creator purifies our spirits, minds and bodies. The emphasis must be on purification, not demonstrating how many songs you know, and how well you can sing them.

As with most sacred songs, the Sacred Direction song is a prayer. It asks our Creator to send his power from the Four Sacred Directions to help us during the ceremony. However, in reality, that prayer has already been prayed as we placed the first four stones in the fire pit. If our Creator instructs you to sing the Sacred Direction Song at the beginning of the first round, when the song is finished, thank him for answering the prayer and acknowledge his powers of The Four Winds for coming to help everyone in the lodge.

Hold a dipper full of water high above the Sacred Stones and thank our Creator for Mother Earth's blood—her life force—that we can't live without. As you pour the water on the Sacred Stones, thank our Creator for releasing his power into the lodge. Throughout the ceremony, the leader will pour water on the Sacred Stones as our Creator directs.

The first round of the Purification Ceremony honors our Creator's power from the East, the East Wind. Our Creator's power from the East brings us the new day, new life, and new beginnings. It gives us new insights and new revelations about our Creator and his spiritual realm.

Our Creator's power from the East begins the purification process within us. The ceremony leader will ask those in attendance to sit quietly in the lodge's protective darkness and allow our Creator to begin the process of purification within them by focusing on their need for purification. As people sit quietly and the warm darkness surrounds them, the leader will pour more water on the Grandfathers and remind the people of the East Wind's power and what it accomplishes in our lives. He will

97

encourage the people to pray for new insights and revelations concerning our Creator and his power to bring new beginnings into our lives.

Our Creator will let the leader know when it is time to end the round. The leader will also know if another song, such as the Purification Song, should be sung to end the round.

When the people have finished their silent prayers, at the appropriate time, the leader will ask the fire keeper to open the door to end the first round.

THE SECOND ROUND OF THE PURIFICATION CEREMONY

It must be strongly emphasized that this is only a general outline of the rituals conducted inside the lodge. Our Creator is in charge of these rituals. He will instruct you concerning what needs to be done and said. He does the purifying. We don't, the songs don't, the water doesn't and the stones don't. Remember that the power is behind the symbol. The sacred items are symbols of our Creator's power, and the rituals open the door for the power from the spiritual realm to flow into the physical realm—and it is our Creator's power.

If you are having Grandfathers brought in at the beginning of each round, hand the bucket of water out to the fire keeper before he brings the sacred stones to the lodge.

If people go out of the lodge between rounds, don't have the Grandfathers brought in until everyone has returned to the lodge.

Our Creator will tell you if you should start the second round with a song or not. He will also pick the songs you are to sing during the ceremony, and let you know when they are to be sung.

The second round focuses on our Creator's power from the South, and that power is Unconditional Love. He used the South Wind to bring his power of Unconditional Love into the world. Our Creator's power from the South creates unity, peace and harmony among his children within the Sacred Circle of Life. It is his power from the South that heals relationships, creates teamwork, helps turn us into servants of others instead of servants of our own egos, and teaches us the true meaning of Love.

This Purification Ceremony is conducted within a medicine wheel lodge. East is the direction of spring, birth, and new beginnings. South is the direction of summer, growth, and the expansion of ideas into reality. It also teaches us about Love and serving others. The purification process intensifies during the second round.

At the beginning of the second round, point out that our Creator purifies us so we can more effectively serve our relatives within Life's Sacred Circle. Serving the needs of others is Love in action.

As specific needs are mentioned during this round, have a discussion with the people concerning what the group will do to help meet those needs.

During this round, the people are asked to make a commitment to serving others instead of serving self.

The purification of spirit, mind and body is a process. During the first round, the focus was on the need for new beginnings. People were asked to acknowledge to our Creator their need for purification and ask him to remove those things that hinder purification from taking place. During the second round, people are asked to focus on the needs of others instead of on their own ego driven wants and desires.

THE THIRD ROUND OF THE PURIFICATION CEREMONY

The third round focuses on our Creator's power from the West. On the medicine wheel the West is the time of the Fall Season. Our Creator's power from the West, or West Wind, brings us internal truth. It empowers us to be able to be truthful with ourselves, our Creator and our relatives within the great Circle of Life.

The healing process begins with accepting and embracing truth. Truth empowers us with faith, confidence and a sense of "knowing" that is necessary in order to take the actions required to achieve success. Truth is the foundation on which positive results are achieved.

When truth is absent, doubt, uncertainty and negativity slowly take control of our lives. Internal truth, which the West Wind brings to us, is an essential part of the purification process. Unless we are truthful with ourselves, our Creator, and others around us, we can never experience purification.

Our Creator purifies us so that we can more effectively serve others. Serving the needs of others is "Love in action". As specific needs are mentioned during this round, have a discussion with the people concerning what the group can and will do to help meet those needs.

During this round, each person will ask Our Creator to help him or her always be truthful with others, themselves and with our Creator, because purification begins with truthfulness.

THE FOURTH ROUND OF THE PURIFICATION CEREMONY

The fourth round focuses on our Creator's power from the North, which is purity and renewal. On the medicine wheel, North is the direction of winter. Winter is the season of rest and renewal. The purifying snows of winter come and help cleanse the earth. During the Purification Ceremony our Creator's purifying North Wind comes into us, purifying our spirits, minds and bodies.

We cannot purify ourselves—only our Creator can purify us, and that is why he gave us the Purification Ceremony. The ceremony first makes us aware of our need for purification and identifies those things in our lives that have created the impurity. It enables us to release the things hindering purification so that our Creator can fill us with his Unconditional Love, creating within us a commitment to serve others instead of self. And finally, it makes us receptive and eager to receive the purity that is our Creator's gift to those who live lives of service to the Sacred Circle of Life.

100

During the fourth round, people are asked to silently review the issues they have dealt with and the commitments they have made. At some point during the round, the leader will instruct people to silently pray, asking our Creator to purify their spirits, minds and bodies, and empower them to live lives of service to The Sacred Circle of Life.

There is usually time allotted for people to share anything they would like concerning their experience during the ceremony. However, the leader must make sure people understand any public sharing of experiences in the lodge are strictly voluntary and that things shared in the lodge are not repeated by others when they leave the lodge.

Songs that are often sung during the fourth round include The Song of the Four Winds, The Give Away Song, and the Closing Prayer Song. The Closing Prayer Song is generally sung at the end of the fourth round as a prayer to indicate it is time to leave the lodge.

SMOKING THE MEDICINE PIPE OR CORNHUSK PIPE

The ceremonial pipe may be smoked inside the lodge at the end of the fourth round, or outside around the altar after the round is over. After the ceremonial pipe has been smoked, the leader will instruct the people to take their cornhusk pipe home with them and smoke it in private as a "thank you" to our Creator for all he did for them during the Purification Ceremony.

THE CEREMONIAL FEAST

The Purification Ceremony ends with the ceremonial feast. This is a very important part of the ceremony because it is a time of fellowship and thanksgiving. The focus of conversation should be on how wonderful and great our Creator is for giving us the powerful Purification Ceremony. There is no place for negative conversation during the ceremonial feast.

At the end of the feast, everyone should remain to help clean up the area by removing any trash and washing dirty dishes.

CONCLUSION

Two thousand years ago Jesus Christ was highly critical of the religious leaders of his day, telling them that they had a form of Godliness, but that they denied the power of God in their religious activities and ceremonies. In many respects, the same is often true in sweat lodge ceremonies currently being conducted around the country. All too often those leading the sweat lodge ceremony are able to display very impressive "form" during the ceremony. However, the proof of the ceremony's value is in the changed lives of people who regularly attend those sweat lodge ceremonies.

If people regularly attend sweat lodge ceremonies, but there is little— if any---evidence of spiritual growth in their lives, they also have a form of Godliness but they are not allowing our Creator's power of Unconditional Love and purity to change their nature from one of self-centeredness to one of humble service to the Sacred Circle of Life.

The purpose of the Purification Ceremony is to get rid of our self-centeredness and submit our will to our Creator so his Unconditional Love can flow into us and out to meet the needs of others—this is the whole focus of *The Way of The Medicine Wheel*.

Teaching Session – 4
THE GIVE AWAY CEREMONY

Grandfather Old Bear once told me that on this Sacred Path life is to be lived each day as a continuous "Giveaway Ceremony". He explained that each morning the rising sun signals the beginning of our Creator's great Give Away Ceremony to us, and that the ceremony continues until sunrise the next morning. All day long—day after day—our Creator is constantly giving to us. He gave us our lives, our bodies, and a place to call home here on Mother Earth. Everything we have came from our Creator as a gift to us, his children. Therefore, since he so freely meets our needs, we, in turn, should freely meet the needs of others within the Sacred Circle of Life. Each day should be lived as a continuous give away.

The words in the Morning Prayer Song illustrate the purpose and meaning of the Giveaway by stating:

Oh, great Creator, thank you for the rising sun.

Oh, Grandfather, thank you for all that you've done.

Thank you for new life today.

And help me give it back, I pray.

Oh, great Creator, thank you for the rising sun.

That song often brings tears to my eyes as I face the rising sun and sing it as a prayer to our Creator, because, once again, I am made aware that everything around me is a gift from our Creator, even the air I breath and my next heartbeat. Since our Creator is so very good to me, the least I can do is give my life back to him be used in helping restore peace, harmony and balance within The Sacred Circle of Life.

The following story of the first Giveaway Ceremony is an attempt by our ancestors to explain why giving should be the focus of our daily lives.

Far back in the distant past, undoubtedly, various versions of this story were retold over and over again around countless campfires during the long winter nights.

THE LEGEND OF THE FIRST GIVEAWAY CEREMONY

When our Creator got ready to make the two-leggeds, he called all of his children together at the foot of the great holy mountain that reaches up to the sky in that far off place were the direction of the North begins. His children came together and set up their lodges, forming a great encampment along the banks of the sacred river known as The River of Life, which flowed continually from the foot of the holy mountain.

The river's pure, clear water nourished the spirits, minds and bodies of our Creator's children, and empowered them to live in peace, harmony and balance with all of their relatives within the Sacred Circle of Life.

At sunrise the next morning, our Creator met with all of his children and said, "I've decided to make more children, and they will be known as the "two-leggeds".

All of the animals were very happy and excited. "When may we meet our new relatives," they asked.

"Tomorrow, at sunrise," our Creator answered. "You will need to help take care of the two-leggeds, and teach them how to live in peace, harmony and balance on the back of your Mother, the Earth.

Our Creator asked all of his children to come closer, then he continued. "Your new relatives will need lots of help from you in order to learn how to live here on Mother Earth. They will have much weaker bodies than most of you four-leggeds, and they won't be able to fly like you winged people do. They won't be able to run as fast, hear as well, see as far, or smell as well as most of you can. So, you will need to be patient with them as you teach them how to live among you."

"Oh, we will," his children enthusiastically exclaimed. "We can hardly wait to meet them, and we will help you take very good care of them."

The next morning, as the sun rose over the mountains on the eastern horizon and sent its warm rays into the beautiful valley, our Creator asked all of his children to gather along the bank of the River of Life. They were filled with excitement and anticipation as they watched him take some of the mud from the river's bank and form it into a man's body. Then he took more mud and formed it into a woman's body. Our Creator set the two bodies out in the sun all morning to dry, and then, in the afternoon, he took them down to the River of Life and washed them in the clear, pure, Sacred Water. When he was finished washing the two-legged's bodies, he blew his breath on their faces, and immediately they came to life.

Our Creator lovingly hugged his new children and then introduced them to the rest of their smiling and cheering relatives who had gathered around them, eagerly waiting to welcome their new brother and sister into their Sacred Family.

That evening, as the full moon shone down on the lush, peaceful river valley, the Creator of All Things met with his children and reminded them of their responsibility to help their new two-legged relatives learn how to live in peace, harmony and balance with the Sacred Circle of Life. Then he explained to the two leggeds that they were to drink freely from the Sacred Water in the River of Life, because it would nourish both their spirits and bodies.

"As long as you drink from the River Of Life every day, you will never die, and your bodies will always be strong and healthy," our Creator told them. Then he went back up the Holy Mountain and disappeared from sight.

All the animals except the spider loved their new relatives, and were surprised at how fast they were able to learn how to live on Mother Earth. The spider, however, became very jealous of his new relatives because they were getting so much attention.

One day the spider approached the two leggeds as they were walking through a meadow filled with all kinds of beautiful flowers, and said, "Greetings relatives. It's a beautiful day, isn't it?"

"Oh, it's beautiful every day here on Mother Earth," they replied.

"Yes, but it would be much more enjoyable for you if you could eat meat like I do," the deceitful spider lied. She rubbed her large stomach and smiled contentedly, as if to illustrate how full and satisfied she was. "Meat tastes much better than drinking that old water in the River of Life all the time."

She giggled to herself as she hopped away, knowing she had accomplished her purpose.

Later that day, the man and woman killed a small deer by hitting it in the head with a rock. They roasted the meat and ate it. They loved the taste of roasted meat, so the next day they made a spear and killed a large deer to eat. They gave some of the meat to the wolves who happened by. They gobbled it down, and then ran off to find their own deer to kill and eat.

The eagle was flying high in the sky and saw all that had happened, so he flew to the Holy Mountain to tell our Creator all that he had seen.

Our Creator was very upset and disappointed with the two-leggeds because they had disobeyed him, taking the life of one of their relatives, and thus bringing death into the world. The two-leggeds had also convinced some of the other animals that eating meat was much better than just drinking water from the Sacred River of life. Because of this, our Creator caused the River Of Life to stop flowing so his children could no longer drink from it and continue living forever.

Our Creator came down from the holy mountain and told all his children to meet him in what has suddenly become an arid valley where the River of Life had been flowing. When the river dried up, the whole area had instantly become a dry, parched desert. And even to this day, there are deserts in various parts of the earth to remind our Creator's children of all they lost when they disobeyed him long ago there at the foot of the Holy Mountain.

Our Creator's children were reluctant to come to the Holy Mountain and face him because of their disobedience. Also, because they now feared each other since they had started killing their relatives for food. The owl

106

warned his relatives that they could expect to be severely disciplined by their Father, and this upset the Creator's children even more.

When Grandfather came down to the foot of the holy mountain, he remained a great distance away from his frightened, disobedient children as he spoke to them. "My two-legged children have made me very sad," he began. "You disobeyed me by killing and eating your relatives, thus bringing death into the world."

He waved his arm in a wide circle. "Look around you now at this dry, barren desert that just a short time ago was a beautiful valley filled with all kinds of flowers, shrubs and mighty trees because the River of Life flowed through it. Your disobedience caused the River of Life to stop flowing, and now, you also have become like this desert."

His children began to cry as they remembered how beautiful this valley had been only a few moments ago.

Our Creator continued. "When you brought death into the world, you forced me take away the River of Life, so now you can no longer live forever. All of you will eventually die, but until that day comes, you will eat one another in order to stay alive."

Then Grandfather told the eagle to bring him the hides of the two deer the two-leggeds had killed, and he made clothes for them to wear. As our Creator handed the two-leggeds the deer skin clothes, he said, "From now on you will always wear clothes as a reminder to all your relatives that the two-leggeds were the ones who brought death into the world. And, because you brought death to all my children, I will teach you a ceremony that must be performed by you and your descendants for all time. You will call this "The Giveaway Ceremony."

"This ceremony will teach you how to be "givers" instead of "takers" only. It will also teach you the true meaning of love. As long as the River of Life flowed through this land, you had no needs. Now you, and all of your relatives, are weak and hungry. So, from now on, your purpose in life must be to give to those who are in need, and help those who need your help. This Giveaway Ceremony is to be lived as a lifestyle —it is the way you will live your life each day—as a great giveaway. Just

as I have given you all that you have, in turn, you must share all that you have with others."

And so that day long ago at the foot of the great Holy Mountain that reaches up to the sky in that far off place where the direction of the North begins, our Creator taught the first two-leggeds how to conduct the sacred Giveaway Ceremony. The Giveaway Ceremony was to be lived as a lifestyle, and it is at the very center of all that is done on this Sacred Path known as *The Way of the Medicine Wheel.*

THE PURPOSE OF THE GIVEAWAY CEREMONY

As the above story explains, our Creator gave the two-leggeds the Giveaway Ceremony to be lived as a lifestyle. It was given to teach us that the purpose of our lives is to serve others, not self. Our whole focus in life should be to serve the needs of others. If that were everyone's purpose in life, all needs within the Sacred Circle of Life would be met.

The Giveaway Ceremony symbolizes the way we are to live our lives. Contrary to what many people think, the purpose of life isn't to see how much "stuff" we can accumulate while we are living here on Mother Earth. Indeed, just the opposite is true. We are to live our lives for the benefit of others, not to see how much wealth and possessions we can amass. That is the whole lesson of the Giveaway Ceremony. It symbolizes our commitment to a lifestyle of "giving" instead of "getting".

THE RESULTS OF GIVING

Giving is the best investment you can make because it returns more to you than any material investment could ever do, and our Creator and Mother Earth are constantly demonstrating that for us in nature. For example, when we plant a single kernel of corn we get several ears of corn back in return. And the same is true in our daily lives. When we give, we get back more than we gave.

What is your response when people give to you? You want to give something back to them, don't you? So, the more you give to your relatives within the Sacred Circle of Life, the more you get back.

Does that mean we give so we can get? No, certainly not. That is the ultimate expression of greed and manipulation. We give to meet the needs of others, or to show our love and gratitude for our relatives within the Sacred Circle—and we expect nothing in return. However, when we give to meet the need of others, or simply as an expression of gratitude and love, it has the same effect as planting the kernel of corn—we always get back more than we gave. That is a universal law that is constantly being demonstrated all around us by our Creator, and also by Mother Earth in nature. Each day, day after day, our Creator gives us a brand new life as the sun rises over the eastern horizon. He gives us every additional heartbeat, as well as our next breath. All of our food, clothing and shelter are gifts to us from our Mother, the Earth. Both our Father and Mother are constantly giving to us, requiring nothing in return.

Giving, and then expecting nothing back in return is the ultimate expression of love in action. On the other hand, giving as a means of getting is the ultimate form of deceit, greed and self-centeredness—and such actions will eventually lead to your depravation.

THE DOMINANT SOCIETY PROMOTES "GETTING" OVER "GIVING"

Our modern society has a terminal disease call, "affluence", and may people are in the advanced stages of that illness. Unfortunately, most people with the disease are totally unaware that they are sick. In fact, they tend to think that the more material possessions they have, the better off they are. However, just the opposite is true.

The more affluent we become, the more self-sufficient, independent and "in control" we usually think we are—and the less we tend to feel the need for our Creator's help. Therefore, an excess of material possessions and wealth often tends to weaken our connection to our Creator and his

109

Spiritual Realm, while at the same time, it usually strengthens our connection—and reliance on—the physical realm.

Are material possessions evil? No, absolutely not. However, spending all of our time and energy acquiring them is. So I ask you, *"How much time and energy are you spending acquiring material possessions, and how does that compare with the amount of time and energy you spend focusing on your connection to our Creator and his spiritual realm?"* The answer to those questions will help you determine where your priorities are.

You see, there are two kinds of priorities—"real" and "imagined"—and it is easy to determine which ones are real. Our real priorities are the ones we spend most of our time working on. So look at how you spend the majority of your time, and you can easily determine your current priorities.

A few years ago, the twelve-year-old son of a friend of mine asked me if I would buy him the latest computer play station for his birthday. When I told him I didn't know what I was going to get him for his birthday, he got very angry and upset, and turned to his father and said, "If Myron doesn't get me the play station for my birthday, then you have to!" His father smiled and patted him on the head as he replied, "I'm sure someone will get you that play station for your birthday. Don't we usually get you what you want?"

Shortly after that, one of my Native American friends invited me to their reservation to attend their twelve-year-old daughter's birthday ceremony. When I asked him what his daughter would like for her birthday, he replied. "Oh, please don't get her anything. She has been collecting things for months for her birthday giveaway. Her birthday ceremony is a time of giving to her friends and relatives to show how much she has appreciated all they have done for her throughout the year."

Angelitta and I were able to attend the young girl's birthday ceremony, and we came away with a deep appreciation of its value and importance.

A lot of the young girl's friends and family attended her birthday ceremony, as well as several tribal elders. When the ceremony was ready to begin, her parents placed a buffalo robe in the center of the living room floor, and asked their daughter to take off her shoes and stand on it. Then, her father smudged her with sage while her mother tied an eagle feather in her hair.

Her grandfather came forward and fanned her with an eagle feather fan while he smudged her with cedar smoke. As he did this, he told her a brief history of their tribe, and the role her ancestors had played in shaping the past history of her people.

Next, one of the older grandmothers came forward and placed the girl's hands in her own weathered and wrinkled old hands. She smiled warmly at the girl as she told her that her actions, and the way she lived, would help determine the future of the whole tribe. All of the elders present nodded their heads, or verbally confirmed their agreement with what the old grandmother said.

When the old woman was finished, the girl's father came forward and told everyone about her major accomplishments during the past year, how she had learned to do beadwork, how helpful she was to her mother around the house, how well she was doing in school, and so on. Then, her mother went to her side, and putting her arm around her daughter's shoulder, pointed out some of her daughter's mistakes during the past year, but explained that those mistakes had become positive lessons in her daughter's life.

Some of the young people talked about what a great friend the birthday girl was to them, and how much they respected her because she was always there when they needed someone to talk to, or needed help with a problem.

Towards the end of the birthday ceremony, the young girl's parents helped her bring out all the gifts she had collected throughout the year to give to those in attendance. As a way of honoring those who had come to the birthday ceremony, she gave gifts to everyone, starting with the eldest and ending with the youngest. The ceremony ended with a feast, and the birthday girl served the food to all the people.

As Angelitta and I drove back to Colorado, we discussed at length the great difference between that birthday ceremony and the birthday parties conducted by parents within the dominant society. In the dominant society, the emphasis at the birthday party is on "getting". Our Native American friend's daughter had spent the entire year collecting things to give away at her birthday ceremony. The ceremony was a time of instilling within her that she was not only a product of past generations, she would help determine what the tribe's future generations became. It was a time of reflecting on the girl's contributions to her family and the greater community during the past year. And, it was an opportunity for her to continue to learn the importance of giving to others.

On the other hand, birthday parties within the dominant society tend to emphasize fun, games and getting gifts from others. As a result, they help create the mind set in children that asks, "What are you going to GIVE ME for my birthday." It is no wonder we live in a society that is more concerned with "getting" than with "giving". We begin programming our children at a very young age that it is much better to get than to give.

BEGIN FOCUSING ON SIMPLIFYING YOUR LIFE

Affluence is addictive—the more things we get, the more we want. We have convinced ourselves that "more" is "better". We tend to go through life never satisfied with what we have. We want bigger houses, bigger and faster cars, and bigger bank accounts. We build bigger shopping centers, bigger churches and bigger theaters. We construct bigger super highways so we can go faster between our bigger cities. And all the while, our appetites for more and more things gets bigger and bigger.

Our gluttonous materialistic appetites that crave more and more possessions are ultimately reflected in the size of our bulging waistlines. Our houses, garages and storage units are not only over stuffed with all kinds of things we neither need nor use, our waistlines are bulging because too frequently we over indulge at the "all you can eat" restaurants.

As a nation, we have become so obsessed with affluence, our economists have come up the terms like "the consumer index" and "purchasing power" in an attempt to define our buying habits.

The weaker our connection to our Creator, the stronger our connection is to the physical realm. And the stronger our connection to the physical realm, the more self centered we become. The more self centered we become, the more we focus on materialism to meet our needs and make us happy. Unfortunately, happiness derived from material possessions is very short lived. True and lasting happiness only comes from walking in peace, harmony and balance with our Creator and all his relatives within the Sacred Circle of Life.

In order to rid ourselves of this terminal disease called "affluence", we first need to rid ourselves of our excess "stuff" and begin moving toward a more simplistic lifestyle.

I suggest that you conduct your first Giveaway Ceremony by starting to give away the excess "things" you have stored away in closets, attics, basements, garages and storage units. I can tell you from personal experience, this is not as easy as it sounds. Even though you don't actually "need" those things, they tend to "possess" you. You may find that they own you, you don't own them. They often control you, making you feel you must keep them because you just might need them someday.

I speak from personal experience. A few years ago Angelitta and I lived in a big house in the mountains. It was full of all kinds of very nice things. When we moved into a small hogan on Medicine Wheel Mesa, we were forced to give away everything except for what was absolutely necessary for living our very simple lifestyle. Many of the things we gave away have very sentimental value to us. Some were antiques from Indonesia we had brought with us to America. Many could not be replaced, such as the antique "gong" given to us by a medicine man living in a remote high mountain village in the jungles of Indonesia.

Emotionally, it was hard for us to give many of those things away. Some of our possessions are still in storage, waiting their turn to be distributed to others who need them more than we do. When Angelitta and I began the painful process of simplifying our lives, we quickly discovered that the more simply we lived, the stronger our connection with our Creator became.

CONDUCTING THE GIVEAWAY CEREMONY

As I indicated at the beginning of this teaching session, the Giveaway Ceremony is one of the most important ceremonies we perform as we walk this Sacred Path because it symbolizes our lifestyle of "giving" instead of "getting". *The Way of The Medicine Wheel* teaches us to live our lives as a continuous "giveaway", serving others instead of ourselves.

Before describing the rituals in the Giveaway Ceremony, we must first consider the kinds of things we should give away.

Usually, the first things that come to mind when we think of conducting a Giveaway Ceremony are the various "material" items that could and should be given away. Even though it is very important to make material items a part of the things we give away, non-material items are often far more important to give than any material things we could share with others.

For example, if you have new neighbors next door, invite them over for a meal to get acquainted. Show them around the community. Let them know where the best places are to shop. Find out what their interests are and help them meet other people with the same interests. Let them know you are always available to help them in any way possible.

I know what you're probably thinking—that takes a lot of time, and you are already very busy. Ah, next to your health, time is your most important possession. It's much easier to give money than to give time. Your time is your life. When you spend time with people, you are giving them part of your life—and your life is your most important possession. Therefore, the amount of time you are willing to "invest" in others is the true test of how much you are willing to serve the Sacred Circle of Life.

Notice that I used the word "invest" instead of "spend". It is true that you are busy, so *invest* your time in people, don't just *spend* time with them. By that I mean when you are with your relatives, make the time count. Serve their needs. Help them. Do things for them. Demonstrate that you love them for who they are. Make their favorite food for them; help them with their important projects, find out their needs and help meet them.

Today people tend to say, "I'm going to go just 'hang out' with my friends." If that is all you do, you have wasted part of your life and theirs as well. Life is short, and people's needs are many. We have been put on this earth to help meet the needs of our relatives within the Sacred Circle of Life. We are our Creator's children, and children are to obey their parents. When someone prays to our Creator for help, he will often use you and me as his hands and feet to meet that person's needs. Each morning, don't just sing the Morning Prayer Song that says, "thank you for new life today, and help me give it back, I pray." Ask Grandfather to use you that day any way he chooses to help serve the needs of your relatives within the Sacred Circle of Life. In that way you will be investing time in others, not just spending time with them.

Serving the needs of others is often as simple as slowing down and letting the driver in the lane beside you get in front of you so he or she can get off at the next exit. Serving the needs of others can be as simple as smiling at those who have frowns on their faces. And yes, serving the needs of others often means digging deep into our pockets to meet the material needs they have.

On this Sacred Path, our first responsibilities of service are to the old ones, widows, and the young ones among us. They need the most help. We serve the elderly among us to help show our appreciation and respect for them passing on to us what they have learned from life. We serve the young among us by passing on to them the things we are learning from our elders. This is one of the most important ways of helping mend the Sacred Circle of Life that has been broken by the two-leggeds' greed and selfishness.

Never forget that our lives are to be lived as a continuous give away.

We are to develop a lifestyle of serving the needs of others within the Sacred Circle—which is why our Creator has put us here on the back of our Mother the Earth. Long ago, our Creator gave us the Giveaway Ceremony as a reminder of how we are to live each moment of our lives. Therefore, conduct the ceremony often, because it will help keep you focused on the true meaning and purpose of life.

ALWAYS BE MAKING PREPARATIONS FOR YOUR NEXT GIVEAWAY CEREMONY

As I said, conduct the Giveaway Ceremony often because it symbolizes the way we are to live every moment of our lives. We should always be in the process of making preparations for our next Giveaway Ceremony.

Every time we go to town, Angelitta is always looking for things to purchase that people need. Since we don't have lots of money, she frequently looks for nice things on sale that people need, such as blankets, canned foods, and other necessities of life. Our give away items tend to be things that people need and use often, not things that wind up in people's attics or storage areas.

On this Sacred Path, most major ceremonies end with a Giveaway Ceremony. However, it can also be conducted at any time. In our family, Angelitta is in charge of all the Giveaway Ceremonies. She plays a major role in collecting the items to be given away, and she is the one who distributes any items to be given to specific people attending the ceremony.

PREPARING YOURSELF FOR THE GIVEAWAY

In a previous teaching session, we explained that a ceremony actually begins with our personal preparation, and that how well we prepare will have a major influence on the ceremony's effectiveness. Your personal preparation is extremely important when conducting the Giveaway Ceremony.

Never let yourself become puffed up with pride when conducting a Giveaway Ceremony. The purpose of the ceremony is to serve the needs of others, not draw attention to yourself and how much you are giving away. Always perform the Self-Offering Ceremony as a way of properly preparing yourself to conduct the rituals involved in the Giveaway Ceremony.

PREPARING THE ITEMS TO BE USED IN CONDUCTING THE CEREMONY

You will need the following items to conduct the Giveaway Ceremony:

- A buffalo robe or special blanket to place the items on that are to be given away.
- The items to be given away.
- Sage, sweet grass and cedar for smudging.
- A drum.
- Food prepared for a meal at the conclusion of the ceremony.

Begin by smudging the area with sage where the ceremony will be conducted and ask our Creator to keep all negative attitudes away from this area during the ceremony. Next, smudge the buffalo robe or blanket, and then smudge all the items to be given away. As you do this, ask our Creator to use these things to help meet the needs of those in attendance. Place the items to be given away on the robe or blanket before people begin arriving for the ceremony and cover them with a blanket.

CONDUCTING THE CEREMONY'S RITUALS

Smudge everyone as they arrive. If space permits, have people sit in a circle around the giveaway items. If it is summer, and the weather permits, we prefer to conduct the ceremony outside or in our tipi. We conduct the ceremony inside if the weather is bad, and we try to arrange the room so people can sit on the floor in a circle around the buffalo robe.

This is a happy time, and a rather informal ceremony, so we have coffee, tea or cold drinks available for people while they wait for everyone to arrive.

Begin by spending some time discussing the purpose of the Giveaway Ceremony. Remind everyone that our lives should be lived serving our relatives within the Sacred Circle of Life. Point out that everything we have comes from our Creator and Mother Earth, so in reality, the things on the robe or blanket are actually gifts from them. Before actually distributing the items, tell the story of the first Giveaway Ceremony.

There are an almost unlimited number of variations to the way this ceremony can be conducted. You may give the items to the individuals or you may start with the oldest person and end with the youngest and have people come and select the items they need.

The Giveaway Ceremony is often a time of recognizing and honoring individuals publicly by giving them special gifts. In such instances, share with the group why you are honoring the individual as you give him or her the gift.

Once all of the gifts have been distributed, invite everyone to join together in a meal.

The Giveaway Ceremony can be organized as a special time for whole families to come together for a day of "fun and games". Games can be organized for children to participate in while the adults visit and relax. As pointed out earlier, there is no limit to the variations that can be developed for conducting the Giveaway Ceremony.

When Angelitta and I invite people to a Giveaway Ceremony, we usually tell them they are also free to bring items to be given away. However, we make sure to explain that this isn't necessary.

I know it has been emphasized over and over during this teaching session, but it is so important that we must continually remind ourselves— the Giveaway Ceremony was given to us as an example of the way we are to live our lives. Life is to be lived as a continuous giveaway. Our purpose in life is to serve others. Therefore, we need to conduct the Giveaway Ceremony often, because it will help keep us focused on the real meaning of life.

The Giveaway Ceremony teaches us the true meaning of love. Love is an action, not a feeling. Love focuses on serving others, not self. Love gives, expecting nothing in return. All of the major religions of the world tell us to "love one another". The Giveaway Ceremony is love in action, and developing a lifestyle of giving is the purpose of this Sacred Path called *The Way of the Medicine Wheel.*

BOOK TWO

The Purpose and Power of The Medicine Wheel

INTRODUCTION TO BOOK TWO

I grew up in rural Oklahoma, the first-born son of a "half-breed" Pawnee Indian woman and a white man. My uncles on my father's side called my mother "squaw", not only because of her dark complexion, but mostly because she regularly befriended the community of Kiowa Indians that lived nearby on poor, red dirt farms like the one we lived on.

Some of my earliest memories are of my mother taking me to pow-wows out in the cow pasture behind an Indian family's run down shack that was home to several Kiowa families. I also used to love lying on my bed with the window open during the hot, summer nights and listening to the steady, rhythmic beat of the drums off in the distance.

I didn't become serious about the spiritual aspects of my Native American heritage until I went through a very serious and devastating personal crisis many years later. At age 43 I owned a manufacturing company, a direct sales company, a management consulting business, and I was the author of a best selling management book.

That year I bought a new home, two new cars, and finished writing my second book. Also, in November of that year my marriage of 23 years fell apart, and I soon found myself divorced.

At that point in my life I turned my back on the white man's world and moved onto a remote mining claim I owned deep in the Rocky Mountains of Colorado. I became more and more depressed, and one day I decided life was no longer worth living.

The next morning I got up determined to shoot myself before sundown. As I sat staring at my 41 Magnum pistol, trying to get up the courage to blow my brains out, suddenly I saw my mother sitting across the table in front of me. She just sat there smiling, not saying a word.

I started crying as I remembered what a wonderful, loving and caring mother she had been, and how she always helped people, especially the Indian families in our community.

Instead of shooting myself that summer day, I went for a long walk in the mountains, and it was on that walk that I made a decision that forever changed the direction and purpose of my life. That day I decided to learn more about the spiritual aspects of my Native American heritage.

It was about a year later, shortly after I built my first "sweat lodge", that our Creator began impressing upon me that I should also build a medicine wheel. However, I had never even seen a medicine wheel, so I began asking some of the local Native American elders what a medicine wheel was, and how to build one. To my surprise, I discovered that none of the Indians I knew had ever built a medicine wheel, and they seemed to know very little about its actual purpose and use.

Unfortunately, that didn't seem to matter to our Creator, because every time I prayed, from somewhere deep within me, I knew my prayers would be much more effective if they were offered from inside a medicine wheel.

One Saturday morning in late summer, I crawled out of bed long before the first rays of light appeared on the eastern horizon, determined to try to find a place to build some sort of medicine wheel. My frustration level was very high because I had no idea where a medicine wheel should be built, and even if I found what I considered to be a suitable place, I knew even less about what to do next.

That morning, as the sun rose over the mountains to the east, I was slowly making my way along a narrow game trail that followed a small mountain stream. I had just finished another prayer to vent my frustrations and hopefully get our Creator to understand that I had no idea where I was going, or what I should do when I got there, when suddenly I heard the loud, shrill scream of an eagle.

Startled by the piercing sound, I stopped and began looking around, trying to locate where the eagle was. It wasn't until the third or fourth shrill scream that I finally spotted the majestic, sacred messenger from our Creator soaring high over head. In fact, the eagle was so high, it seemed like a small, black dot against the backdrop of a fluffy, white, cumulus cloud.

Just as I spotted the eagle, it began an almost vertical dive, heading straight at me and screaming what seemed to me to be an angry warning. I froze in my tracks, not knowing if I should run in an effort to try and escape this diving missile of feathers and talons, or try to remain stationary in hopes that by some miracle he wouldn't notice me.

Engulfed in terror, and trapped by indecision, I just stood there as if under the magical spell of what seemed to me to be a supernatural being that was propelling itself straight at me at the speed of light. Now he was screaming what I imagined was a message informing me that if I moved, he would surely kill me. To my amazement and utter relief, the eagle suddenly pulled out of the dive just above tree top level and started circling me, all the while continuing to scream a message that I now falsely interpreted as a scolding for intruding into his territory.

Suddenly, the eagle started flying down the trail a ways, then it circled back over my head, continuing the loud, shrill screaming. Finally, it occurred to me that he was trying to get me to follow him, so reluctantly I started off down the trail to see where he was headed. The eagle went around the bend in the trail, then headed up the side of a steep ridge.

I had a hard time trying to keep up with him, so he kept flying back, circling over me and screaming as if to say, "Hurry up, lazy two-legged, we have a long ways to go."

Tired and out of breath, I eventually made it to the top of the ridge. I followed the eagle North for about a quarter of a mile, then suddenly it let out another loud, piercing scream and shot straight up, going higher and higher until it was again just a small, black speck in the dark blue sky overhead.

I stopped to catch my breath, then looked around in amazement. Immediately in front of me to the North was a giant outcropping of huge boulders that formed the shape of an eagle sitting on the ground with its wings held out away from its sides as if cooling itself. In every other direction, row after row of mountains stretching all the way to the horizon, were standing like giant sentinels who had been put there to protect this sacred place.

After drinking in this spectacular view, I realized the eagle had led me to this spot because this was where the medicine wheel was to be built. I burst into tears and dropped to my knees, overcome with emotion as I realized that our Creator had actually heard my anguished cry for help in finding where the medicine wheel should be built.

I don't know how long I cried, but slowly my tears of joy were replaced with sobs of frustration as I remembered, once more, that I had no idea what to do next. Yes, now I knew where the medicine wheel was to be built, but I still didn't have a clue as to how to build it.

In this book we will explore the purpose and meaning of the medicine wheel, the ceremony for building the sacred wheel, the powerful symbolism associated with the medicine wheel, and how to use it.

During these teaching sessions we will also discover the important role the medicine wheel will play in helping people survive the "Time of Great Cleansing" that Mother Earth will soon unleash on our so called "sophisticated society".

Teaching Session – 5
PRINCIPLES OF THE MEDICINE WHEEL

The medicine wheel is the oldest, most sacred, and most powerful spiritual symbol our Creator has given the two leggeds. It contains the ancient spiritual principles and truths that enable us to successfully walk this Sacred Path. It is so simple, yet it contains the answers to all of the great profound spiritual mysteries within the universe and shows us how to once again combine the physical and Spiritual Realms into one, single reality.

GRANDFATHER OLD BEAR TALKS ABOUT THE MEDICINE WHEEL

Grandfather Old Bear's small, tattered lodge came into view as I rounded the bend in the river, and I spotted him sitting on a stump beside the lodge door. I knew he saw me as I approached, but he continued to sit motionless on the stump, staring off toward the far mountains on the western horizon, obviously taking in the inspiring beauty of the sacred sunset.

When I reached his side, without first greeting me or taking his eyes off the mountains in the distance, he said, "Grandson, slowly turn in a circle and tell me what you see around you."

I was irritated by his failure to give his usual warm greeting and hug, but I tried to hide it from him, all the while knowing that was impossible. I had come through the center door into My Private World to see him and ask him about the medicine wheel. However, those questions would have to wait until after we finished whatever guessing game he was playing with me.

I knew better than to question what he had asked me to do, so I slowly turned in a circle and then stopped directly in front of him. "I saw lots of tall, beautiful trees behind your lodge. I saw the long valley stretching North and South with the river winding its way through it. I also saw the high mountains framed against the brilliant red of the setting sun in the West," I replied, happy with myself that I hadn't left out any major details of the surrounding topography.

"Huh!", grandfather replied. "I might of known." He shook his head in resigned disbelief. "I see a medicine wheel," he continued. "Every time I turn in a circle, I see myself standing at the center of a medicine wheel with its edges reaching out to the far horizon in every direction." He paused for a moment, apparently to see if I understood the meaning of what he had just said, then continued. "That's the difference between you and me. You like to talk about this Spiritual Path I refer to as The Way of The Medicine Wheel, but I see myself living it."

You could have knocked me over with a feather. Once again, this Ancient One had known why I was coming to see him, and once again, he had read me like a book.

I hung my head in shame as I sat down on the stump next to him. "Tell me, grandfather," I began without taking my eyes off the ground at my feet, "Will I ever learn to walk this Sacred Path the way you walk it?"

"No," he emphatically replied, to my surprise. "You live in a different time and place than I lived in, but if you really work at it, you might come close—maybe." He laughed loudly, and slapped me on the back. "Don't look so dejected, grandson. I could have just said, 'no'!" He laughed again, and I feigned a smile, trying to no avail to cover up my frustration.

We sat there in silence for a while. I assumed he was giving me a chance to start over. Finally I was ready to try again. "I came here to talk to you about the medicine wheel and its role on this Sacred Path you keep referring to as The Way of the Medicine Wheel."

"I know," he replied. "And I just explained it to you, but it hasn't soaked into your head yet because your brain has become all scrambled *up by too much exposure to that man-made electricity back in your world."*

When I frowned and shook my head in confusion, he continued. "Forget it. That discussion is for another time. You certainly aren't ready to deal with that issue yet."

He stood up and stretched. "Let's go for a walk down by the river and we'll talk about the medicine wheel and how it relates to this Sacred Path."

As we walked along the path by the river, grandfather continued. "As I've told you many times, The Way of the Medicine Wheel is the term I use to define the sacred path all people in ancient times traveled as they made their way toward the Creator Of All Things. As you know, the purpose of the Sacred Path is to help us learn to live in peace, harmony and balance with our Creator and all of his Creation. This Sacred Path is a "lifestyle". It's a sacred lifestyle that corresponds with—and flows with— the Four Sacred Seasons. It's the way we live season by season. We live in such a way that we actually become one with, and part of, each Sacred Season."

He took a deep breath and slowly exhaled. "I'll explain that in more detail later, but grandson, you can only fully understand it by living it. No amount of talking about it, and explaining it will make you really comprehend it. You must live it, then you'll know what I'm talking about. Okay?"

I nodded my head, but inside my frustration and confusion was growing.

The Old One knelt down by the river and drew a circle in the moist sand with his long, bony finger. Then he began again. "This Sacred Path is a never ending circle. The medicine wheel is also a never ending circle that defines in detail this Sacred Path." He looked up at me to make sure I was paying attention. "This Sacred Path is broken down into four sacred 'lifestyle ceremonies' that correspond with the Four Sacred Seasons. Likewise, the medicine wheel is broken into four parts."

He slowly drew a line East and West, and a line North and South that

129

intersected at the center of the circle and extended out to its edges. Next, he poked his finger into the sand where the lines crossed at the center of the circle. "Our Creator is at the center of all we do on this Sacred Path, and that is symbolized on the medicine wheel by the lines crossing in the center of the circle."

We spent the rest of that day, and many days thereafter, discussing the medicine wheel. Grandfather explained in great detail how the medicine wheel relates to this Sacred Path, and a summary of those conversations—and others—are presented on the following pages of the next four teaching sessions.

WHAT IS A MEDICINE WHEEL?

Many years ago I built my first medicine wheel high atop a long, rocky ridge, deep in the heart of the Rocky Mountains of Colorado. I must admit that I had no idea what I was doing at the time. I knew even less about the layer upon layer of meaning shrouded within the powerful symbolism enshrined within the medicine wheel. However, our Creator used that event to open my Spiritual Awareness to the fact that the rest of my life would be devoted to the on-going process of learning what the medicine wheel is, and how it is to be used.

Our Creator taught me many things back then, including the ceremony for constructing the medicine wheel. He also began the process of teaching me the powerful sacred symbolism associated with the medicine wheel. As I look back now, I can see that during those years he was actually preparing me for the time when I would meet grandfather Old Bear, and my education about the medicine wheel would begin in earnest.

Grandfather Old Bear helped me understand that the medicine wheel isn't just a powerful symbol; it actually represents and explains the ancient Sacred Path that the two-leggeds everywhere used to travel as they made their way to our Creator. It describes the lifestyle that is required in order to combine the physical and Spiritual Realms into a single reality.

So what is a medicine wheel? It is many things. However, its most important function is to combine into one powerful symbol all of the major principles associated with walking the Sacred Path referred to as *The Way of the Medicine Wheel.* At the same time, it is much more. It is a road map for walking this Sacred Path. It shows us, step by step, how to walk in peace, harmony and balance with our Creator and his entire Sacred Circle of Life.

Before our Creator gave the two-leggeds sacred writings and scared scriptures, he gave them the medicine wheel to teach them how to live in accordance with his Universal Laws of Right Living that produce peace, harmony and balance in our daily lives. The medicine wheel is the oldest and by far the most important sacred symbol that reveals to the initiated the hidden mysteries of the Spiritual Realm.

The land is sacred. However, the earth within the medicine wheel is not only sacred, it is Holy Ground. A properly constructed medicine wheel concentrates and focuses our Creator's power onto a small, round spot of earth in much the same way a magnifying glass can focus the light from the sun.

If you take a piece of paper outside on a bright, sunny day and hold it up to the sun, nothing happens. But, if you hold a magnifying glass the proper distance above the paper it will focus the powerful energy from the sun onto a single dot on the paper, and the concentrated energy from the sun will quickly catch the paper on fire. This is an excellent illustration of how a medicine wheel works. In much the same way as the magnifying glass focuses the sun's light, the medicine wheel focuses our Creator's power within the small area of the circle of stones, thus creating a very holy and spiritually powerful place where we can meet with our Creator.

When we enter a medicine wheel we are totally surrounded by our Creator's power of Unconditional Love in a concentrated form. Our Creator used his power of Unconditional Love to create the universe, and he still uses it today to accomplish all of his work. In a medicine wheel we are in our Father's presence and totally engulfed in his wonderful creative power of Unconditional Love.

Our Creator's Unconditional Love heals hurts, removes pain, solves problems, restores relationships, offers forgiveness, removes guilt, forgets past mistakes, offers hope, promise and success for tomorrow, and makes the impossible a reality—and that is why the medicine wheel was such a wonderful gift to us from our Creator. It is a place where we can enter his presence and more effectively commune spirit to Spirit with him. It is a place where his power of Unconditional Love can enter us and empower us to live in peace, harmony and balance with him and all of his Sacred Creation. It is a place where we can go to learn the great spiritual mysteries that, for the most part, remain hidden from those living in the "fast lane" of this modern day, high tech world system.

So why has most of the medicine wheel's ancient hidden wisdom been lost? The answer is both simple and sobering. The deep, spiritual meaning of the medicine wheel was lost because the two-leggeds began placing greater priority and value on the things in the physical realm than on the things of the Spiritual Realm.

The Way of the Medicine Wheel brought the physical and Spiritual Realms together into a single reality. On that Sacred Path, our Creator maintained a personal, intimate relationship with all of his children. However, somewhere far back in antiquity, the two-leggeds decided to place their own self interests ahead of our Creator's Universal Laws For Right Living that govern his relationship with his children. And, since that time, the two-leggeds have been steadily moving farther and farther away from their Spiritual Father, our Creator. As a result, today most two-leggeds have very little understanding of the true meaning of the medicine wheel.

A few books have been written in an attempt to define the medicine wheel and its secrets, and some of those books have been able to effectively present a few of the medicine wheel's basic principles. On the other hand, some have greatly missed the mark, actually leading people astray concerning the purpose of the medicine wheel and how to use one by suggesting that "the wheel" is some sort of elaborate astrological chart.

One of the things I've learned from grandfather Old Bear is that

132

important truths need to be repeated over and over because they must never be forgotten. During the course of these teaching sessions I will likewise repeat myself over and over in an attempt to help you never forget the most important principles of this Sacred Path.

As I said, and will continue to emphasize, the medicine wheel is a composite of the most important powerful symbolic meanings that reveal this Sacred Path. Therefore, *the medicine wheel is a sacred road map, revealing the path to our Creator, and how to maintain a strong connection to his Spiritual Realm. It is holy ground, a place where we enter our Creator's presence and become engulfed in his Unconditional Love that empowers us to live in peace, harmony and balance with all our relatives within the Sacred Circle of Life.*

A superficial examination of a medicine wheel usually leads one to conclude that it is a very simple symbol. However, one may spend a lifetime studying it and never reach the end of its layer upon layer of hidden powerful and profound revelations into the mystical aspects of our Creator's Spiritual Realm. In fact, as grandfather Old Bear has pointed out to me many times, most of those revelations can never be discovered and understood by simply "studying" a medicine wheel. Their hidden spiritual principles and truths must first be lived—then, and only then, will the medicine wheel's powerful and profound hidden meanings and truths be unveiled, understood and experienced by the two-leggeds.

THE "MEDICINE" BEHIND THE MEDICINE WHEEL

When we talk about *The Way of the Medicine Wheel, some of* you are thinking, "Where's the pill I take that will suddenly enlighten me concerning this Sacred path?" I assure you, the word "medicine", as it is used in the term "medicine wheel" does not mean the same as the word "medicine" as it is used in the field of modern day medicine currently practiced in the dominant society.

When we attempt to talk about and define the infinite, mystical realm of the Spiritual World, we quickly discover that the words used on this finite, physical level fail miserably in our effort to communicate the working and "activity" occurring in the Spiritual Domain. As a result, when we use mere words from the physical plane we often create more confusion than clarity as we attempt to discuss principles and laws that relate to and govern the infinite Spiritual World.

For example, the Webster's Collegiate Dictionary defines medicine as "a substance or preparation used in treating disease." It states that medicine is "the science and art of dealing with the maintenance of health and the prevention, alleviation, or cure of disease." The uninitiated or uninformed person might wrongly assume a medicine wheel is a device used by a pharmacist to dispense pills.

Even though it falls far short of properly and effectively communicating what we mean, we use the word "medicine" in an attempt to communicate the mystical and unexplainable results that occur when the bridge is formed between the physical and Spiritual Realms. We also use the term "medicine" to describe the sacred items or symbols associated with forming that bridge—thus such terms as "medicine pipe" or "medicine wheel" are created in an attempt to define the purpose for which those specific objects are used.

In the dominant society, a "doctor" is a person practicing scientific medicine within the physical realm. On the other hand, a "medicine man" may be practicing Spiritual Medicine that comes from the Spiritual Realm as well as medicine in the physical realm. In both cases, the individuals are working for the benefit and well being of those they treat.

The term "medicine wheel" is used in an attempt to communicate that this is an object used to create a bridge between the physical and Spiritual Worlds. It is an object created for the benefit and well being of those who use it. It is one of the many doorways providing an opening between the physical and Spiritual Realms.

We call it a "medicine" wheel in an attempt to communicate that this is a circular object that works on a Spiritual level for the benefit and well being of those who know how to properly use it. Do we thoroughly understand how it works? No. Therefore, it can't be properly explained.

Do we know that it works? Yes, because we have seen and personally experienced the results of using the medicine wheel.

The medicine wheel is a physical tool used to create a bridge to the Spiritual Realm. *The Way of the Medicine Wheel* is the Sacred Path we walk toward our Creator that is defined by the layer upon layer of symbolism that is brought together to make up the one great symbol we call the medicine wheel.

THE MEDICINE WHEEL'S PROFOUND MYSTICAL SYMBOLISM

It needs to be repeated over and over throughout these teaching sessions that symbolism is the bridge over which we walk to get to the power behind the symbol. In itself, a symbol has no power. However, it represents, or symbolizes, power. In order to tap into that power we first must understand the meaning of the symbol, because the symbol defines and communicates what the power is.

As we explained in the first teaching session, symbolism both hides as well as reveals power. If we know and understand the meaning of the symbol, we may experience the benefit of the power represented by that symbol. On the other hand, if we are unaware of the meaning of a symbol, we will not even be aware that the power exists. To effectively walk this Sacred Path, we must learn all we can about the symbolism contained within the medicine wheel.

The medicine wheel is a composite of layer upon layer of symbolism that has been brought together into one comprehensive symbol that defines the Sacred Path called T*he Way of the Medicine Wheel.* Within the medicine wheel lies buried under symbolism, all of the spiritual principles and truths of all the great religions of the world. In order to discover and properly understand them, we first must discover and understand the symbolism that conceals them.

I repeat—and will continue to emphasize over and over—that *The Way of the Medicine Wheel* is the most ancient of all Spiritual Paths that bring us into a personal relationship with our Creator and all of his

Creation. It was the Spiritual Path all ancient tribes and clans everywhere followed in developing that special personal relationship with their Maker and his Sacred Circle Of Life. That is why today we still find the remains of medicine wheels scattered across all the continents, on many islands and even on the ocean floor.

In order to walk this Sacred Path, we first must understand the powerful symbolism contained within the medicine wheel. Therefore, we will spend a considerable amount of time examining that symbolism so that you will be better prepared for your exciting and rewarding journey along this Spiritual Path toward our Creator. However, first I want to emphasize that no one will ever discover and understand all of the symbolism associated with the medicine wheel and the Sacred Path it represents, because acquiring spiritual knowledge and enlightenment is a never ending, lifelong process.

THE CIRCLE

The circle is the most sacred and profound symbol our Creator has given us. In addition, it is the shape most often found in creation. For example, the microscopic atom, the building block for everything found in creation, is in the shape of a circle. The entire universe is made up of circles—including suns, stars, planets and moons. As far as we know, even the universe is a circle of such vastness that we are still searching for its outer limits—if it has one.

The human body is a composite of circles, including our heads, arms, legs, fingers, eyes and all of our bodies' orifices. The trunks and limbs of our relatives, the trees, are also circular in shape. The list goes on and on.

From antiquity, tribal holy people from around the world have understood that the circle also symbolizes our Creator—and rightly so. Just as the Creator of All Things has no beginning and no end, so the circle is without beginning and end. More than any other symbol, the circle depicts the infinite. All other symbols are contained within the circle, and likewise, our Creator possesses all knowledge, wisdom and understanding.

The circle also symbolizes the peace, harmony and balance that result from walking this Sacred Path. The medicine wheel circle symbolizes our Creator and all of his Sacred Creation. Therefore, the medicine wheel represents all that our Creator has made. The medicine wheel circle also contains within it all of the hidden knowledge needed in order to walk this Sacred Path.

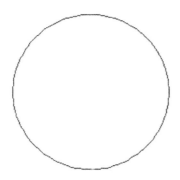

Figure 1

The circle is the oldest and most perfect symbol we have of the Creator and His sacred circle of life.

THE MEDICINE WHEEL'S
SACRED PATHS

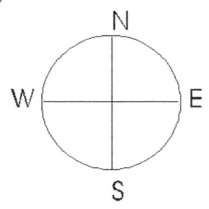

Figure 2

This diagram depicts two of the medicine wheel's most important symbols; the east-west line symbolizing female energy, and the south-north line symbolizing male energy.

The medicine wheel contains two sacred paths. One runs East to West and the other runs South to North. These two sacred paths cross each other in the very center of the medicine wheel.

The "East-West" path is controlled by female energy and symbolizes constant change while the "South-North" path is controlled by male energy and symbolizes unbending tradition.

The sun rises in the East and sets in the West every day. The rising sun brings us the new day and new life. The setting sun brings us the night that erases the day's activities. The East-West line symbolizes the path of the sun as it travels across the sky. The rising and setting sun bring many changes in our lives each day.

East is the direction of Spring and West is the direction of Fall. These two seasons are dominated by female energy (much more will be said about this in a later teaching session).

On the medicine wheel, South is the direction of Summer and North is the direction of Winter, and these two seasons are dominated by male energy.

The East-West line also symbolizes the physical realm and the South-North line represents the spiritual realm.

Within the medicine wheel, both of these paths lead us to our Creator. The medicine wheel teaches us that our Creator is not only at its center, but he also wants to be at the center of all we do every day of our lives.

The medicine wheel is a symbol of our entire lives from birth to death. It is also a symbol of our lives on a daily basis. The East symbolizes our birth. South represents our youth. West symbolizes adulthood, and North is the time of our old age. East is also the time of morning. South is the time of mid-day. West represents sundown, and North is the time of midnight.

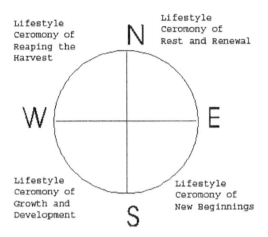

Figure 3

The medicine wheel consists of many layers of symbolism. In this diagram, it symbolizes
the four lifestyle ceremonies that coincide with the four sacred seasons.

Our Creator's power from the East is the source of all new things.
The sun rises in the east each morning bringing us a new day and new life.
Therefore, on the medicine wheel circle, East symbolizes new beginnings.
The Lifestyle Ceremony of New Beginnings begins in the East on the
Spring Equinox and continues around to the South until the Summer
Solstice.

Our Creator's power from the South is the source of Unconditional
Love and it enables us to grow and work together with one another as a
team in peace and harmony. This is the time of mid-day when the sun is at
full strength. Therefore, on the medicine wheel the South symbolizes the
time of harmonious growth and development for all things within the
Sacred Circle of Life. The Lifestyle Ceremony of Growth and
Development begins in the South at the time of the Summer Solstice and
continues to the West until the time of the Fall Equinox.

The power from the West brings the night and empowers us with internal truth. Our Creator's power from the West brings us the night, a powerful time for spiritual awakening and work. The power from the West enables us to see things as they really are and avoid the many deceptions that can trip us up and lead us away from our Creator.

The Fall Equinox occurs in the West on the medicine wheel and signals the start of the Lifestyle Ceremony of Reaping The Harvest. This ceremony continues until the time of the Winter Solstice.

Our Creator's power from the North is the source of purity and wisdom. The Lifestyle Ceremony of Rest and Renewal begins in the North at the time of the Winter Solstice and continues until the Spring Equinox. Our Creator's power from the North enables us to learn from our many experiences throughout our lives. It empowers us with our Creator's wisdom and purity so we can truly live as "hollow bones" in service to our relatives within the Sacred Circle of Life. Our Creator's power from the North also enables us to hear our Creator's voice, as well as the voices of his helpers (or angels) as they speak to us and teach us how to live in peace, harmony and balance with all Creation.

These four Lifestyle Ceremonies will be covered in detail in later teaching sessions.

THE CENTER OF THE MEDICINE WHEEL

As illustrated above, the two sacred paths intersect at the very center of the medicine wheel, and this spot symbolizes the place where our Creator resides. The medicine wheel is a symbol of our lives. Therefore, it is only fitting that our Creator is represented as being at the center of all we do each day. The four Lifestyle Ceremonies were given to us as a way to keep our Creator at the center of all we do as we perform our daily activities.

During one of my discussions with grandfather Old Bear about the medicine wheel he said, *"Every time I look at a medicine wheel I am reminded of how I am to live my life. I see our Creator at the center of my life. I see the two sacred paths that influence my every action. I see the sun rising in the East bringing me new life. I see the night covering the day's activities in the West. I see our Creator's Unconditional Love spreading over me from the South, and I see his wisdom and purity coming to me from the North. I also see the four great Lifestyle Ceremonies that make up the seasonal cycle of my life—and it reminds me of the sacredness of everything I do because our Grandfather is at the center of all my actions.*

"You see, grandson, our whole lives are described for us within the medicine wheel. It is the most sacred tool our Creator has given us for teaching us how to live in peace, harmony and balance with him and all of his Sacred Creation. It is like your sacred books in your modern day religions." *He chuckled to himself, then continued.* "However, it seems to me the medicine wheel is much simpler and easier to understand than those big books.

"That's the problem with people in your modern day world, grandson. They complicate everything—even their relationship with The Creator of All Things. This is a simple path—not necessarily easy, but simple. The medicine wheel is simple, and yet it communicates more about how we are to live than we can comprehend in a lifetime of living. So, grandson, simplify your life and then you can see more clearly all of the wonderful teachings that are hidden within the layer upon layer of symbolism in the medicine wheel."

The Old One from the ancient past looked deep into my eyes, and with sternness in his voice said, "Understand this well, grandson. Even though the teachings of the medicine wheel are simple, you will never comprehend them unless you are also willing to simplify your life. The medicine wheel teaches us how to walk this Sacred Path, and it is the path of simplicity. Therefore, in order to understand the simple—yet powerful —teachings of the medicine wheel, we must be willing to simplify our lives because that is the end result of following this Sacred Path toward our Creator."

I have never forgotten that conversation with grandfather Old Bear, and I am learning that what he said that day is true. The more I simplify my life, the more I begin to understand the simple—yet profound—teachings woven into the layer upon layer of symbolism within the medicine wheel.

As we continue through these teaching sessions, step by step we will discuss these layers of symbolism in great detail.

KNOWLEDGE WITHOUT APPLICATION LEADS TO DECEPTION

There are lots of great books on spirituality. However, as grandfather Old Bear has warned me over and over, to simply have spiritual knowledge is of no benefit unless that knowledge leads to application of the information. In fact, spiritual knowledge without application leads us into deception because we tend to "talk the talk", but we aren't "walking the walk". We have the information in our heads, but it isn't in our hearts where it changes the way we act and live.

There is no value in reading this information on *The Way of the Medicine Wheel* unless the knowledge is then put into practice. Our Creator is not concerned about how much knowledge we have of this Sacred Path. He is interested in what we DO with what we KNOW. And this is especially true concerning the medicine wheel.

The more we apply the knowledge we learn about the medicine wheel, the more our Creator reveals new knowledge and power hidden behind the additional layers of symbolism with the wheel. I challenge you to immediately start putting into practice the Spiritual Truths our Creator reveals to you. Otherwise, you run the risk of becoming deceived by talking about what you know when you're not actually applying or doing what you know to do.

We are giving you information in these teaching sessions, but only our Creator can reveal Spiritual Truth to you. Therefore, again I challenge you to listen to your heart as you read this material. Don't implement this information simply because we put it in print. Ask our Creator to reveal to you what you should do. Ask him to give you Spiritual Enlightenment and then put into practice the things he tells you to do.

Teaching Session -6
THE CEREMONY FOR CONSTRUCTING THE MEDICINE WHEEL
(The Circle of Stones Ceremony)

Just as not all pipes are "medicine pipes" and not all individuals with pipes are "pipe carriers", so not all circles of stone are medicine wheels. A pipe may look like a medicine pipe and an individual may act like a pipe carrier and a circle of stones may appear to be a medicine wheel, but appearances can be deceiving. Our Creator's power creates a medicine pipe. He empowers the individual to become a pipe carrier, and it is our Creator's power that turns a circle of stones into a medicine wheel.

Medicine wheels are situated on the most holy ground on Mother Earth. That knowledge alone should tell us that we two-leggeds cannot create a medicine wheel. What two-legged is capable of creating holy ground? Only our Creator can turn a circle of stones into a medicine wheel. We do the physical work of creating the circle of stones. However, it is our Creator's power that turns that circle of stones into a medicine wheel that encircles the most holy ground on Mother Earth.

I want to make sure you clearly understand the above statement. Our role in The Ceremony for Constructing the Medicine Wheel is that of a "laborer". We do the physical labor of preparing the spot where the circle of stones will be placed. We collect the stones and place them in a circle. However, it is our Creator who turns that circle of stones into a holy place where his power can reside. His power will reside in a medicine wheel only if we properly follow his instructions in creating the circle of stones, and his power remains in the medicine wheel only as long as we continue to work within that wheel in the way he instructs us. Please never forget that. Always follow every detail our Creator asks of you in creating the stone circle, and always work within the medicine wheel exactly the way he requires you to.

Don't do this just because I ask you. Ask our Creator if you also should follow the step by step process for creating the circle of stones presented in this teaching session. The following ceremony for creating the stone circle is the one our Creator gave me many years ago after I followed the eagle to the spot I described at the beginning of the previous teaching session. I have continued to follow the details of that ceremony each time I construct the circle of stones. However, I am not suggesting that this is the only way to create the circle of stones. As I said, ask our Creator, yourself, if this is the ceremony you should perform to construct the circle of stones and do what he says you should do.

You should always follow our Creator's guidance, not ours. I pass on to you the same advice grandfather Old Bear has given me. Many times he has said, *"Grandson, never blindly follow my instructions or advice. Always ask our Creator of All Things if you should follow what I suggest to you, then do what he tells you to do. In that way you will be obeying our Creator and not me."*

THE TIME REQUIRED TO COMPLETE THIS CEREMONY

Unlike many other ceremonies, it is impossible to know how long this ceremony will take. However, I can assure you it will take several days, if not weeks—or sometimes even months. Please understand that you are not in control of how long it will take to construct the circle of stones— our Creator is. Therefore, don't worry about how long it will take to make the stone circle, because it will take exactly as long as it is supposed to take.

THE STARTING POINT

The starting point is to begin praying for our Creator to show you where to construct the circle of stones. Our Creator determines where the medicine wheel will be located, we don't. Our job is to pray, asking him to reveal to us where he wants the medicine wheel to be.

In all probability, the medicine wheel won't be situated in your "favorite spot". Our Creator already knows where he wants the wheel to be located, and he will reveal that location to you when he determines you are ready to receive the information.

Be patient. Our responsibility is to wait for our Creator's instructions, not charge off on our own to put the circle of stones where we want it, or think it should be located.

Even though we do the physical work of creating the circle of stones, the actual medicine wheel belongs to our Creator. He knows where the medicine wheel is to be located, and he is just as interested in revealing that location to you as you are in wanting to find it. However, we must clearly understand that he will not let us know where to create the circle of stones until we are properly prepared to do the work.

This ceremony isn't just about creating a circle of stones that will become a medicine wheel. It is also about preparing us to be worthy of being in our Creator's presence when we enter that sacred circle and walk on holy ground. It is very important that we understand this.

In order for us to create a circle of stones that our Creator is willing to put his power in, we first must be willing to let him be in total control of every action we take while creating that circle. We actually become his hands and feet. We become transformed into his servants, doing his bidding, following his orders and directions, because this is his medicine wheel, not ours.

So continue to pray, asking our Creator to reveal to you where he wants the medicine wheel to be located. How long should you pray? Keep praying until our Creator tells you where the spot is. How long will that take? I have no idea. The first medicine wheel I worked on took several weeks of prayer before our Creator sent the eagle to show me where the spot was. The medicine wheel located on our land at Medicine Wheel Mesa was several months in the making. I can't tell you how long it will take to find the spot and construct the circle of stones, but I can

147

assure you that however long it takes, it is exactly the right amount of time.

Don't worry about getting the circle of stones completed. Instead, worry about obeying every instruction our Creator gives you so that the circle of stones will be worthy of containing our Creator's power, and that you will be worthy to enter the sacred circle and stand on holy ground in his presence.

PREPARING THE SITE FOR THE CIRCLE OF STONES

Our Creator will reveal to you where the circle of stones is to be located only after you have acquired the proper amount of the Five Spiritual Medicines-Courage, Patience, Endurance, Alertness and Humility. The more of these Five Spiritual Medicines we develop, the more of our Creator's sacred knowledge, wisdom and power we will be entrusted with.

Once our Creator has shown you the spot where the circle of stones is to be created, you will perform the Self-Offering Ceremony and the Purification Ceremony for four consecutive days before you begin preparing that spot for the stones. This is extremely important to your personal preparation to be of service to our Creator. Remember that we must be his humble servants. We must be good listeners so we can hear his instructions. We must have courage to perform this ceremony exactly as he instructs. We must be patient, letting him always be in control. And, we must have the endurance needed to continue to perform our tasks to the end, no matter how long it takes.

During one of my trips to grandfather Old Bear's lodge to further discuss the medicine wheel, we had the following conversation:

"I know you want to learn all you can about the medicine wheel," grandfather said as he stoked up the little fire in the center of his lodge. *"So listen carefully and I will explain one of the most important reasons*

for us performing the Circle of Stones Ceremony (that is what he calls the ceremony for constructing the circle of stones that our Creator will turn into a medicine wheel).

He could see that I was hanging onto every word he spoke, so it seemed to me he deliberately paused a long time to let my anticipation build, then he continued. "Grandson, if you properly perform the Circle Of Stones Ceremony, our Creator will be building a medicine wheel within you at the same time you are building the circle of stones." He stared deep into my eyes with that penetrating look I have come to expect from him when he is discussing something of great importance.

I frowned. "What do you mean? How can a medicine wheel be created inside of me?" I asked.

He smiled as he continued playing with the small fire with a willow stick. "Do you know what our Creator wants from you, grandson?"

After pondering his question a little while, I replied. "I'm not sure."

He laughed. "You're not sure? Either you know or you don't—which is it?"

I hate these kinds of probing questions from him because he never lets up until I say exactly what I'm thinking or feeling. "Well then, no—I guess I don't," I admitted.

He laughed even louder. "It's hard for you to admit it when you don't know, isn't it?" Now he was laughing so hard his skinny frame was shaking all over. "Obedience, grandson—our Creator wants obedience from us.

"Every ceremony we perform is a test of our obedience. The level of our obedience is the measure of our faith. The level of our obedience is the measure of our commitment. The level of our obedience is the measure of our trust and love. The level of our obedience is the measure of our Spiritual Courage, Patience, Endurance, Alertness and Humility."

"But what if I obey simply out of fear?" I asked.

"Ah, good question, grandson." His eyes were beaming with love for me as he continued. "You see, if I obey simply out of fear, eventually my fear will cause me to flee in order to escape from my master. That is why I

said, 'the level of our obedience is a measure of our trust and love'. If I obey because of my trust and love, I will do what is asked of me, no matter what the consequences. On the other hand, if I obey because of my fear, I will eventually try to escape my master because I see him as my captor."

"I think I understand," I replied. "But what does that have to do with the medicine wheel?"

"You see, grandson, when I faithfully and obediently follow all of our Creator's instructions in creating the circle of stones, I am demonstrating to him that I am putting his will and his plans first in my life. I am showing him that I love him more than I love myself. My continued obedience is a demonstration of my love for, and trust in, our Creator. Therefore, just as I place the center stone in the circle of stones to symbolize that our Creator is in the center of all things, including my life, my obedience makes that a reality. Our Creator dwells within me at the very center of my life, and his powers from the Four Winds find a home within my spirit. I become that circle of stones. I become the place where our Creator resides. He resides at the center of my being, just as he is at the center of the great Sacred Circle of Life, which is symbolized by the circle of stones.

"I tell you all of this, grandson, to help you understand how important it is to faithfully obey all that our Creator asks of you when you construct the circle of stones. Give your full attention to every detail. Follow his every instruction, leaving nothing undone. Take no shortcuts. Do you understand what I'm telling you, grandson?"

I share with you that very personal conversation I had with grandfather Old Bear because of the profound truth of what he had to say. If we faithfully and obediently follow all that our Creator instructs us to do in creating the circle of stones, we aren't just creating a stone circle; we are becoming a medicine wheel—the place where our Creator resides. Therefore, make obedience to our Creator the top priority in your life. Every day seek his will over your own.

This is especially important as we prepare ourselves to make ready the ground where the circle of stones will be placed. As you conduct the

Self-Offering Ceremony and the Purification Ceremony for four consecutive days prior to preparing the ground, your goal is personal purification so that your own ego doesn't get in the way as you strive to obey all that our Creator asks.

Items You Will Need to Conduct the Ceremony

You will need the following items to conduct this ceremony:
• Lots of natural tobacco (3-5 pounds, depending on the size of the circle).
• Lots of sage, sweet grass and cedar for smudging.
• Lots of red cotton cloth (5-10 yards, depending on the size of the center stone).
• Clean stream water and a whole fish.
• Raw fresh vegetable (such as a green bean, carrot, or ear of corn).
• Raw buffalo meat (a small chunk)
• A fresh fruit with the seed still in it (an apple, pear, etc.).
• Corn husk and natural tobacco for making a cornhusk pipe.
• Rake, hoe and shovel for clearing the spot for the circle of stones.
• A tape measure, or long string, for marking off the size of the circle.

The first thing you do in preparing the ground where the medicine wheel will be located is to thank our Creator for revealing to you this wonderful place. Next, thank Mother Earth for the use of this sacred area. She is also excited about having another medicine wheel on her body, and it is extremely important to show her the honor and respect she deserves.

Now you are ready to smudge the entire area with sage. As you do this, continue to thank our Creator for the honor and privilege of constructing the circle of stones, and ask him to help you always obey his directions as he guides you in your work.

The next step is to ask our Creator to show you how big the circle will be. Slowly walk around the area as you ask Grandfather what size to make the circle of stones, then listen carefully to that small inner voice, for it will impress upon you exactly where and how big the circle should be.

Use a tape measure or long string to mark off the circle in the dirt. Smudge this area again with sage, and then smudge it thoroughly with cedar, as you continue thanking our Creator for allowing you to participate in this wonderful ceremony.

Once the size of the circle has been marked off on the ground, you will then need to clear the inside of the circle of any small bushes, sharp stones, stickers, etc., because you will be walking barefoot on the ground inside the circle. If you have to remove any live plants, offer tobacco to them first and try to transplant them to an area outside the circle so they can continue to live. They are your relatives, so treat them gently.

When you have finished cleaning the area within the circle, smudge it again with sage and sweet grass, then with cedar. Next, sprinkle a generous amount of tobacco over the entire area. As you do this, affirm your commitment to our Creator to faithfully follow all of his instructions as you continue to perform this ceremony.

It is important that you now spend some time contemplating what the circle of stones will become. This is where our Creator will come to meet with you. In some ways, the area within the medicine wheel circle is like the most holy area behind the curtain in the old Jewish temple. That area was where the Ark of the Covenant was kept and only the high priest could go there because that was where our Creator came to talk with him.

The medicine wheel is the place our Creator comes to meet with us. It is the most holy ground on Mother Earth. It is imperative that you properly prepare yourself before entering this most sacred and holy site. Spend lots of time contemplating the sacredness of this spot. Ask our Creator to help you fully understand what it means to enter that sacred circle. I want to warn you, only the humble in spirit should ever be allowed inside the medicine wheel. We should always strive for pure thoughts and right intentions while in the medicine wheel, and we should make sure that all we say there brings honor to our Creator and his Sacred

152

Circle of Life. Once you fully understand that, you are then ready for our Creator to lead you to the center stone.

THE CENTER STONE

Holding a pinch of tobacco up to the sky, ask our Creator to lead you to the place where the Center Stone lives. The Center Stone will be the first stone brought to the circle because it symbolizes our Creator—the Father of all creation. It is brought to the circle first because without our Creator, there would be no creation. Likewise, without the center stone there can be no medicine wheel.

As a symbol of our Father, the Creator, the Center Stone is the most important, most sacred, and largest stone in the medicine wheel. It symbolizes our Creator and the totality of his Power and Unconditional Love.

The shape of the Center Stone will be generally round or oval. It will have a smooth surface without any sharp edges.

I don't know how long it will take you to locate the Center Stone. It could take an hour, a day, a week or longer. Don't worry about how long it takes because you will be led to the Center Stone at exactly the right time. Keep in mind that our Creator is in charge of creating the medicine wheel—you are just the worker. You also need to understand that our Creator will have been in communication with the Center Stone concerning its new responsibility. The stone will know that you are coming. In fact, it will find you. You will not find the stone.

When praying to be led to the Center Stone, also thank our Creator for the important role it will play in creating the medicine wheel. Talk to the stone even before you meet it. Thank it for its participation in creating the medicine wheel.

Keep in mind that this sacred stone is part of Mother Earth's body. Remember to thank our Mother for the use of one of her bones.

Ask our Creator to search the depths of your mind and spirit, removing all negativity, and properly prepare you to meet this sacred stone and touch it. *Never forget that this sacred stone symbolizes our Creator. Therefore, when you touch that stone, it symbolizes you actually touching our Creator!* The stone symbolizes our Creator, but remember that the power is behind the symbol. The symbol either hides or reveals the power it represents, depending on our knowledge, understanding and spiritual connection with the symbol. It is absolutely essential that you are properly prepared to meet the Center Stone, and our Creator will not guide you to it until you are properly prepared—please understand that.

If you think it is taking too long to locate the Center Stone, you need to examine yourself—your motives, intentions and personal preparedness. Keep in mind that our Creator doesn't need to find the stone. He already knows the stone and where it lives. He isn't "hiding" the stone from you as if this is a game of hide-and-seek. He is waiting for you to become worthy of meeting such a sacred and powerful symbol—the symbol of the Creator of All Things.

When our Creator leads you to the Center Stone, first smudge yourself before approaching it. As you approach the stone, smudge the area around you as you walk toward it. Stop a little way from the stone and offer tobacco to the Four Sacred Directions, Mother Earth and our Creator, thanking him again for bringing you to the stone. As you approach the Center Stone, introduce yourself, telling it your name and that it is a great honor to finally meet it.

Approach the Center Stone from the West and smudge the area all around it. Then, sprinkle a generous amount of tobacco around the stone and all over it. Talk to the other relatives living around the stone and explain to them that our Creator has chosen this relative to symbolize him within the medicine wheel. Explain to them that you are sorry to have to take this relative of such great importance away from them, but that this sacred stone will help lots of two leggeds learn to live in peace, harmony and balance within the Sacred Circle of Life.

Smudge a piece of red cotton cloth that is large enough to wrap the Center Stone in and then lay it on the ground beside the stone. Gently lift or roll the Center Stone onto the cotton cloth and wrap it up, making sure none of the stone is showing. Offer tobacco again and sprinkle it over the area where the stone lived, then take it to the site where the medicine wheel will be created.

Smudge the area with sage where you plan to temporarily let the Center Stone rest while you prepare the spot that will become its permanent home at the center of the circle. Sprinkle tobacco, then sage, on the ground, and place the stone on top of it. Next, smudge the Center Stone with cedar smoke.

Go to the center of the circle and ask Mother Earth's permission to dig a small hole (five or six inches deep) in her skin in which to place the sacred food. Sprinkle tobacco over the spot where the hole will be dug. Also sprinkle tobacco in the hole after it has been dug.

Place a small piece of buffalo meat along with some water in the hole. After sprinkling more tobacco in the hole, fill it in with dirt.

Next, offer a prayer to the Four Sacred Directions, Mother Earth and our Creator, thanking them again for leading you to the Center Stone. Then, sprinkle a generous amount of tobacco in the site where the Center Stone will be placed. Remove the red cloth before placing the Center Stone on top of the tobacco.

You are now ready to begin praying for guidance in finding the Four Directional Stones.

THE FOUR DIRECTIONAL STONES

Once the Center Stone is in place, ask our Creator to lead you to the Four Directional Stones. You will find the stone for the West first. The second stone will be placed in the North, the third in the East and the fourth in the South.

These Four Directional Stones will also be round or oval and have a smooth surface, but they will be smaller than the Center Stone.

As was the case with the Center Stone, Grandfather has already been communicating with these four stones, and they are anxiously awaiting your arrival to bring them to their new home within the circle of stones.

These four stones may not all be in the same location. However, like the Center Stone, they will communicate directly with your spirit and you will be drawn to each of them like a magnet is drawn to iron.

You will follow the same procedure for collection of the Four Directional Stones that you used to get the Center Stone. Before placing each stone in the circle, dig a small hole in the earth to place the sacred food items. Water will be poured in the hole in the West, a piece of raw buffalo meat in the hole in the North, a raw vegetable in the hole in the East and a fresh, uncooked fruit with the seed in it in the hole in the South. Follow the same procedure you used for digging and filling the hole for the Center Stone.

Starting in the West, place the stones around the circle in a clockwise direction with the second stone positioned in the North, the third in the East and the fourth in the South.

Once the Four Directional Stones are in place, you are ready to find the stones that will fill in the perimeter of the circle.

THE PERIMETER STONES

The perimeter stones that fill in the rest of the circle symbolize the totality of creation. They also represent the Sacred Circle of Life, and the "Guardian Spirits" that fight against the forces of evil on our behalf. These stones will be considerably smaller than the Four Directional Stones. Some may be round and smooth like the directional stones, while others may have sharp points on them. I can't tell you what the perimeter stones of your circle will look like.

Offer tobacco as you did before looking for the Center and Four Direction Stones, asking our Creator to lead you to the stones he has chosen as perimeter stones, and follow the same procedure you used in collecting the previous stones.

Start enclosing the stone circle by placing the first perimeter stone on the North side of the Directional Stone for the West. This stone must touch the Directional stone. Likewise, all of the perimeter stones must touch each other as you place them around the circle in a clockwise direction.

You won't place sacred food under these stones; however, you will sprinkle tobacco on the ground before placing each stone and then sprinkle more tobacco on the stone after it is placed in position.

As you place each perimeter stone in the circle, thank it for forming the boundary of the medicine wheel and protecting it's Holy Ground. The perimeter stones are guardians of the Holy Ground within the medicine wheel, protecting it from all negative forces or influences that might try to contaminate it with negative energy. These stones symbolize our Creator's Guardian Angels or spirits that fight against the forces of evil in the world. Take great care in placing the perimeter stones as you form the sacred circle.

After placing all of the perimeter stones in the circle, offer tobacco to the Four Winds, Mother Earth, and our Creator, and sprinkle it all over the ground within the circle. Once the circle of stones has been completed, you are ready to find the stones marking the two Sacred Paths within the medicine wheel.

CREATING THE TWO SACRED PATHS

The next step is to find the stones that will mark the two sacred paths within the medicine wheel. The path that travels from East to West on the medicine wheel symbolizes constant change, and the path that travels from South to North symbolizes unbending tradition. In reality, the paths originate from Our Creator, symbolized by the Center Stone, and travels out to the Four Sacred Directional Stones.

These two sacred paths cross one another in the center of the medicine wheel, dividing each path into two equal parts. Collectively, these four parts become the boundary lines of the four Sacred Seasons. This means that each lifestyle ceremony, or Sacred Season, is bounded on one side by constant change and on the other side by unbending tradition (or stability).

The Sacred Path Stones will be much smaller than the perimeter stones; however, that in no way diminishes the important role they play in the medicine wheel. As stated above, they symbolize the two sacred paths we travel within the medicine wheel—and also while living life each day. They also symbolize the power needed in order for us to maintain balance and harmony in our daily lives.

Like the Center Stone and Four Directional Stones, the Sacred Path Stones will be smooth, with no sharp edges. When looking for and collecting these stones, follow the same procedure you used for finding and gathering the Center Stone and Directional Stones. Once they have been collected, store them just outside the western edge of the circle of stones until you are ready to begin work on the two sacred paths within the wheel.

When you are ready to begin working on the two sacred paths, sprinkle a pinch of tobacco on the ground next to the western side of the Center Stone and then place the first Sacred Path stone on the tobacco. Make sure the stone is touching the Western side of the Center Stone and that it is lined up with the Directional Stone in the West.

Repeat this process on the Northern, Eastern and Southern sides of the Center Stone. Continue this routine of placing the Sacred Path Stones until both the East-West path and the South-North path is extended out to the edge of the circle of stones. The last Sacred Path stone for each direction must touch each respective Directional Stone at the edge of the circle.

PREPARING THE CORN HUSK PIPE

Go to the center of the circle and once more offer a large amount of tobacco to the Four Sacred Directions, Mother Earth and up to our Creator. Sprinkle some of the tobacco on the Center Stone. Then, moving in a clockwise direction, walk in circles away from the Center Stone, sprinkling tobacco on the ground all the way out to the circle of perimeter stones. As you do this, reaffirm your commitment to walk in peace, harmony and balance with our Creator and all of his children within the Sacred Circle of Life.

Return to the Center Stone and prepare a Cornhusk Pipe. As you do this, ask our Creator to help you to always obey all he asks you to do. Promise to perform all of the sacred ceremonies associated with this Sacred Path exactly as he instructs you to do.

You will take the Cornhusk Pipe home with you, and for the next four days you will fast and pray. You will also conduct the Self-Offering Ceremony each morning and the Purification Ceremony each evening while you are fasting and praying. Your prayers will focus on asking our Creator to turn the Circle of Stones into a medicine wheel. During this time you will avoid thinking any negative thoughts.

During these four days you will not attend any type of social gathering or activity. You will not entertain people in your home, and, as much as possible, you will remain in solitude while you pray and fast. You may drink water and juice, but don't eat any solid food. As much as possible, spend your time alone in communication with your Grandfather concerning how to live in peace, harmony and balance with him and all of his Sacred Family.

This is a time of intense soul searching. Admit your faults and weaknesses to him and ask him to fill you with his Unconditional Love so that you can more effectively serve others.

At the beginning of the four day fast, ask our Creator to reveal to you a sign that will occur during the four days if he is willing to turn the circle of stones into a medicine wheel. If he is willing to create the medicine wheel, he will give you a strong sign during the four day fast to let you know that. Only our Creator can tell you what the sign will be, and if you ask him he will tell you. Then, at some time during the four days, our Creator will confirm the validity of the sign—making it occur—if he is going to turn the circle of stones into a medicine wheel.

After the Purification Ceremony on the evening of the fourth day, go straight to the Center Stone and smoke the Cornhusk Pipe there. Offer tobacco to the Four Winds, Mother Earth and our Creator and ask Mother

159

Earth's permission to dig a small hole in her skin at the base of the eastern side of the Center Stone. Sprinkle tobacco on the ground where you will dig and then sprinkle more tobacco in the small hole. Place the remains of the Cornhusk Pipe in the hole and cover it over with dirt.

If our Creator caused the sign to occur during the four day fast, the circle of stones has become a medicine wheel.

Teaching Session – 7
WORKING WITH THE MEDICINE WHEEL

The medicine wheel brings the physical and Spiritual Realms together into a single reality. We create the circle of stones here in the physical world, but, only our Creator's power from the Spiritual Realm can turn that circle of stones into a medicine wheel.

When we enter a medicine wheel, we are not only entering our Creator's presence, we are totally surrounded by his power. We are standing on the physical earth that has been turned into Holy Ground.

The ceremony we perform to construct the circle of stones that our Creator turns into a medicine wheel costs practically nothing, and yet the space within that stone circle becomes the dwelling place of our Creator's power. On the other hand, modern man frequently spends countless millions of dollars constructing religious shrines, temples, synagogues, and churches within which multitudes of people gather to "worship" God. I have been in medicine wheels and I have also been in numerous "religious structures" around the world that are used by the world's major religions for their religious activities.

I have been in awe of the magnificent architecture of some of these religious structures. However, I rarely—if ever—have felt the Creator's presence in those exquisite and very costly buildings. On the other hand, on many occasions, I have been overcome by our Creator's awesome power present in the simple—and practically cost free—medicine wheel.

I have often contemplated why our Creator's incomprehensible power of Unconditional Love fills the medicine wheel but is grossly lacking in the man made structures of the world's institutionalized religions and I have arrived at several conclusions.

First, the ceremony involved in creating the circle of stones requires us to wait patiently and humbly for our Creator to reveal the site where the circle of stones will be placed. Then, our Creator oversees each part of the circle's construction. Grandfather chooses each stone for the circle. He determines when we are ready to receive the information concerning where the stones are located. Every action we take in gathering the stones and placing them in the appropriate place in the circle is designed to demonstrate our humility and service to our Creator and Mother Earth. This is very important because our Creator will only work with and send his power to those two leggeds who demonstrate a spirit of humility and obedience to him.

On the other hand, shrines, buildings, and temples built by the two leggeds to be used by their institutionalized religious organizations are—for the most part—treated like business projects. Large amounts of money must be raised; countless planning sessions are conducted. Numerous committees are formed with great detail given to the political and financial makeup of the individuals assigned to them, and hours of heated debate and argument occur during committee meetings as influential people attempt to promote their personal wishes and desires. Countless sites are considered before one is chosen. Architects are hired. Building contractors bid on the projects. Then, with great pomp and ceremony, the religious organizations hold "dedication services" or meetings to dedicate to God their plans, their wishes, their opinions, their desires and their decisions that went into the creation of their structures.

Now, you tell me which is more pleasing to our Creator—the construction of the circle of stones that he oversees and then turns into a medicine wheel, or the religious structures built by institutionalized religious organizations that are composites of man's ideas and decisions?

Second, only naturally occurring material as it is found in nature is used in the construction of the circle of stones. Therefore, the "building material" is still in its natural, sacred form. On the other hand, most of the materials used in the construction of modern day religious structures were developed using the ingenuity of modern man's "god" of technology. That material is saturated with—and contaminated by—man's ego and pride in his ability to turn pieces of Mother Earth's sacred body into another form of his own creation. In all probability, those creating that material gave no consideration to the fact that the earth is their Mother and her body is sacred.

So one can easily see why our Creator chooses the simple construction of the circle of stones over modern day man-made religious structures as a place to send his power.

THE MEDICINE WHEEL IS THE GUARDIAN OF SACRED TIME

Today's high-tech, money driven business world says that "time is money". That simple statement repeated countless times each day in the corporate board rooms of the world sums up our modern business community's value system—the purpose of each day, each hour, each minute, each second, yes, the purpose of life itself, is to make money.

I call this world you and I live, work and play in "the feel good world" because everything we do is designed to make us feel good. In this "feel good world", money controls our lives. We can't live in the feel good world without money because it buys all the things we think we need to make us feel good. Since "time is money" in the feel good world, our lives are controlled by the time clock.

The time clock tells us when to get up and when to go to work. It tells us when to go to all the meetings during the day at work that are focused on making more money. The clock also tells us when to go home from work, when to eat, when to watch TV and when to go to bed, and then when to get up the next morning so we can do it all over again the next day. The clock tells us when its time to take the kids to school and when to pick them up from school. It tells us when its time to take our next pill to calm our nerves, when we can go shopping and when we can't, and what time our friends are coming over for dinner.

As you can see, in the feel good world, the time clock controls every aspect of our lives.

On this Sacred Path, the medicine wheel is the guardian of time, not the feel good world's time clock. Our Creator established Sacred Time and it travels in cycles. On the other hand, man created linear time and it travels in a continuous straight line. On *The Way of the Medicine Wheel,* time travels in cycles, not linear as it does in the feel good world. The medicine wheel charts our whole lives for us from birth through old age. At the same time, it charts the day and the night for us. It tells us when the Lifestyle Ceremony of New Beginnings starts and when it ends. It also tells us when the Lifestyle Ceremonies of Growth and Develop, Reaping the Harvest and Rest and Renewal begin and end. Therefore, it lays out the cycle of ceremonies for our entire lives.

The medicine wheel tells us when to plant, when to harvest and when to rest. It reveals to us the best time to start new projects and how long those projects should last.

The medicine wheel deals with cycles of time—not years, months, weeks, days, hours and minutes that measure linear time in the feel good world. If we are going to walk this Sacred Path, we must begin the painful and frustrating process of freeing our lives from the control of the linear time clock. We must begin thinking in terms of the cycle of Lifestyle Ceremonies—not years. We must think in terms of seasons—not months. We must think in terms of sunrise and sunset—not days, hours and minutes. This is one of the first steps we learn to take in working with the medicine wheel.

I can tell you from personal experience that it is not easy to begin learning to think in cycles of time instead of in linear time. In the beginning it is very frustrating.

I owned a management consulting business for twenty-five years. I have taught "time management" seminars in twenty-five countries around the world, and my life used to be controlled totally by the time clock. My wristwatch was the first thing I used to put on in the morning and it was the last thing I took off at night (some people even sleep with their wristwatch on).

Several years ago grandfather Old Bear began teaching me about the importance of learning to live my life in harmony with our Creator's cycles of time. Part of that conversation is presented below.

As grandfather Old Bear and I sat on a rocky point overlooking the beautiful river valley below, watching the sun go down behind the distant mountains that formed the jagged western horizon, he suddenly turned to me and asked, "What time is it, grandson?"

I looked at my watch. I was very proud of that watch. Angelitta had bought it for me on a trip to Albuquerque, New Mexico's Old Town. It had a heavy, wide sterling silver band studded with turquoise and coral stones, and the face of the watch was inlaid with a piece of highly polished turquoise. "It's eight thirty," I replied as I once again admired my beautiful watch.

The Old One laughed. "Why do you need to look at that watch on your wrist to know what time it is?" he chided. "It may be eight thirty in your world but it's sunset in mine."

"I know. The sun is setting at eight thirty," I explained.

The smile left grandfather Old Bear's face and was replaced with a stone-like seriousness. "The sun always sets at sunset," he emphatically retorted. "If you expect to learn to walk this Sacred Path then you must first learn the difference between the way our Creator keeps time and the two leggeds in your world keep time."

Apparently realizing the forcefulness in his tone of voice, he smiled and patted me on the leg as if to say that he was not really upset with me. "The medicine wheel is my watch. The seasons are the hour hand and the sunrise and sunset are the minute hand," he said, continuing to smile as he watched the orange glow exploding across the Western horizon as the sun sank behind the jagged peaks.

"You see, grandson, in my world the concept of time as you understand it doesn't really exist. In my world, time is the changing of the seasons. We know time travels in a circle because the seasons travel in a circle. The sunrise and sunset travels in a circle. Our lives travel in a circle." He patted my leg again, then continued. "And we don't need some contraption on our wrist to tell us that."

I was greatly offended that he referred to my beautiful watch as a "contraption" but I tried to hide my feelings from him.

"I wasn't saying your watch looks bad," he chuckled again. "But it isn't nearly as beautiful as my watch," he concluded, as he pointed toward the beautiful sunset, indicating that he considered the sunset to be the equivalent of my watch—only much more beautiful.

Pointing to my wristwatch he said, "That kind of time doesn't really exist. Long ago the two leggeds invented it because they took the wrong trail when they came to a fork in this Sacred Path. Once they had lost their way they became confused and disoriented so they developed the concept of time in an attempt to try to explain what was happening around them. You see, grandson, our Creator's time is Sacred Time because it is nothing more than the cycle of the Sacred Seasons. Time as you define it doesn't really exist in my world.

"In your world, time isn't sacred—it's confining. It controls you, frustrates you and helps keep you disconnected from our Creator. That's why you should get rid of that watch because it's holding you back from beginning your journey on this Sacred Path."

Not long after that conversation with grandfather Old Bear, I took my beautiful watch to Robert Talltree, an Indian friend of mine who makes beautiful jewelry, and asked him to replace the watch with a piece of turquoise, and I haven't worn a wristwatch since. However, I must confess that at first it was extremely difficult for me to not be able to look down at my watch at any given moment and know what time it was. I guess you could say I experienced "wristwatch withdrawal".

Since that time, I have systematically been working on learning to think in terms of our Creator's "sacred cycle of time", and I must admit that approach to time has helped keep me more focused on this Sacred Path. I strongly recommend that you also begin the process of learning to think in terms of the sacred cycles of time instead of the two-leggeds linear approach to measuring time.

As we work with the medicine wheel, we must come to understand that it is our time clock and the time it measures is sacred. When I first started working with a medicine wheel, all I saw was a circle of stones. Now I see the layers of symbolism represented by that stone circle. Instead of seeing the big, round Center Stone, I see our Creator of the universe at the center of all things, including my own life. In the place where the Four Directional Stones are situated I see our Creator's power from the Four Winds coming to my aid and assistance.

The circle of stones that make up the outer edge of the medicine wheel force my attention to the fact that our Creator made all that exists and I am his child—part of his Sacred Family. They also tell me that they are Grandfather's Guardian Spirits, protecting me from the negative forces trying to hinder me from walking this Sacred Path.

The Sacred Paths that travel from East to West and South to North all the way to the outer edge of the circle keep me focused on the fact that I must constantly balance my life between change and tradition.

As I look at the medicine wheel I see the cycles of Sacred Time flash through my consciousness—the Lifestyle Ceremonies of New Beginnings, Growth and Development, Reaping the Harvest and Rest and Renewal. I see myself learning to live those sacred ceremonies in peace, harmony and balance with our Creator and the Sacred Cycle of Life.

The longer I work with the medicine wheel, the more I am aware that I have just begun to scratch the surface of what it has to teach me about walking this Sacred Path toward our wonderful Creator.

HOW TO APPROACH THE MEDICINE WHEEL

In considering how we are to approach the medicine wheel, we first must remind ourselves again of what the medicine wheel is. The medicine wheel is our Creator's "Sacred Petroglyph" that he gifted the Ancient Ones who lived in the far distant past. It contains layer upon layer of symbolism that teaches us the powerful spiritual principles and truths we need to know in order to walk this Sacred Path referred to by grandfather

Old Bear as *The Way of The Medicine Wheel.* It is a symbol of our Creator's time clock, recording the cycles of Sacred Time.

The medicine wheel is also the most Holy Ground on Mother Earth. It is the place we meet with our Creator—spirit to spirit. Within the medicine wheel, we are totally surrounded by our Creator's power of Unconditional Love. It is extremely important that all two-leggeds approaching the medicine wheel fully understand this.

I must repeat again: our Creator's power dwells within the medicine wheel and he will meet with us spirit to spirit within that Holy Place. Understand that. Meditate on that. Let that fact sink deep into your very soul. Our Creator's power resides within a medicine wheel. That fact should fill us with awe and cause us to tremble at the very thought of approaching a medicine wheel. Within that Holy Circle we will enter our Creator's presence and converse with him spirit to spirit. Therefore, to do so requires great preparation on our part.

First, conduct the Purification Ceremony to purify your mind and body. Next, take your Self-Offering bundle and approach the medicine wheel from the West.

We approach the wheel from the West because the West represents our Creator's power of forgiveness. Among other things, the West also symbolizes the source of introspection and internal truth. Therefore, we approach the medicine wheel from the West to show our Creator we are in need of his forgiveness and we will be truthful to ourselves and to him in the admission of our many faults and weaknesses.

By approaching the medicine wheel from the West, we are admitting our unworthiness to enter our Creator's presence. We are asking him to take pity on us, to extend his Grace to us. Just as the night comes from the West and covers the actions and activities of the day, so we are asking Grandfather to cover our mistakes and remove them with his forgiveness and Unconditional Love.

Coming from the West, we approach the wheel quietly, respectfully, solemnly and humbly, fully aware of our unworthiness to enter Grandfather's presence and walk on such Holy Ground.

168

As we approach the Directional Stone symbolizing the West, we drop to our knees and offer a prayer to our Creator, admitting our unworthiness and asking him to purify our spirits and fill us with his Unconditional Love as we conduct the Self-Offering Ceremony.

We lay the Self-Offering rug or mat on the ground at the base of the Directional Stone representing the West Wind. We place the mat facing the East to conduct the Self-Offering Ceremony in recognition of all new things our Creator bestows on us. The sun comes up in the East, bringing us new life and a new day.

The East symbolizes the source of all spiritual enlightenment. It represents the source of new knowledge and information coming to us from our Creator. We face the East while doing the Self-Offering Ceremony in recognition of the fact that as we perform this ceremony, Grandfather will create within us a pure spirit and fill us anew with his Unconditional Love, which will empower us to serve others instead of self.

After you have completed the Self-Offering Ceremony, move in a clockwise direction around to the Northern side of the medicine wheel. The North represents the source of purity. Stop at the Directional Stone for the North and thank our Creator for renewing your spirit with his Unconditional Love and ask him to fill you with pure thoughts, intents, motives and actions in dealing with all your relatives within the Sacred Circle Of Life.

Move on to the Eastern entrance to the medicine wheel. Facing East, thank Grandfather for the new life that he gives you each day. Thank him for the new opportunities he gives you each day and the power he gives you that enables you to accomplish all his plans for your life.

ENTERING THE MEDICINE WHEEL

Turn to the West and raise your arms in thanks to our Creator for you life and ask his permission to enter the medicine wheel. If you are a Pipe Carrier and are bringing the Sacred Pipe into the wheel, hold the bowl in

169

your left hand with the stem point up to the sky. With your arms still raised, slowly turn clockwise in a circle in honor of our Creator's Four Sacred Directions and ask his power from those Directions to always come to your aid and help you learn to live in peace, harmony and balance within the Sacred Circle of Life. Drop to your hands and knees and thank Mother Earth for providing this sacred spot for the medicine wheel. Note: if you are bringing items such as drums, etc. into the medicine wheel, make sure they are smudged with sage and then with cedar before bringing them into the Sacred Circle.

With your head bowed low in humility, crawl on your hands and knees into the medicine wheel to show Grandfather your unworthiness to enter his presence. Stand to your feet and with your head still bowed low walk straight to the Center Stone. This symbolizes your desire and willingness to have our Creator at the center of all you do. Kneel in front of the Center Stone and again ask Grandfather to take pity on you and always be at the center of your life. Admit your unworthiness to be in his presence and thank him for his forgiveness, Grace and Unconditional Love that enables you—even in your pitiful condition—to be in his presence (As I do this, I offer tobacco and then sprinkle it on the Center Stone).

MOVING AROUND WITHIN THE MEDICINE WHEEL

As stated above, when you enter the medicine wheel, always go straight to the Center Stone first. Do this by following the Sacred Path from the East Gate to the Center Stone. Upon entering the medicine wheel, I recommend you spend a considerable amount of time first at the Center Stone talking to Grandfather about the things you will work on while in the wheel.

NOTE: Never sit on the Center Stone! Remember that it symbolizes our Creator. Therefore, it would be the ultimate form of disrespect to sit on the Center Stone. You may kneel by it, lay your hands gently and respectfully on it or sit next to it, but never sit on it.

After spending time with our Creator at the Center Stone, you are free

170

to move around within the medicine wheel. However, you must first follow the Sacred Paths in a clockwise manor to each of the Four Directional Stones. For example, as you leave the Center Stone follow the Sacred Path out to the Directional Stone in the East. Offer tobacco to the East and pray to our Creator, thanking him for new life that he gives you with the rising of the sun each day, and commit yourself to following the plans he has for you day by day. Thank him for the Lifestyle Ceremony of New Beginnings and ask him to help you to live each day of that ceremony pleasing to him. Sprinkle tobacco on the Directional Stone of the East.

Turn clockwise and follow the Sacred Path of Constant Change back to the Center Stone. Turn South and follow the Sacred Path of Unbending Tradition out to the Directional Stone in the South. Offer tobacco to our Creator's power in the South and thank him for his gift of Unconditional Love. Ask him to help you to always pass that love on to others by helping meet the needs of your relatives within the Sacred Circle of Life. Thank him for the Lifestyle Ceremony of Growth and Development, and ask him to help you to live each day of that ceremony pleasing to him. Sprinkle the tobacco over the Directional Stone in the South.

Turn clockwise and follow the Sacred Path back to the Center Stone. Turn West and follow the Sacred Path of Constant Change to the Directional Stone in the West. After offering tobacco to our Creator's power in the West, ask Grandfather to help you to always seek truth and honesty, and to be truthful and honest in all of your dealing with him and his Sacred Circle of Life.   Thank him for forgiveness that is symbolized by the coming of the night.   Also, thank him for the Lifestyle Ceremony of Reaping the Harvest, and ask him to help you to live each day of that ceremony pleasing to him. Sprinkle tobacco over the Directional Stone in the West.

Turn clockwise and follow the Sacred Path back to the Center Stone. Turn North and follow the Sacred Path of Unbending Tradition out to the Directional Stone in the North. Offer tobacco to our Creator's power in the North and thank him for purifying your spirit, mind and body. Thank

171

him for the Lifestyle Ceremony of Rest and Renewal and ask him to help you live each day of that ceremony pleasing to him. Sprinkle the tobacco over the Directional Stone in the North.

Turn clockwise and follow the Sacred Path back to the Center Stone. You are now ready to work within the medicine wheel.

NEVER TAKE SHORTCUTS WHILE WORKING WITHIN THE MEDICINE WHEEL

If you are working in the South and want to go around to the West, never cut across the circle to the West. Always return to the Center Stone and then follow the Sacred Path from the Center Stone to the West. This symbolizes our recognition and understanding that there are no "short cuts" when it comes to our spiritual growth and development. It also symbolizes our acknowledgement that we need our Creator at the center of our lives at all times.

In addition, if you are working in the West and want to go to the East, first return to the Center Stone, then follow the Sacred Path to the North, return to the Center Stone and then follow the Sacred Path to the East. This symbolizes our recognition that we must work with all of the Sacred Directions in order to develop and maintain balance in our lives.

This is a very important rule for us to follow while working in the medicine wheel.

We live in a fast paced world where many people are looking for "a quick fix" and "instant results". Unfortunately, those people have never developed Spiritual Patience nor Spiritual Endurance, two of the Five Spiritual Medicines required for walking this Sacred Path.

There are no "quick fixes" or "Short Cuts" when it comes to walking this Sacred Path. You don't go on your first "Vision Quest" and return a spiritual leader of the people. Spiritual growth and development is a life-long, never-ending process, and there are no short cuts. That is why we never take a short cut to get from one place to another within the medicine wheel. We always return first to the Center Stone and then follow the

Sacred Path to the other Directional Stones as we move around within the circle on our way to our next destination within the medicine wheel.

I can't emphasize enough the importance of following this rule. If we can't take the time to return to the Center Stone before going on to the next destination within the medicine wheel, how can we expect to take the time to keep our Creator at the center of our lives as we live out there in the "feel good world"? If we can't follow the Sacred Paths to the Directional Stones that are between us and where we want to go within the medicine wheel, we also won't take the time needed in the feel good world to do those things that create and maintain balance in our lives.

Remember—symbolism is the bridge over which we walk to get to the power behind the symbol. The Center Stone symbolizes our Creator. We always return to the Center Stone before going on to the next Directional Stone in the wheel to show our recognition for the need to keep our Creator in the center of our lives at all times. If I understand the symbolism of returning to the Center Stone, then I will be more likely to ask our Creator to stay in the center of my life out there in the feel good world. Understanding the symbolism involved in following the Sacred Path to the other Directional Stones that are on the way to my next destination within the Sacred Circle helps me do those things I need to do in the physical realm to develop and maintain peace, harmony and balance in my life.

WALKING THE TWO SACRED PATHS

In a previous teaching session, I pointed out that the medicine wheel contains two Sacred Paths. One Sacred Path extends from the Directional Stone in the East to the Directional Stone in the West, and the other Sacred Path extends from the Directional Stone in the South to the one in the

North. These two Sacred Paths cross each other at the Center Stone. These two Sacred Paths actually extend outward from the Center Stone to the Four Directional Stones because our Creator is the source of the power contained within these two paths.

The East-West path is the path of Constant Change and the South-North path is the path of Unbending Tradition. Each of the Four Lifestyle Ceremonies that make up the medicine wheel's Sacred Circle—or Sacred Cycle of Life—is bounded on each side by one of these Sacred Paths.

These two Sacred Paths within the wheel are symbolic of the ongoing struggle between change and tradition that we continually face in life, and the outcome of this struggle determines the course our lives take.

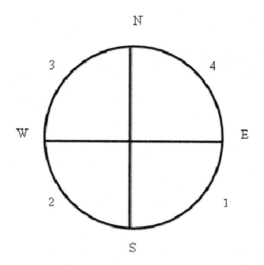

Figure 4

1   The East/West line represents the Sacred Path of Constant Change. The South/North line symbolizes the Sacred Path of Unbending Tradition.

2   The East/West line also represents the physical realm and the South/North line represents the spiritual realm.

3   These two realms meet at the Center Stone within the medicine wheel which symbolizes our Creator.

The numbers 1-2-3-4 represent the Four Lifestyle Ceremonies.

In the above diagram, the number "1" represents the Lifestyle Ceremony of New Beginnings, "2" represents the Lifestyle Ceremony of

Growth And Development, "3" represents the Lifestyle Ceremony of Reaping the Harvest and "4" represents the Lifestyle Ceremony of Rest and Renewal.

The path of Constant Change on one side and the path of Unbending Tradition on the other border each Lifestyle Ceremony.

The Sacred Path of Constant Change

We enter the medicine wheel from the East and walk on the path of Constant Change to the Center Stone. There is a very important reason why we enter the medicine wheel on the path of Constant Change instead of on the path of Unbending Tradition. The work we do within the medicine wheel always focuses on bringing about some sort of change, either changes in our own lives, in the lives of others or within our physical surroundings. As we walk the path of Constant Change to the Center Stone, we thank our Creator for the beneficial changes he will bring about in our lives.

The path of Constant Change is the path our Creator's power of change travels within the medicine wheel. It is also the path we travel as we work on change.

The path of Constant Change begins in the East and ends in the West. This is the pathway of the Sun, which rises each day in the East and sets each day in the West. During the day, the sun is constantly moving across the sky overhead, symbolizing the constant change that is occurring all around us.

Half of the Sacred Pathway of Constant Change, from the Directional Stone of the East to the Center Stone, focuses on bringing about change in the physical world around us. The other half of the Sacred Pathway of Constant Change, from the Directional Stone of the West to the Center Stone, focuses on bringing about internal change within us—both physical and mental.

For example, if we want our Creator to change the weather, we spend time on the Sacred Path of Constant Change between the Directional

Stone in the East and the Center Stone. On the other hand, if we want to work on changing our attitude, we spend time on the Sacred Path of Constant Change between the Directional Stone of the West and the Center Stone.

The medicine wheel can only be used to produce positive change. It can never be used to bring about negative change affecting people. In other words, you can't use the medicine wheel to bring harm to any of your relatives within the Sacred Circle of Life. However, it may be used to prevent harm from occurring either to yourself or to your other relatives within Creation. Keep in mind that our Creator's Unconditional Love works only for the good of his children, never to bring harm to any of them.

The Sacred Path of Unbending Tradition

The Sacred Path of Unbending Tradition begins in the South and ends in the North, and it resists or prevents change. This Sacred Path represents the spiritual realm. We work along this path to enhance our spiritual growth, development and awareness.

Continuous change is occurring within the physical realm. However, our Creator does not change. He is the same today as he has always been and he will always be the same in the future as he is today. The laws our Creator has set in motion to govern the Spiritual Realm are constant and unchanging. On the other hand, the laws he has set into motion that govern the physical realm produce constant change.

The laws of constant change that govern the physical realm produce decay and death. However, the lack of change within the spiritual realm produces eternal life.

The two Sacred Paths are merged into one where they cross each other at the Center Stone. This represents one of the greatest mysteries associated with walking this Sacred Path. This is a powerful symbol of the way our Creator brings together the physical and Spiritual Realms, combining them into a single reality as we faithfully perform all of the sacred ceremonies our Creator has given us.

The sacred ceremonies given to us by our Creator are manifestations of spiritual laws at work here within the physical realm. Therefore, while we are performing sacred ceremonies we are simultaneously in the spiritual and physical realms. Understanding this makes us aware of the ultimate purpose of the Four Lifestyle Ceremonies as we live them day by day as Grandfather intends. Thus, we see that the ultimate purpose of these ceremonies is to combine the physical and spiritual realms together on a daily basis.

That is why the Ancient Ones were able to say that each step they took was a Sacred step. They were keenly aware that they were living simultaneously in both the Spiritual and physical realms.

Don't Become Trapped On These Two Sacred Paths

As we work within the medicine wheel, it is easy to become trapped on one of these two Sacred Paths. For example, we work within the medicine wheel to help produce needed changes in our lives and the surrounding environment. These changes bring about improvements, and, as a result, it is easy for us to focus too much on the path of Constant Change.

Too many changes occurring too fast can lead to chaos instead of improvements in our lives. We not only need to change, we need to take the time to fully incorporate those changes into our lives. That is why when new insights come to us from the East, we move around to the South in the medicine wheel and take the time to develop those new ideas and insights into reality.

In order to develop peace, harmony and balance in our lives we must spend an equal amount of time on both Sacred Paths—Constant Change and Unbending Tradition. In that way we will learn the things that need changing as well as those that should remain as Unchanging Traditions.

If we spend too much time on either of these two Sacred Paths our lives will become dangerously out of balance, and we will eventually become confused and no longer able to walk *The Way of The Medicine Wheel.*

WORKING WITH THE FOUR SACRED COLORS

Different tribes and peoples use different colors to represent the Four Sacred Directions. The colors I use to represent the directions may be different from the colors you use, and that's okay. However, regardless of the colors you use to represent the Four Sacred Directions, it is important that you know the meaning of the symbolism those colors represent.

I use the color black to represent the West, red to represent the North, yellow to represent the East and white to represent the South. Again, you may use different colors and that is perfectly okay—just be sure you know why you use the colors you do, and what they symbolize.

First of all, the Four Sacred Colors, black, red, yellow and white symbolize the four races of two-leggeds, and that those four races are equal. By placing those four colors on the directional staffs located in front of the Four Directional Stones, we are confirming our commitment to equality among all of our fellow two-leggeds. Those four colors are a statement that we will never discriminate in our dealings with our fellow two-leggeds.

That means we do not discriminate between rich and poor, black and white, young and old, male and female, weak and strong or by any other standards of comparison when relating to our fellow two-leggeds. We treat everyone equal—that is an absolute law of this Sacred Path.

Does that mean that we don't bestow honor on individuals? No, of course not. However, we show honor to those to whom honor is due. We honor the lives and deeds of individuals but we don't consider those individuals innately superior to others.

As stated in the first teaching session, the sun shines its light equally on the good and bad alike. This symbolizes the need for us to also treat everyone as equals, regardless of race, culture, religion, age, sex, occupation or amount of wealth (or lack of it) one has.

Unfortunately, today discrimination is rampant among certain groups and individuals that follow our Native American spiritual path, often referred to as "The Red Road". There is inter-tribal discrimination, inter-reservation discrimination, as well as discrimination between and among clans. There is discrimination due to race (or even the amount of Native American "blood" a person has). There is discrimination over the amount of tribal language one knows and uses. There is discrimination concerning who one traces his or her spiritual roots back to (which medicine person or spiritual leader they learned from) and one of the worst forms of discrimination of all is feeling spiritually superior to another person.

There is no place for discrimination in any form on this Sacred Path. We all have the same Spiritual Father and the same Physical Mother. We are all members of the same family (the Sacred Circle of Life). Our Father and Mother love us all equally. What right do we have to think we are better than any one else? None.

Discrimination is a sign of spiritual, emotional and mental immaturity on the part of those doing the discriminating. Unfortunately, such people are deceived because they think they are spiritually, physically, emotionally and/or mentally superior.

We two-leggeds don't just discriminate against other two-leggeds, we discriminate against all the rest of our relatives within the Sacred Circle of Life as well. Most two-leggeds are convinced they are far superior to the rest of creation. In fact, they don't even consider themselves "relatives" to most other two-leggeds, let alone other life forms within the Sacred Circle.

We are not only "related" to everyone within the Sacred Circle of Life, we must also honor and respect all other life forms within that Sacred Circle. People who think they are superior to the four leggeds, winged people, water people, green people and rock people have never taken the time to actually study those other relatives and gotten to know them and their powerful, unique strengths and abilities.

In many ways, we two-leggeds are greatly inferior to some of our other relatives within creation. For example, compared to many of our relatives, we aren't as strong physically, we can't run as fast, see as far, and our sense of smell isn't as good—the list goes on and on. Yet many two-leggeds have a hard time accepting the fact that they are not superior to the rest of their relatives within the Circle of Life. They are quick to say, "But we are far superior mentally." Oh? If that is true, then why are we the ones destroying our physical environment to the point we are endangering the future existence of all life forms here on Mother Earth?

WORKING WITH THE EAST AND LEARNING TO UNDERSTAND ITS POWER AND PURPOSE IN YOUR LIFE

The more we understand our Creator, the easier it becomes to understand the "workings" of the medicine wheel. Unfortunately, our finite human minds are incapable of comprehending more than just a minute fraction of the totality of our Creator and his infinite knowledge, wisdom, purity and power.

Our Creator is omnipotent—meaning he has unlimited and infinite power and authority. In our finite state and with limited mental powers we are unable to fully comprehend what that actually means and entails.

Our Creator is omniscient—meaning he knows all things. He has universal and complete knowledge and understanding of everything that has ever been, is, and ever will be.

Our Creator is omnipresent—meaning that he is everywhere at all times. Being limited to physical bodies, within a physical space, for a limited amount of time, we can't begin to comprehend that aspect of our Creator.

Our Creator is eternal—meaning he is without beginning or end. He always has been and always will be. Being creatures that were born and will someday die, we are incapable of fully understanding the concept of "eternal".

Our Creator is Unconditional Love—meaning all that he has done, is doing and will do is for the benefit of his Creation instead of himself. Being controlled and driven by "self-centeredness", it is impossible for us to either fully understand or totally appreciate the true meaning of Unconditional Love.

Our Creator is unchanging—meaning that he is the same today as he was throughout the past, and he will always be the same throughout the future as he is today. We live in a constantly changing world. We are constantly changing. Therefore, we can't possibly comprehend completely the unchanging attributes of our Creator.

Our Creator is our Spiritual Father—meaning he created us to be his children, members of his family within the Sacred Circle of Life. Having biological fathers and mothers, we are incapable of fully understanding and comprehending what it means to be "children of our Creator". We grew up observing and sometimes reaping the results of our biological parents' weaknesses. Our Creator has no weaknesses. Re-read the above list of qualities and characteristics of our Creator and then reflect on the fact that he is our Father—which also is impossible to comprehend.

As I said above, the more we understand about our Creator, the easier it is to work within the medicine wheel.

Knowing that Grandfather is omnipresent helps us understand the workings of the powers of the Four Sacred Directions. Since our Creator is all-powerful, and he is also everywhere, when we talk of the power of the East, we are talking about that aspect of our Creator and his power that resides in the East. The East represents, characterizes and symbolizes certain aspects of our Creator's unlimited powers. Therefore, we work in the Eastern part of the medicine wheel to call upon and benefit from our Creator's powers symbolized by the East. The same principles apply to the other three Sacred Directions—South, West and North.

The East is the direction of the sunrise. As a result, the sun symbolizes or represents many of the characteristics of our Creator's power that is credited as coming from the East. The rising sun brings the new day and new life. Therefore, we look to the East as being the source of all new things coming to us from our Creator. That is also why the Lifestyle Ceremony of New Beginnings starts in the East on the medicine wheel.

The East represents the source or direction from which all new gifts come from our Creator. As a result, when we are in need of new ideas, new information or any other "new" thing in life, we work on the Eastern side of the medicine wheel and face the East in recognition of our Creator's power coming from the East to provide those "new" things.

Let's remind ourselves again that the symbol is the bridge over which we walk to get to the power behind the symbol. The East symbolizes our Creator's power to create new things or bring new things and new beginnings into our lives. Understanding that, we face the East in recognition of our Creator's ability to bring these new things into our lives —regardless of what the need is.

Facing the East and understanding its symbolism enables me to tap into our Creator's power that the East represents, and as a result, those needs for "new things" become a reality.

The Color of The East

The rising sun, the most powerful symbol of the East, is yellow. On this Sacred Path we use the color yellow to symbolize the direction of the East. We consider the four cardinal directions (East, West, North and South) as being "Sacred Directions" because they symbolize and represent some aspect of our Creator's nature and power. Therefore, the yellow flag that hangs from the staff on the Eastern side of the medicine wheel doesn't just symbolize the East, it actually symbolizes all of our Creator's power that the East represents.

The color yellow represents all new beginnings (new ideas, new information, new projects, new directions, etc.) in our lives. That is why

182

we hang the yellow flag on the staff at the Eastern side of the medicine wheel. When in need of new beginnings, we sometimes use yellow corn meal, or yellow tobacco ties, as we pray to also symbolize our Creator's power to bring those new things into our lives.

The Totem of the East

From antiquity, indigenous cultures around the world have used different totems to represent our Creator's power symbolized by the Four Sacred Directions. The totem you use to represent a direction may be different from the one I use, and that's okay as long as you understand why you are using the totem and its symbolism as it relates to the specific direction. If you don't understand the meaning of the symbolism, you won't experience the power the totem represents.

I hope you are beginning to recognize just how important symbolism is—it is the single most important key to unlocking our Creator's power as we walk this Sacred Path.

It is also important that we understand what a "totem" is and its purpose. When all of us within the Sacred Circle of Life were created, Grandfather put some of his essence or qualities within each family group. Therefore, we two-leggeds possess certain of his qualities, and so on throughout the entire Sacred Circle of Life.

All two-leggeds have been gifted with more of our Creator's creativity than the other family groups were given. In addition, our Creator made each of us as unique individuals, different from all other individuals within our family group of two leggeds. He also put small amounts of his essence that he bestowed on the other family groups within each of us. Therefore, in addition to our creativity, we also may have some of the same qualities our Creator gave to the wolf, deer, hawk, ant and so on.

For example, the Red Tail hawk was created to be an excellent hunter, almost always catching its prey. If a two-legged is also an excellent hunter, usually getting the game he goes after, it may be said that the Red

Tail hawk is his "totem"; that is, the Red Tail hawk's power helps him when he hunts. A "totem" is the unique power our Creator gave to one of his family groups of children that also has been given to us as individuals, or is sometimes given to us on special occasions as we need it.

If you have some of the same power the Red Tail hawk has, before you go hunting or while you hunt, you may often see Red Tail hawks flying around you. As a result, you begin to realize the Red Tail hawk helps you when you hunt. You start to feel a special attachment to, and relationship with, the Red Tail hawk and you start to think of him as your special friend or "helper", not just another bird in the sky. That occurs because the Red Tail hawk is your totem. The power our Creator gave the Red Tail hawk has also been gifted to you. You have a special relationship with the Red Tail hawk—you become more than just "relatives", you are "brothers".

All aspects of our Creator's power are contained within the medicine wheel. In order to describe some of them, the Ancient Ones used certain animals, birds, plants and stones to explain or represent those powers. Each of the Four Sacred Directions was assigned a "totem" to symbolize or represent certain aspects of our Creator's power contained within that Sacred Direction.

On this Sacred Path, the Eagle is the totem of the East. The eagle is considered our Creator's "messenger" because it flies higher than all of the other winged people, symbolizing its closeness to our Creator. When we pray, the eagle represents the messenger taking our prayers to our Creator and bringing his answers back to us. Every time I see an eagle, it reminds me that Grandfather both hears and answers my prayers. That is why eagle feathers are considered the most sacred of all the winged people's feathers.

All new information, insight and enlightenment come from our Creator's power in the East, and the eagle symbolizes the way Grandfather delivers it to us.

The Lifestyle Ceremony of New Beginnings Starts in the East

Our Creator is constantly creating. He creates the new day as the sun rises over the eastern horizon. He is continually creating new life within the Sacred Circle of Creation. All that he creates is for our benefit as a demonstration of his Unconditional Love. He is constantly giving to us so that we can continue living—even our next heartbeat is a gift from Grandfather.

As we have already pointed out, our Creator is omnipresent and omnipotent. That is, he is everywhere at all times and his unlimited power is all around us. If we look to the East, he is there. If we look to the South, he is there, and if we look to the West and North, he is also there. To help us understand that, we use symbolism to represent his presence and power as being everywhere and all around us at all times. From the most ancient of times, our ancestors considered the Four Cardinal Directions as being symbolic of our Creator's omnipresence and omnipotence. That is why the Ancient Ones said the Four Directions were sacred—they recognized Grandfather and his unlimited power was all around them at all times.

As a result, our prehistoric ancestors looked to the East, the direction of the rising sun, as the place from which Grandfather's power created all new things. This is why, when our Creator gave the Ancient Ones the medicine wheel with its Four Lifestyle Ceremonies, East on the wheel symbolized the starting point of the Lifestyle Ceremony of New Beginnings. The Spring Equinox signaled the beginning of that ceremony and it continued around to the South on the medicine wheel until the Summer Solstice.

The Lifestyle Ceremony of New Beginnings is a "sacred dance of life" that honors Grandfather's creative powers. It celebrates the "newness of life". It honors our Creator as being the source of all new things—the birth of new life, the new day, new enlightenment, new information, new wisdom and all new beginnings of every kind.

The Lifestyle Ceremony of New Beginnings starts in the East on the medicine wheel because the East symbolizes the source of our Creator's power that brings all new things into existence. Our Creator and his unlimited power are everywhere. Grandfather revealed to the Ancient Ones that his creative power to make all new things comes from the East and the Lifestyle Ceremony of New Beginnings is a celebration of that creative power.

This is the time of Spring when new crops are planted. Spring is also the time when we begin new projects. The many "event" ceremonies we perform during this time all honor and pay respect to our Creator's unlimited power that gives birth to all new things.

As you start to work with the medicine wheel, spend time in the East. Ask Grandfather to teach you about the layer upon layer of symbolism contained within this very sacred and powerful tool that is the road map for walking this Sacred Path called *The Way of the Medicine Wheel.* However, don't allow yourself to become "trapped" in the East. That is, don't spend an excessive amount of time there before going on to the South to work on the further development of the new things you have learned. In order to develop harmony and balance in our lives, we must learn to work with all of the Sacred Directions as needed.

WORKING WITH THE SOUTH AND LEARNING TO UNDERSTAND ITS POWER AND PURPOSE IN YOUR LIFE

Our Creator's power from the South produces growth and development. Grandfather sends his power from the East to give us new ideas, plans and enlightenment. Then his power from the South turns the new information and plans into reality. On the medicine wheel, the South is the direction of Summer. In the spring we plant our seeds and during the summer they grow to maturity.

The medicine wheel not only plots the cycle of the seasons, it also plots the cycle of the day. The sun rises in the East, bringing the new day and new life. The South represents mid-day when the sun is at its brightest and hottest. The sun sets in the West at evening, and the North represents midnight on the medicine wheel.

186

The sun symbolizes our Creator's power of Unconditional Love. The full measure of Grandfather's Unconditional Love comes to us from the South, during the summer when the sun is delivering the greatest amount of power and energy to the Sacred Circle of Life here on Mother Earth.

Spending time in the South on the medicine wheel will help you experience more of our Creator's Unconditional Love, and it will help empower you with that love so you can pass it on to others.

The Sacred Path of Unbending Tradition begins in the South and travels to the North on the medicine wheel. New ceremony comes to us from the East, but experiencing the depth of meaning shrouded within that ceremony's symbolism comes to us by spending lots of time in the South.

We enter the medicine wheel from the East, symbolically beginning our journey on the Sacred Path. However, the power to walk this Sacred Path comes to us from the South. As we spend time in the South within the medicine wheel, our comprehension of this Sacred Path grows and develops into maturity.

New symbols come to us from the East. However, the full knowledge, meaning and power of that symbol is understood and experienced by spending time in the South.

By now I hope you are beginning to understand how important it is to spend plenty of time in the South within the medicine wheel. The South empowers you to be able to "put into action" the information you received in the East. Therefore, balance the time you spend in each of the Four Sacred Directions because only then will you be able to bring harmony and balance into your life.

The Color of the South

As I mentioned at the beginning of this teaching session, I use the color white to represent the South. However, other people may use a different color. The color White symbolized our Creator's Unconditional Love, which comes to us from the South. It also represents the heat of summer with its power to make things grow. In addition, White represents one of the races of two-leggeds.

White is the color of peace and harmony, an important ingredient in all relationships.

The Totem of the South

On this Sacred Path, the wolf is the totem of the South. The wolf can teach us much about loyalty, commitment, teamwork, self-sacrifice and how to successfully raise a family.

Wolves mate for life, and both the male and female help raise their pups. Both the male and female hunt, however, the young females are usually better hunters than the males because of their organizational and planning skills. The males are stronger and are better protectors of the family and the framework within which it functions.

Wolves have a strong social structure and are extremely loyal and protective of members within their family group. Modern day families within our two-legged dominant society could learn much from wolves about family living.

Wolves work extremely well as a team. They have a team leader (usually the oldest or dominant male) and the other members of the team all know their roles and responsibilities as they work together—an indication of their excellent communication and social skills and abilities.

We could all learn much from wolves concerning how to live and work together as a team. Wolves have great capacity to show love and respect for one another, and they are always ready and willing to sacrifice themselves in order to protect those they love form harm and danger.

The Lifestyle Ceremony of Growth and Development Starts in the South

The Lifestyle Ceremony of Growth and Development begins in the South at the time of the Summer Solstice and continues around to the West

188

until the Fall Equinox. This ceremony corresponds with the season of Summer, and is a time in which much work is done and lots of projects become fully developed.

During this lifestyle ceremony, the emphasis is on putting into practice the things we learned from the East during the Sacred Season of Spring. This is the time "of doing"—turning ideas and dreams into reality.

The Lifestyle Ceremony of New Beginnings is a time of learning. On the other hand, the Lifestyle Ceremony of Growth and Development is a time of putting into practice what you learned. There is more daylight during this Lifestyle Ceremony than at any other time during the Sacred Cycle of Seasons. Our Creator gave us this extended time of daylight so we could be able to accomplish more during this time—and the wolf teaches us that we accomplish far more working together as a team than we do working alone.

WORKING WITH THE WEST AND LEARNING TO UNDERSTAND ITS POWER AND PURPOSE IN YOUR LIFE

Most of our sacred ceremonies begin in the West and there is a very important reason for that. Our Creator's power of Grace and forgiveness comes from the West ("Grace" is the willingness to forgive even when a person is unworthy of forgiveness—this is a condition we all find ourselves in). Grandfather forgives us of our mistakes and wrong doings even when we don't deserve to be forgiven, and his power of Grace and forgiveness comes to us from the West.

That is why we face the West at the beginning of most of our Sacred Ceremonies. We recognize our need to be forgiven, even when we don't deserve it. Therefore, we face the West in recognition of our need and desire for forgiveness and to receive the forgiveness so that we may perform the Sacred Ceremony with the blessing of our Creator.

Grandfather's power from the West also fills us with discernment, personal truth and honesty. It empowers us with internal truth that enables us to be honest with ourselves, our Creator, and our relatives within the

Sacred Circle of Life. Failing to spend enough time in the West within the medicine wheel leaves us vulnerable to all kinds of deceptions, false assumptions and untruths that can be very detrimental and destructive as we walk this Sacred Path. Therefore, as we receive new information and insight from the East and then work on its growth and development in the South, we also need to spend time in the West to insure that we develop the proper perception and interpretation of the information that was received and worked on.

The power to sort out "fact" from "feeling" comes to us from the West. Therefore, it is very important to spend time in the West whenever we are working on emotional issues, because our Creator's power from the West enables us to determine the real truth where emotions are concerned.

Forgiveness is an important ingredient for defusing conflict. When we are working on relationship issues or attempting to resolve conflict, we should spend time in the West in order to discern the truth of the issues and also to receive the power to forgive others when they hurt or wrong us.

The West is also the place all sacred water comes from. It is the resting place of the great Water Spirit that enters the rain, empowering water to become the Sacred Life Force of Mother Earth.

The Color of the West

The color of the West is black. The night comes to us from the West and the night covers over the activities of the day, blotting them out forever.

Many people have great misconceptions concerning the color black. They equate it with evil or with some form of negative power. However, just the opposite is true. The color black helps us block out the physical world and go inside ourselves to make contact with the spiritual realm. In addition, it not only symbolizes forgiveness, it also represents the act of "forgetting" that the offense ever occurred. Just as the night covers the day's activities, true forgiveness forgets the offense ever took place.

190

Forgiveness enables us to erase the effect of the negative words or actions and recreate the conditions that existed before the offense occurred—and our Creator's power to forgive comes to us from the West.

As I said, Black symbolizes forgiveness. It covers the negative actions and energies, removing them as if they never occurred. Black is a wonderful color. It symbolizes the forgiveness we all need to receive from our Creator and it also represents the forgiveness we also need to extend to those who hurt or wrong us.

Receiving forgiveness from our Creator and extending it to those who wrong us is a prerequisite for achieving purity. We can never become pure "hollow bones" that our Creator's Unconditional Love can flow into and then out to serve the needs of others as long as we need to be forgiven from our Creator, or we need to forgive others.

The color black symbolizes our Creator's power to "wipe the record clean". It represents the power to remove all wrongs, which is the first step in creating a life of purity. Black also represents Grace—the act of forgiving even when it isn't deserved or earned. Our Creator is willing to forgive us regardless of the negative things we have done and we must also be willing to forgive others even when we feel they don't deserve our forgiveness.

So you can see that black is a wonderful color and we need to spend time in the West on a regular basis.

In addition, the color black represents the Black race of two-leggeds. Many legends that came to us from ancient indigenous cultures describe the Black race as being the first race of two-leggeds Grandfather Created, followed by the Red race, Yellow race and finally, the White race.

The Totem of the West

The bear is the totem of the West. Its massive, powerful body enables it to perform the role as protector and overseer of Mother Earth's sacred, healing plants. The great bear knows all of the green people who are capable of helping the rest of Grandfather's children live strong, healthy lives.

The bear symbolizes the healing powers of the green people. It knows which plants should be used as medicine when we are sick. Its powerful body also represents the strength and power that our Creator makes available to us for living life to its fullest potential each day.

The bear has no enemies and fears no predator. It symbolizes the way we are to live our lives—free from fear and anxiety. It teaches us the importance of self-confidence. However, the bear is not overbearing nor a troublemaker. It avoids trouble whenever possible. Even though the bear is stronger and more powerful than its relatives, it seeks to live in peace and harmony with everyone, thus becoming a role model for how we two-leggeds should live our lives

The bear never runs from its problems but tackles those problems head on, and it believes there is no problem it can't solve. It never quits or gives up when faced with a difficult situation, and it continues to work on the problem or situation until it achieves its objective.

The bear is one of our best role models for successful living as we walk this Sacred Path. The mother bear is a great provider for her young and she will protect and defend them to the death. Such is the power we receive from the West.

The Lifestyle Ceremony of Reaping the Harvest Starts in the West

The Lifestyle Ceremony of Reaping the Harvest begins in the West with the Fall Equinox and ends in the North at the time of the Winter Solstice. The Lifestyle Ceremony of Reaping the Harvest is performed during the Fall Season. It is a time of reaping the rewards of our work during the Spring and Summer.

During this lifestyle ceremony, we make the final preparations for the Lifestyle Ceremony of Rest and Renewal that will be performed during the Winter months. At this time, we harvest and store up our food supply that will be needed until the following Spring and Summer cycle on the medicine wheel.

All of the projects that were started during the Lifestyle Ceremony of New Beginnings are completed before the end of this lifestyle ceremony. This is an important key to living in harmony and balance with the Sacred Time Cycles. In the Spring, we start many new projects. During the Summer, we further develop those projects, and during the fall we reap the benefit of bringing those projects to completion.

The Lifestyle Ceremony of Reaping the Harvest is one of the busiest times of the year. During this ceremony there is much work to be done to get ready for the time of rest and renewal that occurs during the Winter season. This is also a time of thanksgiving and sharing, a time of rejoicing and happiness, and a time of reaping the benefits of our hard work.

WORKING WITH THE NORTH AND LEARNING TO UNDERSTAND ITS POWER AND PURPOSE IN YOUR LIFE

Our Creator sends us his purity from the North to transform our minds, hearts and spirits so that we are morally without fault and free from guilt in his eyes. Our Grandfather's purifying power is like a refining fire that the North Wind blows into our minds, hearts and spirits to consume all negative and impure thoughts and attitudes so that our actions may become pleasing to him.

Our actions are an outward expression of our thoughts and attitudes. In order to act "right", we first must develop "right" thoughts and attitudes. In order to live in peace, harmony and balance with our Creator and all of his Family within the Sacred Circle of Life, we must first be empowered with our Creator's purity.

Grandfather's purity doesn't make us perfect. However, it does help us develop right and pure motives and intentions. In other words, even with the purest of motives and intentions, we may still say and do things that hurt and offend others.

Purity of mind, heart and spirit is the goal of walking this Sacred Path because it is the prerequisite for living in peace, harmony and balance with Grandfather and his Sacred Family.

Our Creator has placed within each of us the knowledge and understanding of what is right and wrong, good or bad. His purity enables us to consciously choose what is right and good instead of things that are wrong and bad.

In working with the medicine wheel, it is important to understand that we are working with the principles of "cause" and "effect". By that I mean that every "action" produces a "reaction".

For example, before we can receive our Creator's purity that comes from the North, we first must be honest with him and receive his forgiveness that comes from the West. The West empowers us to be honest and truthful which is a prerequisite for receiving forgiveness, which, in turn, is a prerequisite for receiving our Creator's purity.

It is important to understand that spiritual principle because it is a vivid example of how important and necessary it is to work with all of the Sacred Directions contained within the medicine wheel. In order to have balance in our lives, we first must have balance in working with the Four Sacred Directions because their powers are interconnected and interrelated.

The Color of the North

The color of the North is red. Red is the color of fire, and fire symbolizes our Creator's purity. As we conduct the Purification Ceremony, we light the fire to burn the wood that will heat the stones. The fire symbolizes our Creator's purifying power of Unconditional Love coming to enter the Sacred Stones.

Red also symbolizes the Blood of Life. We want our lives to be constantly controlled by our Creator's purity. Therefore, we offer ourselves totally to our Creator to not only be his children, but his obedient servants to help mend the Sacred Circle of Life.

194

In addition, red symbolizes the Red people who in the Western Hemisphere are referred to as "Indians".

The colors black, red, yellow and white are used to not only symbolize the Four Sacred Directions, but to also represent the four races of two-leggeds because in ancient times all people everywhere were given this Sacred Path to follow to our Creator.

The Totem of the North

The buffalo is the totem of the North. The buffalo is a powerful symbol of our Creator's Unconditional Love and provision. In the past, the buffalo provided virtually all of the needs of the American Indian living on the Great Plains. His hide was used as a covering for the people's homes, his meat fed them, his bones provided all kinds of useful tools, his stomach became a water container and, when tanned, his hide became warm, protective clothing to keep out the extreme cold of winter.

The buffalo was a constant reminder to the people that our Creator meets all of our needs. That is why the buffalo skull is still used today in so many of the Sacred Ceremonies conducted by North American Indians.

The Lifestyle Ceremony of Rest and Renewal Begins in the North

Winter is the Season of the North. Winter is a very important season because it was given to us as a time for rest and renewal for the spirit, mind and body. Spring, Summer and Fall are seasons filled with much activity. Therefore, we need the Winter season as a time to rest and renew ourselves for the coming busy lifestyles of Spring, Summer and Fall. Our Creator gave us longer nights in winter so we would have more time to focus on renewing our spirits, minds and bodies.

The Lifestyle Ceremony of Rest and Renewal begins with the Winter Solstice and continues until the Spring Equinox. The harvests have been gathered and prepared so that our basic needs for living have been met for the coming cold months of Winter. We have time available in which to focus our attention and energy on feeding the spirit and mind and not just on feeding the body.

All of the "event" ceremonies conducted during the Lifestyle Ceremony of Rest and Renewal focus on renewing our spirits, minds and bodies, and strengthening our connection with our Creator. This is a time of preparing ourselves for the "new beginnings" coming in Spring.

WORKING IN THE MEDICINE WHEEL AT NIGHT

The energy in the medicine wheel is much different at night than during the daytime. As we have already discussed, the night covers the activities of the day. The night symbolizes our Creator's forgiveness, and his power of night energizes us with introspection.

On the other hand, the day is a time of busy physical activity. The energy of the day is more conducive to physical work, and the energy of the night is more conducive to activities often associated with the Spiritual Realm.

Twilight—that time just before nightfall—is a wonderful time to enter the medicine wheel to prepare yourself to work on issues of personal growth on a spiritual level. Twilight is a time of transition of power. The power of the physical plane is waning and the power of the Spiritual Plane is beginning to grow stronger.

If I am going to the medicine wheel to work on spiritual issues, I enter the wheel at dusk as the sun is setting and use the twilight time to prepare myself for the things and issues I will work on. I go straight to the Center Stone, travel to the South, return to the Center Stone, and then sit with my back against the western side of the Center Stone facing West.

While dusk fades into twilight, I spend the time praying and reflecting on the personal spiritual issues I will be working on in the medicine wheel. I ask Grandfather to help me to be truthful and honest with myself and with him while working on these issues. I also ask him to search the recesses of my mind and spirit and reveal to me personal weaknesses that need to be dealt with, and areas of my life that need to be changed or improved. I ask him to reveal to me people I have wronged and offended and request discernment and wisdom concerning how to make amends. In addition, I pray for enlightenment concerning the meaning and understanding of the vast amount of symbolism associated with this Sacred Path. I ask Grandfather to help me understand omens I encounter or dreams I may have had, and I request guidance in dealing with issues and decisions to be made in the future.

One of the things I always work on at night in the medicine wheel is the expansion of my awareness and understanding of our Creator and my relationship to him. I seek more revelation concerning his will for my life and how to be more obedient to him and his plans for me. I seek forgiveness for past mistakes and ask for the power to not make those mistakes again. I reaffirm my desire and commitment to become a "hollow bone" or "empty vessel" which his Unconditional Love can flow into, through, and out to others. I seek what actions I need to take in order to become more effective in helping mend the Sacred Circle. I plead for wisdom so that I may truly learn to constantly live in peace, harmony and balance with Grandfather and all of his Children.

As the night grows deeper and deeper around us, more and more of our Creator's power is available to us for working on spiritual issues. Do not hesitate to work on spiritual issues far into the night, for I have discovered that the deeper the night, the stronger the spiritual revelations.

WORKING IN THE MEDICINE WHEEL DURING THE DAY

As I said, there is a different energy available to us during the day than during the night. I recommend you work in the medicine wheel at night to prepare yourself for things you will do during the coming days.

The activities of the day are usually focused more on meeting our needs on a physical level and the activities of night are generally focused more on meeting our needs on a spiritual level. The work I do in the medicine wheel during the day usually deals with issues and situations associated with needs within the physical realm.

Examples of issues you might choose to work on in the medicine wheel during the day might include where should you live, what type of job or work should you do, how to improve your business, or when should you go on vacation? You might also work in the medicine wheel on things such as how to improve your health, seeking a soul mate, finding the right car to buy and changing the weather—as you can see, the possibilities are endless.

All of life's issues—both physical and spiritual in nature—can be worked on in the medicine wheel. The question isn't "what can I work on in the medicine wheel;" it's "when will you start?"

Teaching Session – 8
THE FIVE SPIRITUAL MEDICINES

I sat next to grandfather Old Bear and stared into the little fire inside his lodge as I sipped on a cup of hot mint tea. I was wondering why the tea he made always tasted better than the tea back here in this world when he jarred me from my thoughts by asking, "When are you going to start passing on to others the things I am passing on to you?"

"Huh?" I muttered, trying to tear my thoughts away from the wonderful cup of mint tea and focus my attention on what he was saying.

"I said, when are you going to start passing on to others the things I am passing on to you? Do you think you are the only one who should walk this Sacred Path? Are you so self-centered as to think that I spend all of this time with you so you, alone, can have this ancient knowledge to keep all to yourself?"

His sternness shocked me and I quickly forgot all about the great cup of tea he had made for me and gave him my undivided attention.

"Well?" he asked, still pressing me for an answer.

"I don't know," I replied, embarrassed that I was having a hard time focusing my attention on his question, and surprised at the harshness in his tone of voice.

Sensing how uncomfortable I was with the way he was pressing me for a response, he smiled warmly and leaning over and patting me on the leg, he asked, "Grandson, where does corn come from?"

I frowned, trying to make sense out of what he was saying. "It, it comes from a corn plant," I stammered, wondering what this Ancient One was up to with this line of questioning.

"And where does the corn plant come from?" he continued.

"It comes from a kernel of corn," I responded, becoming more

199

confident in my answers, but still wondering where he was leading me with these questions.

He smiled warmly, nodding his agreement. Then his expression became very serious. "But what if people harvested the corn and ate all of it instead of saving some for seed to plant?"

"I guess there would be no more corn."

"You're right—and the people would go hungry." He was silent for a while, letting me contemplate what he had said, then he continued. "The things I share with you concerning this Sacred Path are like kernels of corn being planted within you. They take root and sprout and grow into a strong plant with big ears of corn." His eyes locked onto mine and held me captive within his stare. "Don't eat all of the corn, grandson. You must save some for seed to plant in other people. If you don't, they won't have any corn, and they will go hungry and become weak and frail."

He poured some more tea in my wooden cup, and we both sat near the little fire in silence for a long time while he let me reflect on his statement. Finally he continued. "You must take the spiritual principles I teach you about this Sacred Path and pass them on to others who, in turn, will be faithful in passing them on to the next generation. They, in turn, will pass them on to the next...who will pass them on to the next...who will pass them on to the next. This is the hope for the future. This is how we help mend the Sacred Circle of Life."

Later that day, while we were walking in the woods behind grandfather Old Bear's lodge, he again started talking about the importance of passing the information about this Sacred Path on to others. "Grandson, walking this Sacred Path is far different from following the various religions back in your world. They talk a lot. They have mastered the art of teaching people about their religion, but they don't know how to train people how to live. There is a great difference between "teaching" and "training". Teaching simply passes on information. Training helps people put information into practice. You must train people how to walk this Sacred Path. You train by showing.

You train by doing. You train by setting the example. Do you understand what I'm telling you, grandson?"

Not waiting for me to answer him, he said, "Remember, people do what you Do, not what you SAY—so train by example. YOU MUST LIVE THE WAY OF THE MEDICINE WHEEL—DO YOU UNDERSTAND WHAT I'M TELLING YOU?

"And also, grandson, as you pass things on to people, challenge them to always check with our Creator to determine if he wants them to do things the way you passed it on to them. Keep in mind that they are to always follow our Creator's guidance, not yours or mine. And don't be surprised if he has them do things a little different from the way you do things."

PASS IT ON

I want to challenge you to do what grandfather Old Bear challenged me to do long ago—pass it on. Don't eat all of the corn. Save some for seed to plant in others so they will also have corn to eat. Yes, pass it on. As you learn these principles and put them into practice—pass them on. Train others to follow the principles you follow as you walk this Sacred Path. Don't just talk about the principles involved in living *The Way of the Medicine Wheel*, make these principles part of your lifestyle. Live them every day and show others how to put them into practice in their daily lives. In so doing, you will be making an important contribution in helping mend the Sacred Circle of Life. And, as grandfather Old Bear said, always check with our Creator before implementing any of these principles or ceremonies to see if he wants you to do things this way or a slightly different way.

Medicine Wheel Mesa, located in the remote, high desert area of Southwestern Colorado, is a parched piece of land rimmed by high, tan and red sandstone bluffs, and bordered by rocky canyons. This little mesa is surrounded by hundreds of thousands of acres of public land. Our Creator has made Angelitta and I, along with Alice Brown, caretakers of this little mesa so that we can not only walk this ancient Sacred Path, but help train others how to walk it also. We are committed to passing on to others what has been passed on to us concerning this lifestyle called *The Way of the Medicine Wheel,* and we challenge you to make the same commitment—pass it on!

Not long after grandfather Old Bear talked to me about the importance of passing this information on to others, I had a dream I have never forgotten. I haven't shared this dream with very many people. However, I feel it might help some of you grasp the importance of sharing with others the principles involved in walking this Sacred Path.

In my dream, I was sitting alone at a table inside a very old wood frame building (the type of old, unpainted building you see in western movies). The west wall of the building had plate glass windows that reached from the floor to the ceiling, and the table was next to the window. It was the only piece of furniture in the room.

To the west of the building, there was a large grassy park, and beyond the park there was a row of tall trees. There were lots of people in the park and they seemed to be having a picnic. Children were playing games, and the adults were standing around picnic tables talking, laughing and eating.

As I sat watching the people, suddenly I saw two large objects up in the sky, directly above the people in the park. As I looked closer, I saw that the objects were some sort of "beings", and they seemed to be furiously fighting. They had human faces, but their arms and legs were entirely covered with feathers, and they had large talons for hands and feet.

One of the beings was covered with white feathers and the other one was covered with dull, dark gray feathers. They were locked in violent combat, and the dark one seemed to be winning.

As I watched this war between these two beings, I was shocked that the people in the park below them seemed to be totally oblivious to what was going on directly overhead.

I ran out of the building and yelled at the people to look above them

202

as I pointed up into the sky. However, the people paid no attention to me, and continued on with their party. I ran part way out into the park and yelled louder for the people to look at what was happening above them, but they acted like they didn't even see me.

Finally, in frustration, I ran among the people, shouting for them to look up, but they still ignored me as if I wasn't even there. At last I began walking up to individuals and touching them on the arm and asking them to please look up at the war going on in the sky directly above their heads.

As I touched each person, he or she would stop and look up at the raging battle. Then, that person in turn would touch a friend and ask him or her to look up at what was happening above them.

Suddenly, I noticed that the more people touched those around them and asked them to look up at the war overhead, the more the white being seemed to be winning the war. Finally, when all of the people had been touched and were looking up at the battle, the white being was able to win the war and the dark gray being flew away.

I woke from the dream with a start and couldn't sleep the rest of the night. For the next several days I couldn't get the dream out of my mind. I asked Grandfather to reveal to me what the dream meant, and slowly I began to understand its meaning.

The old, run-down wood frame building symbolized the decay of modern day, institutionalized religion. I was sitting alone inside the old building, separated from the people in the park, but watching them through a large, plate glass window. I represented the way modern day religious leaders isolate themselves from society and hide within their outdated, institutionalized religious systems.

The two beings fighting in the sky above the people symbolized the war going on between good and evil—a war that very few people are aware of today. The white being symbolized "good", and the dark gray being represented "evil".

The people having a picnic in the park represented modern society's obsession with a life of leisure and self-indulgence. The fact that the people having the picnic didn't see the beings fighting in the sky directly above them illustrated how people's pursuit of self-gratification has blinded them to the realities within the Spiritual Realm.

My running out of the building and yelling at the people to look up into the sky, but being ignored by them, symbolized how religious leaders today talk and talk "at" people instead of training them how to put spiritual principles into practice in their every day lives. When I touched individuals and then asked them to look into the sky, they responded and could see the war going on overhead. This represents the need for religious leaders to form relationships with people, not just "preach" at them. It also represents the need to train people how to walk a Spiritual Path, not just talk about the spiritual realm.

As more and more people were touched, the dark being became weaker and weaker and began losing the battle. Finally, when everyone had been touched and could see the battle going on above them, the white being, or good being, was able to win the war and drive the evil being away. This represents the process involved in mending the Sacred Circle of Life.

So I say it again—PASS IT ON. Help others learn how to walk this Sacred Path, and as you do you will be making an important contribution toward mending the Sacred Circle of Life.

As I have stated before, I am not interested in simply sharing information with you concerning this Sacred Path. I want these principles to become a part of your life, guiding your everyday decisions and actions.

It doesn't take a prophet or mystical "guru" to ascertain that current world events are rapidly propelling us into a turbulent and dangerously uncertain future. Economic, environmental, social and political conditions the world over has brought our modern day societies to the breaking point. No one knows the future. However, we can be sure of one thing—increasing rapid change within our surroundings has destroyed the "status quo".

Everywhere I go, I hear people talking about the uncertainty of the future. People say that they "feel something is about to happen that will alter life as we have known it". I consider myself to be a very optimistic person. However, I too have a strong feeling that the world is on the verge of major changes. Do I know what is going to happen? No. Do I know when it is going to occur? Definitely not. Am I convinced that society as we have known it is in for very rough times in the immediate future? Absolutely! In fact, I am convinced that if the masses knew the devastation that is looming on the horizon they would not be able to cope with that knowledge.

That is why this material is being made available to the public, and that is why I urge you—PASS IT ON!

THE TWO WORLDS

There are two worlds—the physical world and the Spiritual World. In the far distant past these two worlds were one. However, far back beyond the eastern horizon, in a time known only to the first people, our ancient ancestors embraced self-centeredness as a lifestyle, thus becoming deceived into thinking that their own thoughts contained more knowledge and wisdom than those of their Creator.

Self-centeredness gave birth to self-will, self-reliance, self-sufficiency and self-indulgence. They began shunning and ignoring our Creator's laws that were shrouded in Unconditional Love and had been chiseled into their consciousness by our Creator's own hands, and instead, replaced them with their own laws that revealed the deceit, arrogance and defiance that began permeating the very core of their souls. By their own willpower, they broke away from the perfect world our Creator had made for all his children, and, with the power of their minds, strength of their hands and backs, they created a new world set apart from the Spiritual Realm.

In their new physical world men were their own gods, subject to no one but themselves. They worshiped and prayed to idols of clay, stone and wood instead of speaking face to face with our Creator as they once had done in the perfect world he had made for them.

So, our Creator made a Sacred Path for his rebellious two-leggeds, so they could find their way back to him, and now we call that Sacred Path *the Way of the Medicine Wheel*. For those walking this Sacred Path, the physical and Spiritual Realms are combined together into a single reality.

THE FIVE SPIRITUAL MEDICINES

There are not only two worlds—the physical and spiritual realms—there are also two powers. There is physical power and there is spiritual power. This Sacred Path not only leads us to the spiritual realm, it brings these the two worlds together, combining them into one single reality.

You can never reach the spiritual realm using physical power. That principle is so important it must be repeated, and please let the truth of those words sink deep into your soul. YOU CAN NEVER REACH THE SPIRITUAL REALM USING PHYSICAL POWER.

What does that mean? We are spirits living within physical bodies with finite physical, mental and emotional powers. We are limited in what we can physically accomplish or endure. However, there are no limits in the spiritual realm. Our Creator is unlimited in what he can do. Grandfather must give us Spiritual Power in order for us to reach the Spiritual Realm, and that is why he gave us the Five Spiritual Medicines.

The Five Spiritual Medicines are "cures" for the physical limitations that hinder us from walking this Sacred Path that combines the physical and Spiritual Realms together into a single reality. These Five Spiritual Medicines are Spiritual Courage, Spiritual Patience, Spiritual Endurance, Spiritual Alertness and Humility.

These Five Spiritual Medicines provide the cure for our human physical frailties and limitations that stand in the way of us achieving our full potential as we walk this Sacred Path. They cure such diseases as doubt, fear, apathy, closed-mindedness and self-centeredness. They help us refocus our attention from the finite physical realm with its human limitations to the infinite Spiritual Realm where nothing is impossible with our Creator.

These Five Spiritual Medicines are like five progressive steps we repeat over and over as we walk this Sacred Path toward our Creator. Repeating these five steps is a neverending process that occurs over and over as we make the journey that finally ends when we reach "the other side" and stand in our Creator's presence.

THE LOCATION OF THE FIVE SPIRITUAL MEDICINES ON MEDICINE WHEEL

The Five Spiritual Medicines are a Sacred Gift from our Creator. He knows it is impossible for us to walk this Sacred Path on our own power, even though we are all tempted to try.

We have emphasized over and over that the medicine wheel contains within it all of the spiritual principles and tools we need to successfully walk this Path and bring the two worlds together into a single reality. It should not be surprising that the Five Spiritual Medicines also have their home within the wheel.

As the following diagram illustrates, Spiritual Courage comes to us from the East. Spiritual Patience comes to us from the South. Spiritual Endurance is located in the West, and Spiritual Alertness comes to us from the North. Humility resides in the center of the medicine wheel, which symbolizes the dwelling place of our Creator.

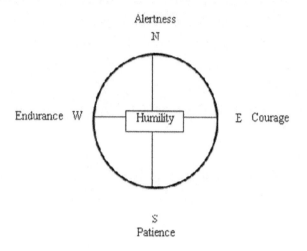

Alertness
N

Endurance W

Humility

E Courage

S
Patience

Figure 5

Spiritual Courage comes to us from the East. Spiritual Patience comes to us from the South. Spiritual Endurance is located in the West, and Spiritual Alertness comes to us from the North. Humility resides in the center of the medicine wheel, which symbolizes the dwelling place of our Creator.

SPIRITUAL COURAGE

The East is the birthplace of all new beginnings. It is also the direction from which we receive Spiritual Courage, which empowers us to start traveling this Sacred Path.

Spiritual Courage is the power to "begin doing". It is the power that enables us to take that first step to start any new endeavor. It takes Spiritual Courage to begin this Sacred Journey. It takes Spiritual Courage to successfully experience a Purification Ceremony for the first time. It takes Spiritual Courage to build the circle of stones that become the medicine wheel. It takes Spiritual Courage to begin simplifying our lives. It takes Spiritual Courage to break away from this materialistic system that drives a wedge between the physical and spiritual realms. It takes Spiritual Courage to obey our Creator as he reveals his plans for our lives.

Spiritual Courage is the "act of doing" for the first time. It is not a belief or attitude. We don't believe in Spiritual Courage, nor do we have an attitude of Spiritual Courage. Spiritual Courage is faith in action. It is the spiritual power that moves us to take the first step in obeying what our Creator instructs us to do.

There can be no progress in our spiritual growth and development without Spiritual Courage. It empowers us to be "doers", not just "talkers". It turns Spiritual Truth into action.

Spiritual Courage is far different from physical courage. Spiritual Courage is Sacred Power from our Creator that moves us to take action. On the other hand, physical courage is based solely on human power. Spiritual Courage is based on the unlimited power of our Creator to help us achieve his will for our lives, whereas physical courage is based on our limited human power to achieve his will.

If you attempt to accomplish our Creator's will for your life based solely on your human courage, you won't get very far. Let me illustrate what I mean. It takes courage to enter a Purification Lodge for the first time. If you enter the lodge using your physical courage, you may overcome your fear, you may endure the heat, you may even stay in the lodge for all four rounds without complaining or leaving; however, that will be your only reward because you are doing it on your own power.

Your faith is based on your own ability to endure that heat and everything else that occurs during the ceremony. So achieving your goal of showing yourself and others that you are capable of staying in the lodge "with the best of them" is your only reward. You used your human power so you only earned human recognition for your effort.

On the other hand, if you admit your reservations and possible fears of entering the Purification Lodge for the first time, but ask our Creator to give you the power to do it, then you are seeking Spiritual Courage, not your own human courage. As a result, our

Creator will empower you to not only participate in the Purification Ceremony, but he will achieve his purpose for your participation—which is purification.

Physical courage contributes to physical results only. Spiritual Courage contributes to both physical and spiritual results. Physical courage is limited by our own willpower, whereas Spiritual Courage has no limitations.

One of the reasons many people participate in spiritual ceremony after spiritual ceremony without seeing any positive results is because they are operating on physical courage instead of Spiritual Courage.

As I said, Spiritual Courage is the "power to try" that comes from our Creator, and that power is Unconditional Love. It is our Creator's Unconditional Love that flows into us, empowering us to do things that are beyond our human ability to achieve. Unconditional Love takes the focus off of us with our human frailties and limitations and places it on our Creator and his unlimited power.

I have entered the medicine wheel many times seeking Spiritual Courage in order to be empowered by our Creator to begin doing the thing he had asked me to do. On such occasions, I would face the East and ask our Creator to send me his power of Spiritual Courage so that I could faithfully and successfully perform the task at hand.

It is important to understand that all of these Five Spiritual Medicines (Courage, Patience, Endurance, Alertness and Humility) are Sacred Gifts from our Creator. He is the one who deserves the credit and recognition for our accomplishments and success in carrying out his plans for us. It is a dangerous thing to be empowered with the Five Spiritual Medicines and then take the credit for the results. When people try to compliment you or praise you in some way for what was achieved, always be quick to point out that it was our Creator who made it possible to accomplish the task, not your own power, knowledge or wisdom.

When faced with an insurmountable problem or situation, always ask our Creator for the power to overcome it, then quickly give him the praise and credit he deserves for the results. Never take credit for what our Creator accomplishes through you. Always remember that physical power and ability is of no value in accomplishing things on a spiritual level. Only spiritual power that comes from our Creator can bring the physical and Spiritual Realms together into a single reality in our lives.

SPIRITUAL PATIENCE

Spiritual Courage is the power that comes from our Creator that helps us begin taking actions needed to accomplish his plans for us as we walk this Sacred Path. Once we begin using the Sacred Medicine of Spiritual Courage we will immediately start seeing results from our efforts.

Taking the "medicine" of Spiritual Courage will make us willing and eager to take action. Therein lies a great danger, and that is why we need and must also take the Sacred Medicine of Spiritual Patience. Without Spiritual Patience, it is easy to go off on our own, take things into our own hands, or get ahead of our Creator's "time table" for implementing or starting what he wants us to do.

Spiritual Courage is the power to begin taking action. Spiritual Patience is the power to "wait" for Grandfather's "right timing" to take that action.

Learning to work with the Five Spiritual Medicines is the key to successfully walking this Sacred Path. Without them, our fears, concerns, reservations, frustrations and doubts will quickly overwhelm us and we will give up or get side tracked, turn around, and abandon our journey on this Sacred Path.

Taking the Sacred Medicine of Spiritual Courage is the first step we take in walking this Sacred Path. Taking the Medicine of Spiritual Patience is the second step that must be taken.

It is extremely important to understand the process involved in becoming empowered with the various aspects of our Creator's Unconditional Love. The first aspect of Unconditional Love that we receive as a gift from Grandfather is the Spiritual Courage to "try" or "begin" to obey his will and plans for us as we walk this Path. Spiritual Courage replaces our own puny and limited human courage. The gift of Spiritual Courage is like the first slice of the pie called Unconditional Love that we "eat" or receive into our being. As I said, it empowers us to get started on this Sacred Path.

The second piece of the pie we receive is Spiritual Patience. It gives

211

us the power to not run ahead of our Creator. It enables us to wait for the next instruction or revelation we will receive from Grandfather. Without Spiritual Patience, we start taking things into our own hands. We try to "make things happen" instead of "letting things happen" in accordance with our Creator's timetable.

We must understand that Grandfather not only has a plan for us, he also has a timetable for accomplishing that plan. Without the Sacred Medicine of Spiritual Patience, we will find ourselves either getting ahead of that timetable or lagging far behind it. If we fail to take the Medicine of Spiritual Patience, we will find that the Sacred Path we thought we were on has quickly become so steep, rocky and dangerous that it is impossible to continue because we have, in fact, lost our way. We will come to one dead end after another until we back track to where we left this Sacred Path, and then take the Sacred Medicine of Spiritual Patience.

Spiritual Patience is a wonderful gift from our Creator. It takes the pressure off of us that produces impatience. It takes the focus off of our own limited abilities to perform and helps us to realize that it is our Creator's unlimited power that will work on our behalf. Instead of feeling we must do things "for" our Creator, we are aware that it is our Creator's power that will accomplish things for and through us.

Spiritual Patience removes the tensions and frustrations that result from impatience and replaces them with peace and calmness that comes from knowing that our Creator has not only given us a plan, but is in control of the results, and will provide all of the power needed to achieve those results.

Impatience is a sign we are assuming control and trying to make things happen on our own. Taking the Sacred Medicine of Spiritual Patience removes our need to use our own power to produce a result and makes us willing to receive that aspect of our Creator's Unconditional Love that makes us willing to let Grandfather be in charge of the situation.

Impatience is not the problem; it is the symptom of the problem. Impatience is a sign we are assuming control instead of letting our Creator be in control. It is a sign we are operating on our own timetable instead of

Grandfather's. Impatience always produces confusion and frustration instead of peace, disharmony instead of harmony and imbalance instead of balance. It creates problems instead of solving them. It replaces faith with fear. It distorts reality, and most importantly, leads to failure.

That is why it is imperative that we take the Sacred Medicine of Spiritual Patience—and we cannot succeed on this Sacred Path without it.

SPIRITUAL ENDURANCE

Once we acquire the Spiritual Courage to "take action", and the Spiritual Patience "to wait for our Creator's leading", we need Spiritual Endurance to not give up. Spiritual Endurance is the power that comes from our Creator, enabling us to keep on taking action and keep on waiting for our Creator's leading, and never give up.

Spiritual Endurance is the Sacred Medicine that wards off the disease of doubt and complacency, and replaces it with confidence and assurance in Grandfather's ability to solve the problem or produce the result.

The gift of Spiritual Endurance enables us to get our eyes off of human frailties and limitations and focus on our Creator's unlimited power and ability to make things happen. Spiritual Endurance is that aspect of Unconditional Love that empowers us to go beyond our human abilities. In fact, it replaces our finite human limitations with our Creator's unlimited power to perform all that is required and needed to produce the result.

Spiritual Endurance knows no limitations because our Creator's power of Unconditional Love has no limitations. Spiritual Endurance removes us from the realm of the "natural" and places us into that of the "supernatural". It strengthens our resolve and commitment to let our Creator's power flow through us to accomplish the things he wants done.

It is important to understand that our Creator's plans for us almost always go beyond our finite human power to accomplish them because they interface with, and are a part of, his overall plans for all of his Children. His plans for us don't just benefit and effect us; they benefit and effect many others within his Sacred Family. Therefore, we must have the help of his power to accomplish his plans for us.

We tend to focus on what we consider to be "personal plans". That is, plans that we come up with generally only involve a very small group of people we associate with. On the other hand, plans our Creator has for us always have a far-reaching impact on a multitude of his family members— many of whom we may never know or meet. That is because Grandfather sees and cares for all of his Creation, whereas, it is hard for us to concern ourselves with the world beyond the immediate surrounding horizons.

As a result, we desperately need our Creator's help to achieve his plans for us, because they are usually much larger in scope than those we would develop on our own. Therefore, it is imperative that we "take" the Five Spiritual Medicines because we could never accomplish our Creator's plans for us without them. They empower us with Grandfather's supernatural, unlimited power. They expand our vision. They strengthen our faith. They are keys to accomplishing things far beyond our limited human power and abilities.

Spiritual Endurance is the Sacred Spiritual Medicine that opens the doorway to the Spiritual Realm, enabling us to become a hollow bone which our Creator's power of Unconditional Love can flow through and out to others within the Sacred Circle. Without Spiritual Endurance it is impossible to achieve the great and wonderful plans our Creator has for us.

Spiritual Endurance builds spiritual strength. It is the food that develops our spiritual muscles. The more Spiritual Endurance we have, the stronger we become spiritually. As we increase our Spiritual Endurance, we expand our spiritual vision. As we increase our Spiritual Endurance, we become more strongly connected with our Grandfather.

The level of our endurance is an indicator of the level of our commitment to obeying our Creator's plans for us. It speaks volumes concerning how serious we are about walking this Sacred Path.

SPIRITUAL ALERTNESS

Just as Spiritual Endurance opens our Spiritual Eyes, so Spiritual Alertness unplugs our Spiritual Ears, enabling us to more clearly hear what Grandfather tells us. Spiritual Alertness is the Spiritual Medicine that develops Spiritual Hearing.

These Five Spiritual Medicines are sequential in nature. That is, the development of one Spiritual Medicine tends to help promote the development of the next. For example, the more we "do" and the more we "wait", the more we promote the development of Spiritual Endurance. At the same time, the more Spiritual Endurance we have, the easier it is to acquire Spiritual Alertness. In fact, it is often while applying Spiritual Endurance to a situation that we begin "hearing" more clearly what our Creator is saying to us.

Spiritual Alertness enables us to discern what our Creator is saying to us in the Sacred Sunrise and Sunset. It whispers the meaning of the symbolism to us all through the day. It "fine tunes" our conscience, and makes us more intuitive. It reveals to us the meaning of dreams and visions. It enables us to hear the Voice of Silence as it speaks to us in the darkness under a star-lit sky.

Many people are spiritually deaf because they have never "taken the medicine" we call Spiritual Alertness. Unless we develop Spiritual Alertness, we have to rely on others to tell us what Grandfather is saying. Therefore, it is imperative that we acquire Spiritual Alertness, for without it we can never achieve our full spiritual potential.

Spiritual Alertness turns our prayers into conversations with Grandfather. It enables us to not only ask him questions, but "hear" his answers as he speaks to us spirit to Spirit.

You may ask, "How does he speak to us?" He communicates to us through circumstances, our surroundings, symbolism, our conscience, that deep inter "knowing" that comes from him, other spiritually alert people—the list goes on and on. However, the real question we should be asking is "Are we listening?"

Spiritual Alertness enables us to listen to what Grandfather is saying when he speaks to us through the sunrise, sunset, symbolism, ceremonies, our conscience and so on. One of my favorite verses in the Old Testament says, "Be still and know that I am God." This is a powerful illustration of Spiritual Alertness in action. Spiritual Alertness involves being still, getting quiet, focusing our attention inward instead of outward, listening to the silence, and listening with our spiritual ears instead of our physical ears.

Grandfather speaks to us Spirit to spirit. His communication with us is often in the form of "enlightenment". He creates within us a "knowing", an assurance, an understanding of his message or plans for us.

Talk to Grandfather and he will talk back to you. We are his children. He is more interested in communicating with us than we are with him. He has big plans for us—plans that affect all of Creation. His plans are perfect for us, helping us to live in peace, harmony and balance with all of our relatives within the Sacred Circle of Life. His plans provide meaning and fulfillment in our lives. His plans involve receiving his Unconditional Love and passing it on to others. However, those plans can only be understood by practicing Spiritual Alertness in our daily lives.

HUMILITY

Humility is the power to not promote or give credit to "self". It is the fifth and most important Spiritual Medicine that we must "take". Spiritual Courage is the power to take action. Spiritual Patience is the power to wait for our Creator's instructions. Spiritual Endurance is the power to continue and never give up. Spiritual Alertness is the power to hear what Grandfather is telling us. If we "take" or acquire these four Spiritual Medicines, great things will begin happening in our lives. We will develop a personal relationship with Grandfather. He will become very real to us and we will start seeing and experiencing his power at work in our lives. We will not only know his plans for us, but those plans will become a reality. Our spirit will be in tune with his Spirit and we will become hollow bones through which his Unconditional Love will flow out to others. Grandfather's power will be evident in our lives—and therein lies the potential problem.

As you begin experiencing more and more of our Creator's power working in and through you, people may begin seeking you out for "spiritual help and guidance". They will see our Creator's power at work in you and may start looking to you as their "spiritual teacher". You may even find yourself being asked to provide answers to people's spiritual questions.

As a result, as time goes by, you will be tempted to start thinking that you are doing spiritual work FOR our Creator instead of him doing spiritual work THROUGH you. If you yield to that temptation, you will become deceived into believing that you are, in fact, a "spiritual leader and teacher". You will start believing that people should follow you and do things on this Spiritual Path exactly as you do. You will start believing that you are the "final authority" concerning this Sacred Path. In reality, you will have become like a "pope" to the people who come to you for spiritual guidance. That is, you will have convinced people that they must always seek you out concerning what is right and wrong as it relates to their spiritual walk.

You may say, "Oh that would never happen to me!" To that I say, "Look around you at so called 'spiritual leaders' in all religions everywhere and you will find many people who have fallen into that trap." I personally have observed many of our own Native American people who were once great examples of "hollow bones" through which our Creator used to work his power. However, over time, many of those individuals started believing that they were the final authority concerning the way things should be done on the Sacred Path often referred to as "The Red Road". They became the judge and jury, determining what people could and couldn't do as they walked that Sacred Path.

As a result, instead of continuing to be hollow bones our Creator's Unconditional Love could flow through and out to meet the needs of others, they slowly became "dry bones", filled only with their own self-serving egos. Some of them began charging people for their "spiritual services" and became spiritual entertainers, with a large fan club instead of our Creator's humble servants.

We cannot serve "self" and our Creator too. One or the other must be in charge and control of our will. If we put self-will above our Creator's will for us, then his Unconditional Love is no longer able to flow through us and out to others because our egos are blocking his love from entering us.

Once Grandfather's power of Unconditional Love stops flowing into us, we are limited to doing things only on the strength of our own knowledge and power. We may continue to perform ceremonies the way we did when our Creator's Unconditional Love was flowing into us; however, that power is no longer operating within the ceremony. As a result, we are simply performing rituals that are powerless. We are putting on a show for the people, but Grandfather's power is absent.

We must never forget that all spiritual power comes from our Creator. Through our own limited human power we cannot heal people, know the future, nor properly advise individuals concerning the mysteries of the Spiritual Realm. Grandfather is the Creator and Master of the Spiritual Realm, and he is our Spiritual Teacher. People are to follow him and do what he tells them, not follow us—and that is what we are to teach those who would want to learn.

Grandfather Old Bear has told me many times that whatever he tells me about this Sacred Path must be taken to our Creator for confirmation. In that way, I will be following and obeying our Creator, not following grandfather Old Bear. That is the test of true humility. We are to live our lives as humble servants of our Creator, daily following his plans for us in helping restore the Sacred Circle of Life. We are to always give him the credit for what is accomplished as we walk this Sacred Path, and NEVER take the credit ourselves.

That is what we are to teach people. That is what we must emphasize, and that is the way we should constantly live our lives. Humility isn't a philosophy of life; it is submission to our Creator. We don't talk about how humble we are; we live our humility before others. If you take credit for being humble, you have just demonstrated that you aren't!

You don't acquire humility by making it your goal. You become humble by submitting your will and plans to our Creator and placing his will for your life above your own. Humility is the result of developing a submissive spirit toward our Creator; it is not a trait we pursue.

Humility is the most important of all the Spiritual Medicines because it is the proof we are truly serving our Creator and not serving self as we walk this Sacred Path. What does it mean to serve our Creator and not self? It means we stop focusing on self and let our Creator's Unconditional Love flow through us and out to others. It means we start focusing on serving the needs of others instead of always focusing on serving our own self-interests. It means we actually live by the Golden Rule—treat other people the way you want them to treat you.

HOW WE ACQUIRE THE FIVE SPIRITUAL MEDICINES

The Five Spiritual Medicines are gifts Grandfather gives us to help us walk this Sacred Path. However, we must earn them; he doesn't give them to us unless we deserve them. For example, it does no good to ask our Creator for Spiritual Courage unless we are willing to do a spiritual activity for the first time.

As was pointed out in an earlier teaching session, our Creator uses volunteers. Therefore, if you want Spiritual Courage, volunteer. Tell Grandfather you are willing to start, but you will need his help to succeed. "Doing" is faith in action. It demonstrates to our Creator that you have faith in his power to help you succeed.

Each of the Five Spiritual Medicines is given to us as a result of a demonstration of our faith. For example, to receive Spiritual Patience, begin waiting for Grandfather's guidance instead of trying to do it on your own.

When you ask our Creator for the Five Spiritual Medicines, you must begin taking the actions that activate their power. Receiving each Spiritual Medicine requires an "act" of faith. This is important because it demonstrates to Grandfather that you believe he truly will empower you with that particular Medicine. Unless you are willing to take the action, you will never receive the Spiritual Medicine.

For example, in order to receive the Five Spiritual Medicines, you must be willing to put yourself in situations you feel are beyond your control or power to produce the desired results. As long as you can control the situation by your power, you don't need our Creator's help. Therefore, receiving the Five Spiritual Medicines requires putting ourselves in situations where we need Grandfather's help to achieve the result. The act of placing ourselves in that situation is a demonstration of our willingness to turn control over to our Creator, and it also illustrates our faith that he will empower us to achieve what needs to be done.

We must never forget that our Creator empowers us with the Five Spiritual Medicines to accomplish his will and plans for us. However, he is under no obligation to give us these Medicines to accomplish our own self-centered plans. His plans for us are always bigger than our ability to achieve them—never forget that. We need his power to achieve his plans because we are powerless to achieve them on our own.

That is why our Creator gives us the Five Spiritual Medicines. They enable us to accomplish what we couldn't achieve in our own strength. However, always remember that when Grandfather empowers you to accomplish his plans, give him the credit for the results. This is very important because it keeps us humble. We must never forget that it is our Creator's power that enables us to walk this Sacred Path. We must always give him credit for what he accomplishes for us and through us on this journey.

BOOK THREE
Keys To Surviving the Coming Earth Changes

INTRODUCTION TO BOOK THREE

It is only fair to warn you that you may find some of the concepts in the following series of teaching sessions hard to accept. However, I strongly recommend that you maintain an open mind and don't make any final judgement concerning the validity of this information until you have thoroughly evaluated and digested the material.

I also want to remind you that I am not trying to convince you to follow this Sacred Path referred to as *The Way of the Medicine Wheel*. The Spiritual Path you follow should be the one our Creator prepares for you, not one someone else told you was right for you.

My job is to simply make you aware of this Sacred Path and it's spiritual principles and ceremonies. Your job is to talk to our Creator and listen to his guidance concerning the spiritual path you should walk.

Some people say that it doesn't matter what spiritual path one follows because all of them lead us to our Creator. That isn't true. Unfortunately, some spiritual paths lead us away from Grandfather and toward the Dark Side. If you want to know if you are on the right spiritual path, check to see if that path is empowering you with more and more of our Creator's Unconditional Love so that you can better serve the needs of your relatives within the Sacred Circle of Life.

All true Spiritual Paths established by our Creator turn their followers into givers instead of takers, servants of our Creator instead of masters over his Creation, forgivers of the wrongs committed against them instead of judges over those who wrong them, and, most importantly, living examples of our Creator's Unconditional Love in action.

Teaching Session – 9
DEVELOPING A LIFESTYLE OF SIMPLICITY

As I sat next to grandfather Old Bear, watching him silently stare deep into the orange flames of the little fire in his lodge, I could tell by the serious expression on his face that I probably wasn't going to like what I was about to hear—and I was right. (And you probably won't like what you read on many of the following pages of this teaching session either).

The longer the Old Wise One sat there in silent contemplation, the more concerned I became. Finally, he cocked his head to one side and looked at me with a funny little grin that seemed to communicate more pity than warmth. He had a great deal of sadness in his voice as he said, "I've watched your world for a long time, grandson, and my heart is very sad and heavy because of what I see happening to your people."

Before I could inform him that they were not my people, he continued. "In your world, people have been deceived into thinking that the more technology they acquire, the easier and better life will be for them— however, just the opposite has proven to be true. The more technology they acquire, the more complicated, stressful and frustrated their lives become. Man-made technology is not leading them to utopia, its leading them into confusion and chaos—and if left unchecked, it will eventually destroy them."

He carefully placed a few more small sticks on the little fire, then looked at me with that warm, loving smile of his that always made me feel safe and secure and said, "In my world, fire was the most important technology we had. It was our Creator's gift to us that truly made us happy and comfortable." He looked directly into my eyes, his thin face drawn tight with concern. "Have you ever noticed how peaceful and relaxing it is to sit around a camp fire, grandson? Fire is the most important gift our Creator ever gave the two-leggeds. It has the power to keep us warm on cold nights, provide light in dark places and cook our food. However, its most important power is its ability to calm us down, help us relax and focus our attention on the spiritual realm.

"In my world fire was sacred. We knew it for what it was—a great sacred gift from our Creator that contained tremendous spiritual power that worked for our benefit as long as we respected it. However, if we failed to give it proper respect, it could become angry and do lots of damage.

"To us, fire symbolized our Creator's power. It was an important part of most of our ceremonies. It was our most important technology because it taught us so much about our Creator and the relationship we have with him. If we followed the rules of working with fire and gave it proper respect, it worked greatly for our benefit. On the other hand, if we disregarded the rules of working with fire, it could become angry and destroy us—and that is also true of our Creator. If we follow his Rules for Right Living, he works in great ways for our benefit. If we disregard those rules, he becomes upset with us and then we may be severely disciplined."

The Old One picked up another small stick and began to gently move some of the sticks around in the fire. As the fire's orange flames rose a little higher, he continued. "My world was more technologically advanced than yours, grandson, because we truly understood the real meaning and power of fire."

As we both sat there staring into the flickering flames of the little fire, a deep, peaceful silence filled grandfather's old lodge, and I found myself never wanting to leave this place.

Finally, grandfather broke the mystical silence by asking, "Have I ever told you the story of how the two-leggeds were given the gift of fire?"

"No," I replied, barely above a whisper, not wanting to disrupt the magic that filled the little lodge.

"Sacred Fire did not exist in the world before our Creator made the two-leggeds," he began. "Our other relatives within the Sacred Circle had no need for fire, so our Creator hadn't given it to them. They didn't

228

need it to keep warm or help them see in the dark, and they didn't cook their food before eating it. And, they certainly didn't need it to help them stay focused on the spiritual realm.

"Not long after our Creator made the two-leggeds, the eagle began noticing that they were having a very hard time living here on Mother Earth. They had thin skin so they got cold easily and their poor sight made it difficult for them to get around in the dark. The eagle felt sorry for his two-legged weaker relatives so one day he went to Grandfather and told him how hard life was for them.

"Grandfather called all of his children to come to a great counsel meeting at the base of the Sacred Mountain located where the world ends there in the far North. This was a very happy occasion and a time of joyful celebration because it wasn't often that all of our Creator's children got to come together for a great gathering with their Grandfather.

"There were always lots of games and competitive events before any serious business was conducted, and these gatherings were sort of like going to a family reunion.

"After the games were over, Grandfather called a meeting of all the elders at the gathering, and he asked for a full report concerning the problems the two-leggeds were having. The spider spoke first, making fun of the way the two-leggeds huddled together shivering on cold nights. He laughed as he hopped around on his skinny legs, showing how the two-leggeds hopped around trying to stay warm when the cold wind blew.

"He said, 'They look like they are doing a dance to the cold.'

"Then the coyote teased them about how easily they became frightened of things they couldn't see in the dark. Old Man Coyote had the spider rolling on the ground with laughter as he demonstrated the two-leggeds' clumsy actions at night by stumbling over a nearby rock and then bumping his nose against a tree and howling as if in pain.

"Finally the owl came to the defense of his weaker two-legged relatives and said, 'I don't think Grandfather called us here to ridicule and make fun of our two-legged relatives. He wants suggestions concerning how to help them live better among us.'

"The debate lasted for days as each elder offered his or her suggestions concerning how to best help the two-leggeds. However, no one came up with a workable solution to the problem.

"The great bear offered to teach the two-leggeds how to hibernate so they could stay warmer during the long, cold winter months, but they refused the offer, saying that hibernation seemed such a boring way to spend the winter.

"When the elders from the geese family said that the two-leggeds could go south with them during the cold winter months, everyone laughed and the elder representing the deer clan said, 'They can't even run fast so how could they ever learn to fly?'

"Even if they could fly, they can't see so good at night, so you geese could only fly during the day,' the mouse chuckled.

"For days, the animals discussed how to help the two-leggeds, but no one really had a workable suggestion. Finally, our Creator said that if his children were unable to solve the problem for their two-legged relatives, then he would have to do it for them.

"So Grandfather called the clouds to come and join the meeting and said, 'I am going to place a very sacred power in your keeping. I have chosen you because, even though you live high above the earth and look down on all of your relatives, you have remained humble, never bragging about the lofty status that has been given to you.

" 'When you send this sacred power down to the earth, it will have the ability to make fire. This new power is called lightning. Each time you send it to the earth, you must offer a prayer of gratitude in a loud voice. This prayer of thanks for being the caretaker of Sacred Lightning is called Thunder. Whenever my children hear the Thunder, they will stop and offer their own prayer of thanks for this wonderful sacred gift of Lightning that brings the Sacred Fire to the two-leggeds.'"

Grandfather Old Bear put another small stick on the little fire and smiled. "Every time I sit around a camp fire I think of this story and it reminds me again of just how sacred fire is."

When he thought the campfire was burning just right, he continued

230

the story. "Grandfather had all of his children gather at the base of the Great Sacred Mountain to witness the bringing of Sacred Fire into the world. Following the instructions of our Creator, the cloud moved directly over a large, dead pine tree standing near the base of the Sacred Mountain, and at our Creator's command, it struck the tree with a bolt of lightning. The dead tree instantly burst into flames as a loud clap of thunder rolled across the valley.

"Grandfather's children gasp in awe at the sight of the burning tree, although the loud noise made by the thunder caused some of them to run away in fear. But, their curiosity quickly drew them back to watch the fire burning the dead tree.

"Then Grandfather said to the cloud, 'I will now give you the power to make rain fall from the sky so you can put the fire out. Otherwise, if left uncontrolled, the fire would burn up the whole world.'

"So the cloud was given the power to make rain and it sent the rain down on the fire and it was quickly put out.

"From that time on the clouds were held in high esteem by all of Grandfather's children because they had the honor of being the Keeper of Sacred Lightning and Sacred Rain," the Old One said as he carefully took a small burning stick from the edge of the little fire.

As grandfather Old Bear slowly raised the little burning stick up toward the sky and gently offered it to the Four Sacred Directions, he said, "This is the most sacred gift our Creator has given us. It is also our greatest technology, far surpassing any technology that has been developed by the two-leggeds in your so-called modern world."

He looked directly at me as he reverently placed the little burning stick back into the small fire and continued. "To understand fire is to understand the very nature and character of our Creator. Nothing can for long stand against fire and survive. It has the ability to consume the whole world. On the other hand, it also has the ability to serve our needs, making life much more enjoyable.

"The Sacred Camp Fire was at the very center of our daily lives. It helped keep us focused on our Creator and the Spiritual Realm. The *ground around the Camp Fire was Holy Ground because it was a great symbol of our Creator's power."*

The Old Holy Man stared deep into my eyes as he continued. "The reason the Camp Fire was so important to us, grandson, is because it kept us focused on a life of simplicity."

The Old One silently stared into the little fire for a while, seemingly lost in deep thought. He then folded his arms across his chest and closed his eyes. About the time I thought he had drifted off to sleep, he started talking again.

"Simplicity," he said, then fell silent again. After a while he started repeating it over and over. "Simplicity---simplicity---simplicity." Then after another short pause, he said, "That's what The Way of the Medicine Wheel is all about—learning to live a life of simplicity."

He opened his eyes and looked at me again. "A campfire is the gift of simplicity. If you want to walk this Sacred Path, you must make the campfire the focal point of daily living because it has the power to help you maintain a lifestyle of simplicity."

Grandfather Old Bear spent a lot of time talking to me about the importance of creating a lifestyle of simplicity, and the next several pages of this teaching session contain an overview of what he told me concerning the need to live a simplistic lifestyle.

PERSONAL ACKNOWLEDGEMENT

Before continuing on with our discussion of the importance of creating a lifestyle of simplicity, I want to confess to you that Angelitta and I have struggled a great deal in our personal lives with the issue of living a simplistic lifestyle. We still have a long way to go in developing the kind of simplistic lifestyle that illustrates the way we should live as we walk this Sacred Path. However, step by step, we are working toward the kind of simplistic living that is enabling us to maintain a stronger and stronger connection to the Spiritual Realm.

CHANGING OUR VALUES

Most people in our modern societies have a value system that is strongly influenced by materialism. In fact, it is safe to say that most people's time in the industrialized world is consumed by either making money or spending it to acquire more material possessions.

Modern man has been deceived into believing more is better. We tend to measure a person's level of success by the quantity of material possessions he or she has acquired. What we refer to as our "standard of living" is defined, for the most part, by the quantity of material possessions we are able to amass, and acquiring more and more faster and faster is the goal of many people.

Grandfather Old Bear is adamant in his belief that modern man's obsession with materialism will be the cause of Mother Earth bringing about the Time of Great Cleansing. He once said, " *Just as every good mother disciplines her children in a effort to help them grow up to lead respectful lives, Mother Earth also disciplines her children when they need it. However, the two-leggeds have not learned from her discipline.*

"Grandson, people in your world have become obsessed with acquiring more and more 'things'. They have developed an unquenchable thirst for more material possessions. They have become drunk with greed and stagger blindly in their quest for MORE.

"Many times Mother Earth has tried to get your people's attention. She has begged. She has pleaded. She has warned. She has threatened— all to no avail. I tell you, grandson, she has reached the end of her patience. In order to stop the continual rape, pillage and defilement of her body by her modern two-legged children, she will soon sweep away their societies and return the small remnant that remains to their original state of simplistic living that produces peace, harmony and balance within the Sacred Circle of Life."

Modern man is also consumed with SELF. We live in a "me first" society. Most people in the industrialized world place a far greater priority on serving their own needs, wants and desires than on what is best for their local community or the environment. In the ancient world—the world of grandfather Old Bear—people placed greater value on family and community than they did on the individual. Family and community had priority over individual needs and desires. Village elders made decisions concerning what was best for the clan or village first and for the individual second.

On numerous occasions, grandfather Old Bear has said to me, *"Grandson, if you are going to walk this Sacred Path, you must learn to put the needs of the Sacred Circle of Life ahead of your own selfish interests. Never forget that your purpose in life is to help strengthen and support the Sacred Circle—it is your true family. Your allegiance must be to your Sacred Family and not to your own selfish interests.*

This issue is of such great importance that the entire next teaching session will be devoted to a discussion of the role of the Sacred Family as we walk this Sacred Path. The Sacred Family is the foundation on which every society is built—destroy the family and you will soon destroy the society.

THE SACRED CIRCLE OF LIFE MUST TAKE PRIORITY OVER SELF-INDULGENCE

The starting point for developing a lifestyle of simplicity is to understand with your mind and commit with your heart that the Sacred Circle of Life must take priority over self-indulgence. This is not an option if you are serious about walking this Sacred Path. Traveling this Path means we not only "talk" about the importance of the Sacred Circle of Life; our "actions" communicate our commitment to placing its needs ahead of our own interests.

234

"How do I do that?" you may ask. It is a daily process that requires continual vigilance. It starts with what many consider small, insignificant actions, and includes the most important decisions of our lives. For example, instead of throwing trash on the ground because that is the easiest thing to do at the time, we make the extra effort to put the trash in the trash container. Rather than flatten the top of a hill, or remove lots of green trees just so we can have a good view for a home site, we pick a location that will have the least impact on our relatives (the green people and rock people) who already live there. Instead of going hunting just for sport, or for a trophy, we hunt only for food and eat all we kill. In other words, we take the collective needs of all of our relatives within the Sacred Circle of Life into account when making decisions, and don't decide based solely on our own desires and self interest.

We have said it many times, and will continue to repeat it regularly during these teaching sessions, *The Way of the Medicine Wheel* is a lifestyle. It is the way we live, not just a philosophy of life or a religion.

If we are going to be successful in walking this Sacred Path, we must begin putting the well being of the Sacred Circle of Life above our own self centered wishes and desires. To fail to do so will eventually lead to the demise of life as we know it today.

NEVER TAKE THINGS FROM MOTHER EARTH BY FORCE

Grandfather Old Bear once said to me, *"Grandson, living a life of simplicity means we never take things from Mother Earth by force. That's one of the big differences between my people and yours. We took from Mother Earth only what she willingly gave us. Your people steal from her to get what they want."*

When he saw the confusion on my face, he said, "We never dug even the smallest hole in our Mother's skin, moved even the smallest rock or collected dead wood for our fires without first making an offering to her and asking her permission. On the other hand, your people build giant earth moving equipment to rip her body apart, blast away the sides of mountains just so they won't have to go around them when driving on their concrete trails, dig huge holes deep into her body looking for what they call "minerals" and cut down whole forests of live trees." He paused for a moment and I thought I saw tears in his eyes as he continued. "And I've never heard your people ask our Mother's permission for any of that! No. They take and take and take from our Mother and never once ask for her permission—and that's STEALING! Your people are so greedy they steal from their own Mother!"

I have never forgotten the sad, painful look on the Old One's face that day as he spoke those strong words of condemnation against our so-called highly advanced and sophisticated society, and I hung my head in shame and avoided eye contact with him for several minutes.

Since that day, I have tried to always remember to take nothing from Mother Earth without first offering her tobacco or cornmeal and asking for her permission before taking anything from her body. On Medicine Wheel Mesa we are taking great care to build small hogans and other dwellings and structures where Mother Earth wants them, not where we want them. We ask her permission to move every rock, collect every piece of firewood, and dig even the smallest hole in her skin.

As we work at paying proper respect to Mother Earth and our other relatives within the Sacred Circle of Life, we are noticing that more and more winged people, four leggeds and other relatives are coming to our land and the area around it.

Medicine Wheel Mesa is high desert country with only about four inches of precipitation a year, and yet we are seeing more and more deer, elk, bear, desert big horn sheep, coyotes, eagles, hawks, rabbits, ground squirrels, all kinds of birds and other relatives coming into the area. We feel this is due, at least in part, to our commitment to always hold Mother Earth and our relatives within the Sacred Circle of Life in the highest regard.

I strongly urge you to make the same commitment we have made to never take anything from Mother Earth without her permission. In doing so, you will be taking important first steps in developing a life of simplicity.

START THINKING "SMALL" INSTEAD OF "BIG"

We live in a society that tends to think that BIGGER is BETTER. As a result, many people are constantly trying to acquire bigger houses, cars, TV's, sound systems, computers, etc. If you are going to be successful in developing a lifestyle of simplicity, you must start training yourself to think small when it comes to material possessions.

The bigger the house, car, TV and so on, the more of our Mother's body and our relatives' lives it took to make those things. I know many single people who live in 3-4 bedroom homes and have 2-3 cars, 3-4 TV's and more than two computers. Their closets are full of clothes they seldom, if ever, wear, and their garages and storage areas are full of things the have forgotten they bought.

How tragic! Usually such people aren't even aware that all of the "things" they possess came either from their Mother, the Earth, or their relatives who live on the Earth. They tend to be oblivious to the fact that their unquenchable thirst for more and more material possessions is contributing greatly to the rapid approach of the Time of Great Cleansing that Mother Earth is preparing to unleash on her self-indulging, two-legged children.

BECOME DEBT FREE

You must work at becoming debt free if you plan to truly simplify your life in preparation for the coming Earth Changes. As long as your time is being controlled by the "money system", it is impossible to develop the kind of simplistic lifestyle required in walking this Sacred Path.

In the industrialized world, most people's appetite for more and more material possessions has led them deep into debt. They borrow money to buy cars, houses, furniture and so on. They have credit cards that are "maxed out" because they wanted all the gadgets, high-tech toys, latest fades and modern conveniences offered by the Madison Avenue marketing gurus. As a result, such people have become slaves of the lending institutions. They are spending their whole lives making money to pay off loans on things they purchased that have already worn out, gone out of style, or been replaced by a bigger and "better" model.

As long as you are in debt, your time belongs to your "lenders". You don't just owe them money—you owe them your time. You are not really free to do the things that are required of you in order to live in peace, harmony and balance with the Sacred Circle of Life. As a result, you life becomes filled with stress, frustration and disenchantment. You wind up feeling that you are caught in a trap—that your life is just one vicious circle of going to work, coming home to get some rest so you can go to work the next day in order to pay all the bills that keep appearing in your mail box each month. Unfortunately for many people, the bills add up to more than the paycheck.

This is not a teaching session on money management, but I can tell you from personal experience that the first thing you need to do is throw away the credit cards. Then determine not to buy anything on credit. Buy only what you can pay cash for (and yes, that includes cars, TV's, vacations, etc.). Why spend your whole life making the moneylenders rich? You may say, "Oh, my car is old and all of my friends drive new cars, and I don't have the money saved to buy a new car now."

Soooo. Then drive the old one until you do have the money saved. Why wind up paying more than double the value of the car in interest payments on a loan? No wonder you are always in debt. Remember the Five Spiritual Medicines apply to all of life—including our finances.

Many people have told me it is impossible for them to live debt free. To them I say, "Then it is impossible for you to ever experience the peace, harmony and balance in your lives that our Creator intended for you to have."

I can tell you from my own experience that the issue of becoming debt free was a major barrier for Angelitta and me when we first started trying to walk this Sacred Path. And I can also tell you from personal experience that it is well worth whatever effort it takes to accomplish the goal. Yes, for many of you it will mean radically changing your lifestyle. Well, I can assure you that the lifestyle lived debt free is a far better lifestyle than the one lived as a slave to the financial institutions.

You may be thinking that it will take you a long time to become debt free. To that I respond, "Then don't put it off any longer. Start working toward that goal now."

The sooner you start, the sooner you will be free from your debts and in control of your life. Then—and only then—will you be able to fully walk this Sacred Path in the way our Creator intended.

Over the years, grandfather Old Bear has talked to me a lot about money. Again and again he has reminded me that it was the two-leggeds development of the "money system" that led them away from this Sacred Path.

He would say, *"In my world we had no need for money. Mother Earth provided all we needed to live in peace, harmony and balance with all our relatives. However, over time, the two-leggeds developed a system of money that was used to get all they wanted. It was the money system that separated the two-leggeds from their Father and Mother. It was the money system that caused the two-leggeds to lose sight of this Sacred Path, and now they can't find their way back to it."*

DEVELOP A PLAN TO BECOME MORE AND MORE SELF SUFFICIENT

In one of my conversations with grandfather Old Bear, he said,

239

"Young One, never forget this. One of the major differences between your world and mine is that people in my world relied on themselves for their daily needs, but people in your world are dependent on others to meet their needs each day.

"When we got hungry we went hunting or gathered food from the Green People. However, when your people get hungry, they have to go to the supermarket and buy food. When we needed a new lodge to live in we tanned the hides and gathered the wood and made it ourselves, or found a good cave to live in, but when your people need a house, they have to buy it from a builder of houses. When my people needed new clothes, they made them. When your people need new clothes, they go the place that sells clothes and buy them.

"We had no need for money because we were self-sufficient. Your people can't live without money.

"Money has become the god of your world, grandson, and your people worship it every day. They trust it to meet all of their needs, desires and wants, and they have concluded that they can't live without it."

He took a deep breath and slowly exhaled. "You must work hard at becoming less and less dependent on money, grandson. As long as you are totally dependent on money for your existence, the god of this world has you firmly in his control.

"On the other hand, the more self-sufficient you become, the less need you will have for money, and the less need you have for money the less control the god of this world—the money system—will have over you. This is one of the most important principles people must learn in order to successfully walk this Sacred Path and experience what it truly means to live in peace, harmony and balance with the Sacred Circle of Life.

By now, many of you are probably becoming extremely frustrated with what you are reading in this teaching session. Don't feel bad. I became just as frustrated when The Old One shared this information with me, and Angelitta and I still experience a certain amount of frustration as we continue to work at applying some of these concepts in our lives.

You may be tempted to quit reading and not even try to apply these principles to your life. That is understandable. However, I urge you to not pass judgement on this information until you have attempted to apply it, because that is the only way you will be able to prove for yourself if these principles should be adopted into your life or not.

No doubt you are wondering what you should be doing in order to become more self-sufficient. Below are several suggestions for you to consider incorporating immediately into your lifestyle. The main thing to keep in mind is that you can't—nor should you try to—incorporate all of the principles in this teaching session into your life over night. Trust me, it will take a considerable amount of time to change your current lifestyle into a lifestyle of simplistic living. No matter how long it takes, Angelitta and I want to assure you that the journey is well worth the effort.

Start drying some of your food for storage instead of buying canned or frozen food. While you are working to reduce your personal financial debt, start drying food for storage and stop buying canned or frozen food. Drying fruits, vegetables and meat is fun and easy and much better for you than canned or frozen food. And if you buy in bulk when fruits and vegetables are in season, or when meat is on sale, you will save lots of money as well as eat more wholesome food.

You can purchase small, inexpensive food dehydrators from such stores as Wal- Mart or K-Mart, and they will have step by step instructions on how to easily dry food right on your kitchen counter while you are at work or doing other activities around the house. Better yet, make your own food dryer out of rubber coated window screen attached to a simple wood frame. It requires no electricity and works great. You will discover that dried fruits, vegetables and meats are not only better for you, but also have a much better taste than canned or frozen food. Dried food, properly stored, will last a very long time—for years in most instances. It takes up much less space when stored, retains its "live food" qualities, and has far more nutritional value than canned or frozen food.

Start growing some of your food. Even if you live in a small apartment, you can still grow some of your food. Vegetables such as sprouts can easily be grown right on your kitchen counter. Small planters can be purchased or easily constructed to grow larger food plants such as tomatoes, peppers, lettuce and so on.

There are also several types of "garden co-ops" in most urban areas that you can join that enable you to grow even more of your food supply. Your local health food store can often be a source for finding out how to contact such groups.

Buy "do-it-yourself" books, and start making things and fixing things you would normally pay someone else to do. It is easy to learn to do small repairs around the house such as painting, fence repair, etc. Places such as Home Depot can even advise you on how to undertake bigger projects such as finishing a basement, building a patio and so on. The point is, you need to start developing a mindset of self-sufficiency instead of relying on others to meet your needs. The more self-sufficiency skills you acquire, the more independent you can become from the money system that is controlling your life. The less need you have for money, the easier it will be to develop peace, harmony and balance in daily living.

GET RID OF THINGS YOU DON'T NEED

One of the first things we all need to do as we work at developing a lifestyle of simplicity is to get rid of all the "stuff" we don't really need. You will be amazed at the things you have acquired over the years that are stored away in closets, garages and storage units that you are keeping but not using. Get rid of it! Have a great Give Away and give the stuff to people who need it, or take it to the Goodwill or other service groups that can sell it or pass it on to those in need.

If you get serious about this, you will discover that it is harder to do than you think. You have lots of "stuff" that you are simply emotionally attached to but never use. Get rid of it! Most of us don't really need all the clothes hanging in our closets and stuff that has been stored away in the attic or garage for years. Get rid of it!

As grandfather Old Bear told me, *"Simplify...simplify...simplify"* your life. Start thinking smaller instead of bigger, and less instead of more".

You'll be amazed at all the things you have that you don't really need. Get rid of it. Go through closets, drawers and storage areas and get rid of everything that you don't really need.

WARNING!   WARNING!   WARNING!
                WARNING!

If you think most of the information shared with you up to this point in this teaching session seems a little farfetched, then you will most certainly be convinced that what you read on the following pages is ABSOLUTELY IMPOSSIBLE to do! However, I encourage you to read the following information with an open mind—even though, for most of you, it will be a shock to your entire value system. In fact, it will challenge most of what you believe concerning the purpose of life and how to find fulfillment in living.

THE DAY I ALMOST WALKED AWAY FROM THIS SACRED PATH

All of us approach many crossroads as we walk our individual paths through life. At each crossroad, there is a decision to make—which way will we go? Some of those decisions have very little impact on our future. On the other hand, some of the decisions we make at life's crossroads have a profound impact on the rest of our lives, and even on the lives of other people.

The fourth year I Sun Danced, I found myself at a crossroad that would change the course of Angelitta's and my life forever. I had looked forward to my fourth year of Sun Dance for several months. Angelitta and I had collected many items to be given away at the end of that dance. As the date for Sun Dance approached (June 17-21), we found ourselves getting more and more excited. But, if we had known in advance what would happen there, we probably would not have gone.

We arrived at the Sun Dance grounds in the Black Hills of South Dakota a few days early to help with the many preparations involved in putting on a Sun Dance. Things such as repairing the arbor, cleaning the Sun Dance grounds, putting up tipis, building and repairing sweat lodges, gathering fire wood, etc.

The routine was no different that fourth year than it had been the three previous years. Angelitta and I were both Sun Dancers. My fourth year of dancing was her third.

The Sun Dance lasts for four days. The fourth year I Sun Danced, the first day began much like the first day the previous three years. We got up before sunrise and went into the sweat lodge for a time of prayer and preparation; came out and dressed for the dance; lined up at the "West Gate" of the Sun Dance circle and then the "Entry Round" began.

Once the other dancers and I were inside the Sun Dance Circle, suddenly I realized that grandfather Old Bear was dancing beside me. In fact, he was dancing right next to me! I was so shocked that I almost fell down. I quickly looked around at the other dancers to see if any of them saw this Ancient One from the distant past dancing next to me, but none of them seemed to notice.

Several times I tightly closed my eyes and then opened them, thinking (and hoping) his image would be gone, but each time he was still dancing next to me. I began sweating profusely, even though it was still very early in the morning and quite cool at that altitude. After a while, grandfather Old Bear started talking to me. What he said is presented below.

"I came to talk to you about electricity, grandson. I figured that since this is the most sacred event you participate in all year, this would be a good place to talk to you about such an important topic," he said as he smiled at me with his warm, loving eyes.

At the sound of his voice I almost panicked. I quickly looked around to see if the other dancers had heard him, but it appeared no one had.

"Electricity, grandson. We must talk about electricity," he was saying.

I was about to tell him to go away and leave me alone, but fearing the other dancers might hear me and think I was talking to myself, I remained quiet, trying to ignore him. Then I couldn't believe what he said next.

"You must stop using electricity, grandson, if you are truly serious about walking this Sacred Path we call The Way of the Medicine Wheel. The two-leggeds stole electricity from the Cloud People and they have tried to make it their slave. What they don't know is that they have become a slave to electricity and it will soon cause the destruction of your so-called modern world".

I was so appalled at that ridiculous statement I was about to shout at him to shut up and leave, but before I could form the words to scream at him, he was gone.

My head was spinning. At first, I was confused by the Old One's statement, but that confusion quickly turned to anger as I realized just how absurd and ridiculous it was. I was also somewhat alarmed that he had suddenly appeared to me in this "reality". Until that moment in the Sun Dance Circle, he had only appeared in that place I go when I walk through the doorway from inside that stone cave in the mountain and out into a world, the location of which I am unable to explain.

I have very little memory of the rest of that first day of Sun Dancing. However, later that night as I lay awake in my sleeping bag while the other Sun Dancers slept, I made a decision to never again listen to anything that old, pathetic, whatever-he-was had to say. I was determined to stop our preparations to move to a remote location and begin living what he had called a "Sacred Lifestyle", and passionately referred to as *The Way of the Medicine Wheel*. I was still so upset, I considered going to the women Sun Dancer's lodge and waking Angelitta and leaving the Sun Dance in the middle of the night.

During the remaining three days of the Sun Dance, I talked to no one about what had happened that first day, and I tried to act as normal as possible. However, inside I became more and more frustrated with each passing day. I became angry with myself for wasting all of that time I had spent listening to that old, antiquated, out-of-touch-with-reality idiot.

A few days after returning home to Colorado Springs, Colorado from Sun Dance, I was sitting on the front porch one evening watching a large group of bugs swarm around the street light across the street from our house. Suddenly, I heard grandfather Old Bear say, *"Even the bugs are frustrated with the two-leggeds' man made electricity."*

I jerked around in my chair and there sat the old codger in the chair next to me,smiling as if we were still the best of friends.

Before I could speak, he continued. *"I know you are upset with me, but you don't have a right to be."* *He paused a moment, still smiling his warm, disarming smile.* *"Actually, you should be down on your hands and knees thanking me for being willing to share Sacred Knowledge with you that very few people are ever privileged to hear."*

"Leave me alone," I shouted, and started to get up and go into the house to get away from him.

He reached out and put his bony hand on my shoulder, and with the most serious expression I had ever seen on his face said, "I don't blame you for being upset at what I told you at your Sun Dance. I would have been shocked if you hadn't been upset when you heard that you were being asked to give up the most important thing in your life."

I stared at him and angrily shouted, "Electricity is far from the most important thing in MY life!"

Just as I again started to get up, he stared deep into my eyes and I froze in my seat. "Before you go running away from the truth, you at least owe it to yourself to hear what the truth is," he said. The warm, loving smile suddenly had been replaced by a stern, serious expression that caused me to stop and give him my full attention.

"As I said to you at your Sun Dance, the two-leggeds stole Sacred Electricity from the Cloud People with the intention of making it their slave. Sacred Electricity—what we call lightning—is a very Sacred Power that came to the earth long, long ago as a gift from our Creator so we

two-leggeds could have Sacred Fire. However, man made electricity is not sacred. It is contaminated and puts off negative energy.

"The two-leggeds use man made electricity to make their life easier. They make man made electricity work for them. They treat electricity like a servant. It sweeps their floor, does their dishes, washes and irons their clothes and cooks their meals. They say electricity has ushered in the great age of technology. It has enabled them to go into outer space. It is the power behind what they call great medical advancements. It gives them the ability to turn winter into summer and summer into winter in their homes, cars and skyscrapers. They think there is no limit to what they can use electricity to do for them."

He leaned over in his chair and looked straight into my eyes. "Unfortunately, grandson, they are totally unaware that they are the ones enslaved by electricity," he said. Then, sliding his chair around until he was facing me, he continued. "Modern day two-leggeds, living what they think is the 'good life', have become so addicted to electricity they can no longer live without it—did you hear what I said, grandson? THEY CAN NO LONGER LIVE WITHOUT IT! They have become slaves to their addiction. They are now addicted to electricity. They can't imagine a world without electricity."

*The Old One sat there in silence for a while. He then leaned close to me, and, in little more than a whisper, as if wanting no one else to hear him, he said, "**Grandson, the day is soon coming when electricity will be taken away from the two-leggeds and then the cities they once thought were such wonderful places to live in will become giant death traps where few will be able to escape.**"*

That conversation with grandfather Old Bear occurred several years ago, and since then he and I have had numerous discussions about man-made electricity. The remainder of this teaching session will contain the main points the Old One has shared with me concerning man-made electricity and how it—more than anything else the two leggeds have made—has contributed to the widening gulf between the physical and Spiritual Realms.

I also want to repeat that Angelitta and I had an extremely difficult time accepting what we have been told about the negative effect man-made electricity has on people's ability to maintain a connection to our Creator and the Spiritual Realm.

Angelitta and I can tell you from our own experiences that, for us, the most difficult aspect of walking this Sacred Path has been the struggle to wean ourselves away from using man-made electricity in the routines of our daily lives. We are, however, committed to continue the process of freeing ourselves from the perceived need for man-made electricity to do certain things for us.

MAN-MADE ELECTRICITY "CONTROLS" EVERY ASPECT OF MODERN SOCIETY

Both Angelitta and I spent the early years of our lives living in communities where there was no electricity. My family didn't get electricity on our little farm in central Oklahoma until I was twelve years old (1952), and the Indonesian village Angelitta grew up in didn't get electricity until just recently.

I remember how excited everyone in our little farming community was when they found out electricity was coming to the area. Farmers got together and helped each other wire their houses, and some even ran electric lines to their barns and set poles in their yards to hang electric yards lights on.

Everyone started looking in the Wards and Sears catalogues at the latest electrical appliances they wanted to order to make life easier on the farm. As each house got electricity, all of the neighbors would gather there to watch the light bulbs light up when the power was turned on.

People in our little farming area were so excited about all of the good things electricity was going to do for them they were not expecting the negative effects it would have on the community. Before the people had electricity, they were a very close knit community. Farmers were always visiting each other and helping one another during planting and harvesting seasons, or any other time people needed assistance. People readily loaned one another farm equipment, tools and even money if they had any. However, after electricity came, the feeling of community quickly faded, and rivalries developed almost overnight.

When one family got a refrigerator, all of them felt they had to get one whether they could afford one or not. When people got a TV, visiting with other families in the community quickly stopped because everyone was glued to the TV set in the evenings and didn't have time for friendly socializing. Tensions ran high in families who couldn't afford to buy all of the modern conveniences for their home and farm, and when the electric bills started coming each month, many were unable to pay them.

Even as a young child of twelve, I was very aware of the negative effect electricity had on our once peaceful, happy and cooperative little farming community. However, my children grew up in a world where man-made electricity has always existed and they think the individual isolation it produces in communities is a normal way of life. They cannot conceive of a world in which TV, electric lights, dishwashers, electric washers and dryers, microwave ovens, computers, video games and the multitude of other electrical gadgets and "toys" didn't exist. Space travel, heart transplants, knowing ahead of time if your baby will be a boy or girl, and cell phones is commonplace in their reality.

In fact, my children have never lived in a world in which man-made electricity didn't control every facet of daily living, and electricity's strangle-hold on society is getting stronger with the passing of each day of their lives.

All that has to happen for us to suddenly realize how dependent we are on man-made electricity is for the electricity to suddenly "go off" in our part of town. People quickly panic and the utility company is flooded with calls demanding that the power be immediately restored.

Just imagine what would happen in your city or community if suddenly there was no electricity for a day…then three days…then a week…then a month! You wouldn't be able to buy gas at gas stations to get to work or to even get out of town if your gas tank was empty. The food in your freezers would soon spoil, and so would the food in the freezers at the supermarkets. You wouldn't be able to get money out of an ATM machine or out of your bank. The water system in your community would be shut down, so there would be no running water in the city. Computers would no longer work. The places where people work would not be able to carry on their daily business functions. All food in the supermarkets would soon be gone. The city or community would be almost totally dark at night except for candles, flashlights or oil lamps, so crime would skyrocket, causing people to fear going out at night. Armed gangs would roam the streets, plundering stores and homes, robbing, raping and killing defenseless people.

Now, expand the above situation to the whole country, and try to imagine the state of total chaos that would develop overnight if we lost all man-made electrical power at once. The strongest nation in the world would almost overnight cease to exist. The national, state and local governments, along with our military and law enforcement agencies would be powerless to function because man-made electricity powers all aspects of their ability to operate. All forms of transportation, except horseback and by foot, would cease. Money (except for what you had in your pocket or at home) would not be available, so the national economy would no longer exist in any form or at any level.

The chaos created by the lack of man-made electricity would be so great that so called sophisticated people would resort to a mindset of the survival of the fittest. As grandfather Old Bear said, our cities, towns and communities will become *"giant death traps where few will be able to escape!"*

MAN-MADE ELECTRICITY IS ADDICTIVE

When Angelitta and I finally made the commitment to move to a remote location in order to walk this Sacred Path, at first we were reluctant to talk about our decision for fear our friends and acquaintances would

250

think we are crazy. So, when we did start talking about it, we weren't surprised at most people's reaction.

As we explained the remoteness of the place were we were going to live, and that there was no electrical power there, many people's response was "Oh, that's OK. Electrical power generated by solar panels is very affordable now. You will have lots of sun where you are moving so you can generate lots of electricity."

Then, when we would explain that we were going to live without electricity, and also without any of the other utilities found in the city, people would usually stare at us in disbelief. Many women even told Angelitta that they felt very sorry for her; some even suggested that she should leave me because it was obvious I had lost my mind.

Modern man is not only convinced it is impossible to live without electricity, he is addicted to it. In fact, that addiction grows stronger with each passing day. We are a society obsessed with electrical gadgetry. We are continually buying new electrical gadgets that now do for us what we used to do for ourselves. They do such simple things as brush our teeth, comb our hair, shave our face, turn the coffee pot on before we get out of bed, raise and lower the windows of our cars, turn the TV on and off, open cans for us—the list goes on and on.

Unfortunately, in most cases, the more dependent we become on electricity to do things for us the less capable we become of doing those things for ourselves if electricity is not available. Without electricity, modern man truly experiences a state of helplessness.

MAN-MADE ELECTRICITY FILLS OUR MINDS WITH NEGATIVITY

People spend a large percent of their time entertaining themselves by listening to the radio, watching TV, playing video games or watching movies. A close examination of the songs on the radio, programs on TV, video games and movies reveal that the information presented is mostly negative. For example, many Rap songs on the radio encourage rape, drug use and disrespect of women, family, government and any other form of authority. Many TV programs promote and glamorize lying, cheating and stealing, immorality, divorce, drug use and even murder. Most popular video games and movies promote all kinds of violence. In fact, it seems the more violent they become the more popular they are.

All day long people in our so-called modern world are being bombarded with negativity that is powered by man-made electricity. Negative input tends to produce negative output. It is no wonder we are experiencing such erosion of moral values in the societies of our modern world—erosion that is brought on, for the most part, by the use of man-made electricity.

MAN-MADE ELECTRICITY ALLOWS US TO TURN NIGHT INTO DAY

During one of my conversations with grandfather Old Bear about man-made electricity he said, *"Grandson, one of the greatest negative aspects of man-made electricity is its use to turn night into day. Our Creator gave us the night as a time for spiritual growth and physical renewal. He also gave us the Sacred Campfire as a way to light the night with positive, sacred energy and power. At night, the Sacred Campfire drew us into the Sacred Spiritual Realm of our Creator and his Helpers and renewed and empowered our spirits. The night also provided a time of rest from the days activities, and it renewed us physically.*

"On the other hand, just the opposite is true of nights in your cities. Man-made electricity not only turns the night into day, the negative energy it emits tends to stir up the negative attitudes, thoughts and feelings in many people. Some of them resort to all kinds of negative deeds and activities that serve to help undermine and weaken their society. People in your world even have a name for it—they call it 'the night life'.

"In my world night was looked forward to as a time for powerful spiritual ceremonies and sacred celebrations. It was a time of telling and re-telling the sacred stories. It was a time in which the extended family

came together to strengthen the bonds of love, friendship, togetherness and family. However, man-made electricity has destroyed all of that for your world.

"In your world, families may sit together at night, but they are really all alone because each person's eyes and mind is glued to and controlled by the TV in the corner of what you call a 'living room' or 'family room'---however, it is neither. In your world, people don't really know how to actually 'live' and family is almost non-existent, and you can thank man-made electricity for that."

Every time I am in a city at night I am reminded of that conversation with the Old One and I have to agree with his analogy. I have spent time in the city at night and I have also spent time sitting around the campfire in the remote desert area where Medicine Wheel Mesa is located—the place Angelitta and I now call home. I can tell you from first hand experience that the nights spent around the campfire at home on Medicine Wheel Mesa are far more spiritually uplifting and physically restful than any night I have ever spent in a city lit up by the wonders of man-made electricity.

THERE IS NO PLACE FOR MAN-MADE ELECTRICITY IN SACRED CEREMONY

You can easily experience the difference between the energy man-made electricity puts off and the energy sacred fire emits by conducting this simple experiment. Sit in a room at night with the electric lights on and concentrate on the feeling you get with the lights turned on. Then light two or three candles and place them in different parts of the room and then turn the electric lights off. Now notice the great difference in how you feel sitting in the candle lit room.

I won't suggest to you the difference candlelight makes you feel as compared to electric lights, because I don't want to influence your reactions. However, I assure you, it will be easy to feel the difference between the atmosphere in the room when the electric light is on and when the candles are lit.

Man-made electricity has a very negative effect on Sacred Ceremony. That is why we always turn the electric lights off during Sacred Ceremonies when they are conducted in houses in the city. On the other hand, Sacred Fire almost always plays some role in our Sacred Ceremonies. I want to suggest to you that even when the Medicine Pipe is smoked in a house in the city the electric lights should be off in the room and candle light used instead. I can tell you from personal experience that the Sacred Pipe Ceremony is much more effective at night when it is done in the presence of Sacred Fire.

HOW DO YOU FREE YOURSELF FROM YOUR ADDICTION TO ELECTRICITY?

I can assure you that the process of freeing yourself from the addiction to man-made electricity is by far the most difficult aspect of walking this Sacred Path. Angelitta and I still struggle with the effects the addiction to man-made electricity has had on our lives. Once a person has been exposed to the so-called comforts offered by man-made electricity there is always an enticement to give in to the "electricity addiction". However, I can assure you that to do so is to walk away from this Sacred Path.

The materialistic world system that is in control of the world today is directly opposed to this Sacred Path. In fact, it has passed all kinds of laws trying to insure that people don't walk this Sacred Path. For example, if you build a house today in the city, it must have electricity, plumbing and all of the utilities required by city building codes. A building permit will not be issued by the city and a bank won't loan money to buy the house unless it has all of those approved utilities. The same is true of houses out in the countryside.

Cities' laws and regulations even prevent people from having a "sweat lodge" in their back yard if an open fire is used to heat the "Grandfathers". If you use a drum in the city and sing Sacred Song too loud, your neighbors will probably call the police, who will then come and force you to stop making excessive noise. Almost none of the Sacred Ceremonies associated with walking this Sacred Path could be performed in the cities because, for one thing, they would be in violation of some city law or ordinance.

So where do you begin in the process of freeing yourself from the addiction of man-made electricity? First of all, notice that I said it is a "process". It is extremely difficult to go "cold turkey" and stop using any electricity at all. I recommend that you start by making a list of all of the electrical appliances, gadgets and toys you have that are powered by man-made electricity. Next, decide which ones you will begin replacing first with manually powered items.

For example, if you have an electric can opener, it is easy to replace it with an old fashioned manual can opener that requires human power instead of electrical power. Next, what about electric toothbrushes and razors—they can easily be replaced with the much cheaper versions requiring no electricity.

Up to this point, we have been dealing with the easier electrical items that could be eliminated. Now come the harder ones. Electric clocks and electric coffee makers can easily be replaced with ones requiring no electricity to operate. You don't really have to have an electric garage door opener, and did you know you can actually make a cake without an electric hand mixer—we do it all the time.

Well, it's getting a little more difficult, isn't it? Now you are really beginning to feel the effects man-made electricity has on you. You are becoming keenly aware that maybe you are addicted after all. Lets keep going. We're just getting started. The really hard part is still to come.

How many TV's do you have in your house? First, get rid of all but one (later that one will have to go also). You don't really have to have a microwave oven in order to live—get rid of it. You can actually eat better if you don't have one.

Well, my job isn't to tell you the order in which you need to start freeing yourself from the addiction of man-made electricity, but you can see by the above examples where you might begin. And you can also see by these examples that it becomes more and more difficult as you start eliminating more and more electrical items from your life. In fact, it is totally impossible to free yourself from man-made electricity as long as you choose to live in a town or city.

IT IS NOT EASY TO CREATE A LIFESTYLE OF SIMPLICITY

As you are well aware by now, a lifestyle of simplicity is not easy to create in this modern world. First, people don't want to give up all of the good things modern life offers them. And second, the world's materialistic system does not want people to create a lifestyle of simplicity because to do so would eventually put it out of business.

Unfortunately, we are no longer able to live exactly the way the Old Ones lived. Grandfather Old Bear has reminded me of that on numerous occasions. However, he has also assured me that we can come close— maybe—if we are really committed to the process. He also has made it very clear that the closer we come to the "old way" of living, the stronger the connection to our Creator may become, and the more we will be able to merge the physical and Spiritual Realms together into a single reality. And that is the purpose of walking this Sacred Path.

I told you in the beginning of this teaching session that you would not like most of the things you were about to read. You are now standing at an important crossroad in your path of life, and you have information that you may not have had before. The question is—what will you do with that information? You will either choose to ignore it or start implementing it to some degree in your daily life.

We are now living in a very unstable and dangerous world that is getting more and more unstable and dangerous as time goes by. Even the casual observer of world conditions is aware that things are rapidly deteriorating on the world scene. There are serious warning signs everywhere. Political unrest is at an all time high. The threat of terrorism is ever increasing on a global scale. The environment is becoming more and more polluted. The global economy is becoming more and more unstable. There is an increase in violence everywhere.

The home—the foundation on which a stable society is built—is in rapid decay. Disrespect for authority is not only at an all time high, but it is encouraged in our movies, TV programs and popular songs. The list of warning signs go on and on, and I haven't even mentioned the ever increasing way our Mother, the Earth, is beginning to lash out at modern man with the increase in severe earthquakes, volcanic eruptions and more violent storms.

I'm not trying to scare you. I'm simply trying to draw your attention to the reality of conditions in the world today. I have never been a believer in the theories of "doom and gloom". I see all of these signs as a very positive thing because it means we are getting ever closer to the Time of Great Cleansing. I look forward to that time because it will eliminate all of the barriers that hinder us today from living in Peace, harmony and balance with our Creator and his Sacred Circle of Life.

There are those who tell us that if we can get more people to change, we can reverse the process of deterioration and ward off the coming Time of Great Cleansing. At this point in time, I honestly don't know if that is still possible. I do know that people who are floating down a river toward a waterfall reach a point in which the river current is so strong they can't reach the riverbank and will plunge to their death over the falls.

I think the same is true of our modern society. We eventually reach a point of decay in our modern world as we get ever closer to the Time of Great Cleansing that the pull of the current is so great nothing we can do can prevent it from happening. Are we there yet? I honestly don't know, but I suspect we have already crossed the line from which there is no escape.

Before concluding this teaching session, I want to confess to you that

I never wanted to write this book on *The Way of the Medicine Wheel.* My intention was to take the information grandfather Old Bear shared with me and simply go to a remote area and walk this Sacred Path to the best of my ability. However, the Old One made it very clear to me that this information was not being given to me alone, but it was to be shared with others in hopes some would be open to these concepts and willing to also walk this Sacred Path.

I resisted putting this information in print for a long time, but I finally yielded to the increasing pressure grandfather Old Bear put on me to pass it on to others. I am not responsible for how you react to this information, or what you do with it. I am simply trying to the best of my ability to be obedient to what our Creator says and confirms to me about this information given to be by The Old One.

I encourage you to spend lots of time talking to our Creator about the information in this book and do what he tells you to do, not what other two leggeds encourage you to do.

Teaching Session – 10
THE SACRED FAMILY

I have had numerous conversations with grandfather Old Bear about the Family and the way it functions on this Sacred Path. As a result of those discussions I have learned that this Sacred Path was constructed for every member of the Family, from the youngest to the oldest. This Path was created for entire Families to walk together, not for individuals to walk alone. And individuals who have no Family are adopted and become part of the Family that walks this Sacred Path.

I have also learned that each Family of two-leggeds is a part of Grandfather's great Sacred Family of Life, and how a Family lives and functions has a great impact on the Sacred Circle Of Life.

I want to inform you at the very beginning of this teaching session that many of the Principles of Living, followed by the Family walking this Sacred Path, are contrary to what is currently considered to be politically correct ways of social behavior practiced by so-called modern day enlightened people. As a result, some of you may take offense to some of the ways the Family of two-leggeds functions on this Sacred Path.

HOW THE TWO-LEGGEDS WERE TAUGHT TO LIVE AS A FAMILY

Grandfather Old Bear told me the following story concerning how the two-leggeds were taught to live as a Family.

One day long, long ago, during the time two-leggeds and four leggeds still understood each other's language, the children of the first two-leggeds were out playing in a large puddle of water that had formed in a low place between two hills after a big rain. They were having lots of fun splashing in the water, chasing each other through the mud and smearing it all over their bodies, then splashing in the water to wash it off.

Most of the four leggeds children tried to avoid the children of the two-leggeds because the two-legged's children always had to have their way when they played games with the four legged's children. If the two-legged children didn't get their way, they would start fights with the other children and call them all kinds of bad names. The four legged children tended to keep away from the two-legged children because they were considered bullies and spoiled brats that didn't know how to get along with their other relatives.

The parents of the two legged children didn't see anything wrong with the way their children played with the four legged children, and in fact, they also thought their own ideas were always far superior to those of any of their adult relatives within the Sacred Circle of Life. Because of the superior attitude of their parents, the two-legged children became more and more arrogant, always imposing their ideas and will on the other four-legged children when they played.

Finally, it got so bad that the two-legged children even had a hard time playing with each other because they would always end up fighting over who was right and who was wrong. And so it was no surprise that before long the two-legged children who were playing in the big puddle of water had actually stopped playing and were pushing and shoving each other in the mud, fighting because someone had done something the others didn't like.

A young girl wolf had been standing on the hill above the two-legged children watching them play in the water, and even though she had wanted to go down to the puddle and play with them, she was glad she hadn't when she saw them start fighting one another.

When the young girl wolf got home that night, she told her mother about how she had wanted to play with the two-legged children, but didn't because playing with them always ended up in some sort of argument or fight if they didn't get their way. That evening, when the father wolf came home from hunting, mother wolf told him what their daughter had said and asked him if he could do something to help solve the problem that had developed between the children of the two-leggeds and the four leggeds.

The next day, father wolf went to the eagle and told him about the problem and asked him to go to Grandfather and ask for help. That evening, as the wolf was returning home, he saw the owl sitting on a low branch of a cottonwood tree and, as the wolf went by, the owl said, "I hear the children of the four leggeds are having problems with the two-legged children."

"Yes, it seems so," the wolf replied as he stopped under the tree to talk to the owl.

"Well, it seems to me you should invite the two-leggeds to come and live with your family for a while so they can learn from you how Families should live together," the owl said. "All of us have such great respect for the way you wolves live together as a Family. I think you're the ones who should show the two leggeds how a Family should act and live together. I noticed that the two-leggeds have a hard time getting along with everyone, even themselves. I think its because no one ever taught them how a Family is supposed to live together."

"Oh, I don't think that's a very good idea," the wolf answered. "I don't seem to be able to get along with their adults too well, myself, and our children are afraid to play with their children."

"Well, it's something to think about," the wise old owl replied. "If the eagle goes and talks to Grandfather about this problem, I think he will come to see you before long, asking you to help, so you'd better give it some thought."

That evening, the father wolf had a meeting with his family and told them he had gone to see the eagle about the problem and that the eagle said he would talk to Grandfather about it. Then he told them of meeting the owl on the way home and what the owl had suggested about them inviting the two-leggeds to come and live with them for a while so they could learn how a Family was supposed to act and treat one another.

"Oh, I think that is a great idea!" the mother wolf exclaimed. However, their children didn't think much of the idea, saying that the two-legged children were too difficult to get along with.

Well, just as the wise old owl had predicted, the next day the eagle

261

delivered a message to both the two-leggeds and the wolf Family, telling them that Grandfather wanted them to come to the Sacred Mountain for a meeting with him.

When the two-leggeds and wolf Family arrived at the Sacred Mountain, Grandfather told the two-leggeds they were to move in with the wolves so they could learn to live as a Family like the wolves do.

So, the wolves and the two-leggeds lived together for a long time as one Family. The wolves taught the two-leggeds how to live and work together as a Family unit, and as long as the two-leggeds walked the Way of the Medicine Wheel, they lived and functioned as a Family the way the wolves had taught them.

THE PURPOSE OF THE FAMILY IS TO HELP THE GREAT SACRED FAMILY OF LIFE BECOME STRONGER AND STRONGER

The first time grandfather Old Bear talked to me about how the Family that walks this Sacred Path should live, we were walking along the river that flows through my "Private World", where I often go when I want to visit with him.

As we walked along the bank of the river that day, grandfather Old Bear turned to me and said, "Grandson, the purpose of the Family is to help strengthen our Creator's Sacred Family of Life. On this Sacred Path, the two-leggeds must understand that everything their Families do is either strengthening or weakening Grandfather's Sacred Family. Our Families are all part of Grandfather's Great Family of Life, and our Families' purpose is to help his Family of Life grow stronger, not weaker. That is one of the reasons we were given this Sacred Path to walk.

"We must understand that our own Families are also sacred. We are the children of our Creator, so that makes every person in the Family sacred. Each husband and wife symbolizes the Sacred Marriage between our Creator and Mother Earth.

"The wolves, beaver, ants, eagles, willows—and all of the rest of the Families within Grandfather's Great Family of Life—know how to live

262

and work together as a Family. They live the way Grandfather taught them to live, and their lifestyles help make the Great Sacred Family of Life stronger.

However, many of the two-leggeds in your world have forgotten how to be a true Family. They are simply individuals sharing the same house, but they don't share the same goals that are necessary for people to live and work together as a Family. Their primary goal should be to help Grandfather's Sacred Family of Life become stronger and stronger.

"You see, grandson, as long as the Family lives and works together the way our Creator intended, everything goes well for everyone within his Great Sacred Family of Life. On the other hand, if the Family stops living the way Grandfather intended, things go bad for all within our Creator's Sacred Family.

How much thought have you given to your Family's purpose? In our modern world, the purpose of many parents is simply to acquire enough material wealth to pass on to their children so they can have a "better" life than the parents had.

If we carefully examine what grandfather Old Bear said about the purpose of the Family, we see that how it functions has a direct impact on everything within the Sacred Circle of Life. We also discover that a Family's purpose should be to live in such a way that Grandfather's Great Family of Life becomes stronger, not weaker. I want to suggest to you that a Family could not have a more important purpose for its existence than that!

A PERSONAL ACKNOWLEDGEMENT

I must confess to you that during my many conversations with grandfather Old Bear concerning the Family, I became more and more frustrated with myself for doing such a poor job as a parent. If I had known the things the Old One has shared with me before I started mine, I could have avoided many mistakes.

WHAT CONSTITUTES A "FAMILY" ON THIS SACRED PATH

In modern society we tend to think of "the immediate family—meaning the father, mother and their children, or "the extended family"—meaning grandparents, aunts, uncles, cousins, etc. of the immediate family. On this Sacred Path, we don't think in terms of an extended Family. Any person that is willing to be subject to the authority of the Head Man and Head Woman (oldest married man in the group and his wife), and they accept (adopt) that individual into their group through proper ceremony, that person becomes a member of the Head Man and Head Woman's Family.

For our purposes here, the term "Head Man" means the man who has the final responsibility for the Family and is the final authority concerning all matters related to the males in that Family. The Head Man is always the oldest married male in the group. The term "Head Woman" is the wife of the Head Man and shares the final responsibility for the Family with the Head Man. She also is the final authority concerning all matters related to the females in the Family. The Head Man and Head Woman maintain their positions as long as they are physically and mentally capable of performing their responsibilities for, and obligations to, the Family.

The Head Man and Head Woman are the counterparts of the Alpha Male and Alpha Female in a Family (or pack) of wolves.

On this Sacred Path the Family lives and works together. The people may or may not all live in the same dwelling. This will depend on the number of married couples in the family. Each married couple has its own private dwelling, located near other couple's dwellings. Adult single people also have their own private dwellings. Children live with their biological parents. However, adopted children usually live with the Head Man and Head Woman unless they assign the children to live with another couple. Children are adopted into the Family; not to biological parents within the Family.

As the Family grows to the point the local area can no longer support it, the next eldest couple in the Family will take some of the younger

264

couples and relocate to another area where a new Family can be started and supported from the land's resources.

The Head Man and Head Woman of the original Family perform the New Family Ceremony to initiate the next eldest couple as the Head Man and Head Woman of the newly formed Family. The New Family Ceremony is always conducted in the Spring during the Lifestyle Ceremony Of New Beginnings.

THE ROLE OF THE HEAD MAN IN THE FAMILY

The Head Man is responsible for, and in charge of, all males within the Family. He is responsible for seeing that all of the physical needs of the family are met, such as food, shelter and safety, and he delegates authority and responsibility to other men as needed.

The Head Man is always the oldest married man in the Family. If his wife dies, or if he or his wife can no longer perform their respective roles due to physical or mental illnesses, the Head Man must relinquish his position to the next oldest married man whose wife is physically and mentally fit to perform the duties of Head Woman.

The Head Man is responsible for insuring that all annual ceremonies associated with this Sacred Path are performed appropriately and on schedule.

The Head Man is responsible for overseeing the Circle of Stones Ceremony (the construction of the Circle of Stones that will become a medicine wheel). He is also responsible for the preparation and maintenance of all altars and other sacred sites used for prayer or sacred ceremony, including sites used for Spirit Questing, the building and care of the Purification Lodge and all other ceremonial sites pertaining to men. The Head Woman is responsible for all ceremonial sites pertaining exclusively to women.

The Head Man may delegate to other males any responsibility pertaining to men, and the Head Woman may delegate to other females any responsibilities pertaining to women. Therefore, it is necessary for the

Head Man and his wife, the Head Woman, to communicate daily with each other concerning the on-going needs of the Family and how those needs will most effectively be met.

The Head Man is responsible for seeing that all male members of the Family receive proper education and training concerning all the ceremonies in which males participate.

He is also responsible for the preparation of the land used for planting all the crops. However, he works closely with his wife in determining where the crops are to be planted and must have her approval of the site. He insures that all the tools and equipment needed for planting, harvesting, drying and storing of food are available and in good repair. He must also make sure that the Family has enough firewood for cooking and heating as needed.

He and his wife oversee the harvesting of all food crops.

The Head Man is a true servant of the Family, and his life should be lived above reproach at all times. To the best of his ability, his life should be an example of the way our Creator's Unconditional Love flows into a person and out to meet the needs of others in the Family. He is also a living example of how the two-leggeds are to live in peace, harmony, and balance with our Creator's Sacred Family of Life. And finally, he must be an example of the Five Spiritual Medicines at work at all times in a person's life.

THE ROLE OF THE HEAD WOMAN

The Head Woman is always the wife of the Head Man, and may or may not be the oldest woman in the Family. She is responsible for, and in charge of, all of the females in the Family, and she, along with the Female Counsel of Elders, pick all camp sites and permanent communal dwelling sites.

Even though the Head Man is responsible for the construction of a dwelling place for him and his wife (the Head Woman), she actually owns the dwelling place and all things in it except the Head Man's personal belongings and Sacred Ceremonial items. She is also the final authority concerning where their personal dwelling place will be located. The Head Man lives with the Head Woman in her dwelling and at her invitation and consent.

Like the Head Man, she is responsible for overseeing the education and training concerning all of the ceremonies in which females participate. She is responsible for the proper storage and care of all seed used for growing food and she is the overseer of the Spring Planting Ceremony as well as the Sacred Water Ceremony. In addition, she helps her husband plan and oversee the Harvest Ceremony and the actual gathering of the harvest. She has the responsibility for choosing the storage place for the food supply and makes sure the storage area remains clean, safe and secure.

The Head Woman is a symbol of Mother Earth and as such, she must be a very loving and caring person. Like her husband, she must live a life above reproach and be an example of the way our Creator's Unconditional Love flows through a person and out to serve others.

THE FAMILY COUNSEL OF ELDERS

The three oldest males in the Family make up the Male Counsel of Elders, of which the Head Man is the leader, and the three oldest females make up a Female Counsel of Elders, which the Head Woman leads. From time to time, as needed, these two Counsels meet together to deal with the general needs of the Family. These two Counsels handle all issues, problems, personality conflicts and disciplinary matters relating to their respective genders and the Family in general.

MARRIAGE

While discussing with me the meaning of marriage, grandfather Old Bear once said, *"The Marriage Ceremony is the most Sacred ceremony ever given to the two-leggeds because it symbolizes the marriage relationship between our Creator and Mother Earth."* He was smiling from ear to ear as he continued. *"You did know they were husband and wife, didn't you, grandson?*

"In the marriage relationship, the man symbolizes our Creator and the woman symbolizes Mother Earth. Our Creator and Mother Earth have the perfect marriage. They never fight or quarrel, and that is the way the man and woman are to live together as husband and wife. Our Creator's love for Mother Earth is eternal and therefore the love between a husband and wife must be eternal.

"The sexual relationship between the husband and wife symbolizes the sexual relationship between our Creator and Mother Earth that results in all of our Sacred Relatives living here on the Earth. Just as our Creator and Mother Earth join together to create Sacred Life, so the husband and wife join together to create children. I tell you, grandson, the sexual act between a husband and wife is not only sacred, it is Holy. Therefore, it must not be desecrated by either the husband or wife becoming involved in sexual relationships outside the Sacred Marriage."

The Old One looked at me with that penetrating stare of his that seemed to say, "I know all about you, grandson." Then he said, "You do understand the importance of what I'm telling you, don't you?"

I nodded my head, indicating that I clearly understood what he was saying, and then he continued. "It is a tragedy the way people in your world have such little respect for marriage and the sacred sexual union between the husband and wife. On this Sacred Path, when a man and woman decide to get married, they are saying they have the same deep, eternal love for one another that our Creator and Mother Earth have for each other."

He gave me one of his mischievous grins and said, "Because my wife and I deeply understood this, our love-making was truly a Spiritual Experience."

On this Sacred Path, Marriage is for life and is a commitment between a man and woman to learn to love one another with the same kind of deep, eternal, spiritual love our Creator and Mother Earth have for each other. However, a married woman has the right to put her husband and his personal belongings out of her dwelling if he becomes intolerable to live with, but that does not break the marriage vow. In such instances, the married man must live alone during this time of separation and he is still responsible for providing food and firewood for his wife (and children if they have any).

If the husband is put out of his wife's dwelling, neither he nor she is free to become sexually intimate with another man or woman. As stated above, sexual relations are allowed only between husbands and wives; however, it is not allowed between the married couple as long as the wife forces the husband to live alone due to his abusive actions. On the other hand, the husband may not move out of the house if his wife abuses him. Instead, he takes the problem to the Head Man who, in turn, explains it to his wife, the Head Woman, and she works with the disagreeable woman while the Head Man works with her husband to resolve the problem.

In instances where the husband has been put out of the dwelling by the wife, the Head Man and Head Woman are responsible for working with the couple to resolve the problem so that the man is invited to move back in with his wife. The wife has the final say as to when the problem is resolved and her husband is permitted to return to the dwelling. When this occurs, a public ceremony is performed by the Head Man and Head Woman to reaffirm the disputing couple's marriage vows.

CHILDREN

Children are Sacred Gifts from our Creator given as rewards to the whole family for their faithfulness in walking this Sacred Path. Even though the children have biological parents who are ultimately responsible for raising them and educating them in the Ways of walking this Sacred Path, all of the adults in the Family are responsible for assisting in this process as the parents request help.

Once the children become adults, the Family helps them construct their own dwelling place.

ADOPTION INTO THE FAMILY

From time to time, people outside the Family may be adopted into the Family. Men being considered for adoption always meet with the Head Man first, and women always meet first with the Head Woman. If the Head Man or Head Woman feel it would be mutually beneficial for the respective individuals to become part of the Family, he or she is brought before the entire Family Counsel of Elders for further consideration. The adoption occurs only if both the person being considered for adoption and all members of the Counsel of Elders are in agreement.

The Adoption Ceremony is always conducted during the Lifestyle Ceremony of New Beginnings, and it occurs only after the entire Family has helped the person being adopted prepare himself or herself a new dwelling place.

OLD AGE

Old Age is considered a reward from our Creator for faithfulness in walking this Sacred Path. The longer people live, the more honor and respect they receive from Family members as a way of showing their gratitude for the contribution the older ones have made to the Family and to our Creator's Sacred Circle of Life.

The appointment of the oldest married man in the Family to the position of Head Man is a way of showing honor and respect for the aging process. It also insures that every man and woman in the Family potentially could some day fill the position of Head Man and Head Woman, depending on their gender. Therefore, each Family member should spend his or her life preparing for that possibility. The fact that every person in the Family could potentially become a Head Man or Head Woman helps motivate Family members at a very early age to start learning all they can about how the Family walking this Sacred Path is to function and properly perform all of the ceremonies associated with each of the Four Sacred Lifestyle Ceremonies.

As adults become too old to properly care for their own physical needs, their children assume the primary responsibility for their care. However, the entire Family also helps in the process of caring for the needs of the Old Ones among them. The Head Man oversees this process for older disabled males and the Head Woman insures that the needs of the older women are being met.

WORK

The Family works together to meet the needs of all within the Family. Planting, harvesting, drying of food, hunting and building of dwellings is done as a Family. The women prepare and cook the food and the Family eats together except on cold, winter days when it is more convenient to cook and eat inside their respective private dwellings.

Almost all work is considered to be a Sacred Spiritual activity. This includes preparing the ground for planting, planting and care for crops, harvesting, hunting, building dwellings to live in, drying food for storage, the preparation and cooking of food, keeping dwellings clean, tanning hides and making items out of tanned hides, preparing all ceremonial sites, and so on. As a result, appropriate Sacred Ceremonies are performed before conducting the work activities mentioned above.

Harvested food is considered Family property, and the Head Woman is responsible for its care and distribution. When individuals go hunting or fishing, the food is shared with all members of the Family, and the elderly are given their portions first. The hide becomes the property of the person who killed the animal and it must be tanned and put to good use.

THE SACRED CAMPFIRE

An arbor with a place for a Sacred Campfire is located in the center of the dwellings and this is the focal point for meals, socializing and many of the Family's ceremonies. However, each dwelling also has its own small arbor and Campfire site for personal work and private family activities.

Fire is a Sacred Gift from our Creator, and the Sacred Campfire is held in great respect. Once the Campfire is lit, the immediate area around the Sacred Campfire becomes Holy Ground. When people come together around the Campfire, they should never engage in negative or disrespectful conversation. The Campfire site is a place that promotes peace and harmony among people and, therefore, it is no place for foul language, off colored jokes or disrespectful conversation.

On this Sacred Path, the Campfire is one of the many "bridges" that help connect the physical realm with the Spiritual Realm. It is a place for the telling of Sacred Stories, socializing and sharing of positive experiences, conducting various Sacred Ceremonies, Singing Sacred Songs, preparing, cooking and feasting on Sacred Food, playing games (except gambling games), and general relaxation.

The Head Man appoints a young man and the Head Woman appoints a young woman to be in charge of always keeping the Sacred Campfire site clean, with an available supply of firewood and water for drinking and washing dishes. This is a responsibility that carries with it great honor, and only young people who have proven themselves worthy of such important responsibility are chosen.

All Campfire sites are ceremonially cleaned on the last day of each Lifestyle Ceremony. On the morning of the first day of each Lifestyle Ceremony, new Sacred Coals of Fire are brought from the Fire Pit at the end of the Purification Ceremony and placed in all of the campfire pits.

PRIVATE DWELLINGS

Private Dwellings are circular in design with the doorway facing East. There are four earthen altars outside the dwelling, one for each of the Four Lifestyle Ceremonies. Inside the dwelling, there is an altar in the west, opposite the door.

The inside of the Dwelling is considered a Sacred Site since everything our Creator has made is sacred and those living in the Dwelling are our Creator's children. All Family activities within the Dwelling, even casual conversation, are conducted with the utmost respect. If arguments involving anger develop between Family members while inside the Dwelling, those arguments are taken outside the Dwelling in respect of the sacredness of the inside of the home. The individuals are expected to resolve the argument, or at least overcome their anger, before going back inside the Dwelling.

Since the inside of the Dwelling is considered a Sacred Site, everything is kept neat, clean and orderly.

The preparation, cooking and eating of food is also considered to be a Sacred Activity, since all food is a part of the Sacred Family of Life. Therefore, before beginning the food preparation and cooking process, the person or people involved must first smudge themselves and offer prayers of thanks to their relatives who will become the meal. Meals are eaten with a great deal of thanksgiving and celebration, and negative conversation should be avoided during mealtime.

The inside of the Dwelling consists of an open circular area with a dirt or stone floor. The structure contains both male and female energy. The female energy resides in the area from the entrance, moving around to the left (south), all the way to the altar in the West. The male energy makes up the area from the altar moving around to the North and all the way to the entrance in the East. The entrance and Altar contain both male and female energy.

If a single adult male that is getting married has his own Dwelling, before the wedding he must remove everything from it and during the Wedding Ceremony give ownership of his house to his new wife. Before he is permitted back in what is now his new wife's Dwelling, she, accompanied by some of her female friends, smudges first the inside and then the outside area around the home. She then returns inside and offers prayers, asking our Grandfather's Blessings on the Dwelling and their marriage. She then determines what personal belongings her new husband may or may not bring back into her Dwelling.

RITES OF PASSAGE

The most important Family Ceremonies are referred to as Rites of Passage, and consist of ceremonies conducted at the time of pregnancy, birth, naming, adulthood, marriage, certain special times of recognition, and death. These Rites of Passage ceremonies are conducted at major times of change in an individual Family member's life.

Adoption ceremonies are also considered to be very important, but are not recognized as a Rite of Passage.

There are many other lesser ceremonies associated with Family living. In addition, there are ceremonies associated with one's change of status or position within the Family due to personal accomplishments on both the physical and spiritual plane. However, space will not permit a discussion of these lesser ceremonies.

Teaching Session – 11
LEARNING HOW TO GET TO YOUR "PRIVATE WORLD"

In this teaching session I will share with you the techniques I use to go to that place—a place I call "My Private World"—where, for many years now, I have been meeting with grandfather Old Bear to learn from him how to walk this Sacred Path. The place you travel to will be your own Private World. It will be different from mine, and yet, I am convinced it is also the same place.

Do I know where that place is? No. However, I go there often. Can I take you to my place? I don't know. I asked Willard Fools Bull, a Lakota Medicine Man, to meet me there, and he did. I asked Mr. Gan, a Chinese businessman living in Indonesia, to meet me there, and he did. However, neither of these men have any memory of what transpired during their meeting with me in My Private World.

I want to assure you at the outset that I do not use meditation to get to My Private World, and neither will you. I do not know how to meditate and it is my understanding that the process of getting there is in no way similar to meditation.

WELCOME TO MY PRIVATE WORLD

Let me take you on a quick tour of My Private World. I pull open a heavy stone door that is in the side of a mountain, and step out into a wonderful world that is like this world, except it is a lot more peaceful. It has a bright blue sky and sometimes clouds float lazily overhead. In My

Private World there are rivers, small streams, high, jagged, snow covered mountains and rolling hills, thick forests and grassy meadows.

Animals, birds and fish live there, just like in this world. However, there is no pollution in My Private World. There are no towns or cities. There are no man made roads, only small game trails. There are no jet planes in My Private World to clog the sky with vapor trails, or automobiles creeping along crowded freeways. And there is no man made electricity there. It reminds me of the way our world surely must have been before the two-leggeds desecrated it.

And, based on the feedback I have received from other people I have taught how to travel to their own Private World, I'm sure you will find that your Private World is very similar to mine.

THE PURPOSE FOR LEARNING TO TRAVEL TO YOUR OWN PRIVATE WORLD

Even though I don't know where My Private World is, I know how to get there, and I'm convinced it connects the Spiritual Realm with the physical realm.

My Private World serves many purposes. I go there to conduct the Spirit Quest ceremony (explained in detail in book four). I also go there often to talk to our Creator, and I have discovered that praying there seems to be much more effective than when I pray here in the physical world because when I talk to our Creator there I actually hear him talking back to me. Sometimes I go there to relax and get away from the pressures of this fast paced physical realm. I go there to get information from the Spiritual Realm that will help me live more effectively here in the physical realm. For the past several years I have gone there to meet with grandfather Old Bear to learn from him how to walk this Sacred Path he refers to as *The Way of the Medicine Wheel.*

Over the years, I have come to believe that the purposes for going to our Private Worlds are endless.

IS YOUR PRIVATE WORLD A "REAL PLACE"?

I have often been asked if My Private World is actually a real place, or is it simply a make believe place that I have created in my mind. I want to share with you two personal experiences I had shortly after I learned to go to My Private World that proved to me that it is a very real place that connects us to the Spiritual Realm.

I had a management consulting business for twenty-five years, and many years ago, while Angelitta and I were living in Indonesia, I was trying to land a management consulting contract with a large Indonesian company. A young Chinese man named Mr. Gan owned this company. The night before I was to present my consulting proposal to Mr. Gan, I went into our bedroom, closed the door and laid down on the bed. I went to My Private World to try and contact Mr. Gan to find out what he thought of the proposal I was about to discuss with him the following day.

To my surprise, Mr. Gan came to My Private World when I called him, and during our conversation, he told me that, in his opinion, the greatest need was training for his field managers. I hadn't included that type of training in the proposal, so I asked him what he thought the contract would be worth with that component added. He told me that he would be willing to pay $70,000 with field manager training added to the contract.

The next morning I got up very early and went to the office and added the field manager training to the proposal and changed the budget from $35,000 to $70,000. When I met with Mr. Gan the next day and presented the proposal, he accepted it without any negotiations. After the meeting, he said with a smile, "I was afraid you weren't going to include the field manager training, and when I heard you include it at the end of your presentation, I was thinking that the whole program would be worth about $70,000."

Two years later I told Mr. Gan how I had arrived at the need for field manager training and the budget for $70,000. He was so impressed, he had me conduct a week-end training session with all of his top managers, including himself, to teach them how to go to their own Private World.

Not long before Angelitta and I moved back to America, my sister, Judy, called me and said that when we returned to the States, I should meet a Lakota medicine man named Willard Fools Bull that she had heard interviewed on a talk radio program.

Later, I went to My Private World and asked for Willard Fools Bull to come and visit me. After a short time, I saw a large Indian man with long, black hair walking up the hill toward me. He was wearing old, faded blue jeans and a faded, red tee shirt. When he got near me, he gave me a warm smile and said, "What did you want with me?"

I explained I was going to be moving back to the United States soon and my sister had suggested that I come to meet him, so I just wanted to see who I was going to meet when I got back to the States.

When we got back to the U.S., I went to the Rosebud Indian Reservation in South Dakota where Willard Fools Bull lived. When I met him, I discovered he was a large man with long, black hair, a warm, friendly smile and he was wearing old, faded blue jeans and a faded, red tee shirt. He looked exactly like the man that came to meet me in My Private World while I was living in Indonesia.

Even though I don't know where My Private World is, I know how to get there, and I have had so many experiences like the two mentioned above that I am convinced it is a very real place somewhere that connects us to the Spiritual Realm.

OUR MIND DOESN'T DISTINGUSH BETWEEN WHAT WE VISUALIZE AND WHAT IS REAL

People often say that I am just doing visualization when I go to My Private World, and visualization isn't real, it's just make believe. It's true that I do visualization in order to get to the three doors in the side of the mountain. However, when I walk through those doors, the world I walk into effects my five senses just like the "real" world here does.

278

Our brain can't tell the difference between visualization and what we call reality. To illustrate that, I would like to do the following experiment with you.

Close your eyes and visualize a big, yellow lemon. Now, see yourself taking a knife and slicing that lemon in half and putting half of the lemon in your mouth and squeezing out the juice. As you see yourself doing that, your brain will tell your saliva gland to rush saliva into your mouth in order to help wash the sour lemon down your throat.

You see, the brain can't tell the difference between what we visualize and what is real. It thinks the visualized sour lemon being squeezed into your mouth is real so it sends saliva to help wash it down.

The Old Testament of the Bible tells us that "as a man thinks in his heart, so is he." That statement suggests that our mind has the power to create our own personal reality. My own experiences in My Private World have taught me that this passage in the Bible is true. Many times, I have experienced things in My Private World that later happened in the physical realm, just as I had previously seen them or experienced them in that World.

HOW I GET TO MY PRIVATE WORLD

I will describe for you the step-by-step process I use for getting to My Private World. However, as time goes by, you may be given a slightly different method.

Step One

I begin by finding a place that is quiet where I will be undisturbed. In the beginning, I used the bedroom and lay on the bed. However, now I can do this most anywhere. Because I started out lying on the bed in my bedroom, I suggest that you consider lying on your own bed to do this. It worked well for me and I'm sure it will for you also. As you lay on your bed, close your eyes and take seven deep breaths, each time slowly exhaling. This will help you relax and get focused.

Step Two

Visualize yourself standing at the very edge of a deep, very narrow canyon that is filled with a black fog right up to the top of the canyon. You are standing so close to the edge of the canyon rim that the black fog is almost touching your feet.

Step out onto the black fog and feel yourself slowly descending down through it. You will descend through red fog next, then yellow fog, white fog, green fog and finally blue fog.

As you come out of the bottom of the blue fog, you will be just above the tops of very tall evergreen trees. You will continue to slowly descend down through them and gently touch the ground on a narrow path (approximately four feet wide).

You will hear water running nearby and will follow the path toward the sound of the water. You will come to a small, shallow mountain stream (about ten feet wide), and you will walk across the stream on the tops of rocks that are sticking out of the water.

When you are on the other side of the stream, you will continue following the path up a small hill to a large, diagonal crack that is in the rock face of a cliff at the base of a mountain. You will walk through that crack and out into a large cave-like room inside the mountain. The room is dome shaped and has rock walls, ceiling and floor. On the west side of the room, there are three large stone doors. As you face the doors, the door on the left takes you to the future, the door in the center takes you to the present and the door on the right takes you to the past.

You will walk through the center door and out into your own Private World. I cannot tell you what is in your Private World. You will have to go there yourself to find out.

Step Three

After exploring your Private World, you will come back through the door, go out
of the cave and back down the path and across the stream. You will continue on down the path short ways until you come to seven steps that have been cut into the side of a dirt bank.

You will walk up those steps, and when you get to the top, you will open your eyes and find yourself back here on this side in the physical realm.

I have just described how I get to my Private World and back. I suggest you try this and feel free to use any variations our Creator seems to be suggesting to you. You may have to try this several times before successfully making it to the cave and beyond the center door.

I had to try several times before I was successful in getting to My Private World each time I tried. So don't get discouraged if you don't make it the first, second, third, or even the tenth time you try. Keep trying —you'll make it.

Remember the Five Spiritual Medicines and apply them to this assignment. You will need Spiritual Courage, Patience, Endurance, Alertness and Humility to get from the physical realm to your Private World. It takes Courage to try this, Patience to wait until the proper time to try, Endurance to not give up trying, Alertness to hear what is being told you when you get to your Private World, and Humility to not let your pride convince you that you have acquired some great spiritual power that makes you spiritually superior to those who have not yet learned to go to their own Private World.

WHAT TO DO WHEN YOU GET TO YOUR PRIVATE WORLD

The first time or two you go to your Private World, I suggest you simply explore it to see what is there. However, once you start to get familiar with your Private World, you should start going there to pray.

I have found that prayer is much easier and far more effective when I pray in my Private World because I am able to actually carry on a conversation with our Creator there. I talk to him and he talks back to me.

I am sometimes asked if I actually see our Creator there when we carry on a conversation. No. However, I have seen a bright light in the forest that seems to expand until it almost fills up my whole Private World. The times that has occurred, I have felt so close to our Creator, and such peace, that human words can't properly express what actually occurred within me.

I also suggest that you go to your Private World to work on real life situations. By doing that, you will have real evidence of the results you get. I think there is very little benefit in going there and asking if the universe is round. What difference does it make what shape it is, and how could you prove it once you were back here in the physical realm?

I also suggest that any information you receive there, you ask our Creator when you get back here if it is correct or not. If our Creator tells you something in your Private World, he will also confirm it to you here in the physical realm. I would never follow through on something told me in my Private World that could not be confirmed to me by our Creator as truth here in the physical realm.

A WORD OF CAUTION

I don't want to scare you. However, I feel it is important to remind you that there are both positive and negative powers within the Spiritual Realm. Some people call this negative power demons or evil spirits; others refer to it as Satan, and some just refer to it as negative energy. It doesn't matter what you call it, the fact is, there are powerful negative spirits at work within the Spiritual Realm, and we need to protect ourselves against them. Therefore, I suggest you always do the Self-Offering Ceremony before going to your Private World.

The Self-Offering Ceremony will insure that you are entering your Private World with pure motives and purpose, thus protecting yourself

282

from the negative spirits that may try to tempt you to follow their evil ways.

Just as we are confronted with choices between good and evil in the physical realm, we are also sometimes offered choices to follow either good or evil power within the Spiritual Realm. With that in mind, I strongly recommend that you always enter your Private World with pure motives and intentions for good; otherwise you are leaving yourself open to be enticed by evil spirits to follow an evil path—and all evil paths eventually lead to self-destruction.

When I am given information in My Private World, I always ask our Creator if that information is correct and if I should act on what I have been told. I suggest you do the same. Our Creator will protect us from being led astray by false information.

WE ARE SPIRITS LIVING IN A PHYSICAL BODY

It is important to understand who you really are—you are a spirit living in a physical body. Without a physical body, you would be unable to relate to and interact with the physical realm. However, your physical body is not really YOU. Your spirit is the REAL YOU, and your spirit needs to interact with and relate to the Spiritual Realm. That is why it is so important to learn to travel to your Private World—it is your contact point with the Spiritual Realm.

Our Creator is Spirit. We are spirits. Therefore, we communicate with and relate to our Creator on a Spiritual plane—Spirit to spirit.

Unfortunately, we cannot take our physical bodies into the Spiritual Realm. We must leave them behind and let our spirits (the real us) travel to the World of The Spirits.

When I met with Willard Fools Bull and Mr. Gan in my Private World, I met with their spirits, not with their physical bodies. Their physical consciousness was not aware of the meeting. That is why, on a physical level, they had no memory of our meetings. The meeting took place on a Spiritual level. I could remember the meeting because here, in the physical realm, and while still in my physical body, I consciously decided to go to My Private World and try to meet with them. That is why, when I returned, I could bring the memory of that meeting back with me to my physical body.

Understanding this makes us aware of how important it is to have a "purpose" when we go to our Private World.

ALWAYS HAVE A "PURPOSE" FOR GOING TO YOUR PRIVATE WORLD

I always go to My Private World to work on something tangible. In other words, I always have a clear purpose for going there. I decide in advance what I will work on while I am there. Here in the physical realm and within my physical consciousness, I state exactly why I am making the trip.

When I open the center door and step into My Private World, to my left is a giant pine tree beside a very small stream (about a foot wide) that flows from the mountain behind me down to the river in the valley below. At the bottom of the pine tree there is a flat rock that is just big enough to make a good seat. I go immediately to that rock and sit under the pine tree and state out loud my purpose for coming to My Private World. Stating out loud my purpose for being there seems to set things in motion on a Spiritual level so that I can accomplish the things I came to do.

I firmly believe that stating my purpose for going to My Private World with my physical consciousness while I am still here in the physical realm enables me to remember on a physical level what my spirit worked on while it was in the My Private World. That is why I always tell people to make sure they have a clear purpose for going to their Private World and state that purpose here in the physical realm before they go and again as soon as they arrive in their Private World.

Earlier, I stated that the process of going to your Private World does not involve meditation, and that I do not know how to meditate. As I understand it, meditation involves emptying your mind. Going to your

Private World involves making a Spirit Journey with a clear purpose and intent to work on something that will be applied and used back here in the physical realm. As I said, I go there to "work on something tangible." I know why I'm going, and here in the physical realm I always remember what I worked on while I was there. I strongly recommend that you always have a clear purpose for going to your Private World.

I think it would be very dangerous to go to your Private World without a clear understanding as to why you are going. I fear that to do so would leave you vulnerable to the deceptive and evil temptations suggested to you by evil spirits within the Spiritual Realm.

OUR CREATOR HAS A PURPOSE FOR US WHILE LIVING HERE IN THE PHYSICAL REALM

It seems that these days more and more people are asking the question, "Who am I, and why am I here?" Grandfather Old Bear once said to me, *"If you don't know who you are and why our Creator has put you on Mother Earth, it means you haven't been spending much time listening to what our Creator is saying to you."*

Let me ask you the same question grandfather Old Bear once asked me, "How much time do you spend LISTENING to what our Creator says to you?" Notice I didn't ask, "How much time do you spend PRAYING?"

Most people's concept of prayer is asking our Creator for something. Many people pray only when they have a problem or want something. Such people's prayers usually focus on GIVE ME-GIVE ME! Those kinds of prayers are rarely—if ever—answered. Why? Because, such prayers are coming from self-centered brats who tend to think only of themselves and rarely—if ever—of the needs of others.

Real prayer is a CONVERSATION we have with our Creator. It involves DISCUSSION. We ask our Creator a question and then listen to his answer. He tells us something and we respond to what we have been told. Prayer is dialogue between you/me and our Creator.

One of the most important things our Creator wants to talk to us about is his purpose for our lives while living here on Mother Earth. Our Creator didn't just put you here to see what you would do. He put you here for a reason. He has a purpose and plan for your life. The question is, do you know what our Creator's plan for your life is?

In the broadest sense, our purpose in life is to live in peace, harmony and balance with the Sacred Circle of Life. However, Grandfather also has a specific plan, or job, for each of us, and the achievement of peace, harmony and balance in our lives can only be accomplished as we live according to his plan for our lives. In other words, peace, harmony and balance in life are the RESULT of living life according to the Life Plans our Creator has for us.

Do you want to know the plans our Creator has for your life? I ask that question because our Creator will not waste his time trying to communicate Life Plans to people who aren't interested in knowing what those plans are and then living life according to those plans.

Below is a step-by-step, simple process for knowing our Creator's personal plans for our lives, and this should be one of the specific projects you work on with our Creator in your Private World.

HOW TO KNOW OUR CREATOR'S PLANS FOR YOUR LIFE

Step One:
Believe our Creator has a personal plan for your life,
And be committed to follow it.

The first step in knowing our Creator's personal plan for your life is to believe he has such a plan, and be committed to following it. If you don't believe Grandfather has a specific plan for your life, then you won't be open to listening to him if he tries to communicate it to you.

It isn't enough to intellectually accept the possibility that our Creator has a plan for your life. You must also be committed to obeying that plan when he shares it with you.

Let me explain what I mean when I say our Creator has a specific Life

Plan for you. He created you as a unique individual. There is no one else like you. He created you with a specific set of gifts, skills and abilities, and he did that for a reason—he has something specific he wants to accomplish through your life. Therefore, you should go to your Private World with the purpose of telling Grandfather that you believe he has a specific Life Plan for you and that you are committed to following it as he reveals it to you.

Be honest. Don't tell Grandfather you are committed to following his plan for your life if you aren't. You may deceive yourself and others, but you can't deceive our Creator. Never forget that. Also, don't try to negotiate with him. Don't say that you'd like to know what his plans for your life are so you can decide if you want to follow them or not. Grandfather never negotiates! He isn't interested in compromises. He doesn't deal in partial plans. He has a specific Life Plan for each of us and he expects total acceptance on our part. If we aren't willing to obediently follow the whole plan, he isn't obligated to tell us what it is. On the other hand, if we are sincerely committed to obeying his plans for our lives, then he is obligated to communicate those plans to us. You see, he is actually more interested in us knowing his plans for our lives than we are.

Once you have communicated to our Creator that you believe he has a specific plan for your life and you are committed to following it, you are ready to implement Step Two.

Step Two:
Ask Grandfather to begin revealing his plan
For your life to you.

Once you have met the prerequisite stated in step one, the next step is to ask our Creator to start revealing his plans for your life to you. As you do this, keep in mind that knowing Grandfather's plans for your life will occur only as you take the Five Spiritual Medicines. To know our Creator's plans for your life will involve the personal application of Spiritual Courage, Patience, Endurance, Alertness and Humility on your

287

part, and Grandfather may choose to test you to see if you have these Five Spiritual Medicines or not.

How long will Grandfather take to start revealing his plans for your life to you? I don't know. But you can be assured that those plans will be revealed to you on Grandfather's schedule, not yours, and when he concludes that you are ready to begin implementing those plans, not necessarily as soon as you think you are ready and able to begin. Once you clearly understand this, you are ready for your next assignment.

Go back to your Private World and specifically ask Grandfather to begin revealing his plans for your life to you, and reaffirm your commitment to following those plans as they are revealed to you.

Keep in mind that Grandfather not only has a plan for your life, he also has a timetable as well. Therefore, be content to let him control the timetable for revealing and implementing those plans.

Your commitment to following Grandfather's plans for your life is extremely important because he isn't willing to waste his time communicating Life Plans to people who are unwilling to follow them. He is looking for people who volunteer to follow the plans he has for their lives.

Keep in mind that he is our Spiritual Father, and, like any father, he wants the very best for his children. We know that his plans for us are the very best plans—far better than any plan we could come up with on our own. Just as we want the very best for our children, he wants the very best for us, his children. His plans are designed to produce true peace, harmony and balance in our lives.

It is also important to understand that our Creator's plans for our lives are so big that we will not be able to accomplish them on our own power or with our own resources or resourcefulness. Our Creator's plans for us are so big they always require his help in accomplishing those plans. It is very important to understand this.

Following the plans our Creator has for your life will require you to put your faith in him and his ability to help you accomplish those plans. That is one of the main reasons he has plans for our lives. He wants to personally demonstrate to us how much he loves and cares for us, and that nothing is impossible for him to accomplish.

Step Three:
After you ask Grandfather to begin revealing his plans to you, begin examining the desires of your heart.

After you have met the prerequisite stated in step one and two, begin examining the desires that start to form within you. Keep in mind that these are our Creator's Life Plans for you; they are not plans you concoct based on your own self-centered ego. The question is, "How does Grandfather communicate his plans for our lives to us?"

If we truly believe our Creator has a specific plan for our lives, and we communicate to him our honest commitment to follow those plans, and then we ask him to start revealing those plans to us, the next step is to start examining the desires that start to develop within us.

For example, when I moved back to the United States with Angelitta in 1994, I knew that in a few years I wanted to retire from my management consulting business, but we had no idea what we wanted to do with the rest of our lives. We began to talk to Grandfather, telling him we knew he had a plan for the rest of our lives and that we were committed to following that plan as he revealed it to us.

It wasn't long before we started getting a desire to purchase land in a remote area of western Colorado known as the Paradox Valley area. As we discussed this, we both agreed that someday we wanted to live away from the hustle and bustle of city life, and we both thought this area of western Colorado would be an ideal place to start looking for land.

Even though at the time we had no idea of our Creator's specific plans for our future, we believed Grandfather had given us the desire to someday buy land in the area of Paradox Valley, so we began believing that was a part of his future plans for us.

Not long after that, I had my first encounter with grandfather Old Bear who began revealing to us the Sacred Path he called *The Way of the*

Medicine Wheel. Through a series of almost unbelievable events, we now own Medicine Wheel Mesa near the south rim of Paradox Valley with a dear friend, Alice Fae Brown, and we are learning to walk this ancient Sacred Path. Did our Creator reveal his plans for the rest of our lives all at once? No.

The starting point was the desire to someday live near Paradox Valley. As we began acting on that desire, step-by-step, our Creator began revealing the rest of his future plans for us.

But how do we know if a desire is from our Creator or from our own selfish ambitions and interests? The answer is given in the next step of this simple process for knowing Grandfather's will for our lives.

Step Four:
Begin acting on the desires and watch
For doors to open or close.

When you go to your Private World to talk to our Creator about his plans for your life, he may speak to you verbally or he may choose to speak to you by placing his desires within you to motivate you to action on his plans.

It has been my personal experience that here on the physical plane he almost always communicates his plans for our lives to us by giving us desires to do what he wants done. It is important to always keep in mind that his plans for us produce peace, harmony and balance in our lives. Therefore, they are GOOD plans, not some kind of plan that will make our lives miserable. Think about it—would you want your children to have a miserable life? Certainly not—and our Creator doesn't want his children to have a miserable life either. Like us, he wants the very best for his children.

Our lives become miserable, frustrating, and out of control when we try to come up with our own plan for our lives. However, when we follow our Creator's plans, we will discover that they always produce peace, harmony and balance in our lives. I tell you this because it is important to understand that once we become committed to following our Creator's plan for our lives, we will have a desire to do those plans.

Our Creator made each of us as unique individuals and he has a personalized plan for each of our lives that involve the utilization of our uniqueness to accomplish those plans. His plans for our lives are tailor-made for the gifts, skills and abilities he gave us. Therefore, when he begins making known his plans for our lives, we will have a desire to do those plans because they "feel right for us." They feel right for us because they are right for us.

I say all of that to let you know that once we are committed to following the Life Plans our Creator has for us, and we have communicated that commitment to Grandfather, the next step is to start examining the desires that begin forming within us, and then start acting on those desires.

If we are truly committed to following the Life Plan our Creator has for us, we will not only start having desires that move us in the direction of those plans, but the doors will open for us to accomplish those desires (plans) if they are actually from our Creator. What am I saying? I'm saying that if a desire is from our Creator, he will also give us the ability (needed resources, etc.) to accomplish those desires. He will never give us a Life Plan without the resources or means to accomplish those plans. And keep in mind that his plans for our lives almost always are beyond our own ability to personally accomplish those plans without his direct help.

As doors of opportunity open for you to begin accomplishing the desire, walk through them. By that I mean keep taking action that moves you toward accomplishing the desire as long as you have PEACE IN YOUR SPIRIT that you are doing the right thing. On the other hand, if the door does not open for you to begin fulfilling the desire, WAIT. DON'T TRY TO FORCE THE DOOR OPEN! Remember: it takes Spiritual Courage to walk through the open door and Spiritual Patience to wait if the door remains closed.

Following our Creator's plans for our lives always involves faith. Faith involves ACTION, not just BELIEF. Faith produces action. If I truly have faith that something is Grandfather's plan for me, I will begin taking action to achieve that plan. And no plan is ever accomplished without action. Therefore, I must begin acting on the desires forming within me in order to see if those desires are truly from our Creator or just my own desires based on my own personal interests.

This leads us to the next step in the process of knowing our Creator's plans for our lives.

Step Five:
Knowing when to take action and when to wait

As our Creator begins placing his desires within you to work on his plans for your life, he will open doors of opportunity for those desires to be accomplished. However, not every desire is from our Creator, and he may not have had any thing to do with opening an open door. We are also capable of opening some doors of opportunity on our own.

So how do we know if the door was opened by our Creator or maybe by our own power? As we walk through the open door, we will experience a deep peace about what we are doing, if our Creator created that opportunity. On the other hand, if we forced a door open by our own power, we will experience frustration, anxiety, doubt and even fear as we walk through the door of opportunity, and it will later prove to have been a mistake. Therefore, always check to see if you have peace as you work on each opportunity that presents itself. If the opportunity is from our Creator, we will experience a deep, reassuring peace that we are doing the right thing (no matter what others may say about what we are doing).

That peace is from our Creator. He always gives us a deep—almost spiritual—peace as we work on the opportunities that present themselves as part of his Life Plans for us. We experience a deep KNOWING within our spirits that we are doing the right things, and that this is our Creator's plan for us. The rule I have set for myself is that I keep moving ahead as long as I have peace about what I'm doing. If there is no peace, I stop and ask our Creator what I should do next.

Sometimes, we have a desire that we are convinced is from our Creator but the door of opportunity is not open for us to move ahead, so what do we do in cases like that? There are times we know our Creator wants us to do something, but the opportunity or means of accomplishing it just doesn't exist.

For example, several years ago Angelitta and I concluded that our Creator wanted us to buy a certain remote piece of land near Paradox Valley in western Colorado. We met a realtor named Jay Brown who found a very remote piece of land that we thought was where our Creator wanted us to move. We spent more than a year working to get the land, but one roadblock after another kept developing even though we had agreed to purchase the land at the seller's price. Finally, it became clear to us that we were not going to be able to buy the land, and at first we were very disappointed.

We knew our Creator wanted us to move to a remote area in that part of Colorado. This was the only piece of truly remote land we had found that seemed to be acceptable for what we knew we had to do. But the door remained tightly closed to get the land.

I went back to My Private World and talked to our Creator, reaffirming my commitment to follow his plans for our lives. I reminded him that I had done all I could do to get the land and that I was just going to wait until he provided a piece of remote land that could be purchased.

Within a week Jay called me very excited about another piece of remote land he had found that was far better than the one we had been trying to buy, and it was also cheaper. Our Creator immediately opened the door for us to get the land and after we purchased it we discovered that it already had a 1500-foot deep water well on it that flowed 15 gallons per minute!

You see, our Creator sometimes provides what seems to be an opportunity, but is actually a TEST to see if we are willing to apply the

Spiritual Medicine of Patience and wait for our Creator to open doors, instead of trying to kick the doors open ourselves.

When our Creator closes a door of opportunity, it is always because he has an even better opportunity for us than the one we are trying to take advantage of. Therefore, never try to kick down closed doors. If you do, I can assure you from my own personal experiences that you will regret it later.

If a door of opportunity is open, walk through it, and as you do, check to see if you have peace. If the door is closed—wait for our Creator to open it or provide the next door of opportunity. You will always find the closed door was for your protection and the next open door will provide a far better opportunity than the one that remained closed to you.

Step Six:
You will experience peace, harmony and balance in your life.

Our Creator's Life Plan for you is far, far better than any plan for your life you could come up with on your own. Grandfather has a purpose for your life. He has a specific Life Plan for each of us, and that Life Plan produces peace, harmony and balance in our lives.

The sixth and final step is to examine our lives on a regular basis to see if we are experiencing peace, harmony and balance in our lives. If we are, we know we are accomplishing Grandfather's plan for us. If we are experiencing a lack of peace, harmony and balance in our lives, we know we are getting off track, and some area of our life is not being lived according to Grandfather's plan for us.

I encourage you to make regular trips to your Private World to talk to our Creator about his Life Plans for you. Keep in mind that once he reveals to you his plans for your life, it is even more important to communicate with him regularly about those plans. He not only has plans for your life; he produces the results.

In Book Four, you will be given the process involved in conducting the Spirit Quest Ceremony. That ceremony will help you put the six steps mentioned above into action each Sacred Season.

ALWAYS THANK OUR CREATOR FOR WHAT HE ACCOMPLISHES THROUGH YOU

Notice these are our Creator's plans for your life—not your plans. He has something he wants to accomplish through you. These are not plans that he gives you and then they become YOUR plans. They always remain his plans for you. So, the results are his results—not yours. He produces the results through you, so never try to take the credit for what he accomplished as you implemented his plans for your life.

It is a dangerous thing to try to take the credit for what our Creator accomplishes through us. We are to become "hollow bones" through which our Creator's power flows to accomplish his plans for us. Always give him the credit for the results. Thank him for what he accomplishes through you. Again I say, never take the credit for what is accomplished.

Our Creator's plans for you are BIG plans that encompass the entire Sacred Family of Life. These plans will produce GREAT results. They will be great because our Creator not only has the plan, he also is responsible for accomplishing the results through you. Be quick to give him the credit. Don't let pride enter in and destroy your humility. That is why we must make sure we take the Spiritual Medicine of Humility.

As long as we remain humble and give our Creator the credit for the results he produces, he will continue to give us new plans to be accomplished. However, if we start taking the credit for what is accomplished, our pride will prevent his power from flowing through us to accomplish the results.

I go regularly to My Private World to ask Grandfather to evaluate me —my weaknesses, motives, intentions, strengths, and so on, and I ask him to reveal to me all the areas of my life that need to be worked on. I ask him to help me improve where I need improvement, and above all, I ask him to give me the power to walk humbly on this Sacred Path.

King David, that ancient king of the Old Testament, prayed a prayer that I have tried to incorporate into my conversations with our Creator. He told God, "Search me and know my heart, try me and know my thoughts, and lead me in the path of Right Living." (My paraphrase). That is a prayer we should pray to our Creator regularly, because it will help insure that we remain Hollow Bones through which our Creator's plans can be accomplished.

As I said earlier, there are an unlimited number of ways to use our Private World, and as you go there on a regular basis, our Creator will reveal more and more of what's available in your Private World that can be used to help strengthen the Sacred Circle Of Life.

Teaching Session – 12
PREPARE YOURSELF FOR WHAT'S COMING

I have had many conversations with grandfather Old Bear concerning the Time of Great Cleansing that is fast approaching. I didn't like what he told me, and I don't like passing on to you what he said—however, I feel compelled to do so. Most of this teaching session will be a summary of what the Old One has told me concerning the Great Cleansing of Mother Earth, and how people should prepare themselves for what is about to happen.

NEITHER GRANDFATHER OLD BEAR NOR I CLAIM TO BE A PROPHET

No one knows the future. No one knows exactly when this Age will end and the next one will begin. Jesus Christ told his followers that not even he knew when the end would come, only his Father in heaven knows that time (see Matthew 24:36 in the New Testament).

However, our Creator has given us "signs" to let us know that this Age is winding down and the next one will soon begin. He has given all of us the ability to recognize those signs if our spiritual eyes are open to what he is showing us and our spiritual ears are listening to what he is telling us. Unfortunately, many people are roaring down the fast lane of life and spending their time chasing what the Madison Avenue Marketing Gurus have convinced them is the "good life". As a result, they are oblivious to what our Creator is trying to show them and say to them about the coming devastation they are about to run head on into—and you don't have to be a prophet to see that occurring.

Will such people wake up in time to change the way they are living before it is too late? I don't know. I hope so. However, grandfather Old Bear doubts that they will.

Talking about such people, he said, *"Man made electricity has caused them to go blind and deaf, and it has almost completely destroyed their connection with the Spiritual Realm."*

WHY THE TIME OF GREAT CLEANSING MUST COME

According to grandfather Old Bear, there have been other Ages before this one, and I'm not referring to Geological Ages. Our Creator's Sacred Family of Life has gone through several previous Ages or Cycles of Life.

The Old One said, *"In the First Age, the two-leggeds could communicate directly with our Creator and with the rest of his Sacred Creation. In the Second Age, giants of all kinds walked the earth, and some of those giants were two-leggeds. A great flood that covered our entire Mother ended the Third Age. And now, this Fourth Age is about to come to a close.*

"Each Age came to an end because the two-leggeds living in that time eventually became addicted to their own self-centered greed. Their lust for more and more material possessions drove them mad. In every Age, the two-leggeds' greed has eventually caused them to try to take by force all Mother Earth has. She patiently puts up with her spoiled children's selfishness as long as she can, but eventually she has to destroy most of them in order to prevent her own death."

THERE HAVE BEEN PROPHETS OF "DOOM" THROUGHOUT RECORDED HISTORY

Throughout history, people have been claiming the world is about to come to an end. Some of these so-called prophets even predicted the actual day the end would come.

As I stated above, no one knows when this Age will end and the next one will begin, and we should be wary of people who emphatically claim they know exactly when and how this Age will end. However, as previously stated, there are specific signs that serve as warnings that this Age is drawing to a close, and we should all pay close attention to what those signs are saying to us.

THE "SIGNS" THAT THE END IS NEAR

This is the first time in recorded history that all the major religions of the world agree that we are nearing the end of this Age. Even the spiritual leaders within our old indigenous religions agree that the end is near.

In the twenty fourth chapter of the New Testament's book of Matthew, Jesus Christ was asked what the signs would be of the coming end of this Age and he said that the signs would be like the "birth pangs" of a woman in labor. As the end gets closer and closer, the signs would be more frequent and more severe. He said that as the end draws ever nearer, the frequency and severity of earthquakes, famines and war will increase and if those days were not shortened, no one would be left alive, but our Creator will shorten those days of destruction so that all life will not be destroyed.

These signs are general signs in that throughout history there have always been earthquakes, famine and war. However, what makes these things a "sign" is their ever-increasing severity and frequency, like the birth pangs of a woman in labor.

These birth pangs become more frequent and more severe the closer the time comes for the baby to be born. Jesus was saying that as earthquakes, famine and war become more frequent and more severe, they will serve as a sign that the end of the Age is near, and the nearer we come to the end, the more frequent and more severe these signs will become. However, he stated that only our Creator knows the exact time when the end of the Age will occur.

THE "END" IS COMING FOR ALL OF US

Even though none of us know when the end of this Age will occur, we all know that someday we will all die, and that will mark the end of our physical lives. Therefore, we should all make sure we are living our lives here in the physical realm in a way pleasing to our Creator. In the previous teaching session we shared with you the simple steps for knowing the Life Plan our Creator has for each of us. We should make knowing and following the Life Plan Grandfather has for each of us the top priority in our lives.

It would be a sad thing to die and then discover we had not known and followed the plan our Creator had for our lives here in the physical realm. With that in mind, I encourage you to follow the simple steps for knowing our Creator's Life Plan for each of us.

SAFE HAVENS ARE BEING SET UP AROUND THE WORLD

We don't know when or how this Age will end. However, we do know our Creator is in the process of creating SAFE HAVENS around the world in preparation for the end of this Age. On numerous occasions, grandfather Old Bear has told me that these Safe Havens are being set up in remote areas around the world as places where people will return to the principles of living according to *The Way of the Medicine Wheel*. He has said that those currently setting up Safe Havens will be gifted the Sacred Ceremonies once practiced by the Ancient Ones who used to live in those respective areas.

The Safe Havens are places where people can go to learn how to escape the stranglehold the materialistic system has on their lives and begin implementing the principles of this Sacred Path. Within each Safe Haven, people will once again learn how to live in peace, harmony and balance within our Creator's Sacred Family of Life. The ancient Sacred Ceremonies that were gifted to the indigenous peoples of that area will once again be learned and implemented as a means of helping people create a lifestyle that merges the physical and Spiritual Realms together into a single reality.

300

These Safe Havens will help prepare people for the coming Time of Great Cleansing that has already begun in some areas of the Earth. People will learn to live a life of simplicity the way the Ancient Ones lived and thus help prepare themselves for the great devastation that is soon to come upon all people living on Mother Earth.

Will all people living in Safe Havens survive the Time of Great Cleansing? Probably not. However, few—if any—will survive outside the Safe Havens. Most of those who do survive will make the transition into the Dawn of the Next Age.

WHAT ABOUT THE IDEA THAT THERE WILL BE A "GREAT SPIRITUAL AWAKENING?"

There are those who believe (and teach) that we are on the verge of a great spiritual awakening, and mankind will evolve into an age of spiritual enlightenment that will lead to utopia. The idea is that man will become better and better until he "breaks through the barriers" and becomes an Enlightened Being.

When I asked grandfather Old Bear about that his only comment was, *"That's wishful thinking."*

GRANDFATHER OLD BEAR'S PREDICTIONS OF THINGS TO COME

Every time grandfather Old Bear discussed with me the Time Of Great Cleansing coming on Mother Earth, he reminded me that he does not know the future and only our Creator knows when and how this Age will end. However, he has told me things that he feels strongly about concerning the events leading up to the end of this Age, and I will pass them on to you as he shared them with me.

"Our Creator, working in concert with Mother Earth,
Will produce the Time of Great Cleansing."

Grandfather Old Bear told me that our Creator and Mother Earth are working hand-in-hand to produce the Time of Great Cleansing. Our Creator will use the Time of Great Cleansing to discipline his two-legged children for their rebellion against his Sacred Laws of Right Living. On the other hand, Mother Earth will use the Time of Great Cleansing to discipline her two-legged children for their rape and pillage of her Sacred Body.

"The Cities will become giant death traps
that devour their inhabitants."

According to the Old One, our Creator never intended for his two-legged children to congregate in cities, because it is impossible to walk this Sacred Path in a city. He said, "The Forces of Evil enticed the two-leggeds to build cities because they knew city living *would destroy people's connection with our Creator and Mother Earth."* He went on to say, *"Cities are the work of man's hands. Nature is the work of our Creator's hands. Cities are monuments to man's self-centered egos and reflections of his evil desires. Nature is a monument to our Creator's holiness and a reflection of his Unconditional Love. So tell me grandson, which place would you rather live? On the polluted ground in the city, or on the Sacred Ground in Nature?"*

Grandfather Old Bear contends that because the two-leggeds disobeyed our Creator by building cities, thus turning their backs on his Sacred Land, at the close of this Age the cities will become giant death traps that devour their inhabitants. The two-leggeds are drawn to the cities because they believe the "good life" awaits them there, but at the close of this Age, too late they will discover the cities are their burial grounds.

"The two-leggeds greatest addiction is to electricity.
At the close of this Age our Creator will
Take man made electricity away from the two-leggeds,

Which will mark the beginning of the end
Of this Age as you know it."

In previous teaching sessions, I have shared with you grandfather Old Bear's feelings concerning the evils of man-made electricity and how, more than anything else, electricity has been responsible for the two-leggeds spiritual death.

The Old One has told me over and over that at the end of this Age our Creator will take man-made electricity away from the two-leggeds. When that occurs, the cities will become "hell on earth", and graveyards for the materialistic societies of the world.

When and how will that occur? If grandfather Old Bear knows, he hasn't told me. However, the question isn't when and how will that occur, it's what are you doing to prepare yourself for what's coming? If you do nothing to prepare yourself for the destruction looming on the horizon, in all probability you won't be one of the survivors. The choice is yours to make. However, I urge you to spend time with our Creator in your Private World, seeking his guidance concerning how you should prepare for the coming devastation soon to change the world as we know it.

"The two-leggeds who survive the Time of Great Cleansing
Will enter the next Age with only the clothes
On their backs, the seeds in their pockets
And the Sacred Ceremonies in
Their heads."

The governments of many countries around the world have built huge underground facilities and stocked them with large quantities of food and water, thinking that these giant underground bunkers will be the equivalent of their own safe havens in case of severe national emergencies.

These underground facilities have their own self-contained electrical power sources, and all of the world's scientific knowledge is stored on hard drives there so that life can go on as usual after the disaster is over.

When I asked grandfather Old Bear if people chosen to live in those cities would be able to survive the Time of Great Cleansing, he laughed and replied, *"Our Creator and Mother Earth have planned the Time of Great Cleansing to deal with just that sort of human arrogance. During the Time of Great Cleansing, the two-leggeds will be taught that no amount of human technology can withstand the powerful forces of nature that will be unleashed against humanity. The two-leggeds will also discover that they are their own worse enemy, because they will destroy more of their own people than are destroyed by the forces our Sacred Mother turns lose on them."*

The Time of Great Cleansing will cleanse Mother Earth of all human technology. It will wipe the world's great cities off the face of the Earth. It will reshape and remold Mother Earth's skin, making the Earth's surface clean and new again. It will make the Earth warm where it has been cold, and cold where it has been warm. It will create—as the Bible predicts—"a new heaven and a new earth". In describing this Time of Great Cleansing, the Bible says that even some of the stars will fall from the sky.

According to grandfather Old Bear, each time a previous Age came to an end, similar things happened. Mother Earth not only destroyed the civilizations that existed during those Ages; she made herself new again so that our Creator's Sacred Family of Life could truly have a new start in a New World. And the same thing will happen during this Time of Great Cleansing.

The Old One told me, *"The two-leggeds who survive The Time of Great Cleansing will enter the next Age with only the clothes on their backs, the seeds in their pockets, and the Sacred Ceremonies in their heads."*

At the dawn of the next Age, the surviving two-leggeds will walk out into a New World. In that world, all traces of the mistakes made by the two-leggeds during the previous Age will have been buried. Because of his undying love for his Sacred Family of Life, once more our Creator will give his two-leggeds another chance to start over in a perfect world free of man-made contamination. In that new world, the two leggeds will once again live in peace, harmony and balance with all of the Sacred Family of

Life until their egos once again destroy the perfection that will exist in that future time.

OUR SECURITY IS IN CREATOR'S UNLIMITED POWER OF PROTECTION

Every time grandfather Old Bear talks to me about the coming Time of Great Cleansing, he always ends by reminding me that no matter how bad things get in the future, our Creator's power of protection is greater than any power of destruction that can be unleashed against us. Therefore, we should not spend our time worrying about what is coming in the future, but should be putting our trust and faith in our Creator's unlimited power to protect us if we are following the Life Plan he has chosen for our lives.

Keep in mind that our Creator has a plan for your life, and that plan includes how to take care of you during The Time of Great Cleansing. Seek our Creator's plan for your life with your whole heart. Commit your whole being to following that plan as he reveals it to you. The greatest security in the world is knowing that you are following the Life Plan our Creator has for you.

BEGIN PREPARING YOURSELF NOW FOR WHAT'S COMING

Today's societies the world over are constantly being warned of the probability of cataclysmic disasters that loom on the horizon of time. We are told that global warming could cause the destruction of our modern way of life. We are warned that huge volcanic eruptions could throw the world into another ice age. We are constantly reminded that huge earthquakes could create gigantic tidal waves capable of destroying all life for miles inland along our coastlines. We are told that new diseases could wipe out huge segments of the world's population. And, if all of that were not enough to get our attention, we are informed that there are countless asteroids out in space that may be on a collision course with the earth. If one of the larger ones hit our planet it, would end all life on Mother Earth. However, even with all of the warnings of possible cataclysmic disaster that comes regularly from both the scientific and religious communities, most people still refuse to change the way they live, or prepare themselves to deal with the possible destruction of their way of life.

When I ask people what they are doing to prepare themselves for the coming Earth Changes, most shrug and say that it's all out of their control, so they don't feel there is anything that can be done to prepare for it. Even when people are confronted with the possibilities that the cities probably won't be a safe place to be when these disasters strike, most refuse to consider moving out of them. It seems most people truly are trapped in the death grip of THE SYSTEM. However, it doesn't have to be that way.

It isn't our Creator's plan for you to perish during The Time of Great Cleansing. Those who perish will do so because they didn't heed the warnings and follow the Life Plan our Creator has for them. Therefore, I challenge you to WAKE UP! Listen to what our Creator is whispering to your spirit. Obey what he tells you to do. Follow the Life Plan he has for you, even though it will mean drastically altering your current lifestyle. Put your faith in our Creator to meet your needs as you follow his plan for your life, and stop trusting in the feel good world's money system to take care of you.

If you have concluded that it is impossible to break away from the control the money system has over your life, then you probably won't survive the Time of Great Cleansing. On the other hand, if you are willing to truly put your faith in our Creator and obey all he tells you to do to prepare yourself for what's coming, then you may be one of those who will be present at the dawning of the next Age. The choice is yours to make, and it truly may be a life or death decision.

At this point I want to remind you again that you should always ask our Creator if what you read on these pages are true or not. ALWAYS FOLLOW WHAT OUR CREATOR TELLS YOU TO DO AND NEVER BLINDLY FOLLOW THE RECOMMENDATIONS OF TWO-LEGGEDS. I don't know where you should live and what you should do

—but our Creator knows. Ask him and he will tell you what you should do. Go to your Private World and spend time discussing with our Creator his plans for your life. He not only knows what those plans are; he is eagerly waiting to discuss them with you.

One thing you can be sure of, though. Our Creator's plans for your life will involve big changes in your current lifestyle. Our Creator planned for his two-legged children to live a life of simplicity, not a life of greed and materialistic gluttony. Our Creator planned for us to live in peace, harmony and balance with all of our relatives within the Sacred Circle of Life, and not to try to use all other life forms to satisfy our own selfish desires and interests.

Our Creator wants us to obey his Sacred Laws for Right Living; not disregard those laws so we can satisfy the lusts of the flesh. Our Creator wants us to submit our will to his will and plan for our lives. Then—and only then—will we learn to live in peace, harmony and balance with his Sacred Family of Life, and become prepared to face all that lies ahead as the world is plunged into The Time of Great Cleansing.

BOOK FOUR:
The Four Lifestyle Ceremonies of the Medicine Wheel

INTRODUCTION TO BOOK FOUR

On this Sacred Path, most activities associated with daily life are performed ceremonially. In fact, life is lived as one continuous ceremony. For example, modern man considers sunrise and sunsets as nothing more than mundane, routine times of day. However, they are powerful, sacred events with great spiritual meaning for those walking *The Way of the Medicine Wheel*.

This book will explain a few of the major activities and ceremonies as they are performed during the Four Lifestyle Ceremonies that make up the annual Cycle of Life for those following this Sacred Path. However, space limitations will not permit a detailed description of all ceremonies performed during the course of the annual Cycle of Sacred Seasons.

The Four Lifestyle Ceremonies correspond with the Four Sacred Seasons, and they keep us focused on living in peace, harmony and balance with our Creator and his Sacred Family of Life.

The Sacred Campfire lights our way as we travel along this Sacred Path. It symbolizes our Creator's power and presence among us. On this Sacred Path, life revolves around the Campfire. This has powerful symbolic meaning because our lives also revolve around our Creator and his Life Plan for simplistic daily living. As you study the following pages of this book, you will discover that the Sacred Campfire plays a very important role in all aspects of Life as we travel this Sacred Path.

The Way of the Medicine Wheel creates a lifestyle of simplicity and the Campfire is a symbol of simplistic living. I want to emphasize again that this Sacred Path is NOT a religion—it is a lifestyle. There is a great deal of difference between *The Way of the Medicine Wheel* and religion.

All religions are man made. Religion consists of organized activities that are repeated over and over until they become religious "traditions".

Religions revolve around man made organizations. Religions own real estate. Religions have members. Religions collect money from their followers. Religions have what they call sacred writings and religious dogma.

On the other hand, this Spiritual Path has no organization. It doesn't own real estate. It doesn't have members, and it doesn't collect money from people. There are no sacred writings associated with this Sacred Path, and there are no religious leaders for you to follow. However, this Spiritual Path does contain Four Lifestyle Ceremonies that, when properly performed, help us live in peace, harmony and balance with our Creator and his Sacred Family of Life.

Far back in antiquity, our Creator laid out this Sacred Path to help us avoid the pitfalls waiting to ensnare us as we travel through the thick jungles and deadly marshes of self-centeredness. *The Way of the Medicine Wheel* leads us away from self-centeredness, and back to our Creator, the Spiritual Father of all Life.

This Sacred Journey takes an entire lifetime. When we arrive back at our Creator's home in the Holy Mountain that reaches up to the sky; in that place in the far North were the world ends, we will shed our self-centered nature once again, cross over into the Spiritual Realm, and live in Perfect Union with him.

In the meantime, the Four Lifestyle Ceremonies described in this book will help keep us focused on this Sacred Path where, step by step, we will learn what it means to live in peace, harmony and balance with our Creator's Sacred Circle of Life.

Teaching Session – 13
THE LIFESTYLE CEREMONY OF NEW BEGINNINGS
(SPRING)

The Lifestyle Ceremony of New Beginnings starts with the arrival of the Spring Equinox and continues until the Summer Solstice. It begins in the East on the medicine wheel and continues around clockwise to the South. The Eagle is the totem of the Lifestyle Ceremony of New Beginnings. Yellow is its sacred color; Spring is its Sacred Season; and Courage is its Spiritual Medicine.

The Lifestyle Ceremony of New Beginnings is the way we live during all of the Sacred Season the modern two-leggeds call Spring. Spring is the time of New Beginnings in Nature. The trees develop new leaves, the dry, brown grass turns green, and new flowers appear all across the countryside. New babies are born to the four leggeds and winged people, and the new cycle of life and activity begins for many of our relatives within the kingdom of insects.

In Book One we explained that there are two kinds of ceremonies on this Sacred Path—lifestyle ceremonies and event ceremonies, and all of life is lived as one continuous spiritual ceremony. Lifestyle ceremonies are the way we live season after season. During each lifestyle ceremony, or season, we perform many event ceremonies. Event ceremonies focus on one specific aspect of the lifestyle ceremony and are of short duration, lasting from a few minutes to a day or longer.

THE PURPOSE OF THE SACRED SEASONS

The Seasons are Sacred Gifts from our Creator. They are our teachers, revealing to us the Great Mysteries contained within the Sacred

Cycle of Life. Just as there are Four Sacred Directions, there are Four Sacred Seasons.

The Seasons receive their power from the Directions, and the Directions receive their power from our Creator. As was explained earlier, our Creator is Omni-Present. That means he is everywhere. If you go to the East, he is there. If you go to the West, he is there. He is everywhere all the time, and the Four Sacred Directions symbolize certain aspects of his nature and power.

The East symbolizes Grandfather's creative nature. It represents his ability to bring forth New Life and give us new insights, revelations, enlightenment and awareness. That is why we say that all new things come from the East, and that is why Spring is designated as the Sacred Season of the East.

The Sacred Seasons are visual expressions of our Creator's Sacred Power in action. For example, Spring is the visual aid that reveals to us our Creator's power to create New Life. As we mentioned earlier, Spring is the time of New Beginnings, a time of birth and New Life. Those walking this Sacred Path recognize that during the Sacred Season of Spring, life is to be lived as a celebration of new beginnings. During Spring, our daily activities create a Lifestyle of New Beginnings, and all of the activities contained within that lifestyle are performed as one continuous sacred ceremony.

The Sacred Seasons are truly one of our most important Spiritual Teachers. They teach us about our Creator's power, provision, and personal attributes. They reveal to us the various aspects of his nature and show us how to live in peace, harmony and balance with our Creator and all of our Relatives within his Sacred Circle of Life.

SPRING: THE LIFESTYLE CEREMONY OF NEW BEGINNINGS

During the Sacred Season of Spring, starting with the Spring Equinox and continuing until the Summer Solstice, our daily activities create a lifestyle of new beginnings. This is the season for preparing the Sacred

Ground for planting and then planting our seeds. During the Spring, the seeds that lay dormant during the winter bring forth new green life. This is the time for starting new projects. This is the time for building new dwellings. In fact, everything we do during this Sacred Season should focus on new beginnings.

Keep in mind that our goal is to live in peace, harmony and balance with our Creator and his Sacred Circle of Life. Therefore, since the rest of our relatives within the Sacred Circle are focusing on new beginnings during the Spring Season, then we should also. This is one of the important keys to living in peace, harmony, and balance with all of Creation.

MEETING WITH GRANDFATHER OLD BEAR

Grandfather Old Bear always gets very excited when he talks about the Lifestyle Ceremonies and their corresponding Sacred Seasons. It seems that sunset is his favorite time of day to begin discussing them, and these sessions usually go far into the night.

As the sun was going down behind the jagged mountains on the western horizon, grandfather Old Bear started building a little fire in his lodge. When he decided it was burning just right, he motioned for me to join him on the tattered old buffalo robe that was spread out on the ground behind the little fire pit.

"Grandson, it's time I started teaching you about the Cycle of Sacred Seasons," he began, "because they are very important teachers on this Sacred Path. The first thing you must learn about the Seasons is that each one contains its own Sacred Power. Each Sacred Season gets it power from a Sacred Direction, which, in turn, received its power from our Creator."

I knew I was in for a long night with the Old One when I saw him place several small, round stones in the fire to be used later to heat water for tea. "You must understand, grandson, that the Sacred Seasons are actually visual aids that demonstrate certain aspects of our Creator's nature, character and power. I could tell you that Grandfather has the power to Create, but the Sacred Season of Spring shows us that he does."

He gave me that questioning look that told me he wanted to know if I understood what he was saying, and I nodded to let him know that I was not only listening intently, I also understood.

"Good!" he exclaimed. "Because that is the first step in understanding the importance of the Cycle of Sacred Seasons—our Creator reveals his power and nature to us through them."

As he poured me a cup of mild mint tea, he continued. "The Lifestyle Ceremony of New Beginnings—Spring—is the time of birth and new life. Therefore, we know it is controlled by female power. That is why during the Spring, so many of our ceremonies are led or performed by our women. Women bring forth New Life. Spring brings forth New Life. That is how we know the Lifestyle Ceremony of New Beginnings that we live during the Sacred Spring Season is controlled by female power, and that is why our women have the highest place of honor throughout that time of year.

"You see, grandson, on this Sacred Path there is a time when women are in charge, and there is also a time when men are in charge. During the Lifestyle Ceremony of New Beginnings, and again in the Fall during the Lifestyle Ceremony of Reaping The Harvest, women are in charge of most of the Sacred Ceremonies, and therefore they hold the place of highest honor in the village during those Seasons.

"On the other hand, during the Lifestyle Ceremony of Growth and Development that corresponds with the Sacred Season of Summer, and again, during the Lifestyle Ceremony of Rest and Renewal during the Winter, men are in charge of most of the Sacred Ceremonies. They hold the place of highest honor during those times."

He smiled and got that mischievous gleam in his eyes as he continued. "So on the medicine wheel the Sacred Path of Constant Change is the path of female power and the Sacred Path of unbending Tradition is the path of male power." His smile expanded into a quiet chuckle. "So it's no wonder women are constantly changing their minds, *grandson. Their power moves along the Sacred Path of Constant Change. Likewise, we men have a right to be hard headed because our power moves along the Sacred Path of Unbending Tradition."*

Then the Old One's expression suddenly became very serious. "When the two-leggeds stopped walking this Sacred Path they lost their understanding concerning the Sacred Roles men and women are to play in life. That is why there is so much competition between women and men in your modern world. Each feels a need to be in charge of something, but they don't understand what our Creator has put them in charge of, so they compete for power over one another."

Grandfather Old Bear's mood became even more somber, and he seemed to be talking more to himself than to me, as he muttered almost under his breath. "When people walked away from this Sacred Path, they lost far more than the Sacred Knowledge associated with the medicine wheel—they forgot how they are to live!"

He looked up at me with eyes full of sadness. "Grandson, I feel sorry for people in your world. Most of them think the Old Ways are no longer relevant in their modern, fast paced lifestyles with so many electrical gadgets and electronic marvels at their finger tips. However, your people will never find peace and personal fulfillment by chasing after technology. True peace and fulfillment in life comes only by following the Principles of Living given to the Ancient Ones by our Creator far back in time. Those Principles of Living apply to all two leggeds in all ages regardless of how technologically advanced they think they become.

"The Lifestyle Ceremonies are just as relevant and just as necessary today as when they were first given to us, grandson. Spring is still the Sacred Season that honors female power to bring forth Life, and most of the Sacred Ceremonies contained within the Lifestyle Ceremony of New Beginnings still need to be performed or led by our women.

"You see, the Lifestyle Ceremonies, and the Event Ceremonies contained within them, not only kept the two-leggeds living in peace, harmony and balance with all of our Creator's Sacred Circle of Life, those

317

ceremonies also helped maintain harmony and balance among the Sacred Seasons.

"The Sacred Water Ceremony performed each Season by the women helped insure that there would be enough rain during Spring, Summer and Fall and enough snow during the Winter to keep the rivers and lakes full for the water people, and that there would be enough moisture for the green people to grow.

"The Sacred Seed Ceremony helped insure the seeds would remain strong and healthy during the long, cold Winter. The Sacred Planting Ceremony assisted Mother Earth in her effort to push the Cold Winds of Winter back into the far North. It also helped the weather to be warm and the rains to come at the right time so the seeds could give birth to green plants during the Spring.

"The Fertility Ceremony helped insure the days would be long and hot during the Summer, so the plants would grow, pollinate and produce their fruits for food—and so it went on and on, grandson.

"The Sacred Ceremonies helped keep harmony and balance between the Sacred Seasons. We knew that when the Sacred Seasons operated in harmony and balance, that ultimately produced harmony and balance within all of the Sacred Circle of Life. Therefore, we faithfully performed these very important Sacred Ceremonies because we understood that to fail to do so weakened the balance in Nature, and if the balance in Nature was weakened, our very existence was also weakened and might even come to an end."

The Old One poured himself another cup of mint tea, and sat quietly staring into the little fire for a long time. Finally, he looked up at me and said, "All over the world, most of the Ancient Sacred Ceremonies have been discarded by those who once practiced the Old Ways. They stopped because they decided they would rather heat their tea in a microwave oven than heat it the ancient sacred way."

Then, his piercing eyes looked deep into the very center of my being. "Grandson, these Sacred Lifestyle Ceremonies are crying out to people to come back to them while there is still time. The Sacred Campfire pleads with people to come and sit around it once again and rediscover the joys of simplistic living."

He paused for a moment as if gathering his thoughts. "I beg you, grandson, faithfully obey all our Creator tells you to do as you walk this Sacred Path."

Cold Chills ran up and down my spine as this Ancient One's words echoed in my ears. Finally I whispered, "I'll do my best, grandfather. I promise I'll do my best."

He shook his head and said, "Your best won't be good enough. You can't do this on your own power. You must ask our Creator to help you, and let him guide your step along this Sacred Path. That's the trouble with most people in your world, grandson, who try to follow a Spiritual Path. They spend too much time trying to do things for our Creator, then start thinking they deserve the credit. But if you get your ego out of the way and let our Creator do things through you, then he gets all of the credit."

The Old One leaned over close to me and said, "Grandson, never forget what I'm about to tell you—**you have no power to make the Sacred Ceremonies work. The power to make a Sacred Ceremony work comes only from our Creator, and never from a two-legged.** You must always focus on that as you and the people perform the Sacred Ceremonies associated with The Way of the Medicine Wheel."

Over the years, grandfather Old Bear has spent lots of time with me talking about the Sacred Seasons and their corresponding Lifestyle Ceremonies, and the remainder of this fourth book will contain a small portion of what he has told me concerning them.

THE SACRED FIRE CEREMONY

The Sacred Fire Ceremony is one of the most important ceremonies on this Sacred Path. There are several reasons why this is so. First, The Sacred Fire Ceremony forms the bridge that connects one Lifestyle Ceremony, and the Sacred Season it represents, to the next, thus keeping in tact the constant flow of peace, harmony and balance that exists within the people and the Sacred Seasons. Second, and most important, the Sacred Fire Ceremony symbolizes and acknowledges our Creator's presence throughout the duration of the Sacred Seasons and the corresponding Lifestyle Ceremonies. Third, the ceremony serves as a reminder that it is our Creator's power, and not the two-leggeds power, that moves within all Sacred Ceremonies and makes them work. And finally, the Sacred Fire Ceremony serves to remind the two-leggeds of our Creator's love for them and his willingness to meet their needs and solve their problems.

The Sacred Fire Ceremony is performed four times a year. It begins the afternoon of the last day of each Sacred Season, and concludes around noon the following day, which is the first day of the next Sacred Season. It is both the first and last Sacred Ceremony to be performed during each Lifestyle Ceremony.

As stated above, the Sacred Fire Ceremony helps keep peace, harmony, and balance flowing within the people and the Sacred Seasons from one Lifestyle Ceremony to the next.

How The Ceremony Begins

When the Sun is at its highest point in the sky on the last day of a Sacred Season and its corresponding Lifestyle Ceremony, the people gather at the Purification Lodge and participate in a Purification Ceremony (as described in Book One). However, the wood from all the Campfire Sites will be used to heat the Sacred Stones.

The people will take the wood from the Campfire Sites with them as they make their way to the Purification Lodge. Additional wood will be used as needed.

The Ceremony begins with the ceremony leader loading the Sacred

Medicine Pipe or Cornhusk Pipe. The Pipe will not be smoked until the end of the next Purification Ceremony, which will occur the next morning. During this Purification Ceremony, the entire First Round is conducted in a cold, dark Lodge without the presence of Sacred Grandfather Stones.

The Ceremony leader begins the First Round by singing the Sacred Fire Song, and then reviews with the people the purpose and importance of the Sacred Fire Ceremony. Next, he reminds people that the dark, cold lodge symbolizes our lives without the presence of our Creator, and he asks for one or two volunteers to share experiences in their lives during this past Sacred Season that helps illustrate that point.

When the people are finished sharing hardships they encountered when they failed to follow our Creator's Life Plan for them, or they tried to accomplish things without relying on his help and guidance, the Ceremony leader begins telling the Sacred Fire Story. He continues with the story until he gets to the part where our Creator calls the clouds to come to the meeting and is ready to give them the Gift of Sacred Lightning.

At that point, he calls for the lodge door to be opened and the round ends. The Fire Keeper brings in the heated Stones; the door is closed and the Second round is started. The Ceremony leader draws attention to the difference in the atmosphere within the lodge with the presence of the Sacred Stones and how that symbolizes the difference in us when our Creator is present in our lives. He resumes telling the Sacred Fire Story at the point where our Creator gifted Sacred Lightning to the clouds.

At the end of the story, the lodge door is opened the second time. During the Third Round, the Ceremony leader has people offer prayers of thanks for all our Creator did for them during the past Sacred Season that is now ending. At the end of the prayers, the Thank You song is sung and the lodge door is opened.

The Fourth and last round consists of prayers of thanks for our Creator gifting the two-leggeds Sacred Fire, and reaffirming the people's commitment to always obey him as they walk this Sacred Path. At the end of the round, the Ceremony leader gives instructions for the removal of the ashes in the communal Camp Fire and personal Camp Fire pits. Then he asks the Head Woman to close the Purification Ceremony with prayer. At that point, she takes over the responsibilities for the remainder of the Sacred Fire Ceremony.

Selecting A Keeper of the Sacred Fire

Once the people are outside the Purification lodge, the Head Woman appoints a woman to be in charge of keeping the Sacred Fire going in the Purification Lodge's Fire Pit throughout the remainder of the Sacred Fire Ceremony, which will conclude the following day around mid-day. This is a very important job, and women consider it a great honor to be chosen for the position. During the remainder of the Sacred Fire Ceremony, this woman will be known as The Keeper of the Sacred Fire, and she will stay at the Fire Pit and keep the fire burning until the Sacred Fire Ceremony ends the following day.

The woman chosen as The Keeper of the Sacred Fire will carry that title throughout the entire next Sacred Season and corresponding Lifestyle Ceremony. As she tends the Sacred Fire during the Sacred Fire Ceremony, she will pray for the women who are removing the ashes from the Sacred Campfire sites and for the men gathering new fire wood for those Sacred Sites. She will not eat or drink as she tends the Sacred Fire, nor will she sleep. She will spend her time praying for the welfare of the people during the coming Sacred Season.

During the next Sacred Season, the Keeper of the Sacred fire will insure that all Sacred Campfire Sites, including Campfire Sites at private dwellings, are well kept and properly maintained. If she observes a messy Campfire Site at a private dwelling, she will go to the woman in charge of that Campfire Site and remind her of the need to keep the Campfire Site very clean and orderly. She will assist the Head Woman in the selection process of any girls that may be chosen during the next Sacred Season to help care for and maintain the communal Sacred Campfire Site.

For this ritual, the following items are needed and must be available at the Purification Lodge Fire Pit area.

- For each woman, a strip of colored cotton cloth (the color of the Sacred Season currently ending). The piece of colored cloth must be big enough to be worn as a belt around the waist.
- For each woman, a strip of colored cotton cloth (the color of the Sacred Season that will begin the following day). This piece of colored cloth must be big enough to be worn as a headband.
- For each man, two strips of colored cotton cloth (the color of the Sacred season that is ending). These pieces of colored cloth must be big enough to be worn on each wrist as a wristband.
- For each man, a strip of colored cloth (the color of the Sacred Season that will begin the following day). This piece of colored cotton cloth must be big enough to be worn as a headband.
- Sage and Cedar, and a seashell for smudging.
- Tobacco and cornmeal.
- All items used to clean the Campfire Site, such as buckets, shovels, broom, etc.
- All items used to cut and gather fire wood, such as axes, saws, etc.
- Enough water in a container for all the people to have a drink of water.
- A wooden cup or bowl for people to drink out of.

The Head Woman will smudge all of the items listed above, even the container of

Drinking water. Each woman will tie the appropriate color of cotton cloth around her waste as a belt and around her head as a headband, and the men will tie the appropriate strips of cotton cloth around their wrists and heads. These pieces of cotton cloth will be worn until the Purification Ceremony the next day.

Facing the direction representing the Sacred Season that is coming to an end, the Head Woman will offer a prayer of thanks to our Creator for all he did for them during the Sacred Season that is ending. Next, she will face the direction representing the Sacred Season that is about to begin, and ask our Creator to come into the camp, and into each person present, and help them accomplish his Life Plan for them each day. She will then kneel down to the Earth and thank Mother Earth for her provisions during the Sacred Season that is ending, and ask for her continued provision during the coming Sacred Season.

The Head Woman will then dip the wooden cup or bowl into the water and hold it up to the West and thank our Creator for sending the gift of Sacred Rain when he gave the two leggeds the gift of Sacred Fire. She will then offer the Sacred Water up to each Sacred Direction and ask our Creator to always send the Sacred Rain as it is needed. Then, starting with the oldest person in the group, she will give each person a drink of water. This will be the last water that the people drink until the feast on the following day. The Head Woman will then pour any remaining water on the ground, and as she does, she will thank our Creator for sending the Sacred Rain to water all the earth.

The Head Woman will then distribute the tools for cleaning the communal Campfire Site to the women, and they will make their way there. The Head Man will distribute the tools for wood cutting to the men, and they will proceed to the area where wood will be gathered for the first communal Campfire Site, and then for each family's personal Campfire Site.

The Ritual For Cleaning The Communal Campfire Site

The following items will be needed to conduct this ritual at the communal Campfire Site.
- The items for cleaning the Campfire Site.
- Tobacco and cornmeal.
- Sage and Cedar for smudging the area.

When the women reach the communal Campfire Site, the Head Woman will mark the perimeter of the site with a circle of cornmeal, and then smudge the entire area with sage.

Starting with the Head Woman, then in descending order of age, each woman will offer a prayer of thanks to our Creator for the gift of Sacred Fire and for always living among them and guiding them in all their activities each day.

When the prayers are completed, the Head Woman will sprinkle tobacco over the ashes in the Campfire Site. She will thank our Creator for the Sacred Fire's provision of light during the dark nights, and for the warmth it provides during cold days and nights. She will also give thanks for its ability to cook their food, and for the wonderful times the people have enjoyed together. The Sacred Campfire remains the center of the group's life and activities.

This is a very sacred ceremony and, therefore, it is important that there aren't any negative attitudes or degrading talk during this ritual. This is a time of joy, happiness, and thanksgiving for our Creator giving us the gift of Sacred Fire, so all attitudes and conversations should be happy and uplifting.

The women will first clean all of the Ashes out of the Fire Pit and take them to the place that has been set aside for the Ashes from all the Campfire Sites. These Ashes are considered sacred because they symbolize our Creator's provision during the past Sacred Season and Lifestyle Ceremony. They represent the way our Creator has kept us warm when the cold winds blew, provided light into the dark places, and provided Sacred Fire to cook our food. They are handled with great respect as they are removed from the Campfire Site and taken to the place designated for the Ashes.

The women clean the Campfire Site and surrounding area thoroughly, removing the ashes and any other debris that may be in the area. They also make sure all cooking utensils are clean and properly stored.

When the Head Woman determines that the Sacred Campfire Site has been properly cleaned, she offers tobacco to the Four Sacred Directions and sprinkles a generous amount in and around the Fire Pit area and then, once again smudges the area, this time with Cedar smoke.

Once this is accomplished, each woman returns to her home and follows the same procedures stated above as she cleans her own Campfire Site.

Ritual For Gathering The Campfire Wood

The men go to the site that has previously been chosen by the Head Man for gathering Sacred Campfire wood. This wood is very special, in that it will be used to start the first Sacred Campfires of the new Sacred Season. Great care is always taken to make sure none of the wood selected for these Campfires is rotten or split open.

The group of men will gather enough firewood for the communal Campfire Sites' needs for the following day, and then each man will gather enough firewood for his family's needs for the following day.

The following items are needed to conduct the Ritual For Gathering The Campfire Wood.

- Wood cutting saws and axes.
- Tobacco
- Sage for smudging.

The Head Man leads the men to the site selected for gathering the firewood and, when they arrive, he offers tobacco to the Four Sacred Directions and then sprinkles it on the ground as he prays, thanking the Green People for participating in this Sacred fire Ceremony.

He also thanks our Creator for the gift of Sacred Fire and its many benefits to the two-leggeds, and then smudges the tools to be used in cutting and gathering wood.

The wood symbolizes all of the gifts our Creator will give the people during the next Sacred Season. Therefore, it is treated with great respect as it is gathered and taken to the Campfire Site.

The Prayer and Fasting Ritual

Once the women and men have completed their respective duties, they will return home and spend the rest of the evening and night fasting and praying for the coming Sacred Season and Lifestyle Ceremony that will begin at sunrise the next day.

During the evening and night, the people will reaffirm their commitments to following the Life Plan our Creator has for their lives. They will pray for him to guide them during the coming Sacred Season and Lifestyle Ceremony, and will thank Grandfather in advance for all the things he will do for them in the days to come.

If people have disagreements with one another, or if they have offended other people, they will go to those people and ask for forgiveness and make amends. All unpaid obligations will be paid, and if they cannot be repaid, they will be forgiven.

Married couples will reaffirm their marriage vows to one another and commit to making the marriage even better during the coming Sacred Season. Parents will discuss with their children areas in their lives that need to be improved during the coming Sacred Season, and they will also praise them for the positive things the children learned or accomplished during the Season that is ending.

The adults will remind each other and their children that in order for harmony to exist between the Sacred Seasons, there must first be harmony among all the members of our Creator's Sacred Family of Life. Conversely, disharmony among the people will produce disharmony between the Sacred Seasons and they will not respond favorably toward the Sacred Family of Life.

The Sunrise Purification Ceremony Ritual

At sunrise the next day, the first day of the new Sacred Season and Lifestyle Ceremony—in this case, Spring and the Lifestyle Ceremony of New Beginnings—the people will meet at the Purification Lodge to conduct the Purification Ceremony.

The women will remove their waistbands and the men their wrist bands and put them into the fire. They will put the headbands in the fire at the conclusion of the Purification Ceremony.

During the first round, the ceremony leader will have all of the Grandfather Stones brought in to honor our Creator's gift of Sacred fire. Since this is Spring, which is dominated by female energy, the ceremony leader should be a woman. She will remind everyone how different the feeling is in this first round compared to the first round the day before. She will offer a prayer of thinks for Sacred Fire, for the Sacred Season of Spring, and the Lifestyle Ceremony of New Beginnings.

During the Second Round, she will have people announce when they will go on their respective Spirit Quests for this Sacred Season, and then, during the Third Round, they will pray for people's success on their Spirit Quest.

During the Last Round, the ceremony leader will have the people pray that the Event Ceremonies to be performed during this Lifestyle Ceremony will be successful, and then the Cornhusk Pipe will be smoked.

After the Purification Ceremony is over, everyone will put their headbands in the fire and the women will take some of the hot coals from the Fire Pit to be used for starting the communal Campfire. They will then go prepare the celebration feast.

While the women prepare the feast, the men will prepare for the Give Away Ceremony in which they will give items to the women to honor them in their role of leadership during the Sacred Spring Season in which female energy is very strong.

328

The Sacred Feast Ritual

The Sacred Feast will occur around mid-day of the first day of the new Season (in this case, Spring). The Head Woman and her female helpers will be in charge of the feast, and the oldest woman and oldest man will be served first; then, the rest of the people will be served in descending order of age.

This is a time of great celebration in anticipation of the wonderful success the people will have during this Lifestyle Ceremony of New Beginnings.

The Give Away Ritual

The Head Man and his male helpers will be in charge of the Give Away Ceremony, and this will be a time to honor the women and the important role they will play during the Sacred Season of Spring. The Ceremony will begin with the telling of the story of The First Give Away. The men will give gifts to the women. Married men will give special gifts to their wives, and single men may give gifts to any females of their choosing. The boys will give gifts to the girls, and all of the giving will be done to honor the presence of strong female energy during the Spring Season.

The Sacred Fire Ceremony officially ends at the conclusion of the Give Away Ceremony. However, at sunset, a bonfire will be built, and a time of dancing, feasting, storytelling, and celebration may go on well into the night.

COURAGE: THE SPIRITUAL MEDICINE OF NEW BEGINNINGS

Spring and its corresponding Lifestyle Ceremony of New Beginnings is the time of year when we further develop the Spiritual Medicine of Courage. It takes Courage to take our lives in new directions, start new projects, embrace new beginnings, and soar to new heights of spiritual awareness.

The Sacred Season of Spring is the time of year when we focus more on exercising and increasing our Spiritual Courage. Spiritual Courage is the power that moves us to start new endeavors and begin new spiritual journeys. It is the Sacred Seed of Change. It gives birth to all new things and launches us on the Sacred Path of Constant Change.

Courage is the power that enables us to take the first step in walking this Sacred Path we refer to as *The Way of the Medicine Wheel.* During the Lifestyle Ceremony of New Beginnings, we become keenly aware of the need to exercise the Spiritual Medicine of Courage so that it may grow and become stronger, because the stronger our Spiritual Courage, the more involved we become in the newness of Spring.

The Spiritual Medicine of Courage is the seed that produces faith. Faith is more than belief—it is belief in action. We prove we have faith by taking action. Courage produces action. Therefore, Courage is the seed that produces faith.

It is important to understand this, because, without Courage, we would not perform the rituals involved in our Sacred Ceremonies. For example, when we plant our seeds, the rituals performed in the Sacred Planting Ceremony demonstrate our faith in our Creator and Mother Earth to cause the seeds to grow. Courage is the power that moves us to action, and the action is the demonstration of our faith in the power symbolized in the ceremony.

The stronger our Courage, the greater our faith. The greater our faith, the more our Creator works on our behalf.

The Spiritual Medicine of Courage is the foundation on which this Sacred Path is built. It is the seed of New Beginnings. It is the starting point for all achievements and accomplishments in our lives. And, it is a very important key to helping us live in peace, harmony, and balance with the Sacred Circle of Life. The more Spiritual Courage we develop, the more potential we have for New Beginnings and greater accomplishments. During the days of Spring, we should stay focused on developing and strengthening our Courage—the Spiritual Medicine that empowers us to begin all new projects and activities.

SPIRIT QUESTING: STRENGTHENING OUR CONNECTION TO THE SPIRITUAL REALM

As we have discussed throughout these teaching sessions, there is a Spiritual Realm and a physical realm, and we are spiritual beings living in physical bodies. Unfortunately, our physical bodies tend to keep us trapped within the physical world and separated from the Spiritual Realm —the dwelling place of our Creator and his Spiritual Helpers.

In a previous teaching, I explained how you can make contact with the Spiritual Realm by traveling to your Private World. However, it isn't enough to just establish contact with the Spiritual Realm. We must be able to strengthen our connection with it.

Why is it so important to create a strong connection with the Spiritual Realm? The answer is simple—because we are spirits, and our Creator is a Spirit (the Great Spirit). The stronger our connection to the Spiritual Realm, the easier it is for us to communicate with our Creator and his Helpers Spirit to spirit.

The Way of the Medicine Wheel is a Spiritual Path that travels through a physical world. However, it is much, much more. It is a Spiritual Path that merges the Spiritual Realm and the physical realm together into a single reality. It removes the scales from our physical eyes and helps us see more clearly into the world of the Spirit. It reveals the Spiritual Power behind the physical symbol. It transforms even the most mundane of life's activities into exciting Spiritual Experiences.

The first time grandfather Old Bear talked to me about Spirit Questing, he said, *"Young one, you're not spending enough time communicating with our Creator. It isn't enough to pray a couple of times a day, or when you have a need. You must spend lots of time talking with Grandfather—you need to learn how to do Spirit Questing the way it was done back in my time.*

"At least once during every Sacred Season, we went out all alone to a special, private place and performed the Spirit Quest Ceremony. During the Lifestyle Ceremony of New Beginnings (Spring) our Spirit Questing focused on discussing with our Creator the New Beginnings in our lives, and during the Summer, it focused on the growth and development that needed to occur in what was begun during the Sacred Season of Spring. During the Sacred Season of Fall, our Spirit Questing focused on giving away part of the harvest we had received, and during the Winter the Spirit Quest was all about spiritual, physical, mental and emotional renewal.

"Our Creator has a specific plan for your life, grandson, but you'll never know what that plan is unless you spend lots of time Spirit Questing. Our Creator has given us Four Sacred Seasons that form the Great Sacred Cycle of Life. Just as each Sacred Season has its specific purpose and role in the Cycle of Life, so also each of us has been given a specific purpose for living during each Sacred Season.

"In order to live in peace, harmony and balance with our Creator and his Sacred Cycle of Life, we must come to understand what our specific purpose is during each Sacred Season. That is why we perform the Spirit Quest Ceremony at least four times a year; once at the beginning of each new Season.

"The Spirit Quest forms a strong connection between our spirit and our Creator, so that he can reveal all of the details of his plans for us during each Lifestyle Ceremony."

CONDUCTING THE SPIRIT QUEST CEREMONY

PREREQUISITES

The Spirit Quest Ceremony can't be performed until you first learn how to travel to your Private World (as explained in Book Three), because that is where we receive the information concerning the specific plans we are to accomplish during each Lifestyle Ceremony and Sacred Season. Therefore, make sure you are able to go to your Private World before attempting to do the Spirit Quest Ceremony.

PURPOSE OF THE SPIRIT QUEST CEREMONY

Our goal in walking this Sacred Path is to learn to live in peace, harmony, and balance with our Creator and his Sacred Circle of Life. Our Creator not only has a specific purpose for each Sacred Season; he also has a specific Life Plan for us as we live during each of those Seasons. Following that Life Plan Season after Season is the key to living in peace, harmony, and balance with Grandfather and his Sacred Family.

The Spirit Quest Ceremony strengthens the connection between our spirit and our Creator so that we are more effectively "tuned in" to what he is communicating to us on a daily basis—either directly or through the symbolism that is constantly all around us.

Symbolism is one of the Sacred languages of the Spiritual Realm. Through symbolism, our Creator reveals to us the great mysteries of Life. During the Spirit Quest, our Creator often teaches us in more detail the purpose and meaning of the symbolism that is all around us all the time.

WHEN THE SPIRIT QUEST CEREMONY IS CONDUCTED

The Spirit Quest Ceremony is conducted a minimum of four times a year—once sometime during the first week of each Sacred Season; the exact time may vary slightly during each Season. It may be conducted more often as special needs arise; you will know what those special needs are when they occur.

PICKING THE LOCATION TO CONDUCT THE CEREMONY

When selecting a location for the ceremony, make sure it is a very private, secluded place where there will be no interruptions, distraction or influences from the "feel good world" that most people live and work in. You should pick a place as far away from a city or town as possible. In fact, you should not even be able to see any physical evidence (such as man made structures or man made light at night) as you conduct the ceremony, and the location should be as far away from electrical power lines as possible.

Grandfather Old Bear told me that he often used small caves or rock overhangs along canyon walls, but that may not be possible for most of you. However, it is extremely important to get as far out in nature as possible and away from all man made influences when conducting the Spirit Quest Ceremony.

ITEMS YOU WILL NEED TO CONDUCT THE CEREMONY

You will need the following items when conducting the Spirit Quest Ceremony:

- Eight stones about the size of your head.
- One stone about twice the size of your head.
- Enough cornmeal to form the two-inch wide border of the circle approximately ten feet in diameter.
- A shell, Sage and Cedar for smudging.
- Blankets or a buffalo robe to keep warm on cold nights.
- (Optional) a drum.

PERSONAL PREPARATION

The day the ceremony begins, spend the morning praying, fasting, and preparing the items to be used in the ceremony. Conduct a Purification Ceremony during the early part of the afternoon.

CONDUCTING THE CEREMONY

Approximately two hours before sundown, arrive at the site you have chosen to perform the ceremony. Smudge yourself, the ground around the ceremony site, and the items to be used during the ceremony. First, use a sage smudge, and then a cedar smudge. As you do this, thank Grandfather for the ceremony and what you will learn from it.

Mark out the circle approximately ten feet in diameter and place the stone about twice the size of a human head in the center of the circle. Next, mark the edge of the circle with cornmeal. The corn meal should form a border about two inches wide.

Next, starting with the direction represented by the current Sacred Season, place two of the stones about a foot apart on the edge of the circle that marks the Sacred Direction of the current Sacred Season. As you face the Sacred Direction, hold each stone up to the sky and ask our Creator to send his power represented by that direction to the Sacred Circle to aid you in your Spirit Quest. Continue clockwise around the circle, repeating this process until all of the stones have been placed in their respective Sacred Directions.

The stones are placed about a foot apart as a "gate" or opening in each Sacred Direction for our Creator's power to travel through. When praying facing a particular direction, always stand or sit in the "doorway" between the stones.

A great deal of the time spent in the circle should consist of going to your Private World and talking to our Creator about his Life Plan for you during the current Lifestyle Ceremony. You will find that the more time you spend in your Private World praying, the stronger the connection will become between your spirit and our Creator. And that is the purpose of the Spirit Quest.

THE IMPORTANCE OF LISTENING

There is a verse in the Old Testament of the Bible that says, "Be still and know that I am God". When Spirit Questing, we should spend a lot of time being still—remaining silent—listening to what our Creator speaks to us from the Sacred Silence.

If we do all the talking (what we call praying) while on our Spirit Quest, we may never hear what our Creator says to us in response to our prayers. When you go to your Private World, spend a lot of time listening. You may be surprised at what you hear in the Sacred Silence.

Keep in mind that our Creator not only has a Life Plan for you to accomplish during each Sacred Season or Lifestyle Ceremony; he also wants to communicate that plan to you. Go on your Spirit Quest expecting to hear directly from our Creator concerning what he wants you to focus on or accomplish during the current Sacred Season.

LENGTH OF THE CEREMONY

People often ask how long the ceremony lasts. I will tell you what grandfather Old Bear told me. *"It lasts until you feel you have accomplished what you went there to accomplish. We don't think in terms of how long the ceremony is to last; we think in terms of what is to be accomplished. When you feel you have received from our Creator what you went there to learn, the ceremony is over.*

THE GIVE AWAY

After the ceremony is over, conduct a Give Away Ceremony as a thank you to our Creator for strengthening the connection between him and you.

SPIRIT QUESTING IS A VERY PERSONAL CEREMONY

The purpose of the Spirit Quest is to strengthen the relationship between you and our Creator and to understand more clearly what he wants you to be focusing on during the current Sacred Season (Lifestyle Ceremony). You may or may not wish to discuss with others what was revealed to you during the ceremony. We should never ask people about their Spirit Quests. They will share some of the things they learned and experienced if they feel it is appropriate.

On the other hand, if you have questions and concerns about your experience during a Spirit Quest, feel free to seek out someone you trust and respect to discuss those questions, concerns or experiences.

THE SACRED WATER CEREMONY

Like the Sacred Fire Ceremony, the Sacred Water Ceremony is conducted four times a year, once during the first part of each Sacred Season. The Sacred Water ceremony is always led by a woman, even during the seasons dominated by male energy.

The Water Spirit is very sacred. Without water we will all die. Water has great power. It can put out fire, wash away the land, erode away the hardest rock, and when it freezes, it is capable of splitting the largest boulders.

In ancient times, the two leggeds bestowed great honor on the Water Spirit that lived in all water, and they recognized its tremendous Sacred Power. The Bible describes an angel stirring up the water in a pool so that those who entered the pool could be healed of their sickness and disease, and even today, all major religions still use Holy Water in many of their ceremonies. A ceremony known as Baptism involving the ritual use of water for spiritual purification continues to be common practice in many religions.

ITEMS NEEDED TO CONDUCT THE CEREMONY

The following items will be needed to conduct the Sacred Water Ceremony:

- Sage and Cedar for smudging.
- Yellow corn meal to be used to form a sacred circle.
- Tobacco for an offering to the Water Spirit.
- A glass or stoneware jar, at least one gallon in size, with a water tight lid.
- A wooden dipper.
- A drum.
- A spring where potable water can be collected.

CONDUCTING THE SACRED WATER CEREMONY

STEP ONE

At sunrise, the woman conducting the Sacred Water Ceremony (usually the Head Woman), will first perform the Self-Offering Ceremony, and then the Purification Ceremony to insure that she is properly cleansed and worthy to communicate with the Sacred Water Spirit. Those women assisting her will also join in the Purification Ceremony.

Men may attend the Sacred Water Ceremony; however, they aren't allowed to assist the woman in charge.

Prior to conducting the Purification Ceremony, the water container, corn meal, tobacco, wooden dipper, and drum will have been smudged and placed on the altar. Following the Purification Ceremony, those items will be taken to the spring where the Sacred Water will be collected.

STEP TWO

When the ceremony leader arrives at the spring she, or a woman she has appointed, will sprinkle corn meal in a circle around the spring. The circle will be large enough for the ceremony leader to stand in while performing the rituals at the spring.

STEP THREE

Once the corn meal circle is complete, the ceremony leader will enter the circle from the West and offer tobacco to the Four Sacred Directions, Mother Earth, the Sacred Water Spirit living in the spring, and our Creator. The leader will thank them for this Sacred Ceremony, and ask our Creator's help in communicating with the Sacred Water Spirit.

When her prayer is completed, she will sprinkle the tobacco around the edge of the spring and in the water flowing from it as an offering to the Sacred Water Spirit. As she does this, she will pray to the Water Spirit, thanking it for its past help in conducting Sacred Ceremonies and then thanking it for the help it will provide during this Sacred Season's many ceremonies.

STEP FOUR

The ceremony leader will sing the Sacred Water Song, then, kneeling beside the spring and placing her hands in the water, she will pray again to the Sacred Water Spirit that lives in all naturally flowing, pure water. She will thank the Water Spirit for its power in assisting all our Creator's children within the Sacred Circle of Life to continue living. She will acknowledge that water is the Life Force of Mother Earth and that our Mother's children can't continue living without it.

She will express her sorrow that her two legged relatives have desecrated and polluted much of the water that flows through Mother Earth's veins, and that is one of the reasons the two-leggeds have become so weak in both spirit and body. She will ask permission from the Sacred

Water Spirit to take some of the Sacred Water that flows from the spring. She will then ask it to send a concentrated amount of its power into the water she takes, so that the Sacred Water can be used to help strengthen the Sacred Circle of Life during the current Lifestyle Ceremony.

STEP FIVE

After completing her prayer to the Sacred Water Spirit, the ceremony leader will take the wooden dipper and gently dip it into the water flowing from the spring. She will then offer the dipper of water to the Four Sacred Directions. As she does this, she will pray to our Creator, asking him to send his Holy Power into the water to help his children within the Sacred Circle of Life have strong bodies, minds, and spirits as they continue to serve him.

The ceremony leader will repeat this process until the water container is filled. She will then securely tighten the lid on the water container.

STEP SIX

The ceremony leader will first thank Mother Earth for sharing her Sacred Life Force with her children. Next, she will thank the Sacred Water Spirit for sending a concentrated amount of its Spirit into the container of water. And finally, she will thank our Creator for sending his power into the water, making it truly Holy Water.

STEP SEVEN

The ceremony leader will lead those in attendance in singing the Sacred Water Song again, and then the Thank You Song.

WHERE THE HOLY WATER WILL BE KEPT

The Holy Water will be kept on or next to the altar in the Head

Woman's home. She is the only one allowed to touch the container of Holy Water and dispense it for ceremonial use.

HOW THE HOLY WATER WILL BE USED

Small amounts of the Holy Water will be added to regular water to be used in such ceremonies as the Planting Ceremony, Purification Ceremony, healing ceremonies, the ceremony for blessing sacred streams, rivers and lakes, Rites of Passage Ceremonies and other ceremonies when Holy Water is needed to perform them.

Holy Water would be used in its concentrated form only as our Creator instructed such use. We will not suggest here when such instructions might occur.

The Sacred Water Ceremony is one of our most important ceremonies. It not only honors Mother Earth's Sacred Life Force, it enables us to truly experience the cleansing, purifying, and healing power of Holy Water as it works in our daily lives.

CONCLUSION

There are many other ceremonies conducted during the Life Style Ceremony of New Beginnings, however, as stated in the introduction, space will not permit a description of all of them. Therefore, we will explore only a few of the basic "event" ceremonies in this fourth book.

It would take an enormous amount of time and space to properly explain all of the sacred event ceremonies that are conducted as we walk this Sacred Path. Please don't assume that the ceremonies presented in this book are the most important ones. All event ceremonies are important. The ceremonies described on these pages certainly aren't more important than the Planting Ceremony, Sacred Home Ceremony, Circle of Fire Ceremony or Circle of Life Ceremony—none of which are explained here.

Teaching Session – 14
THE LIFESTYLE CEREMONY OF GROWTH AND DEVELOPMENT
(SUMMER)

The Lifestyle Ceremony of Growth and Development begins with the coming of the Summer Solstice and continues until the Fall Equinox. It corresponds with the Sacred Season of Summer, and is the busiest time of the year. During the Spring, new projects were started. During the Summer, those projects are in full development.

The Lifestyle Ceremony of Growth and Development begins in the South on the medicine wheel and continues around to the West. This is the time of year the sun is the warmest and the green people grow the fastest.

The sun symbolizes our Creator's Unconditional Love that is given freely to all of his children in the Sacred Circle of Life. Therefore, during the Sacred Summer Season, our Creator's Unconditional Love should be very evident in all our actions. The Lifestyle Ceremony of Growth and Development is the time in which we are to focus on increasing the amount of Unconditional Love we share with the rest of the Sacred Circle of Life.

Unconditional Love doesn't say, "I love you because…" or "I'll love you until…" Unconditional Love is never ending. It loves no matter whether that love is returned or not; that is the way God loves us, and that is the way we are to love others.

WORK INTENSIFIES DURING THE LIFESTYLE CEREMONY OF GROWTH AND DEVELOPMENT

The Spiritual Medicine of Patience comes to us from the South on the medicine wheel during the Sacred Season of Summer. In an earlier teaching session, it was pointed out that Spiritual Patience is the power to not get ahead of our Creator's timetable as we work on accomplishing his Life Plans for us.

Our Creator not only has a Life Plan for us; he has a timetable for achieving those plans. At the right time he will make the resources available to accomplish the plans he has for us. As the plans begin taking shape during the Summer Season, we must not fall into the trap of thinking that we are the ones who have to "make things happen". That is the way the "feel good world" thinks.

Most of us have been programmed from childhood to believe we are the ones in control of our own destiny—we are the ones that have to do whatever it takes to make things happen. That kind of thinking is a great ego builder. It promotes self-centeredness. And, it tends to diminish our belief in, and reliance on, our Creator.

Spiritual Patience is the power to wait for our Creator's guidance. It is the power to stop and listen to our Creator instead of charging ahead on our own in an attempt to make things happen by our own power.

The Sacred Work our Creator has for us to do during the Sacred Season of Summer become great learning sessions. It teaches us that our Creator will provide all of the resources and things we need in order to get his Life Plan accomplished on the timetable he has set for us. Learning that is one of the most important keys to being able to walk in peace, harmony, and balance on this Sacred Path.

The Lifestyle Ceremony of Growth and Development focuses as much on our Spiritual growth and development as it does on accomplishing all of the physical work to be done during the Sacred Season of Summer.

THE SACRED SEASON OF SUMMER IS A TIME FOR TEAM WORK

As we have mentioned in a previous teaching session, the wolf is the totem of the South, and a family of wolves can teach us a lot about teamwork.

One of the things we learn during the Sacred Summer Season is our need to work together with others in order to accomplish all that must be done during the Lifestyle Ceremony of Growth and Development. Two people working together as an effective team can accomplish far more than those same two individuals working alone.

Most people living in our modern, crowded cities have forgotten the importance of teamwork, and many of them don't even know the neighbors living next door. For the most part, life for them consists of getting up and going to work and then coming home and hibernating within the walls of their houses until its time to go to work again. Even people living together as so-called families within the same house often have little, if any, real communication with one another and rarely, if ever, do anything together as a family. As a result, teamwork in such homes is non-existent.

Our Creator's Sacred Family of Life is dependent on one another for its continued existence. We need one another. That is the way our Creator has designed his Sacred Family.

Part of our training during the Lifestyle Ceremony of Growth and Development is to recognize our need for help and learn to work effectively with others as a team. For people raised in a society that promotes rugged individualism and self-reliance, this can be a very difficult lesson to learn.

On this Sacred Path, the family, community, or team is more important than the individual. Therefore, the individual submits his will to the will of the team or community. People following *The Way of the Medicine Wheel* put the needs of the team or family ahead of their own needs or desires and, in doing so, it becomes easier to put our Creator's Life Plan for their lives ahead of their own self-centered plans.

Learning to work in peace, harmony, and balance within a team framework helps us learn to live in peace, harmony, and balance within our Creator's Sacred Circle of Life.

THE SACRED SEASON OF SUMMER IS DOMINATED BY MALE ENERGY

As we said in the previous teaching session, Spring is dominated by female energy and Summer is dominated by male energy. The line that runs from South (Summer) to North (Winter) on the medicine wheel is the line of the Spiritual Realm. It is also the line of Unbending Tradition and is dominated by male energy.

During the time of the Old Ones, men shared spiritual leadership with the women. Unfortunately, in our modern western societies today, women tend to have more interest in spirituality, and are much more involved in religious activity than men.

The lack of male involvement in spirituality has greatly weakened the Sacred Circle of Life. The Sacred Circle of the medicine wheel is dangerously out of balance because of the lack of male spiritual involvement on the wheel's Sacred Path that runs from South to North.

Where are our men today? For the most part, they are trapped in the tangled web of materialism, chasing the elusive dream of financial success, and spending all of their time and energy trying to get ahead in the so-called game of life.

As the Time of Great Cleansing draws ever closer, it becomes more and more important for men to make spirituality the priority in their lives. Men will be greatly needed to help women and children make the transition into the dawn of the Fifth World. Therefore, we should all pray that more and more men would begin walking the Sacred Path toward our Creator.

Men are the keepers of Unbending Tradition. There is a direct relationship with the losing of our Sacred Traditions and the lack of men walking the Spiritual Path. The fewer number of men following the Spiritual Path, the faster the Sacred Traditions are lost. Likewise, as more and more men make spirituality a priority, the faster our Creator will restore the Sacred Knowledge to those following the Sacred Path that combines the physical and Spiritual Realms together into a single reality.

Even though Summer is dominated by male energy and men are in charge of most of the ceremonies then, women are still in charge of the Sacred Water Ceremony performed at the beginning of each Sacred Season. In addition, the women also help with various ceremonies during the Sacred Summer Season as needed.

LIVING LIFE AS A SACRED CEREMONY

On this Sacred Path, we learn to live life as a Sacred Ceremony. That means that every activity we perform each day of each Sacred Season is viewed as part of the overall Sacred Ceremony of Life. The more we view the activities of each day as rituals being performed in the Sacred Ceremony of Life, the more we begin to merge the physical and Spiritual Realms together into a single reality. We also experience what it means to live in peace, harmony, and balance with all of our relatives within the Sacred Circle of Life.

That is why walking *The Way of the Medicine Wheel* is a lifestyle and not a religion. Everything we do each day, Sacred Season after Sacred Season, throughout the days of our lives, is seen as a Sacred Activity with powerful spiritual meaning. As more and more of our physical activity takes on Spiritual meaning, the physical realm begins to merge with the Spiritual Realm, and we become keenly aware of our Creator's power of Unconditional Love at work daily in our lives, enabling us to accomplish his Life Plan for our lives.

THE GREEN CORN DANCE

After the Sacred Fire Ceremony, individual Spirit Quests, and the Sacred Water Ceremony have been completed at the beginning of the Summer season, preparations are begun for the Green Corn Dance. The symbolism and rituals contained within this ceremony communicate the true meaning of the Lifestyle Ceremony of Growth and Development.

The Head Man is responsible for all preparations of the Green Corn Dance, and he is the dance leader on the day of the ceremony. Shortly after the Sacred Water Ceremony is completed, he begins preparation for the dance.

His first task is to pick the location for the dance. Once the location has been chosen and the area cleared so people can dance on the ground barefooted, his next responsibility is to locate the stone that will become the focal point of the Green Corn Dance.

This stone is similar to the Center Stone for the medicine wheel. It will be a smooth, oval shaped stone, and the Head Man will use the same procedure for finding it that is used in finding the Center Stone for the medicine wheel. Once the stone has been located, it will ceremonially be brought to the site selected for the dance and placed in the center of this site.

The Head Man's next duty is to find a healthy stock of corn with a nice tassel on the top because this dance must be conducted while the corn is in its tassel stage of growth.

ITEMS NEEDED TO CONDUCT THE GREEN CORN CEREMONY

The following items will be needed to conduct this ceremony:

- A smooth, oval or round stone for the center of the dance area.
- Corn meal.
- Sage and Cedar for smudging.
- Tobacco.
- A wreath made of sage with a strip of white cotton cloth 3" X 3'.
- Four small, wooden bowls.
- One kernel of corn.
- Water and a healthy leaf from a stock of corn.

- An ear of corn.
- Cornbread.
- A healthy stalk of corn, complete with roots, with a nice tassel on top.
- A necklace made from kernels of corn to be worn by the Head Woman.
- A shovel for digging up the corn stalk.
- Drummers to drum and sing during the dance.

STEP ONE

After the site for the dance has been chosen and cleared, and the stone placed in the center of the dance site, the Head Man will pray for guidance in selecting the stalk of corn to be used during the dance.

STEP TWO

For four days prior to the dance, the Head Man will perform the Purification Ceremony at sunrise and then go to pray for the corn stalk chosen for the Green Corn Dance. He will take a kernel of corn with him the first day and sit on the east side of the corn stalk. He will pray with the kernel of corn in his hand, thanking our Creator for causing all of the Green People seeds to sprout and grow during the Sacred Season of Spring. He will thank our Creator for new life and new beginnings that he brought to the people with the coming of Spring.

The second morning, the Head Man will perform the Purification Ceremony at sunrise. He will then take water with him to the corn stalk and sit on the South side of the stalk of corn. After offering the water to the Four Sacred Directions, he will pour it on the ground as he prays. He will ask our Creator to continue to bring the rains needed to help all the green people grown. He will ask Grandfather to continue to help the people as they work to complete their projects that were started in the Spring.

After performing the Purification Ceremony at sunrise the third morning, the Head Man will return to the corn stalk, taking an ear of corn with him. He will sit on the West side of the stalk of corn and, holding the ear of corn, he will pray for the continued growth of all the Green People and continued help for the people as they work on their summer activities. He will end his prayer by asking our Creator for a great harvest during the Fall Season.

The fourth day, the Head Man will again perform the Purification Ceremony at sunrise. Afterwards, he will go and sit on the North side of the stalk of corn. This time, he will take some corn bread with him and thank our Creator for the wonderful harvest he will give the people in the fall that will enable them to live through the Winter Season while they focus on physical, mental, emotional and spiritual renewal in preparation for the coming of the Sacred Spring Season.

STEP FOUR

The next morning, the Head Man will enter the Purification Lodge at sunrise, along with anyone else who will assist him during the ceremony (including a small male child under the age of puberty). After the Purification Ceremony is completed, the Head Man will give the young boy a shovel and the Head Man will smudge it with sage.

The young boy will carry the shovel as he accompanies the Head Man to the corn stalk. The Head Man will offer a prayer, thanking the Corn People for their help in performing the ceremony and thanking our Creator for all of his wonderful gifts and blessings he gives to his Children within the Sacred Circle of Life. He will thank Mother Earth for giving life to the corn and all the Green People, and thank her for feeding, clothing, and providing for all her children.

The Head Man will smudge the corn stalk with sage while thanking it for assisting the two-leggeds with the Corn Dance. At the end of his prayer, he will have the small child stand on the west side of the corn stalk and begin digging it up, making sure to get all of the roots. If the child is too small to dig up the stalk of corn by himself, the Head Man will assist him.

The Head Man will offer tobacco to the Four Sacred Directions and place it in the hole left by the removal of the corn stalk. Then, he will fill the hole with dirt. On the way to the site where the dance will be performed, the child will carry the stalk of corn on his shoulder, and the Head Man will carry the shovel.

When they arrive at the dance site, the child will lean the stalk of corn against the stone.

STEP FOUR

The Head Man will hold corn meal up to the Four Sacred Directions and then, starting in the West, he will form a circle of corn meal around the stone about eight feet in diameter. He will place the kernel of corn in the wooden bowl and, holding it up to the East, he will offer a prayer of thanks to our Creator for all of the Green People. Then, he will offer a prayer of thanks for all of the new beginnings and new projects our Creator gifted to the people during the Sacred Season of Spring. When he has finished his prayer, he will place the wooden bowl on the Eastern side of the circle of corn meal.

The Head Man will pour water into the wooden bowl and then remove a leaf from the stalk of corn and place it on top of the wooden bowl. He will move around to the South and hold the bowl up to the South as he prays. He will thank our Creator for the Summer's Sacred Season and ask him to continue to provide the rain needed to make all of the Green People grow and become strong. He will ask our Creator for his continued help and guidance as the people work at accomplishing all of their tasks during the Sacred Season of Summer. When he has finished his prayer, he will place the bowl with the water and leaf from the corn stalk on the Southern side of the circle of corn meal.

Next, the Head Man will move around to the West and place an ear of corn in a wooden bowl and hold it up to the West as he prays. He will ask our Creator for his continued blessings and guidance, and also ask that the people always share those blessings with others in need. After finishing his prayer, the Head Man will place the bowl with the ear of corn on the Western side of the circle of cornmeal.

Finally, the Head Man will move around to the North and place a piece of corn bread in a wooden bowl, and hold it up to the North. He will pray to our Creator, thanking him for all of his provisions in the past and the wonderful harvest he will give the people in the Fall so that they may live through the Sacred Season of Winter. He will promise our Creator that he will spend the Winter Season renewing his spirit, mind and body in preparation for the coming of the Sacred Season of Spring, and that he will encourage all of the people to do the same.

When the Head Man is finished placing the wooden bowls in the Four Sacred Directions around the circle of corn meal, he will smudge them and the entire circle of Cedar smoke.

STEP FIVE

The Head Woman will then remove the tassel and the rest of the leaves from the corn stalk while the Head Man places a wreath made from sage on his head so that the white strip of cotton hangs down his back. The Head Woman will place the corn tassel in the sage wreath at the back of the Head Man's head, directly in front of the white strip of cotton. She will then place the remaining corn leafs in a circle inside the sage wreath. The tips of the corn leafs will be placed so that they point up toward the sky. The Head Woman will make sure the corn tassel and leaves are secure and will not fall out during the dance.

The Head Man will place the necklace made of kernels of corn around the Head Woman's neck and place the corn stalk in her right hand to be carried during the dance.

The Head Man and Head Woman will lead the people to the Western side of the dance area, and the people will line up behind the Head Man and Head Woman. When everyone is in line, the Head Man and the people will turn and face the West while he offers a prayer for the success of the dance. He will ask our Creator to provide the people with the strength and resources they need to successfully accomplish all of their work during the Sacred Season of Summer. He will also thank our Creator for all of his provisions and for always taking care of his children within the Sacred Circle of Life. He will reaffirm his and the people's commitment to daily walk in obedience to our Creator's Sacred Laws of Right Living, and to faithfully carry out his Life Plans for each individual.

When the Head Man has completed his prayer, the drummers will begin the first song (the Four Direction Song followed by the Thank You Song). The Head Man and Head Woman will lead the people into the dance area and dance clockwise around the circle of corn meal in the center of the dance area. The drummers and singers will sing the Thank You song four times as the people continue dancing. As the song is sung the fourth time, the people will form a circle around the circle of corn meal and dance in place until the song is completed.

The Head Man and Head Woman will have stopped in front of the wooden bowl on the eastern side of the circle, and the Head Woman will take the bowl and hold it high over her head. As she does this, the Head Man prays for all of the children within the Sacred Circle of Life, asking our Creator to keep them in good health, give them long lives, and help them always follow our Creator's Life Plan for their individual lives.

When the prayer is completed, the drummers will start the next song (the Sacred Seasons song). They will continue to sing the song until the Head Man and Head Woman stop in front of the wooden bowl on the Southern side of the circle of corn meal. When the people have completed forming a circle around the corn meal, the drummers will stop singing and the Head Woman will pick up the wooden bowl containing the water and corn leaf. She will then hold it high over her head as she and the rest of the people turn to face the South.

The Head Man will offer a prayer to our Creator, thanking him for the Sacred Seasons and the things they teach us about how to walk this Sacred Path.

When the Head Man has finished his prayer, the drummers will begin the next song (the Medicine Wheel song), and continue singing until the Head Man and Head Woman stop in front of the wooden bowl on the Western Side of the circle of corn meal. Once the people have completed forming their circle, the drummers will stop drumming and singing, and the Head Woman will pick up the wooden bowl with the ear of corn and she and all the people will turn and face the West.

The Head Man will offer a prayer, thanking our Creator for his unconditional Love that supplies all of the people's needs, and also thank him for the wonderful harvest the people will gather in the fall. He will thank Grandfather for his continued help so that the people may complete all of the work and special projects before the coming of Winter.

When the Head Man has finished his prayer, the drummers will begin the next song (the Sacred Giveaway song), and they will continue to sing as the people dance until the Head Man stops in front of the wooden bowl on the Northern side of the circle of corn meal. When all of the people have finished forming their circle, the drummers will stop singing and the Head Woman will pick up the wooden bowl with the corn meal in it. She and all of the people will turn and face the North as she lifts the bowl high over her head.

The Head Man will offer a prayer to our Creator, thanking him for the rest he will bring the people from all their labors during the Sacred Season of Winter. He will reaffirm the people's commitment to renew themselves in spirit, mind, and body during the Winter Season in preparation for the coming of the Sacred Season of Spring.

When the Head Man has finished his prayer, the drummers begin singing the Song of the Four Winds twice and then the Purification Song twice while the people dance. As the Purification Song is sung, the Head

Man and Head Woman stop at the Eastern side of the dance area where the dance started and the people line up behind them. When the song is finished, the Head Man prays once again, thanking our Creator for giving the people the Green Corn Dance, and thanking him for hearing and answering all of their prayers.

When the Head Man finishes his prayer, the drummers begin singing the Completion Song as the people dance out of the area and get ready for the feast that will be served in the area of the communal Campfire.

STEP SEVEN

The feast is a part of the ceremony and a time of great celebration for all that our Creator does for us as we walk this Sacred Path

STEP EIGHT

The ceremony ends with a give-away in honor of how our Creator is helping us, and as a way to show gratitude to those who have helped with the work during the Sacred Season of Summer.

The Green Corn ceremony serves to remind the people of our Creator's provision throughout the Cycle of Sacred Seasons. It reminds the people of our Creator's continued provision, and reaffirms the people's commitment to trust our Creator to help them and meet their needs as they work on accomplishing his Life Plans for their lives.

SYMBOLISM OF THE GREEN CORN DANCE

Throughout these teaching sessions, we have emphasized over and over the importance of symbolism as we walk this Sacred Path. Symbolism is the bridge over which we walk to reach the power the symbol represents. Therefore, to understand the importance and power of the Green Corn Dance, we first must understand the symbolism used in the ceremony.

The smooth, oval stone in the center of the circle of corn meal: The smooth, oval stone in the center of the circle of corn meal symbolizes our Creator. The stone's presence reminds us that our creator is present at the ceremony. The stone being placed in the center of the dance area reminds us that our Creator needs to always be in the center of our lives as we perform our tasks during the Sacred Season of Summer. Dancing around the stone symbolizes our commitment to never forsake our Creator and his Life Plans for our lives. It communicates that we are committed to remain in his presence at all times through out the Cycle of Sacred Seasons.

The circle of corn meal: The circle of corn meal symbolizes the Sacred Circle of Life. It also symbolizes the Cycle of Sacred Seasons.

The wooden bowl with the kernel of corn placed on the eastern side of the circle: this symbolizes the Sacred Season of Spring bringing us new life and new beginnings—also bringing us new information concerning our Creator's Life Plans for our lives.

The wooden bowl with the water and green leaf from the stalk of corn placed on the Southern side of the circle of corn meal: This represents the Sacred Season of Summer. The water symbolizes the rain our Creator will bring to make things grow strong. It also symbolizes our Creator's Spirit providing the power and resources we need to accomplish all of our work during the Summer Season.

The green leaf from a corn stalk symbolizes the continued growth and development of the Green People during summer and also the continued accomplishments we achieve as our Creator's power works in our lives.

The wooden bowl with the ear of corn placed on the western side of the circle of corn meal: This wooden bowl symbolizes the Sacred Season of Fall. The ear of corn represents the great harvest our Creator provides during the Fall Season. The collection of kernels of corn on the cob represents all of the power and resources our Creator provides in order to make the harvest possible.

The wooden bowl with the corn bread in it placed on the northern side of the circle of corn meal: This symbolizes the Sacred Season of

Winter, and the corn bread represents our Creator's provision during the long, cold months of Winter.

The corn tassel placed in the headband of the Head Man: The corn tassel symbolizes our Creator's power of creation. It also represents reproduction and growth. When worn by the Head Man during the dance, it represents our Creator's power coming to the people to help them accomplish all that needs to be done during the Sacred Season of Summer.

The corn leaves placed in the Head Man's headband: The corn leaves placed in the Head Man's headband symbolizes our Creator's power to feed the people throughout the coming Cycle of Sacred Seasons.

The corn stalk carried by the Head Woman: This symbolizes that the women will have a great harvest during the Sacred Season of Fall.

The sage wreath worn by the Head Man: The sage wreath represents our Creator driving away any negative or evil forces that might try to prevent the people from accomplishing the Life Plan our Creator has for them.

The white cotton flag hanging from the sage wreath: This represents our Creator's protection during the current Sacred Season of Summer.

Digging the corn stalk out by the roots: This symbolizes that the people will waste none of the harvest.

The small boy digging up the corn stalk: This represents the responsibilities the youth must assume to learn the Sacred Ways. It illustrates that the next generation can't just have head knowledge of the Sacred Ways, they must take appropriate actions so those Sacred Ways become a lifestyle, not just a philosophy only.

The four days of Purification prior to digging up the corn stalk: The four days represent the Four Sacred Seasons and the people's commitment to follow our Creator's Life Plans during each Season. They also illustrate the extreme importance of the Green Corn Dance and how necessary it is to properly prepare for such a ceremony.

The four days of purification prepare the ceremony leader to be worthy and spiritually ready to lead such an important ceremony, and it shows that the leader recognizes his total dependence on our Creator and not on his own ability to perform the rituals.

The four days of prayers at the corn stalk prior to taking it to the dance site: The prayers are made while the Head Man faces the Four Sacred Directions around the corn stalk. This is done because the Green Corn Dance not only is being done for the Sacred Season of Summer, but it honors and brings together our Creator's Sacred Power present in the whole Cycle of Sacred Seasons.

CONCLUSION

As in the case with all ceremony, its true meaning can only be understood and experienced by performing the ceremony. We can never learn to fully understand a ceremony apart from participating in it—and that is true of all of the information being presented in these teaching sessions.

We will never understand this Sacred Path by simply reading this material. It must be experienced as a lifestyle, for then and only then can we say we are just beginning to learn to bring the physical and Spiritual Realms together into a single reality.

And the learning never stops. If one were to walk this Sacred Path from childhood to old age, only a fraction of the knowledge and power contained within it could ever be learned and experienced because we are finite; however, our Creator is infinite.

Teaching Session – 15
THE LIFESTYLE CEREMONY OF REAPING THE HARVEST

The Lifestyle Ceremony of Reaping the Harvest begins in September with the arrival of the Fall Equinox and continues to December at the Winter Solstice. The name of this Lifestyle Ceremony would lead one to believe that the emphasis during this season is on getting or receiving, however, as we will see, just the opposite is true. The major emphasis of this Sacred Season of Fall is on giving, not getting—and this is one of the great lessons that Fall teaches us.

The Lifestyle Ceremony of Reaping the Harvest is in the West on the medicine wheel, and occurs throughout the Sacred Season of Fall. Fall is a wonderful time of year. It is a time of change, and where we live in the high desert of the extreme western part of Colorado, that change sometimes occurs very fast.

Fall is a time of transition. It is the time during which Summer begins to lose its grip on Nature, and Winter starts awakening from its long sleep. And likewise, the Sacred Season of Fall is also a time of transition for our Creator's children as well.

During the Summer months, life moves at a rapid pace. Rapid growth is occurring within the family of green people. Babies born to the four leggeds in the spring experience rapid growth and development during the Summer. The two leggeds are busy working on all of the projects they started with the coming of Spring. However, during the Fall Season, the emphasis isn't on growth and development, it is on preparation for the coming Sacred Season of Winter.

THE CYCLE OF SEASONS IS A CYCLE OF PREPARATION

The Sacred Cycle of Seasons is a Sacred Cycle of preparation. And that is one of the great Sacred Teachings given to us by the Seasons. As we walk this Sacred Path, we are to live Life in a constant state of preparation for the next Sacred Revelation our Creator wants to share with us. However, unless we are properly prepared, he will not reveal his Sacred Knowledge to us because we cannot be trusted with it.

Spring is the time of New Beginnings, new birth, new projects, new insights—all given to us in preparation for the time of growth and development that will occur during the Sacred Season of Summer.

Summer is the time of growth, strengthening, and developing what was started or planted in the Spring. This time of growing in the Summer is in preparation for the harvest coming during the Sacred Season of Fall.

Fall is the time of reaping the harvest from what was planted in the Spring and grew and developed during the Summer. The harvest is in preparation for the time of rest and renewal coming during the Sacred Season of Winter.

Winter is the time of quiet rest and renewal in preparation for the time of new beginnings, new birth and new projects coming in the Sacred Season of Spring. And so the never-ending cycle of preparation continues Season after Sacred Season.

If the Sacred Seasons are in a constant state of preparation, we must be also if we want to learn to live in peace, harmony, and balance with the Sacred Cycle of Life. And our preparation must correspond with the preparations that occur during each Sacred Season.

WHAT ARE WE PREPARING FOR?

If the Cycle of Sacred Seasons teach us the need for preparation, then the question must be asked, "What are we preparing for?"

A verse in the Sacred Seasons song says, "The Sacred Seasons are always changing, the Sacred Seasons come and go. They reveal all of life's mysteries that you and I should seek to know". If you don't know that song yet, I highly recommend that you learn it, because hidden within it is one of the keys to learning to walk this Sacred Path referred to as *The Way of the Medicine Wheel.*

As previously noted, the Sacred Seasons are in a constant state of preparation and if we want to learn to live in peace, harmony, and balance with the Sacred Cycle of Life, our lives need to correspond with that same cycle of preparation revealed in the Seasons. But why? What are we preparing for?

As we walk this Sacred Path, we are to be in a constant state of preparation to take the next step in learning how to merge the physical realm and spiritual realm together into a single reality.

As a small child growing up in rural Oklahoma, I attended a little country church with my parents. I still remember one of the old church hymns we frequently sang. One of the verses went like this:

> Just a closer walk with thee,
> Grant it Jesus is my plea.
> Daily walking close to thee,
> Let it be, dear Lord, let it be.

I wasn't aware of it at the time, but that song also talks about the need to merge the physical realm and the Spiritual realm together into a single reality. The whole purpose of walking this Sacred Path is to learn how to merge these two realities into one. That is a never-ending, lifelong process in which each day we are preparing ourselves to achieve that goal. However, we will never learn to totally merge them into one until we shed our physical bodies and our spirits join our Creator in the World of Spirit. But, the more we prepare ourselves, the more of the Spiritual Realm our Creator will entrust to us.

So you may be thinking, "Just how do I prepare myself?" We don't prepare ourselves by seeking out some so-called "guru" or self-proclaimed "spiritual teacher" and blindly following what he or she tells us to do. We don't prepare ourselves by simply filling our heads with what we perceive to be spiritual knowledge.

We begin the process of preparation by first submitting our will to our Creator's will; by getting self out of the way so our Creator is free to work his will for our lives in and through us. Once we have made that commitment, we simply follow the steps for knowing his Life Plans for our lives that was presented in book three. Then, we apply the Five Spiritual Medicines to our daily lives as described in book one.

Simply stated, we prepare ourselves by listening directly to our Creator as he speaks to our spirits, and then totally obeying what he tells us to do. As we continue doing this on a daily basis, we will discover that he shared more and more spiritual principles and truths with us concerning how to merge the physical realm and Spiritual Realm into a single reality.

However, we must keep in mind that how much our Creator shares with us will depend on how much of our egos and self-will we eliminate from our lives. We can not experience the entire Spiritual Realm our Creator wants to share with us if we try to hang on to control of our lives. The more of our lives our Creator controls, the more of his Spiritual realm he will reveal to us—and that is the purpose and focal point of our preparation.

THE SACRED SEASON OF FALL— THE TIME OF REAPING THE HARVEST

Once, while I was discussing the Lifestyle Ceremony of Reaping the Harvest with grandfather Old Bear, he said, *"The Lifestyle Ceremony of Reaping the Harvest is a reality check. Grandson, you don't plant corn and harvest beans."* He winked at me and chuckled. *"I'll bet you didn't know that, did you?"*

Then, his mood changed and he became much more serious. "The Lifestyle Ceremony of Reaping the Harvest reveals the real you, not who you try to convince others you are. It shows you exactly what you planted in the Sacred Season of Spring, and it shows you how much growth and development really occurred during the Sacred Season of Summer. It lets you know if you properly performed the Sacred Planting Ceremony and if you did the Green Corn Dance the way it was supposed to be done. It yells from the mountain top for all to hear who are listening whether or not you have been walking this Sacred Path in obedience to our Creator or if you have been only playing and pretending, deceiving yourself and others in the process."

He looked sternly at me, and his facial features appeared to be set in stone. "Never forget that, grandson. The Sacred Season of Fall isn't just about the women gathering the corn, squash and beans. It is also our Creator's way of letting us know how obedient we have been in following our Creator's Life Plans for our lives."

He paused a moment, seemingly deep in thought. "We truly do reap what we sow, grandson—yes, we truly do."

I have never forgotten that conversation with the Old One, and it totally changed my perception of the Lifestyle Ceremony of Reaping the Harvest.

Yes, the Sacred Season of Fall is the time for harvesting the corn, beans, and squash. But it is much, much more than that. It is also a time of personal evaluation. It's our grade card, so to speak, concerning how well we have followed our Creator's Life Plan for our lives.

The Sacred Season of Fall is in the West on the medicine wheel, and the West brings us our Creator's power of internal truth and honesty. Fall is the time in which we honestly evaluate our relationship with our Creator, those closest to us and the rest of the Family within the Sacred Circle of Life. It is a time in which we admit our weaknesses and shortcomings. We sincerely and honestly ask our Creator to remove anything in our lives that keep us from becoming true "hollow bones" through which our Creator's Unconditional Love flows out to serve the needs around us within the Sacred Circle of Life.

HOW WE SHOULD VIEW THE TIME OF HARVEST

What does the harvest mean to you? Is it a time of storing up the corn, beans, and squash so that you can live through the long, cold winter ahead? Is it like a payday, in which you now receive what you have earned and is therefore owed to you? Is it a time in which to brag and show off the results of your hard work? Or, do you view it as a time in which you are now able to better help meet the needs of those within the Sacred Circle Of Life who are less fortunate than you? How we view the time of harvest will determine, for the most part, how we spend our time during the Sacred Season of Winter, the Lifestyle Ceremony of Rest and Renewal.

If we view the time of harvest as our payday, then we will be more likely to store up and hoard our harvest for our own rainy day needs— which we will have plenty of during the Sacred Season of Winter. On the other hand, if we view our harvest as resources that will now enable us to better help meet the needs of some of the people around us less fortunate than we are, we will spend the Sacred Season of Winter determining how to best share with others some of the harvest we received during the Fall. The harvest, itself, is a test of who we really are, and whether or not we will put into practice self-centeredness or humility.

THIS SACRED PATH IS A PATH OF GIVING; NOT GETTING

Everything we have is a gift from our Creator and Mother Earth. Grandfather gave us our lives and spirits, and he continues giving us our breath. Mother Earth gave us all the material possessions we have. Did we give birth to the trees that helped build our homes? Did we give birth to the food we eat? Everything we have came to us as a gift.

We may say, oh no, we earned it. What did we do to earn our lives? What did we do to earn our spirits that are the real us? What did we do for Mother Earth to cause her to owe us all the so called natural resources on and in the earth that literally keep us alive? I submit to you that we have no rights to anything on and in the earth. They are gifts given to us by our Creator and our Mother, the Earth.

If all we have, including life itself, is a gift, then what right do we have to think we can keep taking and taking without giving something back? But we may say, "How can we give something back to our Creator and our Mother, the Earth?"

It is true that our Creator doesn't need anything we have. However, there is one thing he greatly desires—he wants us to love him, as he loves us—unconditionally. Just as he gives to us unconditionally, he wants us to learn to give to others unconditionally. That is why he gives us a harvest during the Sacred Season of Fall—so we will have something to share with others around us within the Sacred Circle of Life who have needs.

He doesn't want us to just give to our friends or those we like. He wants us to give to those in need, whoever they are. And we are to give expecting nothing in return from those we gave to.

The "feel good" world defines love this way—I love you because…I love you when…I love you if…I love you until… In the feel good world, love is always conditional. However, our Creator loves us with out any strings attached. He loves us even when we don't love or respect him. And that is the type of love we also are to develop as we walk this Sacred Path.

Unconditional love never ends. It never expects or requires love in return. It doesn't keep a record of how others treat us. It doesn't get even when wronged. It always forgives offences. In summation, it loves when that love is not deserved, and it never stops loving. That is the way our Creator loves us and that is the way we are to love others.

In the Spring, we plant a few seeds and in the Fall we reap a great harvest. And those who walk this Sacred Path recognize that the harvest is a Sacred Gift to us so we can also give to others who need our help. As I said earlier, the harvest is actually a test to determine our true nature. Do we hoard our harvest so we can serve only our own needs, or do we share our harvest with those less fortunate than us? The harvest truly separates the "givers" from the "takers". Which will you be?

THE SACRED SEASON OF FALL
IS DOMINATED BY FEMALE ENERGY

The medicine wheel is the perfect symbol of this Sacred Path. As was pointed out previously, the line through the center of the medicine wheel running from East (Spring) to West (Fall) is the line of Constant Change, and is dominated by female energy. The line that runs through the center of the medicine wheel from South (Summer) to North (Winter) is the line of Unbending Tradition and is dominated by male energy. Therefore, female energy dominates the Sacred Season of Fall and most of the event ceremonies conducted during the Lifestyle Ceremony of Reaping the Harvest are performed by women.

The women carry within them the power and ability to bring forth new life. That is why they are the ones in charge of the Planting Ceremony conducted in the Sacred Season of Spring. Since they are the ones who planted the seeds, they own the harvest. Therefore, during the Sacred Season of Fall, the women are in charge of overseeing the harvest ,and that harvest belongs to them.

During the Fall, the women choose where the harvest will be stored, and oversee the men in the preparation of the storage site. The women make the decision when it is time to harvest the crops, and the men assist them in the harvesting process.

THE SACRED FAMILY CEREMONY

Once the harvest has been gathered and stored away, it is time to begin preparing for the Sacred Family Ceremony, which will be conducted during the last full moon of the Fall Season. The women are in charge of this very important ceremony, and preparations begin by the Head Woman calling a meeting of the women elders. The purpose of the meeting is to discuss the success of the harvest and to access the special needs of the individuals and families within the village or community.

Not only are personal needs discussed, but also the individual accomplishments of persons within the group since the beginning of the Sacred Season of Spring There is special emphasis on those personal accomplishments that benefited the entire community, such as building or repairing community arbors, etc. The women place special emphasis on those children who have worked hard since the beginning of Spring assisting the adults with the various community projects and activities.

ITEMS NEEDED FOR THE CEREMONY

- Sage and Cedar and a large shell for smudging.
- Tobacco and cornmeal.
- Enough rope that when tied together will form a circle large enough for the people to stand around and hold in their hands.
- Enough wood to keep a fire going throughout the night.
- Wooden bowls to hold samples of the harvest.
- A drumming/singing group.
- A buffalo skull.
- Strips of Four Direction colored cotton cloth that can be tied together to form two belts.
- Enough small cedar branches (about 12" long) for each person to hold one.
- One each of the Four Direction Cotton cloth flags (3" X 3').
- A forked willow staff about six feet long with a black cotton flag (3" X 3') tied to the bottom of the staff's fork.
- Items for a Give Away Ceremony.
- Four oil lamp torches to provide some light in the ceremony area.
- Prepared food for a feast.

CONDUCTING THE SACRED FAMILY CEREMONY

STEP ONE

The afternoon of the day of the ceremony, the Head Woman will lead a Purification Ceremony for those assisting her with the Sacred Family Ceremony. If she chooses not to lead the Purification Ceremony, she can ask someone else to do it.

STEP TWO

Following the Purification Ceremony, the Head Woman and other women elders will make sure all of the items needed for the Sacred Family Ceremony are at the ceremony site. She will supervise the building of the round, earthen altar in the center of the ceremony site and place the buffalo skull in the center of the altar facing West.

Next, she will place the wooden bowls containing samples of the recent harvest around the buffalo skull. She will then place the willow staff with its black flag firmly in the dirt directly behind the buffalo skull. Then, holding a mixture of the tobacco and cornmeal up to the West, she will offer a prayer to our Creator, asking him to join the people as they conduct the Sacred Family Ceremony. After her prayer she will sprinkle the mixture on and around the altar.

After the altar is completed, the Head Woman's helpers will place firewood just to the West of it so a fire can be built during the ceremony.

STEP THREE

The Head Woman and the other women elders assisting her will tie the ropes together to form a circle large enough for everyone to stand behind and hold with their hands. She will lay the rope circle on the ground and then have someone place the oil lamps in the ground a safe distance behind the rope circle. The first lamp will be placed in the West, the second in the North, the third in the East and the last one in the South.

STEP FOUR

The Head Woman will tie the directional flags to the rope circle beginning with the black flag on the western side and continuing clockwise around the circle, attaching the red flag on the northern side, the yellow flag on the eastern side, and the white flag on the southern side.

STEP FIVE

At sundown, the people participating in the ceremony will gather at the ceremonial site and, starting in the West and moving clockwise around to the South, the Head Woman will light the torches. As she lights each torch, she will offer a prayer to our Creator's power represented by the directional torch being lit, asking that our Creator send that power to help the people properly perform the ceremony.

STEP SIX

The Head Woman will have one of the women elders tie the Four Direction colored Cotton belts around the waists of a young girl and boy that have been chosen to lead the people in forming a circle around the rope. As this is being done, another woman elder will distribute a small Cedar limb fan to each person, and have the people line up for entry according to age (from the eldest to the youngest) behind the two young children wearing the Four Direction colored belts.

STEP SEVEN

Standing on the inside of the rope circle, with the rest of the people outside the circle, the Head Woman walks beside the two children chosen to lead the people to form a circle just outside the rope circle on the ground. The drumming group sings the Four Direction song as the people slowly form a circle just outside the circle of rope on the ground. The drumming group will continue to sing until the people have completed forming their circle. Once they have formed their human circle the drummers will sing the Four Direction Song one more time.

STEP EIGHT

Once the people have completed the circle, they reach down in unison with their left hands, take hold of the rope circle, lift it off the ground, and form a tight circle with the rope. The Head Woman reminds the people that the rope circle symbolizes our Creator's Sacred Family of Life, and that by taking hold of the rope, they are committing to honor and help care for that Sacred Family of which they are a part.

She also explains that by taking hold of the rope, the people are also committing to honor and help take care of one another around that rope circle. She then offers a prayer to our Creator reaffirming the people's commitment, and asking him to help each person within the circle to always honor that commitment.

STEP NINE

The Head Woman asks the Head Man to come and build a small Fire just West of the altar from the firewood. When the Sacred Fire is going, the Head Man returns to his place in the circle. However, it is the Head Man's responsibility to keep the Sacred Fire going through out the remainder of the ceremony. Once the Fire is started, the drummers will sing the Sacred Fire Song. When the song is completed, the Head Woman prays again, thanking our Creator for his presence within the Sacred Circle and again reaffirming the people's commitment to always obey him and honor and help care for his Sacred Family of Life.

STEP TEN

After she completes her prayer, the Head Woman will ask the two eldest women to come inside the circle. She will have one of them stand in front of the yellow flag on the circle's eastern side, and the other woman will stand in front of the black flag on the western side of the circle. Once the women have taken their places, she will offer another prayer to our Creator, thanking him for all of the females within his Sacred

Family of Life, and especially for the women participating in this Sacred Ceremony.

When the prayer is completed, the Head Woman will ask the two eldest men to come inside the circle. She will have one stand in front of the white flag on the circle's southern side and the other in front of the red flag on the northern side. When the men have taken their places, the Head Woman will pray again, thanking our Creator for all of the males within his Sacred Family of Life, and especially for the men present at the ceremony.

STEP ELEVEN

Next, the Head Woman will ask the boy and girl wearing the Four Directions colored belts to come inside the circle. The Girl will stand on the eastern side of the altar, and the boy will stand on the northern side. The Head Woman will then offer another prayer to our Creator, thanking him for all of the young ones within his Sacred Family of Life and especially for the children attending this ceremony.

When the prayer is completed, she will turn to the people forming the circle around the rope and ask them to all look at their elders standing inside the circle at the Four Sacred Directions. She will explain that they represent all of the elders who have gone before them and faithfully handed down these Sacred Ways from generation to generation. She will explain that we wouldn't have this Sacred Path if their ancestors down through the past hadn't been faithful in passing the Sacred Ways on to their younger generations. Then, she will challenge the adults within the circle to make a commitment to faithfully pass on these Sacred Ways to the present generation of young people. The people will then make a verbal commitment to do so.

The Head Woman will then pray again, asking our Creator to hold the adults present accountable for following through on their commitment, and to bless their faithfulness in fulfilling that commitment.

The Head Woman will then ask all of the children standing in the circle to join the boy and girl around the altar. She will then talk to the children present, telling them that they represent the future of the people. She will explain that they will determine what the people become in the future. She will point out how important it is that the young people learn all the Sacred Ways of the people and faithfully follow them.

She will then ask all of the children to join hands, forming a circle around the altar. Next, she will have the woman standing in front of the yellow flag in the East come and pray for the children. She will then join hands with them as she stands on the East side of the altar. When she is finished, the man on the South, then the woman from the West, followed by the man on the North, will come and pray for the children. and then join hands with them on their respective sides of the circle around the altar.

The Head Woman will then ask the children if they are willing to learn from the adults to faithfully follow these Sacred Ways. Hopefully, most of the children will commit to being taught how to walk this Sacred Path.

The Head Woman will then ask the adults outside the circle to come inside the rope circle and join hands with the children in the circle around the altar. At this point, the Head Man will make sure the Sacred Fire is burning well.

The Head Woman will then start passing the wooden bowls filled with items from the recent harvest, around the circle of people, starting with the eldest person in line. As the bowls go around the circle on their way to the youngest child, the Head Woman explains that the passing of the bowls symbolize the passing of the Sacred Ways on to future generations and the blessings that will come from our Creator as each generation faithfully follows this Sacred Path. As the youngest child in line receives each bowl, he or she places it back on the altar.

STEP TWELVE

The drummers begin singing the Completion Song, and the Head

Woman leads the boy and girl wearing the Four Direction colors belts, followed by the rest of the people in the circle, past the Fire. Each person throws his or her small Cedar branch in the Fire to seal his or her commitment to always pass on these Sacred Ways to the next generation.

The Head Woman closes this part of the ceremony with prayer, thanking our Creator for his many blessings to his Sacred Family of Life, and then the people proceed to the communal camp site for the feast.

STEP THIRTEEN

Following the feast, the Head Woman has everyone gather around a communal bond fire for a Give Away Ceremony. This is a different type of give away, in that it gives recognition to individuals within the group, and it also is a time in which individuals make commitments to help meet the needs of other individuals or families present.

The Head Woman is in charge of this last ritual of the Sacred Family Ceremony, and begins the give away with a prayer to thanks to our Creator for all that he and Mother Earth give the Sacred Family of Life on a continual basis. After the prayer, the drummers lead the group in the singing of the Sacred Give Away song.

At the completion of the song, the Head Woman leads the group in a time of personal praise and recognition of individuals who have been of great service or shown outstanding deeds of kindness to our Creator's Sacred Family of Life, and specifically to individuals present or within the local community.

Following this time of showing recognition, the Head Woman shares any special needs that she is aware individuals or families within the group may have, and asks for volunteers to help meet those needs. The individuals present step forward to verbally commit to helping meet such needs. An example of needs that might exist within the group is the gathering of a winter supply of wood for the elderly, or helping make repairs on someone's dwelling.

The Head Woman then leads the group in the singing of the Thank

You song and ends the ceremony with another prayer of thanks to our Creator for his continual blessings and provisions day after day.

SYMBOLISM OF THE SACRED FAMILY CEREMONY

The Sacred Family Ceremony is a "bonding" ceremony. It bonds the past to the present and the present to the future. It bonds the parents to the children and the elders to the youth. It bonds the individual to the community and the community to the individual. However, most importantly, it bonds the physical realm to the spiritual realm, and the individual to our Creator and his Sacred Family of Life.

As with all ceremony, the Sacred Family Ceremony can only be understood by understanding the symbolism used during its performance. I hope by now you have become keenly aware that the need to understand symbolism is one of the major themes running through all of these teaching sessions.

The degree in which we are able to merge the physical and spiritual realms together into a single reality depends on the degree in which we understand the symbolism our Creator has placed all around us.

The altar made of earth in the center of the rope circle: The altar symbolizes the connection between the physical and spiritual realms. It represents the union between our spirit and our Creator. The altar draws our attention to the world of the spirit, and it draws our spirits toward our Creator. The earth the altar is made from symbolizes the physical world, and the buffalo skull placed on the earthen altar symbolizes our Creator's power and ability to meet all of our needs here in the physical realm.

The wooden bowls filled with things from the recent harvest are living proof of how our Creator, in union with Mother Earth, is our constant provider. The staff with the black flag on the altar serves to remind us that all of the power represented by the symbolism associated with the altar is at work currently within this Sacred Season of Fall and in the Sacred Family Ceremony now being performed.

The circle made of rope: The rope symbolizes the physical realm, and

374

the circle represents the spiritual realm. Therefore, the circle made of rope symbolizes the bringing together of the physical and spiritual realms into a single reality. In addition, the space outside the rope circle symbolizes the physical world, and the space inside the circle represents the Spiritual World.

As the ceremony begins, the people (except for the Head Woman) are in the physical realm. However, at the end of the ceremony, they have all moved into the Spiritual Realm. The Head Woman is on the inside of the circle the entire time the ceremony is being conducted. In fact, she guides and instructs the people during the ceremony from within the circle (the Spiritual Realm).

The Head Woman symbolizes our Creator's helpers in the Spiritual World as they instruct us in the ways of the Spirit and help guide us along this Sacred Path toward our Creator.

The four torches of Fire placed in the Four Sacred Directions: The lighting of these four torches symbolizes our Creator's power totally surrounding the people during the ceremony.

The boy and girl who led the people in the forming of the circle around the rope: The boy and girl leading the procession to form a circle around the rope symbolize the fact that our youth are the future leaders of the people. They also represent and determine what the people's future will be. Their Four Directions colored belts symbolize their responsibility to follow this Sacred Path throughout the Cycle of Sacred Seasons. The Head Woman walking beside the youth as they led the people to form the circle around the rope symbolizes our Creator's constant help as we walk this Sacred Path.

The small Cedar fans everyone carried: The Cedar fans represent the people's commitment to living a life of purity as they walk this Sacred Path, and their desire to have a strong connection to the Spiritual Realm. At the end of the ceremony, they threw the Cedar fans into the Fire. The Fire symbolizes our Creator's presence at the ceremony, and the people throwing the Cedar fans into the fire symbolize that they will spend the rest of their lives in obedience to living out the Life Plan our Creator has for their lives.

The people holding the rope circle in their left hand as they hold the Cedar fan in their right hand: This symbolizes their commitment to merging the physical and spiritual realms together into a single reality in their individual lives. The Cedar fan in the right hand symbolizes their pure motives and intentions in making that commitment.

The two women elders standing in front of the flags in the East and West: The two woman elders symbolize the women from past generations all the way back to antiquity, who have faithfully walked this Sacred Path and handed it down to the next generation. Their standing in front of the flag in the East and the one in the West symbolizes the female energy that dominates both the Spring and Fall Seasons and the need for the woman participating in the ceremony to faithfully perform their ceremonial roles and duties during those two Sacred Seasons.

The fact that the Head Woman calls the two women elders to come within the circle and stand in front of their respective flags symbolizes that they must be strongly connected to the Spiritual Realm in order to faithfully fulfill their roles and carry out their ceremonial duties during these Sacred Seasons.

The two men elders standing in front of the flags on the southern and northern sides of the circle: This symbolizes the men's ceremonial roles and responsibilities during the Sacred Seasons of Summer and Winter. The men elders symbolize the male elders back through time who have faithfully passed on the roles and responsibilities of men in walking this Sacred Path.

The two children being led by the Head Woman to the altar inside the rope circle: The children represent the future of the people—and in many respects, the future of our Creator's Sacred Family of Life. They will be the ones who determine for the most part, what that future will become. The Head Woman leading the children to the altar symbolizes the fact that the next generation must be strongly connected to the Spiritual Realm and has our Creator at the center of all it does. The elders looking on as the children are led to the altar symbolize the fact that it will be the elders of this generation who must watch over the teaching of the youth and ensure that the Sacred Ways are properly passed on to them.

The elders of each generation have a major responsibility for becoming strongly connected to our Creator. The elders are responsible for insuring that the Sacred Ways are kept intact and passed on to the youth in a pure form, just as they were passed on to the elders of the present generation.

The elders have no right to compromise or change the Sacred Ways on their own—only our Creator can change the way the Sacred Ways are carried out generation after generation. And our Creator will communicate those changes to the youth as they mature if any changes are to be made. The understanding of this also must be passed on to the youth by the elders.

The Fire built on the West side of the altar: This symbolizes the presence of our Creator and his power not only during the ceremony but throughout the entire Sacred Fall Season.

The people going inside the rope circle beginning with the oldest people and concluding with the youngest person: This symbolizes the people living their lives more in the spiritual realm than in the physical realm and that it is the responsibility of the older ones to lead the younger people in achieving this.

The feast: The feast represents the wonderful harvest our Creator gives to us, as well as his continual provision in our lives. It also symbolizes the results of faithfully following this Sacred Path and serves to illustrate that our Creator takes care of our needs as we faithfully obey his Life Plan for our Lives.

The Give Away of recognition and service to others: This symbolizes the true meaning of the Give Away Ceremony. The people end the Sacred Family Ceremony by recognizing and praising those in their midst who have served others in an outstanding way since the beginning of the Spring Season. They then make commitments to one another to continue meeting the needs of those among them. This is the true purpose of walking this Sacred Path.

CONCLUSION

Ceremony is far more effective than books as a teaching tool. When we read a book about Spirituality, we are reading about Spiritual Principles. However, when we perform a Spiritual Ceremony, we are acting out those Spiritual Principles as a visual aid to ourselves and to others observing the ceremony.

Reading these teaching sessions about this Sacred Path provides information. However, conducting the ceremonies allows us to experience this Sacred Path.

Unfortunately, most of these ceremonies can't be performed in the city. There were no cities like we have today when these ceremonies were given to the two leggeds long ago. Back then, people lived in very small groups and the surrounding land sustained their lives. The Ancient Ones who followed these Sacred Ways weren't restrained by all of the local, state and federal governmental laws that currently prohibit the implementation and practice of many of the Spiritual Principles and Sacred Ceremonies associated with this Sacred Path.

Many people will read the information in these teaching sessions and conclude that *The Way of the Medicine Wheel* is no longer relevant in today's modern, high tech world. For those people, these teaching sessions will be like most of the other books on spirituality they read—the spiritual principles presented might be accepted in theory but for the most part they will never be put into practice.

Our goal is not to convince people to implement the Spiritual Principles and ancient Sacred Ceremonies presented in these teaching sessions. Our goal is to simply make the information available to the general public. We then challenge the people who read it to ask our Creator what they should do with the information, and then obey what he tells them to do.

378

Teaching Session – 16
THE LIFESTYLE CEREMONY OF REST AND RENEWAL

The Lifestyle Ceremony of Rest and Renewal begins with the coming of the Winter Solstice and continues until the Spring Equinox. It corresponds with the Sacred Season of Winter. It is located in the North on the medicine wheel. The buffalo is its totem, its color is red, and its Spiritual Medicine is humility.

Spring is the time of new beginnings. Summer is the time of growth and development. Fall is the time for reaping the harvest from what was planted in the Spring and grew during the Summer. These three seasons are filled with lots of activity and hard work. Our Creator gave us the Sacred Season of Winter as a time of rest and renewal in preparation for the coming Sacred Season of Spring in which the cycle of new beginnings starts again.

THE RESULTS OF OUR FAST PACED SOCIETY

Man has convinced himself that the more technologically advanced society becomes the better life will be for its people. However, just the opposite has proven to be true. The more technologically advanced society becomes, the faster the pace our lives become and the more pressure, frustration and exhaustion we experience as we try to keep up with the rapidly increasing demands of work and family.

We are caught in a "giant speed trap". We build faster planes, cars and Internet service, and we eat more and more fast food meals. We use the ever-increasing speed of technological development to fuel our "I want it NOW" appetites, and the results have been devastating.

Rarely do families these days sit down together for a meal, spend evenings or weekends together doing family projects, or even communicate long enough to find out what each other is thinking, feeling or needing. What is even worse is that most people spend even far less time communicating with our Creator to find out his Life Plans for their Lives so they can experience the true peace, harmony, and balance that comes from submitting their wills to him and his Plan for them.

Peace, harmony, and balance in life will never be found in technology. It will only be experienced as we follow the Life Plan our Creator has for us. However, for that to happen, we must first slow down the pace of our lives. We must find a quiet place of solitude, and spend the time necessary for our spirits to communicate spirit to Spirit with our Creator—and that is why he gave us the Lifestyle Ceremony of Rest and Renewal.

REST COMES BEFORE RENEWAL

Most people in our fast paced society don't really know how to rest. In order to rest, we must first be able to relax, and it is extremely difficult to relax in the midst of the hustle and bustle of the city with horns honking, sirens screaming, the noise of planes flying overhead, the bumper to bumper traffic jams on our freeways and the boom! boom! boom! coming from the radio of the car stopped next to us at the red light.

Even in the so-called quiet of our own homes, the TV's and radios keep us distracted, the kids need our attention, our spouses want some of our time, the phone rings and our bosses want to discuss the business meetings at our offices the first thing in the morning.

When and where is there time to really relax in our schedules? And, unless we can find time to relax, we will never be able to get the proper rest we need to prepare ourselves for renewal.

WE SHOULD PATTERN OUR LIVES AFTER THE CYCLE OF SACRED SEASONS

In order to learn to live in peace, harmony and balance with our

Creator and his Sacred Family of Life, we must first pattern our lives after the Cycle of Sacred Seasons he has set in motion. The Sacred Seasons have much to teach us about Sacred Living. They reveal the secrets and Spiritual Mysteries concerning how to walk this Sacred Path toward our Creator.

For example, Spring begins with the arousal of Nature from its Winter rest and sleep and once more starts the Cycle of Life on the road to new beginnings. Summer is the time of growth and increased activity in Nature, and Fall begins the transition from the many activities of Summer to the quiet rest of Winter in Nature's World.

The Cycle of Sacred Seasons is no accident. It was designed and put in place by our Creator so that the Cycle could remain perpetual, never-ending, and always strong, each Sacred Season accomplishing that for which it was created. Therefore, if we want to live in peace, harmony and balance with our Creator and his Sacred Circle of Life, and remain strong and accomplish that for which he created us, we also must pattern our lives after his Cycle of Sacred Seasons.

THE STARTING POINT

After the Sacred Fire Ceremony is completed that marks the completion of the transition from Fall to Winter, within a few days we go on our first Winter Spirit Quest. The purpose of this Spirit Quest is to ask our Creator to reveal the major areas of our lives in which renewal needs to occur, including physical, mental, emotional and Spiritual renewal. What our Creator tells us will become the areas we will spend our time working on during the Sacred Winter Season. In fact, they should be the only things that consume the majority of our time during the Winter months.

WHAT IS RENEWAL?

What are we talking about when we say that the Sacred Season of

Winter is the time for renewal? Webster's Collegiate Dictionary defines renewal as to "M*ake like new. Restore to freshness, vigor, or perfection. To make new spiritually. Regenerate. To restore to existence. Revive. To make extensive changes in. Rebuild. To do again. Repeat. To begin again. Resume. Replace. Replenish.*" That is what we focus on physically, emotionally, mentally, and spiritually during the Sacred Season of Winter.

HOW DO WE ACHIEVE RENEWAL?

In order to achieve renewal, we must first slow down and stop doing the things that depleted us during the Sacred Seasons of Spring, Summer and Fall. We must first rest from those activities. This is also what Nature does.

During the Spring, Summer, and Fall Seasons we expend a lot of physical, mental, emotional, and Spiritual energy. The Winter Season is the time we replenish and replace that spent energy. It is the time we become revitalized physically, mentally, emotionally and Spiritually—all of which is necessary preparation for the new beginnings we will be involved in come Spring.

Renewal can't begin until we first rest from and stop doing those things that depleted us. First we rest; then renewal begins. That is one of the reasons there are very few ceremonies assigned to the Winter Season. The main ceremonies of Winter are the Purification and Spirit Quest ceremonies, and they are performed as often as needed. Both of those ceremonies prepare us for and aid us in the renewal process.

In addition, during the Winter Season, we spend a lot of time traveling to our Private World in order to find out from our Creator and his helpers what aspects of our lives need renewing, and how to proceed in the renewal process.

THE PROCESS OF RENEWAL IS DIFFERENT FOR EACH PERSON

Much of the initial information we need to begin the process of renewal will be given to us during Purification Ceremonies, Spirit Quests, and as we travel to our Private World. Keep in mind that our Creator is more concerned about our renewal than we are. That is why he gave us the Sacred Season of Winter. During the Winter months, the days are colder and the nights longer so that we spend more time inside resting and doing things that will bring about our physical, emotional, mental, and Spiritual renewal. For me, I find that some of my greatest progress in renewal comes at night as I work on the areas our Creator has shown me that I need to work on.

I encourage you to participate in the Purification and Spirit Quest ceremonies often during the Winter Season because you will find that our Creator uses those ceremonies to clarify for you specifically what you need to do during your process of renewal. Your process will be different from mine because our areas needing to be replenished may be different. Our Creator tailor makes a renewal plan designed for each of us. He knows our needs better than we do. He knows our weaknesses better than we do. And he knows how to renew us better than we do. Therefore, we should spend a lot of time with our Creator discussing our needs for renewal, and then follow his guidance during the renewal process.

Much more could be said about the renewal process. However, Webster's definition of renewal not only defines it, but also gives us clues concerning how to achieve it. On the previous few pages, we have enough information to get us started on the process of renewal and, after all, that is the purpose of the material in each teaching session—it just gets us started so we can let our Creator do the teaching and guiding.

CONCLUSION

It is important to keep in mind that renewal is a process—a process that begins following a period of rest.

I have personally found that the Sacred Season of Winter is the most important Season for me because it allows me to get recharged, so that I am eager and anxious for the new beginnings soon to start with the coming of Spring.

The Lifestyle Ceremony of Rest and Renewal makes it possible for us to maintain a high level of achievement throughout all of the Sacred Seasons. I have experienced in my own life that without the Sacred Season of Winter, it is impossible for me to develop and maintain the level and quality of peace, harmony and balance in my life that our Creator intended. I suspect you will discover the same will be true in your own life.

BOOK FIVE

Rites of Passage: Keeping Us Anchored to the Sacred Cycle of Life

INTRODUCTION TO BOOK FIVE
Initiation and Its Role in the Rites of Passage

Every ancient culture had what we commonly call today "Rites of Passage". These Rites were often secret ceremonies and initiations that were performed at various stages of a person's life, including at birth, puberty and death. The Rites of Passage ceremonies for men were usually different from those for women. However, they all had one thing in common—they helped keep the individual anchored to and focused on the Sacred Cycle of Life.

The ancient Rites of Passage ceremonies celebrated life. They taught respect for one's elders and honored the wisdom that comes with old age. They bound one generation to the next and promoted self-respect. They instilled personal responsibility and taught love of family and community. And most importantly, they helped develop a strong connection between the individual and our Creator.

Unfortunately, most people in our modern Western World seem to view the ancient Rites of Passage as barbaric and without value for today's so-called sophisticated and enlightened society. People today tend to believe that the Old Ones from ancient cultures have nothing of value to offer our highly advanced world where technology is often worshiped as the god that can solve any problem. However, it is our opinion that many of the social problems found in our modern world exist today because during the Age of Enlightenment most Westerners discarded the Rites of Passage ceremonies that were once practiced in one form or another by all of their ancient clans and tribes.

On the following pages of this book, we will present some of the major Rites of Passage ceremonies practiced on *The Way of the Medicine Wheel*. We will explain their importance and value and present the step-by-step process that modern man can follow to re-institute these important ceremonies into their families today.

INITIATION

Many years ago Robert Tall Tree, an Ojibwa Indian spiritual leader, took me out into the foothills of the Rocky Mountains in Colorado at sunrise and performed an initiation ceremony for me to become a Pipe Carrier for the people. The initiation involved a commitment on my part to faithfully fulfill my obligations as a Pipe Carrier and to carry on the traditions, duties and responsibilities that went with carrying the Sacred Pipe for the people. Robert performed with me certain rituals, and passed on to me Sacred Knowledge associated with being a Pipe Carrier.

What is initiation? Who should be initiated? Who does the initiating? And how does one's life change following initiation? I will attempt to answer all of these questions during the remainder of this introduction to Book Five.

WHAT IS INITIATION?

Over the years grandfather Old Bear has talked to me a lot about the Rites of Passage associated with this Sacred Path. During these many discussions, he frequently talks about these Rites as "Initiation Ceremonies" in which with each Rite of Passage we are initiated into the next phase of life within the great Sacred Cycle of Life.

What is initiation? Initiation ceremonies are different from other ceremonies in that at the very basic level they mark a new beginning in a person's life. On this Sacred Path, initiations are always conducted in the East on the medicine wheel. New beginnings start in the East and the new Sacred Knowledge that is brought to us during an initiation comes from the East.

All initiation ceremonies are very sacred because they are the most important keys for growth and development that we have on *The Way of the Medicine Wheel*. Initiations unlock our Creator's sacred Knowledge and Power, making it known to us. Initiations are the rungs on the spiritual ladder that enable us to climb higher and higher into the Spiritual Realm. Initiations are the ultimate test of the Five Spiritual Medicines in the lives of those being initiated. And during a successful initiation ceremony, the Five Spiritual Medicines are collectively at work in the initiate's life. Unless The Five Spiritual Medicines are collectively at work in the initiate's life, the initiation cannot and will not be completed.

Initiation marks the beginning of change in the initiate's life. It signals a time of new growth and awareness on a Spiritual level. Initiation brings with it new commitments, responsibilities, obligations, and accountability.

On this Sacred Path, initiations are always for the benefit of others within the clan, tribe or community, not for the benefit of the initiate. During the initiation rites, the initiate makes a commitment to serve some aspect of the needs of the Sacred Circle of Life. The initiate assumes more responsibilities and obligations to meet those needs, and is held accountable by our Creator and the initiate's peers to fulfill those responsibilities and obligations of service.

What is initiation? On this Sacred Path, it is the beginning of increased service to the Sacred Circle of Life. What is initiation? It is increased sacrifice of self for the benefit of others. What is initiation? It is the progressive transformation into a life of giving instead of taking. What is initiation? It is the ultimate proof of how well we have fulfilled our commitment, responsibilities, and obligations in the past. What is initiation? It is proof of our Creator's trust in our commitment to faithfully fulfill our increased responsibilities, obligations, and commitments in the future.

WHAT ARE THE QUALIFICATIONS FOR INITIATION?

In the previous paragraph, we stated that initiation is the beginning of increased service to the Sacred Circle of Life. The most important qualifications for initiation focus on how faithfully the initiate performed his or her previous responsibilities, obligations, and commitments to serving the needs of those in the Circle of Life. We can never be initiated into greater levels of service and Spiritual Awareness if we are unfaithful in properly performing our current responsibilities, obligations, and commitments of service to the Sacred Circle of Life.

The qualifications for future initiations are directly dependent on how well we perform at our current level of initiation. Our Creator will not entrust us with more Spiritual Knowledge and responsibilities until we are faithfully carrying out our current obligations.

So, if you want more of our Creator's Sacred Power flowing through you and out to others to meet their needs, make sure you are faithfully serving others at your current level of initiation. The best way to become qualified for the next level of initiation on this Sacred Path is to faithfully perform all of the responsibilities our Creator is currently giving you, and always make sure you are constantly implementing the Five Spiritual Medicines in your life.

If you are faithful in performing the small responsibilities of service you will be entrusted with greater responsibilities of service. Remember that you must learn to be a good follower before you are qualified to become a good leader. Poor followers make very poor leaders because the follower's main responsibility is to learn how to serve. The best followers are those who learn to serve best. Leaders are the ultimate servants. Therefore, if you want to become a good leader you must first learn how to be an excellent server.

Never seek the "limelight", but seek to be unnoticed as you perform your service duties. What is your motivation for seeking greater levels of initiation? Is it to draw attention to yourself and feed your own ego, or is it to quietly perform greater levels of service within the Sacred Circle of Life? Those who seek greater levels of initiation to feed their own egos will discover that our Creator will not entrust them with more responsibility.

Remember that it is far better to strive for obedience to our Creator than to seek recognition from our peers. The service we faithfully perform in secret will be faithfully recognized and rewarded by our Creator. However, the recognition we seek from our peers will be short lived and without reward from our Creator. Our Creator rewards humility but severely disciplines the proud.

Strive for greater obedience rather than greater responsibility. The more faithful we are in obeying the things our Creator asks of us today, the greater responsibilities he will give us in the future. However, those who seek greater responsibility in the present but ignore the obligations of service they already have will receive little or nothing from our Creator in the future.

So how do we prepare ourselves for initiation? Humbly obey all our Creator asks of us without complaint and without selfish motivation.

WHO DOES THE INITIATING?

Earlier, I mentioned that a close friend of mine, Robert Tall Tree, performed the ceremony when I was initiated as a Pipe Carrier. Robert performed the initiation ceremony; however, it was our Creator who initiated me as a Pipe Carrier.

It is our Creator who initiates us into the next level of service; it is not the initiation ceremony. No two legged can initiate another two legged. We have no Spiritual Power. All Spiritual Power comes from our Creator. He gives us the initiation ceremony to be performed, but the person conducting the ceremony doesn't do the initiating. Only our Creator can initiate us into the next step or level of Spiritual Awareness, Understanding and Responsibility.

All Sacred Spiritual Knowledge comes to us from our Creator. All Spiritual Responsibility is delegated to us from our Creator. Only our Creator has the power to Create. We can rearrange what has already been created, but we are powerless to create something out of nothing.

People who think they have the power to heal or the knowledge to know the future are deceived. The power to heal comes from our Creator —not from ourselves. And likewise, the power to initiate a person into greater levels or realms of Sacred Spiritual Awareness, Knowledge or Responsibility comes from our Creator, not from the one performing the initiation ceremony.

This great Spiritual Truth must permeate every cell of our being. It must be the foundation on which our Spiritual Path rests. It must so saturate our hearts and minds that it controls and molds our every thought, word, and action. A deep awareness of this fact becomes the source of our humility and motivates us to become hollow bones through which our Creator's Unconditional Love can flow into us uninhibited, and out to meet the needs of those within the Sacred Circle of Life.

HOW DOES ONE'S LIFE CHANGE FOLLOWING INITIATION?

I am continually dismayed by the lack of change that seems to occur in some people's lives even though they have participated in Sacred Ceremonies for years and years. As I said earlier, initiation brings with it new Sacred Knowledge, obligations and responsibilities. Our Creator entrusts us with greater obligations and responsibilities of service.

During initiation ceremonies, more and more of our self-centered egos are stripped away so that we can be of greater service to others within the Sacred Circle of Life. Therefore, following initiation, we should be more humble and have more of a servant's heart, not more proud and egotistical.

Greater responsibility brings with it greater temptation. The more responsibility our Creator gives us, the more recognition we receive from our peers. And the more recognition we receive from others, the more we are tempted to become proud, arrogant and even haughty in our dealings with others. If we succumb to such temptations, we quickly become deceived into believing that it is our power—not our Creator's power—

which is helping the people. We must never forget that it is the Five Spiritual Medicines that enable us to resist this great temptation.

Greater obligation brings with it increased accountability. Initiation not only increases our obligations of service; it also increases our accountability for our actions. For example, during the Rite of Passage from adolescence to adulthood, part of the initiation ceremony focuses on the increased obligations and accountability that occurs when an individual's role changes from childhood to adulthood.

Adults have more obligations and are held to higher standards of accountability than children are. And just as that is true within the clan or tribe, it is also true concerning our individual relationships with our Creator. The further we progress on this

Spiritual Path, the greater our accountability is to our Creator for our actions. So how do we successfully fulfill our obligations? We always make sure we are taking The Five Spiritual Medicines—they are the cure for all of our Spiritual weaknesses.

We will now look at a few of the major Rites of Passage that anchor us to this Sacred Path we refer to as *The Way of the Medicine Wheel.* Even though these are ancient rites, they have great meaning and value for our modern societies. It is our prayer that you will benefit as much from these Rites and initiations as we have.

Teaching Session –17
THE RITE OF PARENTHOOD
The Creation of New Life

I followed grandfather Old Bear across the river that flows through My Private World and along a trail that led up into the foothills of the high, rugged mountains that frame the western horizon. I had never been in this area of My Private World before, and I wondered why we were walking so far. Finally, grandfather sat down on a rocky knoll that provided a sweeping view of the upper southern end of the long valley and patted the rock he was sitting on, indicating that I should sit down beside him.

He smiled his warm, loving smile and said, "I brought you to a new area because its time for you to begin learning new things about this Sacred Path. It was a long walk getting here because we are going to deal with the deeper aspects of your journey on The Way of the Medicine Wheel. All you have been taught up to this point has only been preparation for what you must now learn."

He sat there in silence for a long time and I thought he had gone to sleep, but after a while he continued. "This is a beautiful spot isn't it?"

"Yes," I replied, sorry I hadn't done more exploring of My Private World in past years.

"It wasn't time for you to come here yet," he commented matter-of-factly, as if he knew my thoughts. "Each place in your Private World has it own special things to teach you. This is the place you will learn about our Sacred Rites of Passage.

*"One of the reasons your world is in the mess it is in is because it has abandoned the Ancient Sacred Ways our Creator gave the Old Ones long, long ago. Grandson, never forget what I'm about to tell you—**every step***

you take away from our Creator's Sacred Path, your life becomes more and more chaotic, and that is why your world is in the mess it is in today."

He smiled broadly as he looked over at me. *"You do want to escape from all the chaos around you, don't you, grandson?"*

Until I started meeting with this Old One I hadn't thought of the world I lived in as being so chaotic. I had been content with living the way everyone else I knew lived, and I had enjoyed all the "goodies and gadgets" the Madison Avenue marketing gurus worked so hard to convince me that I couldn't live without. However, after meeting grandfather Old Bear, and spending countless hours with him learning about this Sacred Path, I now not only understood what he was telling me, but I also agreed with what he was saying.

Therefore, I eagerly replied, *"Yes, grandfather, I certainly want to escape from all the chaos I find around me in my modern world."*

He nodded as if to indicate that he already knew that, and continued. *"You're now ready to travel further along this Sacred Path and learn the important role the ancient Rites of Passage play in keeping you anchored to our Creator and his Sacred Cycle of Life.*

"Grandson, it is important that you deeply understand what I'm about to tell you because in recent times understanding of the dual purpose and meaning of the Rites of Passage has been lost by most who still attempt to follow the Old Ways."

Then, staring deep into my eyes he said, ***"Our Rites of Passage have a dual purpose and meaning as we walk this Sacred Path. They not only move us from one stage of our physical lives to the next, they also move us from one stage of our Spiritual***

Lives to the next.

"So you see, grandson, the Rites of Passage not only keep us strongly connected to our physical families and communities, they also keep us strongly connected to our Creator and the Spiritual Realm. Each Rite of Passage not only initiates us into more and more commitment, responsibility, obligation, and accountability to our physical families and

communities, it also initiates us into more and more commitment, responsibility, obligation, and accountability in the Spiritual Realm.

"Each Rite of Passage is divided into two parts. The first part deals with the increased commitment, responsibilities, obligations, and accountability the initiate receives in regards to living in the physical realm. The second part deals with the increased commitment, responsibilities, obligations, and accountability he or she receives in regards to serving our Creator and the Sacred Circle of Life from a Spiritual perspective.

"As I have explained to you over and over, this Sacred Path combines the physical realm and the Spiritual Realm together into a single reality. What we do on the physical level effects us on a Spiritual level also, and what we do on a Spiritual level effects us here on the physical level. Therefore, the Rites of Passage are designed to help further fuse these two realms together in our lives. They play an important role in the creation of peace, harmony, and balance as we travel through the Sacred Cycle of Life."

For the most part, the remainder of these teaching sessions contain what I have learned from grandfather Old Bear concerning the Sacred Rites of Passage and the initiation ceremonies associated with these rites. Some of the information may be offensive to those who have been deceived by our modern Western World that constantly strives for political correctness and pushes for the feminization of all males and the "masculinization" of all females. However, I would much rather be Spiritually correct in the eyes of our Creator than politically correct in the eyes of a humanistic society.

The Rites of Passage create strong bonds between children and their parents, between youth and old age, between males and females, between the individual and the community, clan and tribe, between each stage of the Sacred Cycle of Life and between the initiate and our Creator and his Sacred Family.

As stated in the introduction to this book, they are truly anchors that help keep us securely bonded to this Sacred Path as we travel through Life. They are the rungs in the Spiritual Ladder, enabling us to climb higher and higher into the Spiritual realm. Therefore, we strongly encourage all of you to incorporate these Rites of Passage into your personal lives and the lives of your family members.

CONCEPTION
The Rite of Parenthood

The Rite of Parenthood is the first Sacred Rite of Passage. Conception is our Creator's act of placing a Sacred New Life in the womb of a woman. Conception is the result of the Sacred Physical Union between a man and woman. Conception turns women into mothers and men into fathers. Conception is the first step in the preservation of the Sacred Circle of Life. Conception is the means by which the Spiritual Realm becomes bonded with the physical realm, bringing them together into a single reality. Conception is truly our Creator's greatest single Sacred and Holy act of on-going Creation.

During one of our many discussions of the Rites of Passage Old Bear said, "Grandson, you must carefully listen to what I'm about to tell you."

He took a stick from the ground and began slowly and carefully drawing a medicine wheel design in the dirt. Finally, he was ready to continue. "Conception is the point in time in which our Creator sends our spirits into the wombs of our mothers so we can receive our physical bodies. We are spirits, but we have been sent here to live in a physical world. Therefore, our Creator must give us physical bodies so we can function in and relate to our physical surroundings.

"Pregnancy is the time in which our spirits and physical bodies are bonded together. It brings the Spiritual Realm and the physical realm together into a single reality within a Mother's Womb. So you can see that the time of pregnancy is a very sacred and holy time."

The Old One looked up into the deep, blue sky overhead and seemed to be checking with our Creator to make sure he was wording things correctly. Without taking his eyes off the heavens he said, "Before Conception, our spirits live with our Creator." He seemed to be gazing directly into the face of our Creator as he continued. "Grandson, there are no accidents when it comes to Conception. Our Creator sends each spirit here for a specific purpose. We are all here for an important reason. He has a special Life Plan for each of us. That is why the Rite of Parenthood is such an important Rite of Passage.

"At the time of Conception, our spirits bring with us the Sacred Knowledge of Right and Wrong. We already have our Creator's Sacred Laws of Right Living embedded within our consciousness. However, we do not know how to live in and relate to the physical realm. Therefore, it is our parents' responsibility to teach us these skills."

He looked over at me with one of the most somber expressions I had ever seen on his old, wrinkled face. "Unfortunately, all too many parents in your world don't know how to properly relate to the physical world, and most of them know even less about relating to the Spiritual Realm." His face took on an expression of deep pain as he continued. "Each passing generation tends to know less and less of our Creator's Sacred Laws of Right Living and, as a result, it has less and less respect for Mother Earth and the Sacred Circle of Life.

"Parents pass on to their Children both their good and bad habits. If a father uses very bad language, his son will generally use worse language. If a husband physically abuses his wife, their son will usually abuse his wife. That is why the Sacred Rite of Parenthood is so important. It helps insure that our Parents will teach their children how to put our Creator's Sacred Laws of Right Living into action here in the physical world."

THE RITE OF PARENTHOOD

On this Sacred Path, parenthood begins at the time of Conception, not when the infant emerges from the womb into the physical world. Therefore, the Rite of Parenthood is conducted within the first moon cycle following the confirmation of the pregnancy. As stated earlier, Conception turns women into mothers and men into fathers. And if the man and woman are already parents, it turns them into new mothers and fathers. Therefore, the Rite of Parenthood is performed with the Conception of each new Life.

The Rite of Parenthood is the celebration of New Life. The Rite of Parenthood is the celebration of Motherhood and Fatherhood. The Rite of Parenthood is the celebration of our Creator's greatest display of his Love for the Sacred Circle of Life—the gift of a New Life being given to a woman and man to care for, love, and teach the Ancient Sacred Ways.

It is important to understand that it is not the Rite of Parenthood that turns a woman and man into a Mother and Father—a woman and man become a Mother and Father at the time of Conception. The Rite of Parenthood sets forth the responsibilities, obligations, and accountabilities as parents. The new Mother and Father have new responsibilities, obligations, and accountabilities to each other as new parents. They also have new responsibilities, obligations, and accountabilities to the new Life. They have new responsibilities, obligations, and accountabilities to the family and community and most importantly, they have new responsibilities, obligations, and accountabilities to our Creator. All of these are dealt with during the Rite of Parenthood.

Unlike some Sacred Ceremonies, Rites of Passage ceremonies and initiations are very private ceremonies and only those receiving special invitations may attend.

THE RITE OF PARENTHOOD IS A SEMI-PRIVATE CEREMONY

Only those receiving personal invitations are permitted to attend a Rite of Parenthood ceremony because this is a very sacred and private time for the new Mother and Father. Therefore, one of the first things done in preparing for the ceremony is to determine who will be invited. Normally, those in attendance would be the parents and grandparents of the new Mother and Father, immediate family members, special close friends and elders in the community, and the spiritual leader or elder chosen to perform the initiation ceremony. The person chosen to perform the ceremony will be in charge of both the physical and spiritual aspects of the initiation.

PREPARATIONS FOR THE PHYSICAL ASPECTS OF THE CEREMONY

First, the couple must decide where the physical ceremony will be performed. It is almost always conducted inside the couple's home. However, it may be performed in the home of one of their parents or grandparents if they are still living. The Spiritual part of the ceremony will be conducted outside, but the physical aspects of the ceremony are always performed inside.

It will be conducted during the first full moon after the confirmation of pregnancy. It must be performed at night. The exact time will need to be coordinated with the person who is to perform the ceremony.

On the day of the ceremony, the couple will remove all of the furniture from the room where the ceremony is to be performed. They will cover all windows and doors with black or dark blankets so that no light can enter the room from outside the house. The room where the ceremony is conducted symbolizes the mother's womb, and covering the windows and doors symbolizes protecting the new life from the negative forces at work within the physical realm.

ITEMS NEEDED TO PERFORM THE CEREMONY

The Spiritual Elder performing the ceremony will gather together the following items to be used in performing the ceremony.

- Two kernels of corn, one painted green and one painted red.
- Two small "medicine pouches" that can be worn around the neck.
- An ear of Indian Corn.
- Yellow Cotton cloth to wrap the ear of corn in.
- A piece of Yellow Cotton cloth, one inch wide and three feet long.
- A bag of blue cornmeal.
- A bag of yellow cornmeal.
- A black, red, yellow and white cotton flag, each 3" X 3'.
- Sage, Cedar and Sweet grass for smudging.
- A shell for smudging.
- Sacred Water from the Sacred Water Ceremony.
- Red earth paint.
- Blue earth paint.
- Black earth paint.
- A piece of Cottonwood limb ½" X 6".
- Yellow Cotton cloth to wrap around the Cottonwood limb.
- A small, white breath feather.
- Small Cotton cord approximately 2' long.
- Sacred Food (dried meat, water, fresh fruit, and fried cornmeal with sugar and raisins.)
- Sacred tobacco and cornhusks for preparing a cornhusk pipe.
- Tobacco to sprinkle on the floor of the circle.
- Drum
- A gourd to serve as a drinking cup.
- Four candles to be used for light during the ceremony.

PREPARING THE ITEMS FOR THE CEREMONY

The Ceremonial leader will remove the bark from the small Cottonwood limb and round off one end. He will then paint the stick with the red earth paint. After the stick dries, using the blue earth paint, he will paint a zig zag line like a lightning bolt down the full length of the stick. When the line is dry, he will paint two black dots across the face of the rounded end. These two black dots will represent the eyes of the face.

The Ceremonial leader will cover the bottom two thirds of the stick with the yellow cotton cloth. This will represent the clothes on the stick. He will then glue the small, white breath feather on the back of the stick's head. Tacky Glue or Super Glue will work well for gluing the feather. When this is completed, he will smudge the stick and wrap it in a piece of red cotton cloth or a piece of leather. This will symbolize the unborn child. He will present this to the Mother during the ceremony.

He will prepare all of the strips of colored cloth as described above, and then smudge all the items to be used during the ceremony. As he does this, he will pray that the unborn child will be born healthy and grow up to faithfully follow this Sacred Path and obey all our Creator asks of him or her. He will also pray for the Mother to have a safe and easy delivery during childbirth, and that the Father and Mother would nurture the child with Love.

On the day of the ceremony, the ceremonial leader will arrive early at the home where the ceremony is to take place. After the ceremonial room has been prepared for the ceremony, he will smudge every room inside the house and then smudge the area outside house. First, he will smudge the inside of the house with sage and then with sweet grass. As he smudges both the inside and outside of the house he will pray, asking our Creator to remove all negative energy from the area and surround the area with his Unconditional Love.

After smudging the house, he will make a circle on the floor of the room using the blue cornmeal. The circle will be about eight feet in diameter with an opening in the east about two feet wide. Next, he will make a circle of yellow cornmeal just inside the blue cornmeal circle and will leave an opening in the east about two feet wide. The circle of blue cornmeal symbolizes the spiritual realm and the circle of yellow cornmeal represents the physical realm.

Next, the ceremonial leader will place the yellow flag on the floor on the East side of the circle. The end of the yellow flag will touch the circle of blue cornmeal. He will place the white flag on the South, the black flag on the West and the red flag on the North. The flags will be placed on the floor and the end of each flag will touch the blue cornmeal circle.

Once the flags are in place, the ceremonial leader will sprinkle tobacco all over the inside of the circle, and place the bags of blue and yellow cornmeal next to the opening on the East to be used to close the circle once everyone is inside. He will then place the four candles in the Four Sacred Directions. These candles will be lit when the ceremony begins, just prior to meeting with the new Mother and Father in a separate room.

The ceremonial leader is now ready to meet with the new Mother and Father privately in a separate room of the house. He will pray for them, asking our Creator to help them be good parents and an excellent example to the child of the Sacred Laws of Right Living in action. He will also pray that the parents will effectively teach the child how to walk this Sacred Path, and that the child will grow up to be a servant of the Sacred Circle of Life.

The leader will then use some of the Sacred Water to prepare the Sacred Red Earth Paint. The leader will then leave the room while the husband rubs it on his wife's stomach and forehead and the wife rubs it on her husband's forehead and over his heart. As they do this, they will promise our Creator and each other to always be an excellent example to this child of the Sacred Laws of Right Living in action.

Once this is completed, the ceremonial leader will return to the room and load the Cornhusk Pipe and then smudge the couple with cedar smoke. He will walk in front of the couple as he continues to smudge the path in front of them with cedar smoke, while he leads them to the room where the rest of the ceremony will be conducted.

When they reach the ceremonial room, he will lead the group in singing the Four Direction Song and then the Give Away Song. When the songs are completed, he will pray again to our Creator, thanking him for this couple's commitment to follow these Sacred Ways as they raise the child.

When the prayer is completed, the leader will instruct the new parents to sit on the floor on the West side of the circle near the black flag. He will paint the soles of their feet and palms of their hands with the Sacred Red Earth Paint. As he does this, he will explain that this confirms their commitment to always raise the child in the Sacred Ways, and to be a good example of the Sacred Laws of Right Living at all times.

The Ceremonial leader will smudge the couple again with cedar smoke, and then lead them around the northern side of the circle to the entrance of the eastern side. The husband will stand beside his wife so that with his right hand he can hold her left hand. Then, the leader will use the piece of long yellow cotton cloth to tie their wrists together, just above their clasped hands. As he does this, he will say that our Creator has listened to every word of their commitment and is now binding them together in their obligation to raise the child in the Sacred Ways.

He will remind the couple that all of those in attendance are now witnesses to their commitment and are available to help them in any way they can as the couple raises the child to follow the Sacred Ways. Each person in attendance will then come forward and shake the couples' clasped hands and confirm their commitment to help the couple in any way they can as they raise the child in the Sacred Ways.

The leader will then use a small branch of sage to sprinkle the Sacred Water on them before leading the couple inside the Sacred Circle. Once they are inside the circle, he will use the cornmeal to close the circle behind them. He will then explain that these two Sacred Circles symbolize the spiritual and physical realms, and that the couple has made a commitment to our Creator to follow the Sacred Path and teach their child these Sacred Ways.

He will hold the green and red kernels of corn in his left hand and raise them up toward the sky and pray, asking our Creator to empower the Mother and Father to always be united in their commitment to raise the child in the old Sacred Ways. He will put the green kernel in one leather pouch and the red one in the other and tie the green one around the Mother's neck and the red one around the Father's neck.

He will explain that they will wear these leather pouches around their necks until the child is born as a constant reminder of their commitment to raise the child to follow this Sacred Path and to always live according to our Creator's Sacred Laws Of Right Living.

He will then give the Mother the "fetish doll", made from a small Cottonwood limb, and tell her this doll symbolizes their new child and that she is to place it on the altar in their home. She is to then pray for the child every day to be born healthy and strong and to grow up to faithfully serve our Creator and follow the Life Plan he has for the child. The mother will keep the doll and give it to the child during his or her Rite of Passage into Adulthood.

The ceremonial leader will give the ear of corn to the Father and tell him to place it on the altar in their home. He will explain that the ear of corn symbolizes the Father's responsibility and commitment to always provide for his Family including the new child that our Creator has given him. He will also explain that the ear of corn will be kept on the altar until the child's fourth birthday. They will then help the child plant the corn during the Planting Ceremony, and the corn produced from this ear of corn will be saved as seed for the child to plant the first planting season after he or she is initiated into Adulthood. This symbolizes the tying together of the generations and the passing on of the Sacred Ways from one generation to the next. The ceremonial leader will explain that the way parents raise their children determine—to a great extent—whether or not future generations follow the Sacred Ways.

The ceremonial leader will then lead the couple to each of the Four

Sacred Directions, beginning in the West, and offer a prayer for the couple, invoking our Creator's power from each Sacred Direction to help the couple to be good parents and fulfill their commitment to pass on these Sacred Ways to their children.

Following the prayer, the leader will reopen the Sacred Circle in the East and instruct the couple and the rest of those in attendance to form a circle around the cornmeal. He will then light the Cornhusk Pipe and pass it clockwise around the circle of people. After the Pipe has been smoked, he will give the remaining part of the Pipe to the Father and instruct him to place it on the altar at home for four days. On the fourth day, he will bury the remains of the Pipe on the West side of the couple's home.

The leader will lead the group in the singing of the Thank You song and the Completion song, and then the couple will serve a meal to those in attendance. This completes the first part of the Rite of Parenthood ceremony.

The second part of the ceremony will be conducted at another time and will consist of the couple participating in a Purification Ceremony with the ceremony leader. Following the Purification Ceremony, the couple will then participate together in a Spirit Quest to strengthen their Spiritual connection to our Creator and to receive further instructions from him concerning how they are to better prepare themselves as parents during the time of pregnancy.

RESPONSIBILITIES, OBLIGATIONS AND ACCOUNTABILITIES OF THE PARENTS

Grandfather Old Bear once told me that parents have a very great influence on future generations. He said, "If parents realized that how they live and how they raise their children will influence many generations in the future, they would take parenthood more seriously. This Sacred Path begins at the front of the home and ends at the back." He gave me one of his serious looks and then said, "If you don't know what that means, talk to our Creator—he will help you understand its meaning."

At first I didn't understand what grandfather Old Bear was saying. However, after many trips to the Spirit Quest circle, I have come to understand what the Old One was saying that day. Commitment, responsibility, obligation, and accountability are taught in the home by the parents. The home is the place where individuals are knit together into a strong family unit.

The home is the place where every principle of this Sacred Path is put into practice. The home is the place where peace, harmony and balance are to be on continual display. The home is the place where the Sacred Laws of Right Living are taught and lived. The home is the place where the Five Spiritual Medicines are taught and practiced. The home is a Sacred Sanctuary, its walls protect Holy Ground and become a shield against the negative forces at work in the physical realm. The home is a reflection of how well the parents are fulfilling the commitments they made during the Rite of Parenthood.

During the Rite of Parenthood the parents make a commitment to our Creator, the unborn child, each other, the community and future generations to faithfully pass on these Sacred Ways to the child. During the Rite of Parenthood the parents assume all of the responsibilities, obligations and accountabilities associated with passing these Sacred Ways on to the child. During the Rite of Parenthood the parents pledge to support and help each other in fulfilling all of their commitments, responsibilities, obligations and accountability involved in passing these Sacred Ways on to the child. And during the Rite of Parenthood those in attendance also pledge their support and help to insure that the parents are successful in carrying out their commitments, responsibilities, obligations and accountability.

The Rite of Parenthood solidifies the parents' commitment to each other and to our Creator. The Rite of Parenthood is not only the first Rite of Passage on this Sacred Path, more than any of the other Sacred Rites, it helps insure that these Ancient Sacred Ways will be passed on to the next generation in as pure a form as possible.

Teaching Session – 18
THE RITE OF BIRTH

The Rite of Parenthood helps prepare the parents for the birth of their child. People sometimes ask us if one Rite of Passage is more important than another. The answer is, no, they are all equally important and one flows into the next, forming one Great Rite of Passage as we move through the Sacred Cycle of Life.

The Rite of Birth follows the Rite of Parenthood. During the Rite of Parenthood, the focus is on the parents. However, during the Rite of Birth, the focus is on the parent's new baby.

The Rite of Birth is always conducted at the first New Moon following the child's birth unless the New Moon occurs within one week following the firth. If that occurs then the Rite of Birth will be conducted approximately one month later at the next New Moon.

The Rite of Birth celebrates the new baby's entrance into the physical realm. The bonding of the spirit with the its' new physical body has been completed and now it is time to enter the physical world and begin the Sacred Journey back toward our Creator. As with all life, the spirit travels in a Sacred Cycle. It came from our Creator and once it emerges into the physical world with its new physical body it begins its journey back to our Creator.

During one of my conversations with grandfather Old Bear he said, "Our Creator always has a purpose in sending a spirit to live here in the physical world. Each of us has a Sacred Life Plan that focuses on making an important contribution to the Sacred Circle of Life. We are sent here for the specific purpose of following our Life Plans while we are here in the physical realm. We aren't here by accident, grandson. Our Creator doesn't have accidents or make mistakes.

"Parents need to realize that when they hold that helpless little baby in their arms they have a great responsibility to our Creator to raise that child to accomplish his or her Life Plan. In fact, having that baby and raising it to accomplish its Life Plan is part of our Creator's Life Plan for the parents. When parents hold their newborn baby in their arms they need to realize that they are holding the future of the world in their arms. Understanding that one thing will change the way parents relate to their children."

The Rite of Birth is performed outside in a medicine wheel during the daytime at the time of the New Moon. Like the Rite of Parenthood, it is a semi-private ceremony and only a few people are involved.

PREPARING FOR THE CEREMONY

The parents will invite people such as their parents, grandparents, and close personal friends. They will also arrange for an elder to perform the ceremony. If the infant is a girl a woman elder with strong spiritual connections to our Creator will perform the ceremony and if it is boy a man recognized for his strong spiritual standing will conduct the ceremony.

From the time of the infant's birth until the ceremony the parents will closely watch the baby's actions and reactions to its environment. They will also watch the physical environment's actions and reactions toward the infant, including birds and animals that may frequently come near. They will use these "signs" to help determine the first name the baby will receive and that name will be announced during the Rite of Passage.

Usually the child will carry that name until the Rite of Adulthood. However, if some very special event happens in the child's life before the age of puberty he or she may be given a new name in honor of that event.

Unlike new parents in today's modern world who pick a name that they like for the baby, on this Sacred Path the naming of individuals is a very Sacred activity. The name is associated with the individual's character, personality, abilities or a powerful special event that occurred in his or her life. The name always has some spiritual significance that may be known only to the individual and a few close relatives or friends. The name defines who the person is and describes some aspects of the individual's uniqueness.

The parents will also make preparations for the feast and a Give Away at the conclusion of the Rite of Birth Ceremony. For the Rite of Birth, the Give Away will always consist of food items to be given to those in attendance. The food symbolizes the productive life the baby will have and his or her contribution to meeting the needs of the community.

ITEMS NEEDED TO CONDUCT THE CEREMONY

The person chosen to perform the ceremony will gather together the following items for the ceremony.

- New directional flags for the medicine wheel.
- Sacred Water from the Sacred Water Ceremony.
- Tobacco.
- Sage, sweet grass, cedar and a shell for smudging.
- A deer skin or small blanket to wrap the infant in.
- A black, red, yellow, white and blue kernel of "Indian corn".
- A grinding bowl and grinding stone to use for making cornmeal.
- The leather medicine bags the parents have worn around their necks since the Rite of Parenthood.
- The ear of corn given to the parents during the Rite of Parenthood.
- A drum.
- Medicine Pipe tobacco and cornhusks for making the Cornhusk Pipe.
- Sacred Red Earth Paint.

APPROPRIATE CLOTHING FOR THE CEREMONY

The women in attendance will wear long skirts or dresses and shawls to cover their heads during the ceremony. If a female elder is conducting the ceremony, she will wear the same type of clothing described above. The men will wear jeans or casual long pants and long sleeved shirts. Men are not allowed to wear hats during the ceremony. The infant going through the Rite of Birth will wear only a dipper but will be wrapped in a deer skin or blanket.

CONDUCTING THE RITE OF BIRTH INITIATION

STEP ONE

Prior to the start of the ceremony the ceremonial leader will approach the medicine wheel from the West and conduct the Self-Offering ceremony near the stone marking the Sacred Direction of the West.

When the Self-Offering ceremony is completed, the ceremonial leader will replace the Directional Flags at each of the wheel's Sacred Directions. The leader will then enter the medicine wheel from the East and take all of the items to be used during the ceremony to the center of the wheel and place them at the base of the Center Stone. Next, the leader will remove any weeds, sticks or sharp stones that might hurt one's bare feet.

STEP TWO

The Ceremony will begin with each parent conducting the Self-Offering ceremony near the stone marking the Sacred Direction of the West on the medicine wheel. While the parents are performing the Self Offering ceremony, the leader will smudge those in attendance who have gathered along the eastern side of the medicine wheel just outside the Sacred Stone Circle.

STEP THREE

The ceremonial leader and the parents will remove their shoes before entering the medicine wheel. With the mother holding her baby, the leader will lead the couple into the medicine wheel and to the Center Stone. The leader will pray to our Creator thanking him for giving the parents the responsibility of raising the child to follow the ancient Sacred Ways. When the prayer is completed, the leader will place the black, red, yellow and white kernels of corn on the corresponding Directional Stones, each time returning to the Center Stone before proceeding to the next Directional Stone. The leader will then return to the Center Stone and place the kernel of blue corn on it.

STEP FOUR

The leader will then mix Sacred Water with the Red Earth Paint and paint the baby's big toes and thumbs with the red paint while the mother holds the infant. Next, the leader will take the baby in his or her arms and holding it slightly upward will pray, informing our Creator that the parents are giving the infant back to him for service in the Sacred Circle of Life.

The painting of the infant's big toes with Sacred Red Earth Paint symbolizes the infant walking this Sacred Path. The painting of the infant's thumbs symbolizes the child's life long service to the Sacred Circle of Life. The leader will then ask the parents to state the child's new name and then will lift the infant slightly skyward again and announce to our Creator the infant's new name.

The leader will then take the infant to the each of the Directional Stones, starting in the East and going clockwise around to the North, stopping at each Stone and loudly proclaiming the child's name. The leader will then take the baby out of the medicine wheel and hand it to the oldest person present and introduce him or her to the infant, stating its new name. In descending order of age, each person will be introduced to the baby, and the leader will state its name. As each person holds the infant, he or she will pray for it, asking our Creator to give it a long and healthy life of service to the Sacred Circle of Life.

STEP FIVE

The ceremonial leader will return the infant to its parents who have been waiting at the medicine wheel's Center Stone. The leader will give the baby to the Father to hold while he or she takes the mother to gather the five kernels of corn that have been placed on each of the Directions Stones and the Center Stone. The Mother will start with the stone in the East and move around the medicine wheel clockwise, each time returning to the Center Stone before proceeding to the next Directional Stone.

After collecting the kernels of corn from the Four Directional Stones, the leader and mother will return to the Center Stone and take the blue kernel of corn. The kernels of corn will be smudged with cedar smoke and placed in the grinding bowl and the Mother will grind the kernels of corn into fine cornmeal.

These five kernels of corn symbolize the Five Spiritual Medicines. When they have been ground into cornmeal the leader will lead the parents to the Directional Stone in the East. The Father will hold the baby while the Mother holds the bowl of cornmeal.

The leader will take a small pinch of cornmeal and holding it up to the East will pray, asking our Creator to give the infant the Medicine of Spiritual Courage as he or she walks this Sacred Path. The leader will then sprinkle the cornmeal on the baby's head and they will return to the Center Stone and then proceed to the Directional Stone in the South.

The leader will raise a small pinch of cornmeal up to the South and pray, asking our Creator to give the infant the Medicine of Spiritual Patience as he or she walks this Sacred Path and then sprinkle the cornmeal on the baby's head. They will continue this routine, traveling on to the West and then the North. In the West the leader will pray for the child to receive the Medicine of Spiritual Endurance and in the North the Medicine of Spiritual Alertness.

When they return to the Center Stone the leader will hold a small pinch of cornmeal up to our Creator and ask him to give the infant the Medicine of Humility. The leader will save a small pinch of the cornmeal

414

to be placed in the medicine pouch the mother has been wearing around her neck since the Rite of Parenthood. The leader will then take the kernels of corn form the Father and Mother's medicine pouch and grind them into cornmeal and place it in the Mother's pouch with the rest of the cornmeal.

The leader will then place the medicine pouch around the baby's neck. This pouch will be kept on the parent's family altar until the child reaches the age of puberty. The child will wear the medicine pouch during his or her Rite of Adulthood.

The cornmeal in the pouch now symbolizes the parent's commitment to pass these Sacred Ways on to their child. They will frequently hold the pouch as they pray for the child's journey through the Sacred Cycle of Life. The child will also be permitted to hold the pouch while praying for guidance and understanding of the Sacred Life Plan our Creator has for him or her. However, the child will not be permitted to wear the medicine pouch until his or her Rite of Adulthood.

STEP SIX

The leader will then lead the group in singing the Thank You song and the Completion song and they will proceed to the area where the feast and Give Away ceremony will be conducted. Following the feast the leader will tell the story of how our Creator gave the Give Away ceremony to the two-leggeds and the parents will then distribute the food to those in attendance.

As the food is distributed, the leader will explain that it symbolizes the way the child will grow up to serve the needs of the community and the Sacred Circle of Life, and this will conclude the Rite of Birth.

COMMITMENT, RESPONSIBILITIES, OBLIGATIONS AND ACCOUNTABILITY

The parents have the responsibility of teaching the young child the importance of fulfilling his or her commitments, responsibilities, obligations and accountability. The parents' first duty will be to begin teaching the child about our Creator and his Sacred Circle of Life. They will teach the young child the same principles that were presented in the first teaching session of book one in this book.

The parents will begin giving the small child responsibilities at a very young age, and teach him or her the importance of fulfilling their obligations to the family. As soon as possible the young child will begin assuming an important role in family life. If the child is a girl she will begin helping her Mother with all the duties and responsibilities of the woman. If it is a boy he will begin helping his Father with the men's responsibilities.

One of the main problems with many children and young people growing up in our large cities today is that they are not made to feel that they plan an important part in the family's well being. Both father and mother often work outside the home and from a very small age the children are often carted off to day care centers. Rarely do young children in the cities have enough to keep them busy contributing to the family's well being.

On the other hand, on this Sacred Path, the children quickly become an important contributor to daily family life. From an early age the children are given important duties in assisting the Father and Mother with their daily activities. The boys help gather fire wood, help build new dwellings for people in the village, help with the planting and care of the crops, help with the harvesting, participate in hunting trips and the butchering of the game, learn the ceremonies men participate in and at a relative young age go on their first Spirit Quest.

The girls learn to cook, help their Mothers with the duties around the house, assist in the planting and harvesting ceremonies and learn what it means to be a woman on this Sacred Path. By the time the child reaches puberty he or she is well on the way to learning how to live in peace, harmony and balance with the Sacred Circle of Life.

416

Teaching Session – 19
THE RITE OF ADULTHOOD

The more technologically advanced our society becomes, the longer it seems to take children to reach adulthood. Oh, they may be considered adults because of their biological age. However, many of them are not adults in terms of the maturity required to effectively fulfill their commitments, responsibilities, obligations and accountabilities.

There are many reasons why it seems to be taking linger and longer for children to reach adulthood an terms of their ability to stand by their commitments and fulfill their responsibilities and obligations and accept accountability for their actions. We could blame the parents. We could blame the child. We could blame city living. We could blame society. We could blame it on the erosion of our core values—and to one degree or another all of those factors are to blame. However, simply placing blame does not solve the problem. We must ask ourselves, "What is the solution?"

How do we instill within children the motivation to stand by their commitments, fulfill their responsibilities and obligations and willingly accept accountability?

Almost every time I discussed the Rites of Passage with grandfather Old Bear he would say, "The Rites of Passage were the glue that held our clans and tribes together. They bound parents to children and children to parents. They bound youth to old age and one generation to the next. They bound people to our Creator and taught respect for the Sacred Circle of Life. They made people eager to make commitments, assume more responsibilities and obligations and willingly accept accountability. That's why each of our tribes saw themselves as THE PEOPLE.

"Each tribes Rites of Passage instilled great respect for the individual and even greater commitment to the community"

Then he would look deep within my soul as he would say, "Grandson, you must understand that our Rites of Passage initiations kept us firmly anchored to these Sacred Ways and helped prevent people's souls from dying."

In our modern society we tend to identify the age one reaches adulthood as being somewhere between the ages of 18-21, depending on our purpose for considering a person to be an adult. However, in Ancient Times the Old Ones considered a child to be an adult when he or she reached puberty, which for girls could occasionally be as young as 11-12 years of age.

Regardless of the age a child becomes and adult, the Rite of Adulthood marks an important change in a person's life. Adulthood carries with it increased expectations, commitments, responsibilities, obligations and accountabilities. In our modern societies, crimes committed by adults carry with them much more severe punishment than similar crimes committed by children.

We have child labor laws that prevent, or protect, children from performing some jobs that are considered to be too dangerous or too strenuous. We have child pornography laws that protect children against sexual exploitation. We have laws defining how old one has to be to get a driver's license, acquire a loan from a lending institution, or buy cigarettes and alcoholic beverages.

On this Sacred Path the Rite of Passage greatly increases the individual's commitments, responsibilities, obligations and accountabilities to the village or community. The Rite of Adulthood changes the relationship of the individual with his or her parents. The Rite of Adulthood changes the individual's primary focus from the biological family to the greater extended family of the community.

Prior to the Rite of Adulthood the parents and extended family helped care for and "raise" the child to adulthood and his or primary role was to help meet the needs of the biological family. Following the Rite of

Adulthood the individual is expected to primarily focus on helping meet the needs of the entire community.

Before the Rite of Adulthood the parents were responsible for caring for the child. Following the Rite of Adulthood the new adult is expected to help care for his or her biological parents as well as all who have needs within the extended family or village.

The Rite of Adulthood is divided into two ceremonies. The ceremony for girls is called the Rite of Womanhood and the ceremony for boys is called the Rite of Manhood.

CONDUCTING THE RITE OF WOMANHOOD FOR GIRLS

Women conduct the Rite of Womanhood for girls and only women are allowed to attend the initiation ceremony. The first part of the ceremony begins at sunrise during the first full moon following the completion of the girl's first menstrual cycle. If the full moon occurs during the girl's menstrual cycle, the ceremony is conducted at the time of the next full moon. Women never participate in or conduct Sacred Ceremony during their menstrual cycle or "moon time".

PREPARING FOR THE CEREMONY

On this Sacred Path women are held in high esteem. They symbolize Mother Earth from which all life was formed. Therefore, when a girl reaches womanhood it is a time of great joy and rejoicing for not only the girl's parents, but also for the entire village or extended family.

Starting several months prior to the Rite of Womanhood ceremony both the mother and her daughter will be gathering together items for the Give Away ceremony that will be held at the conclusion of the girl's initiation into Womanhood.

During the girl's first menstrual cycle, her mother goes out into the woods and digs up a small cedar tree (approximately twelve inches tall).

419

She then transplants it at the site where the Rite of Womanhood will be performed. This is usually somewhere several feet beyond the directional flag that represents the current season in which the girl's first menstrual cycle occurred.

Before digging up the little tree the mother prays, thanking the cedar people for all they do for the two-leggeds. And she also asks our Creator to help her daughter to live long like the cedar people and always be of service to the Sacred Circle of Life the way they are.

She offers tobacco to the Four Sacred Directions and sprinkles it over the little tree before digging it up.

Once the small cedar tree has been transplanted, the mother prepares a Cornhusk Pipe and takes it to the woman elder she will ask to perform the Rite of Womanhood ceremony for her daughter. She offers the Cornhusk Pipe to the "grandmother" and then asks her to perform the initiation ceremony. At that time, she discusses with the "grandmother" who will be invited to attend the ceremony.

The woman elder performing the ceremony should be a spiritual leader and ceremonial leader among the people and is often the Head Woman of the village. She will spend a great deal of time with both the mother and her daughter prior to the ceremony, learning all she can about the daughter and explaining to her the details of the ceremony and its important symbolism.

The "grandmother" (ceremonial leader) will be the one who gives the girl a new name during the Rite of Womanhood. Therefore, she will spend a considerable amount of time praying about that name and seeking guidance from our Creator in selecting the name.

ITEMS NEEDED TO PERFORM THE RITE OF WOMANHOOD CEREMONY

The woman performing the Rite of Womanhood ceremony will gather the following items for the ceremony.

- Red Earth Paint.

- New Directional Flags for the medicine wheel's Four Sacred Directions.
- Tobacco.
- Sage, cedar and sweet grass and shell for smudging.
- Blue cornmeal.
- Yellow cornmeal.
- A large elk hide or Indian blanket.
- Drum.
- Holy water from the Sacred Water ceremony (about one gallon).
- A new planting stick and a small bag of the seed corn.
- The fetish doll given to the parents during the Rite of Parenthood.
- A pan large enough to hold the gallon of Sacred Holy Water.
- The Rite of Birth medicine bag containing the ground up cornmeal.
- All items needed to conduct the Purification Ceremony.

CONDUCTING THE RITE OF WOMANHOOD CEREMONY

STEP ONE

The first step in conducting the Rite of Womanhood ceremony is to perform the Purification Ceremony for the young girl being initiated into Womanhood. The "grandmother", or woman elder conducting the Rite of Womanhood ceremony, will be the woman in charge of performing the Purification Ceremony at sunrise the day of the ceremony. The girl, her mother and the other women assisting in the Rite of Womanhood ceremony will attend the Purification Ceremony.

The girl's mother will bring the fetish doll, medicine bag of cornmeal, the bag of corn seed and the new planting stick and place these items on the altar in front of the Purification Lodge.

At the beginning of the first round of the Purification Ceremony, the mother will give her daughter the fetish doll and explain that it symbolizes the time of Conception in which our Creator sent the girl's spirit into her mother to receive a physical body. She will explain how it was an important part of the Rite of Parenthood, and how the girl's parents placed the fetish doll on their altar and prayed daily for their baby to be born healthy and to always follow these Sacred Ways.

During the first round, the girl will cradle the fetish doll in her arms like a baby, while the ceremony leader explains the Sacredness of all Life, and that our Creator has a very important Life Plan for the girl to follow as an adult. Those in attendance will offer prayers for the girl that she will always follow the Life Plan our Creator has for her thoughout her adult life.

During the second round the mother will give the girl the small medicine bag containing the cornmeal and explain that it was used during the girl's Rite of Birth ceremony. The grandmother will point out that the cornmeal in the bag symbolizes the Five Spiritual Medicines and the parent's commitment to raise their daughter to live her life according to our Creator's Sacred Laws of Right Living.

During this round the "grandmother" will discuss the Five Spiritual Medicines with the girl, explaining their importance in helping women walk this Sacred Path, and the women will pray that the girl will always apply the Five Spiritual Medicines to her life and live according to these Sacred Ways.

At the beginning of the third round the mother will give her daughter the bag of corn seed and explain that this seed came from an ear of corn used during the Rite of Parenthood after she was conceived. The "grandmother" will explain that the corn seed symbolizes the girl becoming a woman and her ability to bare children so that her people may continue to be a part of the Sacred Circle of Life. She will then explain that the corn also symbolizes how fruitful and productive the girl's life will be as she faithfully follows the Life Plan our Creator has for her.

During this round the women will pray that the girl will live a very productive and fruitful life as a woman, and that like the corn, she will help serve the needs of the community so that it may remain strong.

The ceremonial leader will point out to the girl that just as her mother has passed these Sacred Ways on to her, she also has an obligation to pass them on to her children and teach them to do the same. Using the corn as an example, she will point out that the corn seed, when planted, will produce much more corn. She will explain that like the corn, when the girl passes these Sacred Ways on to her children, and teaches them to do the same, she is helping insure the Spiritual wellbeing of future generations.

At the beginning of the fourth round the mother will give her daughter the planting stick and the ceremonial leader will explain that this symbolizes all of the work the girl will do for the Sacred Circle of Life as a woman. She will explain that it also represents a life of productivity and not a life of laziness.

The group will pray that this new young woman will be a good wife and homemaker, and that she and her family will never go hungry and that all of their physical and spiritual needs will always be met.

STEP TWO

After the Purification Ceremony, the women will change clothes. Then the grandmother in charge will take the group to the young cedar tree the mother has planted a ways beyond the directional flags representing the current season. For example, if the Rite of Womanhood ceremony were being conducted during the Summer, the little cedar tree would be planted South of the directional flag representing the South.

The woman leading the ceremony will first make a circle of blue cornmeal around the cedar tree large enough for all of the women to stand in. The cedar tree will be at the center of the circle. She will then make a circle of yellow cornmeal just inside the blue cornmeal circle. The blue cornmeal symbolizes our Creator's power available to us from the Spiritual Realm, and the yellow cornmeal symbolizes the girl's new life as a woman in the physical realm. Together, the two circles symbolize our Creator's power and presence always surrounding the woman through out her life.

The group will enter the circle from the East, and when everyone is inside, the "grandmother" leading the ceremony will pray, thanking our Creator for the cedar tree's contribution to this Sacred Ceremony. She will also and ask that the two-leggeds always honor the cedar tree for its wonderful contribution to the Sacred Circle of Life.

The grandmother will have the girl stand next to the small tree as she tells the young woman the story of how the cedar tree was chosen by our Creator to be used during this very sacred initiation. The story goes like this:

Long, long ago, during the time of the First People, a young orphan girl became very frightened during her first "moon time" because she thought she had contracted some terrible disease that would cause her to bleed to death. Afraid someone would see her with her terrible bleeding disease, she went out into the forest alone and sat down under a tree and began crying.

The great eagle saw the little girl crying and came and landed on a limb above her head and said, "what's the matter, why are you so unhappy?"

Looking up at the huge eagle the girl replied, "I have a terrible sickness and I think I going to die."

The eagle flew to the ground and looked intently at the child and realized she was very frightened. "Come, get on my back and I'll take you to our Creator and he will make you well," the eagle said.

So the girl climbed on the giant eagle's back and he flew high in the air as they headed toward the great Holy Mountain there in the far, far North at the end of the world where our Creator has his home.

When they arrived at the Holy Mountain our Creator met them, and the eagle explained to him why they had come.

Grandfather smiled as he patted the young girl on the head. "You're not going to die. You're becoming a woman and your female power is becoming very strong. I will give you a ceremony to take back to your people and you will call this ceremony The Rite of Womanhood. As your

424

women perform this ceremony it will be a time of great celebration when a young girl becomes a woman."

Our Creator explained the ceremony to the young girl in detail and then said, "Now go to grandfather Cottonwood, one of the wisest of all the green people, and ask him to participate in your initiation during the Rite of Womanhood."

So the young girl went to the giant grandfather Cottonwood tree and patted his huge tree trunk and called, "Grandfather, grandfather, our Creator told me to come and ask you to participate in the Rite of Womanhood ceremony he gave me to take back to all the two-legged women. Will you please come and help me?"

The great Cottonwood tree looked down at the small girl and said in a gruff voice, "Child, don't you know that the sacred eagle is our Creator's messenger? If he wants me to help you, surely he would have sent the eagle to tell me. So go away child, I'm very busy. Lots of winged people make their home in my branches and I must provide shade for many of our relatives within the Sacred Circle of Life. Now go along and don't bother me. You'll have to find someone else to help you."

So very discouraged, the girl went back to our Creator and explained what the great grandfather Cottonwood tree had said.

Our Creator was very disappointed with the Cottonwood tree for not helping her, but he smiled and said, "Very well, child, go ask the powerful Oak tree. I'm sure he will be willing to participate in your Rite of Womanhood ceremony." So the girl went off to talk to the great Oak tree.

When she arrived at the grandfather Oak tree she patted his strong, powerful trunk and called up to him, "Grandfather Oak tree, our Creator sent me to ask you if you would come and participate in the Rite of Womanhood ceremony he gave me. Will you please come and help me?"

Like the grandfather Cottonwood, the giant Oak tree refused saying, "Oh no, child, I'm far too busy to help you. Can't you see that many of our relatives within the Sacred Circle of Life are coming to gather my acorns? I must stay here and help feed our Creator's children. You'll have to find someone else to help you."

The girl began to cry as she walked back to report to our Creator what the great Oak tree has said. She was so sad because she was sure she would never find anyone to help with the initiation ceremony.

When she told our Creator the giant Oak tree was also too busy to help her he also was very sad and finally said, "I'll send you to the Cedar tree. I'm sure he will be willing to help you."

So the girl set off to find a Cedar tree to ask for help. She searched and searched and finally she came to a small Cedar tree not much bigger than she was. She timidly approached the little tree and said, "Oh, Cedar tree, our Creator told me to come and ask if you would please come and participate in my Rite of Womanhood initiation. I've talked to both the Cottonwood and Oak trees but they are too busy. Can you please come and help me?"

The small Cedar tree smiled at the girl and said, "Why of course, my young relative. It would be an honor to participate in your Rite of Womanhood initiation. I would be delighted to help my little two-legged sister anyway I can."

The girl was so happy she hugged the small Cedar tree then ran to tell our Creator the good news. Our Creator was very pleased with the Cedar tree but very disappointed that neither the Cottonwood or Oak trees would help her. So he sent the eagle to ask the grandfather Cottonwood, the giant Oak and the little Cedar tree to come and meet him at the foot of the Great Holy Mountain.

When the trees arrived, our Creator said to the Cottonwood and Oak tree, "I am very disappointed in you for your unwillingness to help your young two-legged relative perform the sacred Rite of Womanhood ceremony I gave her. Therefore, because you thought you were too busy and your other duties were more important, I will cause your beautiful leaves to fall to the ground every fall, leaving you bare and exposed for all your relatives to see your nakedness. To you, grandfather Cottonwood, I will make the smoke from your wood used in a fire to have an unpleasant smell as a reminder to you of how you failed to serve the needs of one of your young two-legged relatives. And to you, giant Oak tree, I will make your acorns bitter at certain times of the year so they will be uneatable, and your leaves will also fall off every fall. This will help remind you that you should always do all you can to help your relatives in need within the Sacred Circle of Life."

Then our Creator turned to the young Cedar tree and patted it gently on the head. He smiled warmly as he said, "Because you have been willing to serve the needs of your relatives any way you can, I will make your leaves remain green even in the coldest part of the winter. And because you have a pure heart and are willing to serve in anyway you can, I will make you an important part of all of the two leggeds' sacred ceremonies. I will give you a sweet aroma and your leaves will be sacred because when they are burned, the sweet smelling smoke will have the power to help purify anything it touches."

After the story is told the women will discuss with the girl the lessons of life being taught in the story and how all women should strive to live their lives in service to our Creator's Sacred Circle of Life the way the Cedar tree does.

STEP THREE

When the "grandmother" has finished telling this story to the girl, and its meaning has been discussed, she will have her remove all of her clothes and her mother will wrap a large elk hide or Indian blanket around her daughter. The woman leading the ceremony will build a small fire South of the Cedar tree and while the fire burns to make some coals for smudging, using a very small Cedar limb, she will sprinkle the Sacred Water all over the girl's body, beginning at her head and working down to her feet.

As the ceremonial leader sprinkles the Sacred Water on the girl she will pray for this girl, and all of the girls in the future who will become women, that they will live lives worthy of Sacred Womanhood. She will then explain to the girl that women are the "backbone" of the extended family. They are an extension of Mother Earth, and that our Creator has given women the Sacred Gift of giving birth to the two-leggeds' future, and that this is the greatest of all the Sacred Gifts our Creator has given his two-legged children.

She will point out that women—more than men—determine the moral codes and fibers of the Sacred Family and extended community. She will explain that women have greater influence over men than men have over women and that they must always use that influence wisely and for the good of the family—never for their own selfish interests.

She and the rest of the women will explain the sacredness of the sexual union, and that she should save her sexual gifts to be shared only with her husband, because to do otherwise degrades the high spiritual and moral status of all women. She will point out that the sexual experience is a wonderful gift from our Creator and a beautiful way of expressing our love for our mate. She will explain that the women participating in this Rite of Womanhood ceremony are available anytime to further discuss with the girl the sacredness of the sexual relationship between a woman and a man. And, she will point out that as the time approaches for her to marry they will have lengthy discussions with her concerning how to fully experience the joys of sexual union in marriage.

STEP FOUR

The "grandmother" will then take some of the live coals from the fire and place them in the bottom of a shell, and then place lots of cedar leaves over the burning coals to create lots of smoke. She will then ask the girl to stand over the shell and let the Cedar smoke engulf her whole body inside the elk hide or Indian blanket. As she does this, she will remind the girl that she is to always live her life like the sacred Cedar tree—always willing and ready to serve the needs of those within the Sacred Family of Life.

She will ask the girl to make a verbal commitment in front of her mother and the other women elders present to be willing to learn all of the women's ceremonies conducted during the Sacred Seasons of Spring and Fall. She will also promise to faithfully pass them on to her girls in the future so these Sacred Ways will not be lost.

The ceremonial leader will remind the girl that her mother is passing these Sacred Ways on to her, and that she has a responsibility to pass them on to the next generation. She will explain to the girl that as a woman, she will become the Mother of future generations and that how she lives as a Mother, and how she passes on these Sacred Ways, will help determine if the next generation of two-leggeds survive or not.

She will remind the girl that this group of Women Elders are always available to teach her and support her in any way they can as she learns what it means to become a Woman on this Sacred Path.

STEP FIVE

Next, the Mother will mix Red Earth Paint with some of the Sacred Water, and starting at her daughter's hair line, she will paint a red line down between her eyes, along the bridge of her nose, down the center of her chin, down between her breasts and through her navel. Just above the pubic hairline, she will make a fork in the line, drawing it down the front of both legs and out the end of her big toes. She will then draw connecting lines down both arms, beginning at the neck area, extending across the shoulders and down to the tip of her middle finger.

As the mother paints this red line on her daughter, the woman in charge of the ceremony will explain that this red earth line first symbolizes our Creator's and her parents' love for her. It also symbolizes her—as a woman—becoming a hollow bone, through which our Creator's Unconditional Love can flow into her, through her and out to help meet the needs of the Sacred Circle of Life. The ceremonial leader will then ask the girl if she, as a Woman, is willing to become a hollow tube for the Creator's love to flow through and out to others. She will then explain that the red earth line going from the top of her head to her feet and hands also symbolizes her becoming a Woman.

STEP SIX

The ceremonial leader will then lead the mother and girl and the rest of the women over to the Western side of the medicine wheel where they will all perform the Self Offering ceremony in preparation for entering the medicine wheel. When the Self Offering ceremony is completed, the grandmother in charge of the ceremony will lead the mother and daughter, along with the rest of the women, around the Northern side of the wheel to the East entrance.

At the East entrance to the medicine wheel, the ceremonial leader will offer a prayer, thanking our Creator for the Sacred Life Plan he has for the girl and ask him to empower her to live a fruitful and productive life as a Woman. They will sing the Give Away song, then the grandmother will lead the group to the Center Stone where she will offer tobacco to the Four Sacred Directions, Mother Earth and our Creator, and then sprinkle sacred tobacco over the Center Stone.

She will then offer another prayer to our Creator, thanking him for guiding the girl's life as she becomes a Woman. She will sprinkle some of the sacred tobacco over the girl's head as she announces the "Woman's Name" the girl will use as a Woman.

She will then lead the girl to the medicine wheel's East Gate and announce the girl's name to the East Wind. The mother will take a small pinch of cornmeal from the small leather pouch around her daughter's neck and sprinkle it over her daughter's head, as the ceremonial leader prays for the girl to always exercise Spiritual Courage as a Woman.

They will return to the Center Stone and then proceed to the wheel's South Gate where the grandmother will announce to the South Wind the girl's new name. The mother will take another pinch of cornmeal from the small pouch and sprinkle it over the girl's head as the ceremonial leader prays for the girl to always exercise Spiritual Patience as a Woman.

They will repeat this process, going on to the West Gate and then the

North Gate. At the West Gate the ceremonial leader will pray for the girl to have Spiritual Endurance during her life as a Woman and at the North Gate she will pray for her to have Spiritual Alertness. Then they will return to the Center Stone and she will pray for the girl to live a life of humility as a woman.

STEP SEVEN

The grandmother will then have the girl sit on the ground on the North side of the Center Stone and touch the stone with her right hand while facing East. She will tell the girl that she will now tell her about the Four Personal Powers that will either help her or harm her as she lives the life of a Woman.

I will pass on to you what grandfather Old Bear shared with me concerning these Four Personal Powers, and both girls and boys are taught about these Powers during their initiations into Adulthood.

One day while we were walking along a game trail at the edge of the forest in my Private World, grandfather Old Bear stopped and pointed to four, high, jagged mountain peaks in the distance and said, "You see those four sharp mountain peaks over there? They remind me of the Four Personal Powers that either help us or harm us as we walk this Sacred Path."

He found a grassy spot nearby and sat down; then patted the ground beside him, indicating that I should sit down next to him.

As I sat down he continued. "Our Creator has given us all of the tools we need to walk this Sacred Path. However, it's up to us to use those tools wisely. He gave us the Five Spiritual Medicines that enable us to go far beyond our physical limitations as we follow the Life Plan he has for us. And, he also gave us Four Personal Powers and the free will to use those Personal Powers any way we choose.

"These Four Personal Powers originate in our Mind, our Mouth, our Heart and our Hands and Feet. Our mind produces our Thoughts. Our mouth produces our Words. Our heart produces our Decisions. And our

hands and feet produce our Actions. So, grandson, our Four Personal Powers are our Thoughts, Words, Decisions and Actions—these control and determine our destiny. They either help us stay true to this Sacred Path or they create a path of their own, a path that leads to our destruction.

"The dark side is constantly trying to place negative thoughts in our minds which eventually produce negative words from our mouth, wrong decisions from our heart and bad actions from our hands and feet. Therefore, grandson, you must submit your Four Personal Powers to our Creator, asking for his help in keeping negative thoughts, words and decisions out of your mind, mouth and heart, so that you won't take negative actions against our Creator's Sacred Circle of Life."

The ceremonial leader will explain these Four Personal Powers to the girl, informing her that, for the most part, they will determine her future as a Woman. She will explain that these Four Personal Powers are continually at work in our lives, determining our thoughts, words, decisions and actions. They greatly influence who we are and our destiny within the Sacred Circle of Life.

She will then take the girl to the East Gate of the medicine wheel and pray that our Creator will help the girl guard her mind against all negative thoughts through the rest of her life. Then, the grandmother will take the girl to the South Gate and ask our Creator to help the girl always guard her mouth so that she will not speak negative words against anyone during her life as a Woman. Next, she will take the girl to the West Gate, and ask our Creator to help the girl to never make wrong choices and decisions during her life as a Woman. And finally, she will take the girl to the North Gate and ask our Creator to help the girl never take negative actions against any of her relatives within the Sacred Circle of Life.

STEP EIGHT

The grandmother will then lead the group of women back to the Purification Lodge and the girl will be hugged by all of the women. They will tell her they have loved her and enjoyed knowing her, but that the girl is getting ready to disappear and the next time they see her she will be a Woman.

The ceremonial leader will sprinkle Holy Water on the girl again and then the women will hold hands as they form a circle around the girl. The girl's Mother will then enter the circle and hug her daughter and tell her how much she has loved her and that she looks forward to the wonderful relationship they will have together when her "little girl" soon becomes a Woman.

The ceremonial leader will then instruct the girl to enter the Purification Lodge and sit on the eastern side of the lodge facing the door. She will instruct the girl that she will remain in the lodge all night, praying for our Creator to guide her life as a Woman. She will also pray, affirming her commitment to always follow the Life Plan our Creator has for her life, and carry on the Sacred Ways of the people.

Once the girl is situated on the eastern side of the lodge, the door will be closed and the women will build a Sacred Fire in the Fire Pit and spend the night praying for the girl as she lives her life as a Woman. They will also spend part of the night preparing the feast for those special guests who will arrive at sunrise to meet the new Woman.

The next morning at sunrise the Mother will open the Purification Lodge door and ask the New Woman to emerge from Mother Earth's womb. The New Woman will crawl out to take her place as a Woman in the world. Those in attendance will use the holy water to help wash the Red Earth Paint off the young Woman and then she will put on new clothes her mother has made for her.

The ceremonial leader will instruct the New Woman that she is to never discuss with any male—not even her husband—about what happens during the Rite of Womanhood initiation ceremony.

The grandmother will ask the New Woman to offer a prayer of gratitude to our Creator for this Sacred Rite of Womanhood. They will then proceed to the area where the morning meal will be served to the guests who have arrived.

When they arrive at the area where the meal will be served the grandmother will introduce the New Woman to those present by her new name and all of the guests will shake hands with the New Woman, welcoming her into the community.

STEP NINE

Following the morning meal, the New Woman and her Mother will have a Give Away Ceremony consisting of food and clothing to be distributed to those in attendance. At the end of the Give Away, the ceremonial leader will lead the group in the singing of the Completion song, thus ending the Rite of Womanhood initiation ceremony.

THE RITE OF MANHOOD CEREMONY

While discussing the Rite of Manhood Ceremony with grandfather Old Bear, he said, "It will be impossible for you to conduct the Rite of Manhood Ceremony the way my people did it because you live in a different world and a different time. Things in your world are much different than mine was. However, that does not mean the Rite of Manhood ceremony you perform will be any less effective or powerful."

He began laughing so hard that his skinny, old body shook all over as he continued. "Our Creator has a much more difficult time making men out of boys than he does making women out of girls. For the most part, girls are much more ready to become Women than boys are to become Men. Therefore, the initiation of boys into men is harder than the initiation of girls into Women."

He was still smiling and his eyes snapped with delight as he went on. "Girls in my world were much more attracted to the Spiritual Realm than boys. Girls usually grew up into Women who were very powerfully connected to our Creator and this Sacred Path—that is not to say boys weren't when they became Men.

"Our men were usually quite spiritually connected to the Real World

—the Spiritual Realm. However, generally speaking, it was our women who kept the people in line and focused on these Sacred Ways. Our men were much more easily distracted by the physical world than our women. That is why I always enjoyed the Lifestyle Ceremonies of Spring and Fall so much—our women were in charge of most of the Sacred Ceremonies during those two seasons and those ceremonies were very powerful."

STEP ONE

As a boy approaches his thirteenth year, his father begins making preparations for his son's Rite of Manhood ceremony by beginning to collect items for the Give Away that will occur at the conclusion of the ceremony. The Father will take a Cornhusk Pipe to one of the "grandfathers" (an elder who knows the Rite Of Manhood ceremony), and ask him if he is willing to conduct the Rite of Manhood ceremony for his son. Once the grandfather has agreed, they will smoke the pipe together and discuss who will be invited to attend the boy's initiation into Manhood.

Prior to the initiation ceremony, the grandfather meets with the Father and his son several times to discuss the details of the ceremony, including the meaning of the various rituals that will be performed during the initiation. The person conducting the ceremony will also be responsible for determining the name the boy will be given during the Rite of Manhood initiation. The boy is told he is not permitted to discuss the ceremony and its meanings with any other person, including his friends— both male and female.

STEP TWO

During the first New Moon following the boy's thirteenth birthday, the Father will ceremonially plant a small Cedar tree several yards beyond the Directional Gate of the medicine wheel representing the current season. If the boy's thirteenth birthday falls on that month's New Moon, the Rite of Manhood will be conducted at the next New Moon.

STEP THREE

The man conducting the ceremony will collect the following items to be used during the Rite of Manhood initiation.

- The boy's fetish doll from the Rite of Parenthood ceremony.
- The boy's bag of cornmeal from the Rite of Birth ceremony.
- Four Directional Flags.
- Sage, sweet grass, cedar and a shell for smudging.
- One gallon of Sacred Water from the Sacred Water ceremony.
- A pan to hold the gallon of water.
- A small limb from a cedar tree for sprinkling the water.
- Red Earth Paint.
- All items needed for a Purification ceremony.
- All items needed for the Self Offering ceremony.
- Blue Cornmeal.
- Yellow Cornmeal.
- A new hunting knife.
- Corn husks.
- Medicine Pipe tobacco.
- All items needed for a Spirit Quest.
- A new shirt for the young man (preferably a deerskin shirt).
- A bag of corn seeds and a digging stick.

STEP FOUR

At sunrise on the day of the New Moon the person leading the ceremony will take the boy and those assisting with the Rite of Manhood ceremony into the Purification Lodge.

During the first round, the Father will give his son the fetish doll used during the Rite of Manhood, and explain that this doll symbolizes the boy being gifted to the family for them to raise according to these Sacred Ways. The grandfather leading the ceremony will explain that the boy is now becoming a man and his responsibilities will not only be to his parental family, but as a man, he has responsibilities for the extended family of the community.

The ceremonial leader will instruct the boy to break the fetish doll in half, symbolizing his transition from childhood into manhood, and also symbolizing the breaking of his childhood ways and his commitment to learning the ways of manhood.

The men in the lodge will then discuss with the boy what it means to become a man, including responsibilities, obligations and accountabilities associated with manhood. They will emphasize the importance of spending time with men instead of with childhood playmates, so that men can teach him the ways of Manhood. They will let the boy know that they are always available to help him learn what it means to be a man and that he should never hesitate to seek their advise or counsel.

During round two, the Father will give his son the small medicine bag containing the cornmeal from the Rite of Birth ceremony, and the boy will put it around his neck. The grandfather leading the ceremony will inform the boy that the cornmeal in the bag symbolizes the Five Spiritual Medicines the boy will need to acquire as a Man. He will emphasize the need for every man to seek the Life Plan our Creator has for his life and that part of this ceremony will involve the boy going out on a Spirit Quest so our Creator can begin revealing to the New Man the beginnings of that Life Plan.

During the third round, the Father will give the son the new hunting knife and the grandfather will explain that this hunting knife symbolizes the man's responsibility to care for the physical needs of both his biological family and the extended family of the community. He will point out that his first obligation as a man will be to help meet the needs of the elderly within the community. And also, that he will be expected to help meet the physical needs of all of his relatives within our Creator's Sacred Family of Life anyway he can.

During the fourth round the Father will give the son the bag of seed and the digging stick. The grandfather in charge of the ceremony will explain that the seeds symbolize our Creator's power to supply our physical needs and the digging stick represents our responsibilities to perform the work needed to lead a productive life. He will point out that what we call work is actual Sacred Activity our Creator has delegated to us so we can learn the lessons involved in humbly serving the needs of all our relatives within the Sacred Circle of Life.

The grandfather will explain that the seeds came from an ear of corn planted during the boy's fourth year with his parents, and that the seed symbolizes the need for us to pass these ways on to future generations. He will stress the fact that if we don't pass them on to our children, this Path to our Creator will be lost and we will be to blame.

STEP FIVE

Following the Purification Ceremony, the group will change clothes and the grandfather will lead the people to the small cedar tree the Father planted. He will first form a circle of blue cornmeal about ten feet in diameter around the small cedar tree, then a circle of yellow cornmeal just inside the blue circle. All of the men will sit in a circle around the cedar tree and the grandfather will tell the story of how our Creator made the cedar tree a part of the ceremony.

He will emphasize the fact that our Creator first gave the Rite of Adulthood to a girl, and that we must always honor and respect the females in our family and community. He will explain that our Creator made men physically stronger than women, but not spiritually stronger. He will emphasize the need for a man to take care of and always protect his wife, and to constantly show his love for her.

He and the group of men will then explain the sacredness of the sexual union between a husband and wife, and that the sexual act is an act of expressing love, not just sexual lust.

They will smoke the Cornhusk Pipe and then the grandfather will have the Father and son stand next to the small cedar tree and the boy will be instructed to remove his shirt. Using the small cedar limb, he will sprinkle Sacred Holy Water over the boy and then he will mix some of the Red Earth Paint with the Sacred Water. He will paint the boy's forehead red and then paint a red circle around his mouth. Next, he will paint a large red circle over his heart. He will also paint the backs of his hands and the tops of his feet with the Red Earth Paint. He will then sprinkle the Sacred Water over the boy again.

As he paints the boy, he will explain that the Red Earth Paint symbolizes the Four

Personal Powers, and what those powers are and the influence they have on our lives. He will point out that the red paint on the forehead symbolizes the thoughts of the mind. The red circle around his mouth symbolizes the words he speaks; the red paint over his heart represents the decisions he makes; and the red paint on his hands and feet symbolize the actions he takes.

The grandfather will then lead the group to the Western side of the medicine wheel and each person will conduct the Self Offering ceremony in preparation to enter the Sacred Circle. Once the Self Offering ceremony is completed, he will lead the group around to the northern side of the circle to the East Gate. There, he will sing the Give Away song before leading the Father and son and the rest of the group into the medicine wheel.

They will go to the Center Stone and there the ceremonial leader will offer tobacco to the Four Winds, Mother Earth and to our Creator, and then sprinkle the tobacco on the Center Stone. He will whisper the new name the boy will have as a Man in the father's ear, and the Father will announce to the group his son's name as a man. He will hug his son and then the grandfather will lead him around to each one of the men and introduce him as the Newest Man in their community.

The grandfather will lead the group to the medicine wheel's East Gate and take a small leather pouch from the New Man's neck and give it to his Father. Then, in a loud voice, the grandfather will introduce the New Man to the East Wind. The Father will then sprinkle a small pinch of cornmeal over the Directional Stone in the East as the grandfather prays for the New Man to be given the Medicine of Spiritual Courage as he walks the Sacred Path as a Man.

The ceremonial leader will then lead the New Man and the rest of the group back to the Center Stone, and then to the South Gate. With a loud voice, he will introduce the New Man to the South Wind. The Father will sprinkle another pinch of tobacco over the Directional Stone for the South and the ceremonial leader prays for the New Man to receive the Medicine of Spiritual Patience as the walks this Sacred Path as a Man.

This process will be repeated in the West and North. In the West, the grandfather will pray for the New Man to be given the Medicine of Spiritual Endurance and in the North the Medicine of Spiritual Alertness. They will return to the Center Stone where the ceremonial leader will pray that the New Man be given the Medicine of Humility.

The grandfather will then pray, thanking our Creator for the wonderful gift of this New Man to the Sacred Circle of Life. He will ask our Creator to reveal the Sacred Life Plan he has for the New Man, and then he will lead the group to the Spirit Quest site he has prepared for the New Man. The New Man will enter the Spirit Quest Circle and remain there until dawn the next morning, praying for our Creator to begin revealing to him the Sacred Life Plan he is to follow as a man.

At dawn the next morning the grandfather will come for the New Man and take him to the Purification Lodge for his first Purification Ceremony as a New Man. During the ceremony the New Man will share his experiences while in the Spirit Quest Circle and then following the ceremony he will be taken to the ceremonial feast his mother has prepared for the men. Following the feast the father and New Man will conduct a Give Away ceremony.

At the conclusion of the Give Away, the grandfather will lead the group in the singing of the Closing Song and the Rite of Manhood ceremony will be concluded.

THE RITE OF TRANSFORMATION

On this Sacred Path, life travels in a continuous circle. Our Creator sends our spirits into our mothers to receive our physical bodies so we can function in the physical realm. We then follow the Sacred Circle of Life through birth, youth, adulthood and old age. At some point along the Sacred Circle of Life, we go through a Sacred Transformation in which we shed our physical bodies so that our spirits—the real us—are free to return to our Creator and the wonderful Spiritual Realm.

Instead of thinking of our physical bodies experiencing physical death, on this Sacred Path the emphasis is on our Spirits being freed from our physical bodies so that we are free to return to our Creator and his Spiritual Realm. This is called the Rite of Transformation.

As grandfather Old Bear and I walked along the bank of the beautiful river that flows through my Private World, he said, "I want to talk to you about the Sacred Mystery of Life."

He picked up a few small stones and tossed them one by one into the river, seeming to be buying himself time to gather his thoughts. "Our Creator sends us here to the physical realm for a specific purpose. As I have told you over and over, he has a Sacred Life Plan for each of us. We are sent to the physical realm for a purpose—a specific job to do for our Creator."

He paused as we came to a large outcropping of boulders and motioned for me to follow him as he climbed up on one and sat down on its flat top. "Even though we are sent here for a specific purpose," he continued, "we are free to choose whether or not we are willing to follow his Life Plan for us. Our Creator never forces us to follow the Great Plan he has for our lives. We are always free to choose what we do with each day of our lives.

"Remember when I talked to you about the Four Personal Powers?

Those Personal Powers either help us follow that Great Plan or they cause us to go our own way and miss the wonderful Plan our Creator has for each of us.

"I learned the hard way that the only way to truly experience peace, harmony and balance in my life in the physical world was to follow the wonderful Life Plan our Creator had for me."

He patted the flat, smooth spot next to him, indicating that I should move over closer to him. As I did, he put his long, skinny arm around my shoulder and gave me a gentle pat on the back as he went on. " It's a terrible thing when people live their lives only for themselves—ignoring our Creator's Plan for their lives—and then one day have to face him and give account for their disobedience."

He chuckled to himself and said, "The Sacred Mystery of Life is no mystery at all. Life is very simple when we submit our will to our Creator and let him work his wonderful Sacred Life Plan in us. That is the only way to experience peace, harmony and balance in our lives. And that peace remains with us as we experience the Sacred Transition from the physical world back to the Spiritual Realm we came from.

"You see, grandson, what your world calls death is no death at all—it is a wonderful transformation. It is a great time of celebration! It is why we walk this wonderful Sacred Path. This Sacred Path is an exciting journey through the physical realm back to the Spiritual Realm, and the purpose of the journey is to learn how to live in peace, harmony and balance with our Creator's Sacred Circle of Life. But in order to do that, we must get self-will out of the way so we can do our Creator's will and follow his Life Plan of Sacred Service to all of our relatives within his Sacred Family.

"People tend to fear the unknown. So, if people don't know why they have been put here and how they are supposed to live, they usually wind up living in fear all of their lives. They fear life and they fear what they call death. They fear death because they don't know what awaits them on the other side of what they refer to as "death's door".

The Old One was really getting excited about this subject. His smile *broadened and he slapped his knee as he continued. "I tell you, my boy, if you live your life in obedience to our Creator's Sacred Life Plan for you, you will look forward to your Time of Transformation. You won't fear it. No, you'll embrace it with open arms. You'll draw it to your breast and say, 'Thank you, Creator, for this opportunity to live with you in the Spiritual Realm—free from the problems, sickness, worry and decay that exist everywhere in the physical world.'*

"Yes, the Rite of Transformation is to be a time of great joy, a time of celebration and thanksgiving, not a time of mourning and misery—that is, if we have followed the wonderful Life Plan our Creator has for our lives. One the other hand, if we have ignored our Creator's Life Plan for our lives and gone our own selfish way, then we have good reason for concern.

"Just as a father disciplines his children when they willfully disobey them, so our Creator will discipline his children when they willfully disobey him, ignoring the wonderful Sacred Life Plan he has for them. For such people, their Time of Transformation will definitely be a time of great worry and concern."

He patted my leg and smiled warmly at me. "So, young one, as the sun rises each day, face it with uplifted arms and reaffirm your commitment to follow your Creator's Plan for your life that day. If you do, you will find that there are no mysteries in life—only wonderful experiences that produce peace, harmony and balance each day you live. Then when it comes your time to cross over into the Spiritual Realm, you will do it with great joy."

That day grandfather Old Bear explained to me that we cannot perform the Rite of Transformation the way it was conducted long ago among his people because we live in a much different world with strict burial laws that govern burial rituals. However, he made it clear that we can still achieve the purpose of the Rite of Transformation, and emphasized the importance of continuing to perform this very sacred and powerful Rite.

He emphasized the importance of making the Rite of Transformation a time of great joy and celebration instead of a time of sorrow and sadness. He pointed out that we would naturally miss our friends and loved ones when he or she crosses over into the Spiritual Realm. However, the emphasis and focus should be on what they have gained instead of what we have lost.

He taught me the following song to be sung during the Rite of Transformation.

Oh, Creator, guide our journey through the stars.
Yes, Grandfather, guide our journey to where you are.
As we travel along life's way,
Guide our journey every day.
Oh, Creator, guide our journey to where you are.

Grandfather Old Bear said the Rite of Transformation is to be a celebration of Sacred Life, not a bemoaning of death. It is to be a time of commitment and reaffirmation to live life according to our Creator's Sacred Life Plan for each of us. It is to be a joyful time of feasting. At the end of the feast, family members of the one who crossed over to the Spiritual Realm are to conduct a Give Away ceremony in honor of their loved one who has now gone to the "Real World".

He also told me that as long as people followed the above guidelines for the Rite of Transformation, they were free to work out the details of that Rite as they saw fit. It should be a very personal ceremony that celebrated the life of a very special person in their lives.

CONCLUSION

There are many other Rites of Passage that could—and maybe should —be included in this material. There is the Marriage Rite, rites and ceremonies performed when a person joins various groups and societies, naming rites, and rites honoring individuals for various special accomplishments. However, space will not permit a description of all of the above mentioned.

We should keep in mind that the various Rites of Passage collectively make up the one great Rite of Living Life according to our Creator's great Sacred Life Plan for each of us—and that is the greatest Rite of all!

As we said at the beginning of this book, the Rites of Passage are the anchors that keep us firmly connected to this Sacred Path. Our Creator gave them to us to help insure that we live our lives in peace, harmony and balance within the Sacred Family of Life. If we do, when we someday cross over into the Spiritual Realm, we will gladly hear our Creator and Spiritual Father say, "Well done, good and faithful servant! You have been faithful in a few things; I will put you in charge of many things. Come and share your master's happiness." Matthew 25:21 (the Bible).

APPENDIX

The following songs are prayers that we sing during the various ceremonies associated with this Sacred Path. You can order a CD of these songs from our web page at WWW. Medicinewheelmesas.com. The songs on CD also have a brief explanation of when they are to be used.

THE FOUR DIRECTION SONG

Way yi ya hay hay hay ya hay yi ya ha wello hay.
Way yi ya wello hay.
Way yi ya wello, wello, hay.
Oh, Creator, I ask your sacred power in the West,
Please listen to my prayer,
And come and join us here.
Way yi ya hay hay hay ya hay yi ya ha wello hay.
Way yi ya wello hay.
Way yi ya wello, wello, hay.
Oh, Creator, I ask your sacred power in the North,
Please listen to my prayer,
And come and join us here.
Way yi ya hay hay hay ya hay yi ya ha wello hay.
Way yi ya wello hay.
Way yi ya wello, wello, hay.
Oh, Creator, I ask your sacred power in the East,
Please listen to my prayer,
And come and join us here.
Way yi ya hay hay hay ya hay yi ya ha wello hay.
Way yi ya wello hay.

Way yi ya wello, wello, hay.
Oh, Creator, I ask your sacred power from the South.
Please listen to my prayer,
And come and join us here.
Way yi ya hay hay hay ya hay yi ya ha wello hay.
Way yi ya wello hay.
Way yi ya wello, wello, hay.
Grandmother Earth, please listen to this simple prayer.
And come and join us here.
We always need you near.
Way yi ya hay hay hay ya hay yi ya ha wello hay.
Way yi ya wello hay
Way yi ya wello, wello, hay.
Oh, Creator, please come and join us here today.
Give us the words to pray,
Guide all we do and say.
Way yi ya hay hay hay ya hay yi ya ha wello hay.
Way yi ya wello hay.
Way yi ya wello, wello, hay ya yo.

THE THANK YOU SONG

Way ya hay ya, way ya hay ya,
Way ya hay ya, way yi ya hay.
Way ya hay ya, way yi ya hay ya,
Way ya hay, hay, hay ya wello hay.
Oh Creator, how I thank you
That you hear me when I pray.
And I thank you that the answer
Is already on its way.
Way ya hay ya, way ya hay ya,,,
Way ya hay ya, way yi ya hay.
Way ya ha ya, way yi ya hay ya,

Way ya hay, hay, hay ya wello hay.
And Grandfather, how I thank you
For providing for us each day.
So I will help those who are needy
That I meet along life's way.
Way ya ha ya, way ya hay ya,
Way ya hay ya, way yi ya hay.
Way ya ha ya, way yi ya hay ya,
Way ya hay, hay, hay ya wello ha.

CLOSING PRAYER SONG

Way ya hay ya, way yi ya, way ya hay.
Way ya hay ya, way yi ya, way ya hay.
Oh, Creator, thank you for this day.
Oh, Grandfather, guide us on life's way.
Oh, Grandfather, help us not to stray.
Way ya ha ya, way yi ya, way ya hay.
Way ya hay ya, way yi ya, way ya hay.
Way ya hay ya, oh, wello, wello hay ya yo.

MORNING PRAYER SONG

Ya way ya hay, hay ya hay, hay ya hay.
Ya way ya hay, hay ya hay, hay ya ho.
Way ya hay, hay ay ho, wello hay, ya hay ya ho.
Ya way ya hay, hay ya hay, hay ya ho.
Oh, great Creator, thank you for the rising sun.
Oh, Grandfather, thank you for all that you've done.
Thank you for new life today, and help me give it back I pray.
Oh, great Creator, thank you for the rising sun.
Ya way ya hay, hay ya hay, hay ya hay.
Ya way ya hay, hay ya hay, hay ya ho.

Way ya hay, hay ya ho, wello hay, ya ha ya ho.
Ya way ya hay, hay ya ho, wello hay, ya hay ya ho,
Ya way ya ha, hay ya hay, hay ya ho.

EVENING PRAYER SONG

Way ya hay ya, way ya hay ya, way ya hay ya,
Way ya hay yi ya, hay ya hay yi ya hay.
Way ya hay ya, way ya hay ya, way ya hay ya,
Way ya hay yi ya hay ya hay yi ya hay.
Oh, Creator, how I thank you for the morning,
And for watching over us all day long.
And Grandfather, how I thank you for this evening,
And the power it brings to keep our spirits strong.
Way ya hay ya, way ya hay ya, way ya hay ya.
Way ya hay yi ya, hay ya hay yi ya hay.
Way ya hay ya, way ya hay ya, way ya hay ya.
Way ya hay yi ya hay ya hay yi ya hay.

PURIFICATION SONG

Take away all I've done wrong, cleanse my spirit and make it strong,
Way yi hay yi ya, hay ya, hay yi ya hay.
Take away all I've done wrong, cleanse my spirit and make it strong,
Way yi hay yi ya, hay ya, hay yi ya hay.
Take away all I've done wrong, cleanse my mind and make it strong,
Way yi hay yi ya, hay ya, hay yi ya hay.
Take away all I've done wrong, cleanse my mind and make it strong,
Way yi hay yi ya, hay ya, hay yi ya hay.
Take away all I've done wrong, cleanse my body and make it strong,
Way yi hay yi ya, hay ya, hay yi ya hay.
Take away all I've done wrong, cleanse my body and make it strong,
Way yi hay yi ya, hay ya, hay yi ya hay.

Now remove all we've done wrong, cleanse Mother Earth and make her strong,
Way yi hay yi ya, hay ya, hay yi ya hay.
Now remove all we've done wrong, cleanse Mother Earth and make her strong,
Way yi hay yi ya, hay ya, hay yi ya hay yo.

THE SACRED WATER SONG

Way yi ya hay, wello hay, way yi ya hay wello hay,
Way yi ya hay, hay ya hay, way yi ya hay.
Way yi ya hay, wello hay, way yi ya hay wello hay,
Way yi ya hay, hay ya hay, way yi ya hay.
Oh, sacred water, hear our cry, send your rain so we won't die.
Oh, sacred water, please listen to this prayer.
Fill the oceans, lakes and streams, and turn the deserts green,
Oh, sacred water, send your rains everywhere.
Way yi ya hay, wello hay, way yi ya hay wello hay,
Way yi ya hay, hay ya hay, way yi ya hay.
Way yi ya hay, wello hay, way yi ya hay wello hay,
Way yi ya hay, hay ya hay, way yi ya hay.

SACRED EARTH SONG

Way yi ya, hay yi ya, way yi ya hay. Way yi ya, hay yi ya, wello hay.
Way yi ya hay yi ya, way yi ya hay. Way yi ya way ya hay.
Honor our Mother, take care of her land.
Respect her children, give a helping hand.
Honor our Mother, take care of her land, take care of her sacred land.
Way yi ya, hay yi ya, way yi ya hay. Way yi ya, hay yi ya, wello hay.
Way yi ya hay yi ya, way yi ya hay. Way yi ya way ya hay.
I'll honor our Mother and take care of her land.
I'll respect her children, and give a helping hand.

I'll honor our Mother and take care of her land, I'll take care of her sacred land.

Way yi ya, hay yi ya, way yi ya hay. Way yi ya, hay yi ya, wello hay. Way yi ya hay yi ya, way yi ya hay. Way yi ya way ya hay ya hay.

THE MEDICINE WHEEL SONG

Way ya hay ya hay, way yi ya ho, way ya hay, hay ya hay, way yi ya ho. Way ya hay ya hay ya hay, way yi ya ho. Way ya hay, hay ya hay, way yi ya ho.

There's a time to plant, when the warm winds blow,

Way ya hay, hay ya hay, way yi ya ho.

And there' a time for gentle rains, to help things grow.

Way ya hay, hay ya hay, way yi ya ho.

There's a time to reap from what we sow,

Way ya hay, hay ya hay, way yi ya ho.

And there's a time to rest and renew the soul,

Way ya hay, hay ya hay, way yi ya ho.

Way ya hay ya hay, way yi ya ho, way ya hay, hay ya hay, way yi ya ho. Way ya hay ya hay ya hay, way yi ya ho. Way ya hay, hay ya hay, way yi ya ho.

There's a time to be born and a time to grow old,

Way ya hay, hay ya hay, way yi ya ho.

THE SACRED STONE SONG

Oh, these sacred stones, are Grandmother's bones,

And they will soon become our Grandfather's home,

Where he will help us pray, in a sacred way.

He'll take away all our pain, and give us new life today.

He will fill us with his love, to pass on along the way.

He will help us meet the needs of our relatives each day.

He will open up our eyes so that we can see

That these sacred stones, are Grandmother's bones.

THE SACRED PIPE PRAYER SONG

Oh dear relatives, please pray for me, as I fill this sacred pipe for you.
It will send our prayers to the Creator, who knows all we say and do.
So, Grandfather please, take pity on me, and on all of my relatives too.
Give me the words to pray. Guide all I do each day,
And help me to be faithful to you.
So, Grandfather please, take pity on me, and on all of our relatives too.
Give us the words to pray. Guide all we do each day,
And help us to be faithful to you.
Give us the words to pray. Guide all we do each day. And help us to
be faithful to you.

THE SACRED PIPE SONG

Oh, the sacred pipe will watch over you.
It hears what you say, and knows what you do.
So if you do what's right and your words are true.
Then the sacred pipe will watch over you.
Yes, the sacred pipe will watch over you.
It will be your friend and protector too.
If you do what's right and your words are true.
Then the sacred pipe will watch over you.

THE SACRED SILENCE SONG

Oh, the voice of sacred silence speaks to me, and it opens up my eyes
so I can see.
With the setting of the sun, when the night is fully come,

Then the voice of sacred silence speaks to me.

Oh, the voice of sacred silence speaks to me, telling me that I should be all I can be.

It speaks to me down in my soul, warning me to not let go.

Oh, the voice of sacred silence speaks to me.

Yes, the voice of sacred silence calls my name. Telling me that I will never be the same.

It says the cleansing time is near, but I should never live in fear.

\Yes, the voice of sacred silence calls my name.

And the voice of sacred silence calls to you. Telling you how to live and what to do.

It says help mend the sacred hoop, and always live the way you should.

Yes the voice of sacred calls to you.

And the voice of sacred silence speaks to me.

THE GIVE AWAY SONG

Way ya, ha ya, way ya yi yo
Ha, ya, ha ya, yi yeah.
Way ya, ha ya, way ya yi yo
Ha ya, ha ya, yi yeah.
Creator, help me live my life as a sacred give away.
And may I always share your love in all I do and say.
In all I do and say each day, in all I do and say.
Oh, help me always live my life as a sacred give away
Way ya, hay ya, way ya yi yo
Ha ya, ha ya, yi yeah.
Way ya, hay ya, way ya yi yo
Ha ya, ha ya, yi yeah.
(Repeat two times)

SACRED FIRE SONG

Sacred fire is like Grandfather's power
That turns the night into day.
It keeps us warm on cold dark night,
And it drives all the dangers away.
And Grandfather's power is like a sacred fire
That purifies our souls.
It brought his love into the world
As a gift to both young and old.
So keep sacred fire burning in your home
And never let it go out.
For if it does, you'll learn that you
Have forgotten what love is all about.

SONG OF THE FOUR WINDS

There's a sacred wind that blows from the west.
It brings the truth that withstands each test.
It gives us power to do our best.
There's a sacred wind that comes from the west.

And the north wind blows on both young and old.
It renews the mind and purifies the soul.
It brings us rest when the cold wind blows.
Oh, the north wind comes to both young and old.

The east wind blows on both me and you.
It turns the old into the new.
It reveals the path that's straight and true.
Yes the east wind blows on both me and you.

The south wind brings love into the world.
For every man, woman, boy and girl.
It's the source of true peach and harmony.
Oh, the south wind blows on you and me.

Our Creator's power is in the sacred wind.
It's everywhere and has always been.
It gives us life and forgives our sin.
Yes, Grandfather's power is in the sacred wind.

QUESTIONS AND ANSWERS

The following questions are frequently asked concerning the information in these teaching sessions. We have answered these questions to the best of our ability. We include this question and answer section because you may have some of the same questions others have had when they are exposed to this material.

Q: Who is grandfather Old Bear?
I don't really know. I have never asked him what Indian tribe he was from, what time period he lived in, or where he lived, even though I have often wondered what the answer to these questions are. I was afraid of him the first time I met him as a small boy when I went through the door on the right. I still had my doubts about his intentions toward me when he first appeared in My Private World behind the center door. However, I soon grew to love him because it was so obvious that he loved me, and only wanted what was best for me.

Some people have suggested that he is a demon or evil spirit attempting to deceive me and lead me away from our Creator. And, I admit that at first I wondered if that was the case. However, I soon dismissed that possibility because he always challenged me to not do what he told me to do, but always go to our Creator and ask him if I should do it or not. I can't imagine demons or evil spirits challenging us to follow what our Creator said instead of what they told us to do.

I always took grandfather Old Bear's advice and asked our Creator if I should do what the Old One suggested or not. I have yet to have our Creator contradict what grandfather Old Bear tells me or suggests that I do.

Q: Where is this Private World I go to, what is it, and does everyone have such a place they can travel to?
Again I must say that I don't know where or what this place is that I

call "My Private World". However, over the years, I have come to believe it is either the Spiritual Realm or a place that enables me to contact the Spiritual Realm much more easily than here in the physical realm. And yes, I believe everyone has their own Private World they can go to—it is just a matter of learning how to get there.

Q: Where is Medicine Wheel Mesa and can we come to visit it?

Medicine Wheel Mesa is located six thousand, four hundred feet above sea level on the eastern edge of western America's high desert plateau. It is situated on the western edge of southwestern Colorado, near the Utah state line.

From time to time, we do invite people from the general public to attend special ceremonies and events on the land. However, for obvious reasons, the land is not open to the general public for public use.

The desert has a very fragile ecological system, and we are committed to preserving it in its natural state as much as possible. If too many people at one time come to the land, its ecological system will quickly become severely damaged.

That does not mean we are trying to live in isolation and keep all people away from Medicine Wheel Mesa. More and more people are coming to the Mesa for short periods of time to pursue their own spiritual journeys. If you are seriously pursuing our Creator's Life Plan for your Life, and feel that our Creator definitely wants you to contact us to see how you might spend a few days at Medicine Wheel Mesa working on your own personal Spiritual Walk with our Creator, you may e-mail us at: oldbearm@yahoo.com and explain your reasons for wanting to come. Those in charge of handling our e-mail will respond to you in a timely manner.

I must caution you that there is no running water, electricity, telephone service or other modern conveniences on the mesa. We do not allow cell phones, portable radios, I-pods, or wristwatches to be brought on the land. We require people to pack out their own trash because we have no public garbage disposal service that comes to take away trash and garbage. We ask that people bring at least two gallons of water per person per day that they intend to stay on the land, and we do not allow any alcoholic beverages or drugs to be brought on the land.

If you are traveling to and from the land at night, you need to be aware that at certain times of the night it can be as much as 80-100 miles to the nearest open gas station and at least that far to a grocery store. It is also at least that for to the closest hospital. We share that with you so you can appreciate the remoteness of the mesa and that there are none of the conveniences of the city available nearby.

Q: Do you ever permit people to volunteer to come to Medicine Wheel Mesa to help with the general work that needs to be done?

Yes. From time to time, we welcome people to come to the land to help us with some of the work we are doing. We are still in the early stages of developing Medicine Wheel Mesa into what it will become in the near future. We are currently involved in building as many as twelve Navajo style hogans (small circular dwellings) for people to stay in while they are on the land working on their own Spiritual Walk.

We do not charge people to come and stay on the land for Spiritual purposes, but from time to time we do accept volunteer help in building the hogans. It is very labor intensive work and all work is done by hand without the use of power tools (except for the use of chain saws for cutting the trees to be used in building the hogans).

The work of building the hogans begins around the first part of April and continues through the early part of November, and so volunteers for work on this project are limited to those Sacred Seasonal time frames. It needs to be understood that we are not in a position to pay people for their work. However, in exchange for their time working on the hogans, we are available to spend time with the volunteer workers, helping them in any way we can as they work on their Spiritual Journeys toward our Creator.

Q: Do you still meet with grandfather Old Bear to discuss The Way of The Medicine Wheel?

Yes. He has told me that learning to walk this Sacred Path is a life long process, and that I have just begun to learn these Sacred Ways. He has made it clear that he will only continue sharing additional aspects of these Sacred Ways as long as I apply what I have been taught. If I fail to implement what I have been shown, I will not be given additional information concerning how to combine the physical and spiritual realms together into a single reality until I put into practice what I already know.

Q: Why do you make so many references to the Bible, but you never reference other religion's holy books?

I have never studied other religion's holy books. However, I have spent many years of my life studying the Bible, and have been surprised to find that the Bible contains all of the Spiritual Principles involved in walking this Sacred Path. I am by no means an expert on the Bible, but I do consider myself to be a serious student of the Bible, and I am amazed at how far away modern day Christianity's teachings have drifted from it.

I want to make it very clear that I am opposed to all forms of what I call modern day "institutionalized religion". I strongly believe all of the world's major religions, as they are practiced today, are man-made and not "God ordained", and man has greatly distorted and polluted God's original teachings to his children within the Sacred Circle of Life.

I can't speak for other religions and their holy books because I haven't studied them. However, I can speak about the Bible and what it teaches because I have studied it as a serious student and continue to do so to this day. I am appalled at how many people greatly criticize the Bible, yet they have never read it, let alone studied it. I am also amazed at the things people say that are in the Bible but are not there.

As man went through the so-called Age of Enlightenment, he seemed to lose his ability to accept the great mystical teachings that exist in the Bible from cover to cover. For example, God spoke to Moses out of a burning bush. Unfortunately, practically all leaders within Christendom today would say God doesn't speak to people that way today.

However, the green people have taught me much about our Creator and this Sacred Path.

462

I will continue to make references to the Bible where I think they are appropriate, because I am convinced this Holy Book contains within its covers every Spiritual Principle needed to successfully walk the Spiritual Path toward our Creator.

Some people have asked me if I am a Christian. I am a follower of Jesus Christ and his teachings (which he personally summarized as "love God with all your heart and your neighbor as yourself.) Now I ask you, who could disagree with that teaching and be a serious seeker of our Creator's Spiritual Path?

I am a follower of Jesus Christ and his teachings, but I am not a follower of man-made Christianity (or any other religion) as it is taught and practiced today. I have a personal relationship with Jesus Christ but I have never studied Buddha and his teachings, so I don't know anything about him.

I have found that the great Spiritual Principles of the Bible work for me and meet my needs as I walk this Sacred Path. However, I have no right to criticize people who practice and follow other religions and the teachings of their holy books, and I believe if people are truly following our Creator, they will love and accept people who disagree with them— not criticize, hate or condemn them.

Q: Why do you describe the details of ceremonies in these books, making them available to the general public?

I know many "traditionalists" feel that the general public should not have the details of ceremony (especially the meaning of the ceremony's symbolism) explained to them, and in principle I agree. However, the ceremonies explained in these teaching sessions are ones that we frequently invite the general public to attend.

When we invite the general public to a ceremony at Medicine Wheel Mesa, we always have a "talking circle" after the ceremony to discuss its meaning and answer questions about the ceremony. At that time, we explain the general symbolism of the ceremony, because this is one of the ways we feel we can expose people to more of the Spiritual Principles of this Sacred Path.

Not all ceremonies conducted at Medicine Wheel Mesa are open to the general public. Those ceremonies are not even discussed with the general public, and only those people whom our Creator is preparing to duplicate somewhere what is being done at Medicine Wheel Mesa are ever invited to attend or participate in those ceremonies.

Q: Why are you living at Medicine Wheel Mesa?

Grandfather Old Bear (along with many so-called modern day "prophets") are attempting to inform us that The Time of Great Cleansing is looming on the near horizon. I am not a prophet, nor do I make any claims to know the future. However, based on what I have learned from the Old One, I feel compelled to begin preparing for the extremely difficult days ahead as we get ever closer to the end of this Age.

We believe our Creator is preparing places of "Safe Haven" at various spots around the planet to begin bringing back the Ancient Sacred Path for people to follow as a means of preparing themselves to deal with the coming Earth Changes.

We do not recruit people, nor do we attempt to convince people of our beliefs. Our job is simply to live in obedience to what is revealed to us, and encourage people to sincerely ask our Creator what they should do to prepare themselves for the destruction that's coming. Our mission is very simple—to obey what our Creator tells us to do and encourage others to follow the Life Plan he has for their lives.

AUTHORS BIOGRAPHY

Myron Old Bear lives with his wife, Angelitta, on remote Medicine Wheel Mesa, which is located in the high desert area of southwestern Colorado.

Both Myron and Angelitta carry sacred medicine pipes for the people, and they are also Sun Dancers. They follow the Sacred Path called *The Way of the Medicine Wheel,* as described in this book.

Myron and Angelitta live in a Navajo style hogan without electricity or running water, and they cook their meals over an open wood fire. Their closest neighbor is approximately twenty miles away.

Myron brain tans hides for making clothing, and makes ceremonial drums. His wife makes women's traditional dresses and other leather items for sale. They sun dry most of their food for storage and spend much of their time conducting the sacred ceremonies associated with the Sacred Path referred to as *The Way of the Medicine Wheel.*

CPSIA information can be obtained
at www.ICGtesting.com
Printed in the USA
BVOW06*1818291216
472190BV00003B/6/P